# Media/
# Impact

# Media/Impact

## An Introduction to Mass Media

### Second Edition

**Shirley Biagi**
California State University, Sacramento

Wadsworth Publishing Company/Belmont, California/A Division of Wadsworth, Inc.

Communications Editor: Kris Clerkin
Development Editor: John Bergez
Editorial Assistant: Patty Birkle
Production Editor: Karen Garrison
Managing Designer: Ann Butler
Print Buyer: Karen Hunt
Art Editor: Kelly Murphy
Permissions Editor: Bob Kauser
Designer: Seventeenth Street Studios
Copy Editor: Jennifer Gordon
Photo Researcher: Stephen Forsling
Compositor: Thompson Type
Cover: Ann Butler
Signing Representative: Robin O'Neill
Printer: Arcata Graphics/Hawkins

2 3 4 5 6 7 8 9 10 — 96 95 94 93 92

Library of Congress Cataloging in Publication Data
Biagi, Shirley.
    Media/impact : an introduction to mass media / Shirley Biagi, — 2nd ed.
      p.   cm.
    Includes bibliographical references and index.
    ISBN 0-534-16242-8 (acid-free paper)
     1. Mass media.  I. Title.
  P90.B489  1992
    302.23 — dc20                            91-43700

# About the Author

SHIRLEY BIAGI is Chair of the Department of Journalism at California State University, Sacramento. She has been guest faculty at the American Press Institute, the Southern Newspaper Publishers Association, and the Poynter Institute for Media Studies. Author of more than 200 magazine articles, she has written four other books for Wadsworth: *Interviews That Work, Newstalk I: State-of-the-Art Conversations with Today's Print Journalists, Newstalk II: State-of-the-Art Conversations with Today's Broadcast Journalists,* and *Media/Reader.*

# Contents

# The 4 Radio Industry                              111

# 7 The Recording Industry    239

# 8 The Book Publishing Industry    263

# Part Three/Support Industries

# 9  Advertising                                                295

# 10  Public Relations                                          325

## Part Four/Issues and Effects

## Ownership Issues and Press Performance Issues   353

## Media Effects   375

# Legal and Regulatory Issues 13    399

# Part Five/Appendices

## Media Resources     495

## Media Statistics     509

# Profiles and Perspectives

# Preface

**W**ELCOME TO *Media/Impact*. For students, the following notes explain how to use this book to study the media. For instructors returning to this text, now in its second edition, and for instructors who are using *Media/Impact* for the first time, these notes explain the changes from the revised first edition and review the text's continuing instructional features.

## Understanding the Media: Four Key Themes

Studying the mass media is important because of the significant role they play in our society. The media influence our beliefs, tastes, and behavior, and they help to set the agenda for political and cultural debate.

To explain the media and their impact on society, this edition of *Media/Impact* emphasizes four themes:

1. *The media are profit-centered businesses.* This book stresses the idea that *media economics* underwrites the way media industries develop and function. Understanding the decisions of media insiders — why afternoon newspapers are disappearing, which television shows are produced, why so many movies are sequels — requires knowing where the media get their income and how the marketplace affects the way the media operate.

2. The evolution of media is inextricably linked to improvements in technology. As exemplified by compact discs and cable television, advancing technology causes rapid transformation in the way the media work.

3. The organization of a country's political system affects the structure of the media within that country. The interrelationship between government and media defines the media's role.

4. Media both reflect and affect the society and culture in which they operate. The media are social and cultural mirrors, displaying the nation's values. They also are influential participants in the culture, sometimes altering the national dialogue by focusing attention on issues and trends.

These themes are introduced in the first chapter and reinforced both in the discussions of individual media industries and in the extended discussion of media-related issues and effects in Part 4.

## New Features

In addition to introducing these four themes, *Media/Impact* offers several new features to enhance the text's usefulness for students and instructors:

• **Industry Snapshots.** Each of the seven industry chapters in Part 2 features a two-page spread of text and graphics highlighting current trends in each industry.

• **Global Media.** Chapter 15 is an entirely new addition that emphasizes the growing internationalization of the media business.

• **Glossary.** Another addition, the glossary offers quick reference help for terms that may be new to students.

## Continuing Concepts

This edition also continues its emphasis on central concepts from the last edition:

**Media Economics.** The media industries chapters show how the media are driven by economic trends, and then the five chapters in Part 4 examine the effects of changes in media ownership and other economic factors. Throughout the text, data are presented that highlight significant trends in media economics.

**Current Information.** The story of media changes daily, making currency particularly important in the study of mass communication. This text presents the latest data available, updated until the last possible publication deadline, including current developments in ownership, law, ethics, and global media issues. *Media/Impact/Update*, a biannual newsletter for instructors, keeps them up-to-date with timely information.

**Historical Perspective.** Timeliness is crucial in the study of media, but so is historical perspective. Understanding the media means, in part, seeing how economic, cultural, and technological influences have shaped today's media industries. In addition, the text highlights the stories of significant people in media history: Ernie Pyle reporting the events of World War II; Ida Tarbell uncovering the abuses of Standard Oil; and the Hollywood Ten defending their political beliefs before congressional investigators.

**Forecasts.** The media's history and current developments foreshadow their future evolution, and *Media/Impact* includes projections about what lies ahead — technologically and economically — for the media industries.

# Continuing Features

Features that continue in this text because of their usefulness in earlier editions are:

• **Media/Impact Profiles**, emphasizing the contributions of important individuals, past and present, to the media industries;

• **Media/Impact Perspectives**, incorporating a diverse range of critical views by media analysts;

• **In Focus** sections at the end of each chapter, summarizing central concepts for review;

• **Media Resources Appendix** and **Media Statistics Appendix**, which offer help for further research about the media plus 29 tables of data — the most comprehensive listing of up-to-date media statistics available.

# Organization

This edition continues the organization of earlier editions of *Media/Impact*. After the introductory chapter, Part 2 consists of seven chapters describing each of the media industries: newspapers, magazines, radio, television, movies, recordings, and books. Part 3 comprises two chapters devoted to the media support industries — advertising and public relations.

These first ten chapters explain the history and functions of each of the media industries and media support industries as a foundation for the five chapters in Part 4, which analyze the important issues and effects of today's media: ownership issues and press performance issues; media effects; legal and regulatory issues; ethical issues; and a new addition for this edition, global media.

# Instructors' Aids

Accompanying *Media/Impact* is a comprehensive Instructor's Manual, created by Ron Jacobson of Fordham University. The manual includes chapter outlines, multiple choice, completion, and essay questions. A special feature of the manual is a chapter-by-chapter list of videos to enhance the text, compiled by Susanne Roschwalb of American University. Tests are available on disk in IBM and Macintosh formats.

# Acknowledgments

Every detail of this book's format and design is the result of the painstaking care of the Wadsworth team that created this edition of *Media/Impact*. Their names appear on the copyright page, but I feel especially thankful for the help I received from Kris Clerkin, John Bergez, and Karen Garrison. Brett Braidman, Carole Tchinguirian, and Carol Bell contributed research assistance, for which they deserve special mention.

This second edition of *Media/Impact* also reflects the suggestions, contributions and wisdom of the reviewers of this edition and of earlier editions, for which I am very grateful. They are: First edition reviewers: Roy Alden Atwood, University of Idaho; Tom Beell, Iowa State University; Gerald Flannery,

University of Southwestern Louisiana; Ken Harwood, University of Houston; James Hoyt, University of Wisconsin — Madison; Seong H. Lee, Appalachian State University; Alfred Lorenz, Loyola University; Maclyn McClary, Humboldt State University; Robert McConnell, Ball State University; Daniel G. McDonald, Cornell University; Alston Morgan, Oral Roberts University; Marlan D. Nelson, Oklahoma State University; Richard Alan Nelson, University of Houston; John H. Vivian, Winona State University; Donald K. Wright, University of Southern Alabama; and Eugenia Zerbinos, University of Maryland.

Updated first edition reviewers: Michael Carlebach, University of Miami; Danae Clark, University of Pittsburgh; William Miller, Ohio University; David Mould, Ohio University; Ray Newton, Northern Arizona University; Patricia Bowie Orman, University of Southern Colorado; Manny Paraschos, Emerson College; Jim Patten, University of Arizona; Peter K. Pringle, University of Tennessee at Chattanooga; Penny Summers, Northern Kentucky University; Jim Tyman, University of Michigan; and Laura Widmer, Northwest Missouri State University.

Second edition reviewers: Paul H. Anderson, University of Tennessee at Martin; Michael Carlebach, University of Miami; Jack F. Holgate, University of Southern Mississippi; Tom Jacobson, State University of New York, Buffalo; Richard Alan Nelson, Kansas State University.

# A Request for Comments

Four years have passed since the first edition of *Media/Impact*, and the book has been updated every two years to try to reflect the unforeseeable, kaleidoscopic changes in the media industries. The book, like the media business, is now truly global, with users throughout the United States, Canada, and Australia.

In the first and revised first editions, I asked students and instructors to write me with their comments and suggestions. Truthfully, I expected very little response, but I have been thrilled with the results. More than 100 students in a class in Arizona who had used *Media/Impact* each wrote me a letter about the book. A student from Tennessee sent me some very useful technical information for the Recording Industry chapter.

Instructors have sent articles and books for consideration as Impact/Perspectives, and they have suggested videos to use, which I included in one edition of *Media/Impact/Update*.

Students who transfer to CSUS, where I teach, often tell me that they used *Media/Impact* at another college, which is gratifying. (One student told me candidly, "It actually wasn't too bad — for a textbook." I considered his comments high praise.)

I hope you find the book at least as useful as he did. I believe this text offers students the information they need as consumers of the products the media business delivers and, perhaps, as future employees of the media industries.

And again, I ask for your comments and suggestions. Please write to me at California State University, Sacramento, 6000 J Street, Sacramento, California 95819.

*Shirley Biagi*

# Overview

*When was the last time you spent 24 hours without the*

*media? From the moment you get up in the morning until*

*the time you go to bed at night, the media are waiting to keep you company. Radio*

*news gives you headlines in the shower and traffic reports on the freeway; the newspaper*

*offers you national and local news and helps you keep up with the latest college*

*basketball standings and Garfield's attempts to steal another piece of lasagne; maga-*

*zines describe new computer software for work, and dur-*

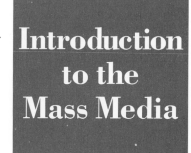

Introduction
to the
Mass Media

*ing your lunch hour they keep you current with the latest*

Within the last 15 years, home video has transformed the movie business by expanding the audience for movies like *Dances With Wolves*, featuring actor-director Kevin Costner.

fashions; after work, the newest paperback novel competes with your videocassette recorder, beckoning you to spend an evening with the hottest video release.

According to industry estimates, the average adult spends more than half of his or her waking life with the media. This is the breakdown of the way Americans divide their time watching, listening, and reading:

• *More than 64 percent of all adults read a daily newspaper; four out of five people read a newspaper at least once a week.*

• *Adults read an average of ten magazines a month.*

• *Adults listen to the radio an average of 3 hours a day.*

• *Each household leaves the TV set turned on an average of 7 hours a day; adults watch TV an average of 4 hours a day.*

• *Adults go to the movies about five times a year; adults with a VCR rent an average of six movies a year.*

• *Adults buy an average of four recordings a year.*

• *Americans buy an average of nine books a year; the average library user borrows six items a year.*[1]

Some form of mass media touches nearly every American every day — economically, socially, or culturally. The mass media can affect the way you vote and the way you spend your money. They sometimes influence the way you eat, talk, work, study, and relax. This is the *impact* of mass media on American society.

This wide-reaching presence distinguishes American media from the media in other countries. In no other country do the mass media capture so much of people's time and attention. In no other country do the media affect so many aspects of the way people live. And in no other country do the media collect so much money for delivering information and entertainment. The American mass media industries earned about $134 billion in 1990 and employed nearly 1.5 million people.[2]

Today's American society has inherited the wisdom and the mistakes of the people who work in the mass media and the society that regulates and consumes what the mass media produce. Consider these situations:

• *You are a newspaper publisher in a small New England town in the 1700s. You publish an article that angers the local council, and they throw you in jail. Yet you want to continue to publish the newspaper. What would you do? (See James Franklin and the* New England Courant, *Chapter 2.)*

• *You have just bought a computer and you want to stay current with new developments in software. You subscribe to* PC World *and* BYTE. *How does your choice of magazines reflect the changes in the magazine industry? (See Second Half of the 20th Century: Specialized Magazines, Chapter 3.)*

• *You have just bought a small radio station in a big-city market and you need programming. How can you program your station cheaply and quickly? (See Formats: Gordon McLendon's Legacy, Chapter 4.)*

• *You are in a bookstore with $10 to spend. You can't decide whether to buy a novel by Stephen King, a book of poems by Emily Dickinson, a travel guide to Mexico, or a collection of "Calvin & Hobbes" cartoons. What are the economic consequences of these decisions by book buyers for the publishing industry? (See Chapter 8 on consumers' book-buying habits.)*

• *You believe you have been misquoted and misrepresented in a major magazine story written by a freelance journalist, so you sue the author and the magazine. The case eventually reaches the U.S. Supreme Court. What implications will the court decision have on the media's liability for the stories they print and broadcast? (See* Masson v. The New Yorker *magazine, Chapter 13.)*

People who work in the media industries and people who watch, listen to, read, and govern what the media offer make choices like these every day. The future of American mass media will be determined by these choices.

*Mass communication* means using a form of mass media to deliver a message rapidly to a large group of people simultaneously. Here, people in the Soviet Union gather around a radio in August 1991 to hear news following the coup attempt by the country's military leaders, which eventually failed.

# The Communication Process

t O UNDERSTAND the mass media, first it is important to understand the process of communication. Communication is the act of sending ideas and attitudes from one person to another. Writing and talking to each other are only two ways human beings communicate. We also communicate when we gesture, move our bodies, or roll our eyes.

Three terms that scholars use to describe how people communicate are *intrapersonal communication, interpersonal communication,* and *mass communication*. Each communication situation involves different numbers of people in specific ways.

If you are in a grocery store and you silently discuss with yourself whether to buy a package of chocolate chip cookies, you are using what scholars call *intrapersonal communication*: communication within one person.

To communicate with each other, people use many of the five senses — sight, hearing, touch, smell, and taste. Scholars call this direct sharing of experience between two people *interpersonal communication*.

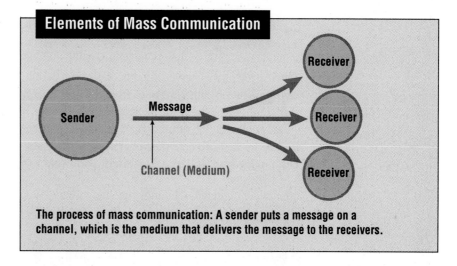

## Elements of Mass Communication

**Sender** → **Message** → **Channel (Medium)** → **Receiver** / **Receiver** / **Receiver**

The process of mass communication: A sender puts a message on a channel, which is the medium that delivers the message to the receivers.

*Mass communication* is communication from one person or group of persons through a transmitting device (a **medium**) to large audiences or markets. In MEDIA/IMPACT you will study mass communication. (The plural of the word *medium* is *media*, so when scholars discuss more than one medium they refer to **media**.)

To describe the process of **mass communication**, scholars draw charts and diagrams to convey what happens when people send messages to one another. This description begins with four easily understood terms: *sender, message, receiver,* and *channel* (Figure 1.1).

Pretend that you're standing directly in front of someone and you say, "I like your hat." In this simple communication, you are the sender, the message is "I like your hat," and the person in front of you is the receiver (or audience). This example of interpersonal communication involves the sender, the message, and the receiver.

In mass communication, the sender puts the message on what is called a **channel**. This channel is the medium that delivers the message. A medium is the means by which a message reaches an audience. Radio is the medium that delivers music, for example; television delivers entertainment shows, and newspapers deliver news stories. The radio, television, and newspaper media are simply delivery systems for the messages they carry.

Using a very general definition, mass communication today shares three characteristics:

*1. A message is sent out using some form of mass media (such as newspapers or television).*

*2. The message is delivered rapidly.*

*3. The message reaches large groups of different kinds of people simultaneously or within a short period of time.* [3]

Thus, a telephone conversation between two people would not qualify as mass communication, but a message from the president of the United States, broadcast simultaneously by all the television networks, would qualify.

Mass media deliver messages to large numbers of people at once. The businesses that produce the mass media in America — newspapers, magazines, radio, television, movies, recordings, and books — are mass media industries.

# Understanding the Mass Media Industries: Four Key Themes

HIS BOOK uses the term **mass media industries** to describe the seven types of American mass media businesses: newspapers, magazines, radio, television, movies, recordings, and books. The use of the word *industries* underscores the major goal of mass media in America — financial success.

But the media are more than businesses: They are key institutions in our society. They affect our culture, our buying habits, and our politics, and they are in turn affected by changes in our beliefs, tastes, interests, and behavior. To help organize your thinking about the mass media and their impact, this section introduces four key themes that will recur in the chapters to come.

## 1. The Media as Businesses

What you see, read, and hear in the American mass media may cajole, entertain, inform, persuade, provoke, and even perplex you. But to understand the American media, the first concept to understand is that the central force driving the media in America is the desire to make money: *American media are businesses, vast businesses.* The products of these businesses are information and entertainment.

Other motives shape the media in America, of course: the desire to fulfill the public's need for information, to influence the country's governance, to disseminate the country's culture, to offer entertainment, and to provide an outlet for artistic expression. But American media are, above all, profit-centered (see Impact/Perspective, The Business of Media).

**Who Owns the Media?** To understand the media, it is important to know who owns these important channels of communication. In America, all of the media are privately owned except the Public Broadcasting Service and National Public Radio, which survive on government support and private donations. The annual budget for public broadcasting, however, is less than 3 percent of the amount of money advertisers pay every year to support America's commercial media.

Many family-owned media properties still exist in the United States, but today the trend in the media industries, like other American industries, is for media companies to cluster together in groups. The top ten newspaper chains, for example, own one-fifth of the nation's daily newspapers. This trend is called **concentration of ownership**, and this concentration takes five different forms.

*1. Chains.* Benjamin Franklin established America's first newspaper chain. This tradition was expanded by William Randolph Hearst in the 1930s. At their peak, Hearst newspapers accounted for nearly 14 percent of total national daily circulation and nearly 25 percent of Sunday circulation. Today's newspaper chain giant is Gannett, with 82 daily newspapers, including *USA Today*.

Broadcast companies also own chains of stations, but the Federal Communications Commission (FCC) regulates broadcast ownership. Today one company can own no more than 12 TV stations, 12 AM radio stations, and 12 FM radio stations, as long as the total number of stations doesn't reach more than 25 percent of the national audience.

*2. Networks.* The four major networks are ABC (American Broadcasting Company), NBC (National Broadcasting Company), CBS (Columbia Broadcasting System), and Fox Broadcasting. Beginning with NBC in the 1920s, the three original networks (NBC, CBS, and ABC) were established to deliver radio programming across the country, and the network concept continued with the invention of television. Networks can have as many affiliates as they want, but no network can have two **affiliates** in the same broadcast area. (Affiliates are stations that use network programming but are owned by companies other than the networks.)

Fox is the youngest network, founded in 1986, and serves only television.

*3. Cross-Media Ownership.* Many media companies own more than one type of media property: newspapers, magazines, radio and TV stations, for example. Gannett, which owns the largest chain of newspapers, also owns television and radio stations. Among the properties of Capital Cities/ABC are the *Kansas City Star, Modern Photography* magazine, San Francisco's KGO radio, KGO-TV, and the ABC network. Rupert Murdoch's News Corporation owns newspapers, television stations, magazines, Twentieth Century-Fox Film, Fox Broadcasting, and HarperCollins Publishers.

*4. Conglomerates.* When you go to the movies to watch a Columbia picture, you might not realize that Sony owns the film company. Sony is a *conglomerate* — a company that owns media companies as well as companies unrelated to the media business. Media properties can be attractive investments, but some conglomerate owners are unfamiliar with the idiosyncrasies of the media industries.

*5. Vertical Integration.* The most noticeable trend among today's media companies is **vertical integration** — an attempt to control several related aspects of the media business at once, each part helping the other (see Impact/Profiles, Four Moguls of the Media). Besides publishing magazines and books, Time Warner, for example, owns Home Box Office (HBO), Warner movie studios, and various cable TV systems throughout the United States. The

# The Business of Media

**Jeff Greenfield**, an ABC News correspondent, describes the hazards of big business involvement in the media.

WHY DO we print bad news? Why do we invade people's privacy? Why do we unsettle our audience who may want only a bit of relaxation with their morning coffee or pre-dinner drink? We do it, we say, because it's our obligation. We have been granted Constitutional exemption from the legal accountability that governs every other major institution in this country, and we have been granted it for a reason.

The bedrock theory of the free press is that once society decides to invest ultimate power in the people, they must have access to the widest possible range of information. James Madison said it concisely enough to satisfy any journalist

Japanese company Matsushita owns MCA Records, Universal Studios, and manufactures broadcast production equipment. Paramount Communications owns TV stations, movie theaters, and cable networks as well as the book publishing company Simon & Schuster.

To describe the financial status of today's media is also to talk about acquisitions. The media are buying and selling each other in unprecedented numbers and forming media groups to position themselves in the marketplace to maintain and increase their profits. In 1986, the first time a broadcast network had been sold, *two* networks were sold that year — ABC and NBC. In 1990, 1,080 radio and television properties worth nearly $2 billion changed owners.

Media acquisitions have skyrocketed since 1980 for two reasons. The first is that most conglomerates today are publicly traded companies, which means that their stock is traded on one of the nation's stock exchanges. This makes acquisitions relatively easy.

A media company that wants to buy a publicly owned company can buy that company's stock when the stock becomes available. The open availability of stock in these companies means that anybody with enough money can invest

looking for a sound bite: "A people who mean to be their own governors must arm themselves with the power which knowledge gives."

. . . The question may now be fairly asked: What public are we now serving?

More and more, I think, media managers are treating the public not as an audience but as markets — as "targets" to be captured almost as if they were our enemy, or at best people who must be tricked into buying a paper or watching the news. . . .

[But] if we look simply to the bottom line, if our chain or corporate owners say, "We don't care what kind of news you do, as long as the return

on investment is 30 or 40 percent," then what happens to our premise? If we behave the same as the purveyor of tires or soda pop, how long do you think it will be before the public starts asking some very hard questions about why we have been given this extraordinary Constitutional privilege and what we are doing with it?

The press exists as part of a remarkable experiment in self-government. Even if we are faithful to our role in this experiment, we need to do a better job of thinking through why we report what we report, and we need to do better in explaining to our audience why we do what we do. We also need to remember that the

First Amendment is not the only value enshrined in our system: privacy and a fair judicial system are among the others.

But if we abandon our role in this system, if we behave as a business and nothing but a business, then nothing we say or do will convince the public that we have any real justification for our acts save the raw claim of the legal power to behave this way. We will have lost their trust because they will have concluded that we did not deserve to keep it.

*Excerpted from "An Abusive Press?" in a speech given to the Colorado Press Association, February 20, 1987. Reprinted by permission of Gannett Center for Media Studies.*

**IMPACT/
PERSPECTIVE**

# Four Moguls of the Media

Behind what has been called a takeover frenzy in the media are four distinctive competitive media moguls. While Rupert Murdoch has concentrated his attention on media properties, the other three moguls hold media businesses along with many other types of investments. Which moguls seem to be most interested in vertical integration?

**Mortimer Zuckerman.** Before he turned 30, he was a millionaire. Zuckerman has accumulated a personal fortune estimated at $400 million.

"After meeting with a difficult person," reports *The Wall Street Journal*, "Mortimer Zuckerman sometimes will draw his antagonist's face on a squash ball and pound the ball through a vigorous game. 'You'd be amazed at how therapeutic it is,' he says."[4]

In 1980, Zuckerman bought *The Atlantic* magazine with profits from his real estate group, which he co-owns. Then he paid $164 million for *U.S. News & World Report*. He spent $8 million on *The Atlantic* and cut the subscription price, which added 125,000 new readers. "Every magazine needs a kick in the ass once in a while," he told *Newsweek*.

Zuckerman is a hands-on owner at *U.S. News*, where he edits the magazine and handles the business side. "There is a natural assumption that people, just because they own something, don't have the intelligence to be involved," he told *Columbia Journalism Review*. "And I'm trying to challenge that premise."

"His friends are journalists, academics and politicians," reports *The Wall Street Journal*. "He plays softball with TV newsman Tom Brokaw and writers Ken Auletta and Carl Bernstein. He owns homes in Boston, Washington, and New York City, plus a weekend estate in East Hampton, New York. When he wanted to learn about the intellectual history of the West, he hired a Columbia University professor to tutor him. At his weekly softball game in Sag Harbor, New

Mortimer Zuckerman, owner of *U.S. News & World Report* and *The Atlantic*.

Ted Turner, the major force behind Turner Broadcasting.

Rupert Murdoch, who owns major media properties in the United States, Australia, and Great Britain.

York, a player used to shout, 'If you can't strike them out, why don't you buy them, Mort?'"[5]

**Ted Turner.** Ted Turner did buy a baseball team, the Atlanta Braves. Then in 1986, he paid $1.5 billion for MGM/UA Entertainment and announced that he would "colorize" several of the major MGM movies so they would be more attractive on TV.

"The last time I checked," he told the *Los Angeles Times*, "I owned the films that we're in the process of colorizing. I can do whatever I want with them, and if they're going to be shown on TV, they're going to be in color."[6] Turner seemed to

relish the controversy over colorization. He said he would colorize *Casablanca* "just for controversy's sake."

Controversy is something Turner invites. In 1980, he launched Cable News Network (CNN) from his "superstation" WTBS in Atlanta. At first critics called the idea Cable News "Nitwork," but Turner revolutionized the cable industry and continues to promote his satellite broadcasts, beamed from Atlanta to worldwide audiences.

The 1986 MGM/UA purchase left Turner so deeply in debt that he immediately sold it back but kept the 3,650-title MGM film library to use

on WTBS. Said one movie-industry analyst, "Hollywood will never be the same."[7]

In 1987, facing more debt problems, Turner was forced to sell some of Turner Broadcasting's stock, in essence giving up control of the company to a newly formed board of directors. Turner still holds 40 percent of the stock, however. In 1989, Turner's wealth was estimated at $1.76 billion, making him one of the nation's wealthiest people.

**Rupert Murdoch.** In 1952, Rupert Murdoch inherited his father's business, a barely profitable Australian newspaper. Today, Murdoch's

# Four Moguls of the Media

**(continued)**

Laurence A. Tisch became chairman of the board of CBS in 1986.

News Corporation owns more than 100 media properties in Australia, Great Britain, and the United States, including San Antonio and Boston community newspapers, Fox Broadcasting, and Harper-Collins Publishers.

A New Yorker who switches on station WNYW, reads *TV Guide* magazine, and watches a 20th Century-Fox film is consuming three Murdoch products. With an Australian accent and an American passport, Murdoch is the biggest newspaper owner in England. (He became an American citizen in September 1985.)

In 1989, Murdoch launched Sky Television to beam satellite broadcasts throughout Europe.

In 1990, Sky Television merged with British Satellite Broadcasting to form British Sky Broadcasting, which holds a monopoly on satellite broadcasts in Britain.

**Laurence A. Tisch.** He owns 24.9 percent of CBS and he's chairman of Loews Corporation. In 1986, CBS's board of directors appointed Tisch to run the company. Soon afterward, the CBS network ratings dropped to third for the first time in CBS's history. The board hoped Tisch would change that.

Some observers called Tisch an opportunist, taking advantage of CBS's decline, but former FCC Chairman Newton

Minow, who also serves on the CBS board of directors, said something else is driving Tisch to control CBS.

"If Larry only wanted to make money, he'd go elsewhere," said Minow. "CBS is not just a business for him. It's an institution of great public weight."[8]

After Tisch became chairman of the board, CBS announced a series of cutbacks, including 700 layoffs in its broadcast group. CBS became profitable as a result of the cutbacks, and in 1991 its prime-time TV programming began to pull ahead of NBC and ABC in the ratings.

in the American media industries, which is exactly how CBS Board Chairman Laurence Tisch joined the media business (see page 14).

The second reason for the large increase in media alliances is that beginning in 1980, the Federal Communications Commission, under the Reagan administration, gradually deregulated the broadcast media. Before 1980, for example, the FCC allowed one company to own only five TV stations, five AM radio stations, and five FM radio stations.

Companies also were required to hold onto a station for three years before the station could be sold, and the FCC approval process for sales was very complicated. The post-1980 FCC eliminated the three-year rule and raised the number of broadcast holdings allowed for one owner.

The issue of concentrated media ownership is important because some critics fear that concentration means control. That is, if only a few corporations are able to direct the media industries in this country, does this limit the outlets for differing political viewpoints and innovative ideas? (See Impact/Perspective, The Effects of Media Alliances.)

**Who Pays for the Mass Media?** Most of the $134 billion a year in income that the American mass media industries collect comes directly from advertisers. Advertising directly supports newspapers, radio, and television. (Subscribers pay only a small part of the cost of producing a newspaper.) Magazines receive more than half of their income from advertising and the other portion from subscriptions. Income for movies, recordings, and books, of course, comes from direct purchases and ticket sales.

This means that most of the information and entertainment you receive from television, radio, newspapers, and magazines in America is paid for by people who want to sell you products. You support the media industries *indirectly* by buying the products that advertisers sell.

Advertising pays most of the bills. One full-page black-and-white ad in *The Wall Street Journal*, for example, costs $105,000. To place a full-page color ad in *Rolling Stone* magazine costs $43,000. A 30-second television commercial in prime time (8 P.M. to 11 P.M.) costs $120,000. Multiply the prices for all these ads in all the media, and you can understand how easily American media industries accumulate the more than $134 billion they collect annually.[9]

You also pay for the media *directly* when you buy a book or a compact disc or go to a movie. This money buys equipment, underwrites company research and expansion, and pays stock dividends. Advertisers and consumers are the financial foundation for American media industries (see Figure 1.2).

This income also pays salaries to employees. More than 1.5 million people work in the media industries, according to the U.S. Department of Commerce.

# The Effects of Media Alliances

In this excerpt from his column as editor of *Harper's* magazine, **Lewis Lapham** says that big media companies all speak with the same voice, telling the public only what the public wants to hear.

THE MASS media increasingly have become less hospitable to the first person singular. With remarkably few exceptions, the news and editorial columns of the big media (*Newsweek*, *The New York Times*, NBC, etc.) sound so nearly alike as to be indistinguishable from one another. Dan Rather's voice (like Peter Jennings' voice or Tom Brokaw's voice) is the voice of a committee, of a syndicate, of an institution. Properly defined, it is nobody's voice, telling nobody's story.

Because of the size of their audiences (measured in the millions instead of the tens of thousands) and because of the enormous sums of money inhibiting any sudden or subversive movement of the imagination, the big media cannot afford to describe the world as it is. The world is too strange, too alarming, too specific, too much at odds with the mythologies in which people would prefer to believe. The mass media have no choice but to flatter the illusions of their audiences and tell the equivalent of fairy tales. "Yes, Virginia, this is the best of all possible worlds; yes, our generals are competent, our armies invincible, our artists busily at work on masterpieces, our statesmen wise, our money safe."

"Notebook," *Harper's* 274, no. 1,642 (March 1987): 10.

**1.2** ➤

## Who Pays for the Media?

| Industry Category | 1990 Spending Shares | |
| --- | --- | --- |
| | Advertisers | Users |
| Newspapers | 79% | 21% |
| Magazines | 55% | 45% |
| Radio | 100% | 0% |
| Television | 100% | 0% |
| Cable television | 12% | 88% |
| Filmed entertainment | 4% | 96% |
| Recordings | 0% | 100% |
| Books | 0% | 100% |

SOURCE: Data from *The Veronis, Suhler & Associates Communications Industry Forecast*, June 1991, p. 38.

This number includes all of the people on the payrolls of media companies: reporters, news directors, book editors, magazine art directors, movie producers, and advertising salespeople, for example.[10]

## How Does Each Media Industry Work?

Books, newspapers, and magazines were America's only mass media for 250 years after the first American book was published in 1640. The first half of the 20th century brought four new media—movies, radio, recordings, and television—in less than 50 years.

To understand how this happened and where each medium fits in the mass media industries today, it is important to examine the individual characteristics of each medium. (For a comparison of income and employment in the media industries, see Figure 1.3.)

*Newspapers.* There are about 1,600 daily newspapers in the United States. Evening papers outnumber morning papers 3 to 1, but the number of evening papers is declining. Papers that come out in the morning are growing in circulation, and papers that come out in the afternoon are shrinking. The number of weekly newspapers is also declining—from 8,714 in 1960 to about 7,550 in 1990. Advertising makes up about two-thirds of the printed space in

INTRODUCTION TO
THE MASS MEDIA

Magazines like *Glamour* can target an audience and deliver a specific market to advertisers. Here, *Glamour* presents itself to advertisers as a good place to sell stereos.

daily newspapers. Newspaper income is expected to remain steady over the next decade, with very little growth.

*Magazines.* According to the Magazine Publishers Association, about 12,000 magazines are published in the United States. This number is remaining steady. To maintain and increase profits, magazines are raising their subscription and single-copy prices and fighting to maintain their advertising income. The number of magazines people buy by subscription is going up, but newsstand sales are going down. Magazine income is expected to decline slightly in the next decade.

*Radio.* More than 12,000 radio stations broadcast programming in the United States, about evenly divided between AM and FM. About 1,700 of these stations are noncommercial, most of them FM. The average American household owns five radios. Radio revenues are expected to grow slightly in the next decade.

*Television.* About 1,400 television stations are operating in the United States; one out of four stations is noncommercial. Many of the stations are affiliated with one of the four major networks — NBC, CBS, ABC, or Fox —

**1.3** ➤

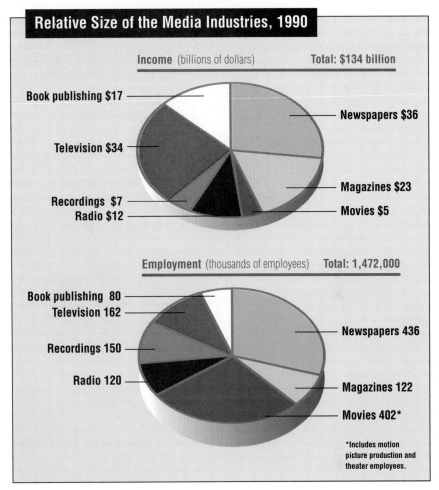

### Relative Size of the Media Industries, 1990

**Income** (billions of dollars)     **Total: $134 billion**

Book publishing $17
Television $34
Recordings $7
Radio $12

Newspapers $36
Magazines $23
Movies $5

**Employment** (thousands of employees)     **Total: 1,472,000**

Book publishing 80
Television 162
Recordings 150
Radio 120

Newspapers 436
Magazines 122
Movies 402*

*Includes motion picture production and theater employees.

SOURCE: Data from *U.S. Industrial Outlook*, 1991; Bureau of Labor Statistics; *Variety*; Federal Communications Commission.

although an increasing number of stations, called *independents*, are not affiliated with any network.

Ted Turner launched Cable News Network (CNN) in 1980 to serve cable companies. More than half the homes in the United States are wired for cable, and half the nation's viewers receive 33 or more channels. Cable receives about 7 percent of the overall money spent on television advertising. Network income is declining, while income to independents and cable operators is going up. Total industry revenue is projected to grow at about 7 percent a year.

*Movies.* Nearly 24,000 theater screens exist in the United States. Only 900 of them are drive-ins. The major and independent studios combined make

**1.4** ➤

## How People Spend Their Media Dollars

Per-person spending per year in the United States

| Medium | 1990 | 1985 | % change |
|--------|------|------|----------|
| Cable television | $71.73 | $42.44 | +69% |
| Books | $64.46 | $45.33 | +42% |
| Home video | $59.64 | $15.16 | +293% |
| Newspapers | $50.37 | $45.33 | +11% |
| Recordings | $41.26 | $25.10 | +64% |
| Magazines | $41.04 | $29.84 | +38% |
| Movies | $27.48 | $21.44 | +28% |
| TOTAL | $355.98 | $224.64 | +58% |

SOURCE: Data from *The Veronis, Suhler & Associates Communications Industry Forecast*, June 1991, p. 14.

about 400 pictures a year. The industry is collecting more money because of higher ticket prices, but the number of people who go to the movies is declining.

The major increase in income to the movie industry in the last decade came from sales of movies for videocassettes. The year 1986 marked the first time that the number of videotape rentals was higher than the number of movie tickets. Industry income is expected to remain unchanged.

*Recordings.* Prerecorded cassettes account for more than half the recordings sold. Another 30 percent of sales comes from compact discs. Most recordings are bought by people who are under 30. The introduction of digital tapes by the Japanese could change the recordings market. The industry is expected to grow at a rate of about 5 percent, boosted by sales of compact discs.

*Book Publishing.* Publishers issue about 40,000 titles a year in the United States, although some of these are reprints and new editions of old titles. About 20,000 retail bookstores are in business in the United States, and these bookstores account for 30 percent of all the money earned from book sales. The rest of the books are sold through book clubs, in college stores, to libraries, and to school districts for use in elementary and high schools. Book publishing income is expected to increase at an annual rate of about 4 percent.

Overall, media industries in the United States are prospering. The division of profits is shifting, however, as different media industries expand and contract in the marketplace to respond to the audience. For example, if the population's interest shifts away from the print media to video entertainment, fewer people will buy newspapers, magazines, and books, which means that these industries could suffer. (For recent trends in consumers' media spending, see Figure 1.4.) Understanding the implications of these changes is central to understanding the business of the media.

# 2. The Media and Communications Technology

The second theme that you will encounter throughout this book is *the effect of technological change on the mass media*. The development of communications technology directly affects the speed with which a society evolves. An entire country with one telephone or one radio may be impossible for people in the United States to imagine, but there are still many countries today where ten families share a single telephone and people consider a television set to be a luxury.

In the United States and other countries such as Japan that have encouraged technological advancements, communications changes are moving faster than ever before. For the media industries, this means increasing costs to replace old equipment. For consumers, this means a confusing array of products that seem to be replaced as soon as they are marketed — compact discs overcoming cassettes, for example.

By today's standards, the earliest communications obstacles seem unbelievably simple: for instance, how to transmit a single message to several people at the same time, and how to share information inexpensively. Yet it has taken nearly 5,500 years to achieve the capability for instant communication that we enjoy today.

**Three Communications Revolutions.** The channels of communication have changed dramatically over the centuries, but the idea that a society will pay to stay informed and entertained is not new. In imperial Rome, people who wanted to know the news paid professional speakers a coin (*gazet*) for the privilege of listening to the speaker announce the day's events. Many early newspapers were called gazettes to reflect this heritage.

The first attempt at written communication began modestly with pictographs. A pictograph is a symbol of an object that is used to convey an idea. If

## The Three Communications Revolutions

The invention of writing, displayed here on clay tablets, has been called the first communications revolution. Johannes Gutenberg is responsible for the second communications revolution, the invention of movable type. Satellite dishes, which use computer technology to transmit information, represent the third communications revolution.

you have ever drawn a heart with an arrow through it, you understand what a pictograph is. The first known pictographs were carved in stone by the Sumerians of Mesopotamia in about 3500 B.C.

The stone in which these early pictographic messages were carved served as a medium — a device to transmit messages. Eventually, messages were imprinted in clay and stored in a primitive version of today's library. These messages weren't very portable, however. Clay tablets didn't slip easily into someone's pocket.

In about 2500 B.C., the Egyptians invented papyrus, a type of paper made from a grasslike plant called sedge. The Greeks perfected parchment, made from goat and sheep skins, in about 200 B.C. By about A.D. 100, before the use of parchment spread throughout Europe, the Chinese had invented paper, which was much cheaper to produce than parchment, but Europeans didn't start to use paper until more than a thousand years later, about A.D. 1300. The discovery of parchment and then paper meant that storing information became cheaper and easier.

Meanwhile, pictographs as a method of communication developed into phonetic writing, using symbols for sounds. Instead of drawing a representation of a dog to convey the idea of a dog, scholars could represent the sounds d-o-g with phonetic writing. The invention of writing has been called the *first information communications revolution.* "After being stored in written form, information could now reach a new kind of audience, remote from the source and uncontrolled by it," writes media scholar Anthony Smith. "Writing transformed knowledge into information."[11]

The Greek philosopher Socrates anticipated the changes that widespread literacy would bring. He argued that knowledge should remain among the privileged classes. Writing threatened the exclusive use of information, he said: "Once a thing is put in writing, the composition, whatever it may be, drifts all over the place, getting into the hands not only of those who understand it, but equally of those who have no business with it."[12]

As Socrates predicted, when more people learned to write, wider communication became possible because people in many different societies could share information among themselves and with people in other parts of the world. But scholars still had to painstakingly copy the information they wanted to keep, or pay a scribe to copy it for them. In the 14th century, for example, the library of the Italian poet Petrarch contained more than 100 manuscripts that he had copied individually himself.[13]

In Petrarch's day, literate people were either monks or members of the privileged classes. Wealthy people could afford tutoring, and they could also afford to buy the handwritten manuscripts copied by the monks. Knowledge — and the power it brings — belonged to very few people.

As societies grew more literate, the demand for manuscripts flourished, but a scribe could produce only one copy at a time. What has been called the *second information communications revolution* began in Germany in 1455, when Johannes Gutenberg printed a Bible on a press that used movable type.

More than 200 years before Gutenberg, the Chinese had invented a printing press that used wood type, and the Chinese also are credited with perfecting a copper press in 1445. But Gutenberg's innovation was to line up individual metal letters that he could ink and then press with paper to produce copies. Unlike wood or copper, the metal could be reused to produce new pages of text, which made the process much cheaper. The Gutenberg Bible, a duplicate of the Latin original, is considered the first book printed by movable type (47 copies survive).

As other countries adopted Gutenberg's press, the price for Bibles plummeted. In 1470, the cost of a French mechanically printed Bible was one-fifth the cost of a hand-printed Bible.[14] This second revolution — printing — meant that knowledge, which had belonged to the privileged few, would one day be accessible to everyone. This key development was one of the essential conditions for the rise of modern governments, as well as an important element of scientific and technological progress.

Before the Gutenberg press, a scholar who wanted special information had to travel to the place where it was kept. But once information could be duplicated easily, it could travel to people beyond the society that created it. The use of paper instead of the scribes' bulky parchment also meant that books could be stacked end to end. For the first time, knowledge was portable and storable. Libraries now could store vast amounts of information in a small space. And because these smaller lightweight books could be easily carried, classical works could be read simultaneously in many cities by all different kinds of people. Another benefit of the development of printing was that societies could more easily keep information to share with future generations.

This effort to communicate — first through spoken messages, then through pictographs, then through the written word, and finally through printed words — demonstrates people's innate desire to share information with one another. *Storability, portability,* and *accessibility* of information are essential to today's concept of mass communication. By definition, mass communication is information that is available to a large audience quickly.

Today's age of communication has been called the *third information communications revolution* because computers have become the storehouses and transmitters of vast amounts of information that previously relied on the written word. Computer technology, which processes and transmits information much more efficiently than mechanical devices, is driving the majority of changes affecting today's media. This means that changes in today's media industries happen much faster than in the past. Satellite broadcasts, digital recordings, and desktop publishing are just three examples of the third information communications revolution.

Although each medium has its own history and economic structure, today all the media industries compete for consumers' attention. Before the century ends, satellite and microchip technology will transform the media business more than we can foresee — quicker transmission of more information to more people than ever before.

# 3. The Media and Government

No institution as sizable and influential as the mass media can escape involvement with government and politics. The media are not only channels for the transmission of political information and debate, but also significant players with a direct stake in government's regulatory and economic policies, as well as government's attitude toward free speech and dissent.

Accordingly, the third theme of this book is that *the way a country's political system is organized affects the way the media within that country operate*. Media systems can be divided into those that allow dissent and those that do not. To categorize the political organization of media systems, scholars often begin with the 1956 book *Four Theories of the Press*, by Fred S. Siebert, Theodore Peterson, and Wilbur Schramm. These four theories, which were originally used to describe the political systems under which media operated in different countries, were: (1) the Soviet theory, (2) the authoritarian theory, (3) the libertarian theory, and (4) the social responsibility theory.

**The Soviet Theory.** Historically in the Soviet Union, the government owned and operated the mass media. All media employees were government employees, expected to serve the government's interests.

Top media executives also served as leaders in the Communist party. Even when the press controls loosened in the 1980s under *glasnost*, the mass media were *part* of the government's policy. Under the Soviet theory, government control came *before* the media published or broadcast; the people who controlled the media reviewed copy and looked at programs before they appeared.

This description of the Soviet press system was conceived before the events of the 1990s challenged the basic assumptions of Soviet government. Many

Eastern bloc countries, such as Romania and Czechoslovakia, which once operated under Soviet influence, based their media systems on the Soviet model. Today, the media systems in these countries are in transition (see Chapter 15).

**The Authoritarian Theory.** Media that operate under the authoritarian theory can be either publicly or privately owned. This concept of the press developed in Europe after Gutenberg. Until the 1850s, presses in Europe were privately owned, and the aristocracy (who governed the countries) wanted some sort of control over what was printed about them. The aristocracy had the financial and political power necessary to make the rules about what would be printed.

Their first idea was to license everyone who owned a press so the license could be revoked if someone published something unfavorable about the government. The first colonial newspapers in America, for example, were licensed by the British crown. Licensing wasn't very successful in the United States, however, because many people who owned presses didn't apply for licenses.

The next authoritarian attempt to control the press was to review material after it was published. A printer who was discovered publishing material that strongly challenged the government could be heavily fined or even put to death.

Today, many governments still maintain this type of rigid control over the media. Most monarchies, for example, operate in an authoritarian tradition, which tolerates very little dissent. Media systems that serve at the government's pleasure and with the government's approval are common.

**The Libertarian Theory.** The concept of a libertarian press evolved from the idea that people who are given all the information on an issue will be able to discern what is true and what is false and will make good choices. This is an idea embraced by the writers of the U.S. Constitution and by other democratic governments.

This theory assumes, of course, that the media's main goal is to convey the truth and that the media will not cave in to outside pressures, such as from advertisers or corporate owners. This theory also assumes that people with opposing viewpoints will be heard — that the media will present all points of view, in what is commonly called the free marketplace of ideas.

The First Amendment to the U.S. Constitution concisely advocates the idea of freedom of the press. Theoretically, America today operates under the libertarian theory, although this ideal has been challenged often by changes in the media industries since the Constitution was adopted.

**The Social Responsibility Theory.** This theory accepts the concept of a libertarian press but prescribes what the media should do. Someone who believes in the social responsibility theory believes that members of the press will do their jobs well only if periodically reminded about their duties.

This theory grew out of the 1947 Hutchins Commission Report on the Free and Responsible Press. The commission listed five goals for the press, including the need for truthful and complete reporting of all sides of an issue. The commission concluded that the American press' privileged position in the Constitution means that the press must always work to be responsible to society. [15]

If the media fail to meet their responsibilities to society, the social responsibility theory holds that the government should encourage the media to comply. In this way the libertarian and the social responsibility theories differ. The libertarian theory assumes the media will work well without government interference; the social responsibility theory advocates government oversight for media that don't act in society's best interest.

Since 1956 when the four theories first were used to describe media systems, critics have contended that these theories are too limiting and that the categories cannot neatly describe all the world's media. In fact, many countries today combine elements of one or more types of media systems.

**Developmental Theory.** A fifth description for media systems that can be added to describe today's media has been called the *developmental* or Third World theory. Under this system, named for the developing nations where it is most often found, the media *can* be privately owned, but are usually owned by the government. The media are used to promote the country's social and economic goals, and to direct a sense of national purpose. For example, a developmental media system might be used to promote birth control or to encourage children to attend school. The media become an outlet for certain types of government propaganda, then, but in the name of economic and social progress for the country.

Although the theory that best describes the American media is the libertarian theory, throughout their history the American media have struggled with both authoritarian and social responsibility debates: Should the press be free to print secret government documents, for example? What responsibility do the networks have to provide worthwhile programming to their audiences? The media, the government, and the public continually modify and adjust their interpretations of just how the American media should operate.

# 4. Media, Society, and Culture

The media industries, as already discussed, provide information and entertainment. But media also can be used to try to persuade the public, and media can affect the culture. These last two functions of media — *persuasion* and *transmission of the culture* — form the basis of the scholarly studies that address the effects media have on society and the culture in which they operate.

This question of the *impact* of the media leads to the fourth theme of this book: *The mass media are cultural institutions that both reflect and affect the society in which they operate.* Although the media can actively influence society, they also mirror it, and scholars constantly strive to delineate the differences.

When the advertising industry suddenly marched to patriotic themes by using flags and other patriotic logos in ads following the United States' claim of victory in the 1991 Gulf War, was the industry pandering, or were advertisers proudly reflecting genuine American sentiment, or both? Did the spread of patriotic themes silence those who felt that the United States overreacted in the Persian Gulf? If you were a scholar, how would you prove your arguments?

This is an example of the difficulty scholars face when analyzing the media's social and cultural effects. Early media studies analyzed the message in the belief that, once a message was sent, it would be received by everyone the same way. Then studies proved that different people perceived messages differently (described as **selective perception**). This is because everyone brings many variables to each message: family background, interests, and education, for example.

Complicating the study of the media's cultural and social effects is the recent proliferation of media outlets. These multiplying sources for information and entertainment mean that today very few people share identical mass media environments. This makes it much more difficult for scholars to determine the specific or cumulative effects of mass media on the general population.

Still, the attempts by scholars to describe media's social and cultural role in society are important because, once identified, the effects can be observed. The questions should be posed so we do not become complacent about media in our lives, so we do not become immune to the possibility that our culture may be cumulatively affected by the media in ways we cannot yet define.

# How MEDIA/IMPACT Works

t HE EFFECTS of media are so interwoven in American society that isolating their influence is difficult. But to help you understand how the American media work together, MEDIA/IMPACT first talks about the development of each medium separately. Then MEDIA/IMPACT expands the discussion to important media effects and media issues.

Chapters 2 through 8 cover each of the seven types of media in America. These chapters explain the historical development of each type of media business and the people and the economics that make each business work. To study an industry's history is to understand the traditions and assumptions that influence how that industry operates today. To study an industry's economics is to understand why each industry makes the financial decisions it does.

Chapters 2 through 5 discuss what are often called the major media: newspapers (Chapter 2), magazines (Chapter 3), radio (Chapter 4), and television (Chapter 5). These media are called the major media because they account for most of the income — 80 percent — the media earn every year. This income is almost entirely from advertising.

Chapters 6 through 8 describe the secondary media: movies (Chapter 6), recordings (Chapter 7), and books (Chapter 8). Although these media are important to the total media business in America, they are not supported by advertising, but by direct purchases. You buy a book or a cassette and you pay admission to see a movie. The secondary media account for about 20 percent of American media income.

Chapters 9 and 10 cover two media-support industries: advertising and public relations. Because advertising pays for most of the American mass media, understanding how the advertising business works is important. A discussion of public relations is included to help you understand how advertising and public relations companies sometimes work together and the role that public relations companies play in garnering media attention for their clients.

Chapters 11 through 14 cover critical arguments about the overall effects of media today and the economic, social, cultural, and political consequences of the American media system on American society. Recent studies of these effects pose many provocative questions: Do the owners and the members of the media have too much power? Why must political candidates spend so much money on campaign advertising, and does it help get them elected? Should high school principals have the power to censor student newspapers? Are reporters too insensitive to people's privacy? Chapter 15 covers the emerging role of global media markets.

The Media Resources Appendix suggests books and magazines to read and lists organizations that compile information about each type of media business. The Media Statistics Appendix gives a selection of historical tables to use for reference to help you understand the media's development.

Throughout the chapters are sections called Impact/Perspectives and Impact/Profiles to focus attention on a particularly interesting person or event or to expand on an important debate about the mass media.

Once you understand the media separately, you can consider their collective effects. After you understand how each type of media business works, you can examine why the people who work in the media make the decisions they do. Then you can evaluate the impact of these decisions on you and on society.

## IN FOCUS

### Introduction to the Mass Media

• According to industry estimates, the average adult spends more than half of his or her waking life with the media.

• The mass media industries in the United States earned $134 billion in 1990 and employed nearly 1.5 million people.

• Communication is the act of sending ideas and attitudes from one person to another. Intrapersonal communication means communication within one person. Interpersonal communication means communication between two people. Mass communication is communication from one person or group of persons through a transmitting device (a medium) to large audiences or markets.

• Many motives shape the American media, including the desire to fulfill the public's need for information, to influence the country's governance, to disseminate the country's culture, to offer entertainment, and to provide an outlet for creative expression. But, above all, the major goal of the American media is to make money.

• Four key themes can be used to study American Media:
1. American media operate as profit-centered businesses;
2. The media are greatly affected by technological changes;
3. The way a country's political system is organized affects the way the media within that country operate;
4. The mass media are cultural institutions that both reflect and affect the society in which they operate.

• Although many media businesses are still family-owned, the main trend in the United States today is for media companies to cluster together in groups. This trend is called concentration of ownership and can take five forms: chains, networks, cross-media ownership, conglomerates, and vertical integration.

• Media acquisitions in the United States have skyrocketed because most conglomerates today are publicly traded companies and because, beginning in 1980, the federal government deregulated the broadcast industry.

• U.S. media industries continue to prosper, but the share of profits is shifting among the industries; different media expand and contract in the marketplace to respond to the audience.

• The communications revolution occurred in three stages. The invention of symbols was considered the first communications revolution; the invention of movable type marked the second communications revolution; and the invention of computers ushered in the third communications revolution.

• Storability, portability, and accessibility of information are essential to today's concept of mass communication. By definition, mass communication is information that is available to a large audience quickly.

• The way a country's political system is organized affects the way the media within that country operate. The traditional four theories of the press divided media systems into the Soviet theory, the authoritarian theory, the libertarian theory, and the social responsibility theory. Recent scholarship has added a fifth theory: the developmental, or Third World, theory.

**II**

**The Media Industries**

**2**

*In 1882, Harrison Gray Otis bought a 25 percent share*

*of the* Los Angeles Times *for $6,000. Today, Times*

*Mirror Company, headed by Otis' great-grandson Otis Chandler, still owns the* Los

Angeles Times, *but also owns* Newsday, *the* Baltimore Sun *newspapers, the*

Hartford Courant *and other newspapers, plus cable and television properties. Times*

*Mirror's yearly income is $3.5 billion.*

*The success of Times Mirror demonstrates the rapid*

*growth of newspapers since their beginnings in the*

**The Newspaper Industry**

**Left:** Benjamin Harris published one issue of *Publick Occurrences* on September 25, 1690. *Publick Occurrences* is sometimes called America's first newspaper. **Right:** John Campbell's *Boston News-Letter*, first published in 1704, is the nation's first consecutively published newspaper.

United States more than three centuries ago. American newspapers began as one-page sheets in colonial America that consisted primarily of announcements of ship arrivals and departures and old news from Europe. Today's large urban newspapers like the *Los Angeles Times* rely on satellite-fed information, and these papers often run to 500 pages on Sunday. (The record for the largest single day's newspaper is held by *The New York Times*. On November 13, 1987, the *Times* published a 1,612-page edition that weighed in at 12 pounds.)[1]

Times Mirror, like all of today's top ten American newspaper chains, has invested in broadcast and cable properties, but continues to devote most of its attention to "newspapering." The huge earnings of these newspaper chains, and their expanding ownership of the nation's smaller newspapers, is a significant theme in the economic evolution of American newspapers.

A second theme in this chapter is how technology changed the role that newspapers play in the delivery of news. For 230 years, newspapers were the nation's major news medium. Newspapers were the only way for large numbers of people to get the same news simultaneously. There was no competition. The invention of broadcasting in the early 20th century changed this exclusive access to news; broadcasting offered instant access to information. Yet despite increasing competition for its audience, the newspaper industry today continues to earn more money every year and employ more people than any other media industry.

A third theme in this chapter is the important part that the newspaper industry played historically in defining the cultural concept of an independent press, based on the belief that the press must remain independent from government to fulfill its responsibility to keep the public informed. Newspapers were the only mass medium for the timely delivery of news from 1690 until the introduction of radio in 1920. Debates about what the public should know, when they should know it, and who should decide what the public needs to know happened during a time when newspapers were the main focus of these discussions.

# Colonial Newspapers: Toward an Independent Press

THE ISSUE of government control of newspapers surfaced early in the history of the colonies. At first, newspapers were the mouthpieces of the British government and news was subject to British approval. Many colonial newspapers were subsidized by the British government, and publishers actually printed "Published by Authority" on the first page to demonstrate government approval.

The first colonial newspaper angered the local authorities so much that the newspaper issued only one edition. This newspaper, *Publick Occurrences*, which was published in Boston on September 25, 1690, is often identified as America's first newspaper. Printer Benjamin Harris, the newspaper's publisher, planned to issue his newspaper once a month with occasional bulletins, but public officials in Massachusetts stopped him soon after he began.

The first and only edition of *Publick Occurrences* was two pages the size of a sheet of today's binder paper (then called a half-sheet), printed on three sides. Harris left the fourth side blank so people could jot down the latest news before they gave the paper to friends.

Along with the news that the Indians had established a "day of Thanksgiving," Harris made the mistake of reporting in his first issue that the French king was "in much trouble" for sleeping with his son's wife. Harris' journalism was too candid for the governor and council of the Massachusetts Bay Colony, who stopped the publication four days after the newspaper appeared.

The nation's first consecutively issued (published more than once) newspaper was *The Boston News-Letter*, which appeared in 1704, one half-sheet printed on two sides. In the first issue, editor John Campbell reprinted the queen's latest speech, some maritime news, and one advertisement, telling people how to put an ad in his paper. Like many subsequent colonial publishers, Campbell reprinted items from the London papers. At one point he apologized to his readers for printing foreign news 13 months late.

Because paper was scarce in the colonies, Campbell used a terse reporting style. On March 18, 1706, for example, he reported: "On Thursday night last, Sampson Waters, a Young man went well to Bed, and was found dead next morning."[2]

For 15 years, Campbell's *News-Letter* was Boston's only newspaper. Then in 1719, Boston became a two-newspaper town when William Brooker launched the *Boston Gazette*. He hired Benjamin Franklin's older brother James as his printer. Campbell, like many newspaper publishers after him, did not welcome the *Boston Gazette*'s competition. "I pity the readers of the new paper," Campbell wrote. "Its sheets smell stronger of beer than of midnight oil. It is not reading fit for people!"[3]

Neither the *News-Letter* nor the *Gazette* could be called exciting. They were loyal to the British crown — on the first page of both newspapers appeared the heading "Published by Authority" — and both Campbell and Brooker depended on England for news and for subsidies. Even though England had ended the policy of licensing the press in 1700, the *News-Letter* and the *Gazette* continued to use the heading (see the *News-Letter*, page 36).

The first challenge to British control came when James Franklin started his own newspaper in Boston in 1721. His *New England Courant* was the first American newspaper to appear without the crown's "by authority" sanction. Thus, Franklin began the tradition of an independent press in this country.

James Franklin argued in print with the local clergy and accused regional authorities of not doing enough to combat pirates. In 1722 the town council charged him with contempt and threw him in jail.

When he was released, the council forbade James to publish his newspaper, so James named his brother Ben the publisher. Sixteen-year-old Ben Franklin, a printer's apprentice, had worked in his brother's shop. He also had contributed articles to the *Courant* under the byline Silence Dogood, who claimed to be the mother of three children.

In 1729, Ben Franklin moved to Philadelphia and bought the *Pennsylvania Gazette* to compete with the only other newspaper in town, the *American Weekly Mercury*, published by Andrew Bradford. The *Pennsylvania Gazette* became the most influential and most financially successful of all the colonial newspapers.

In the same printshop that printed the *Gazette*, Franklin published *Poor Richard's Almanack* in 1732, an annual that sold about 10,000 copies a year for the next 25 years. Franklin proved that a printer could make money without government sanctions or support.

The first New York paper, the *New York Gazette*, was founded by William Bradford (Andrew Bradford's father) in 1725. Bradford's title was "King's Printer to the Province of New York," for which he received a British salary.

The second New York newspaper was *The New-York Weekly Journal*, begun in 1733 by John Peter Zenger. Zenger had once apprenticed to William Bradford, but Zenger quickly established an independent reputation. The *Journal* continually attacked Governor William Cosby for incompetence, and on November 17, 1734, Zenger was arrested and jailed, charged with printing false and seditious writing. (*Seditious* language is writing that could incite rebellion against the government.) While Zenger was in jail, his wife Anna continued to publish the paper.

## The Zenger Trial

Zenger's trial began on August 4, 1735, nine months after his arrest. His defense attorney was Andrew Hamilton (not to be confused with Alexander Hamilton), then almost 80 years old. Hamilton's defense was that truth was a defense against libel, and that if Zenger's words were true, they could not be libelous. (A *libelous* statement is one that damages a person by questioning that person's character or reputation.) Referring to Britain's power over the colonies, Hamilton told the crowded courtroom and the jury:

*Power may justly be compared to a great River, while kept within its due Bounds, is both Beautiful and Useful; but when it overflows its Banks, it is then too impetuous to be stemm'd, it bears down all before it, and brings Destruction and Desolation wherever it comes. . . .*

*The Question before the Court and you, Gentlemen of the Jury, is not of small nor private Concern, it is not the Cause of a poor Printer, nor of New-York alone, which you are now trying: No! It may, in its Consequence, affect every Freeman that lives under a British Government on the main of America. It is the best Cause. It is the Cause of Liberty. . . . The Liberty — both of exposing and opposing arbitrary Power (in these parts of the World at least) by speaking and writing Truth.*[4]

Zenger was acquitted, and he celebrated the victory that night at the Black Horse Tavern, where Hamilton was the guest of honor. The trial established a landmark precedent for freedom of the press in America — the concept that truth is the best defense for libel. If what someone publishes is true, the information cannot be considered libelous. (The issue of libel is discussed in Chapter 13.)

# Women's Role as Colonial Publishers

Colonial women were not encouraged to work outside the home. Therefore, those women who published early newspapers are especially notable because they were relatively rare.

Like Anna Zenger, early colonial women printers usually belonged to printing families that trained wives and daughters to work in the printshops. James Franklin trained his daughter, and after he died his widow Anne managed the business. By the time the American Revolution began, at least 14 women had been printers in the colonies.[5] One of these family-trained printers was the first woman publisher.

Elizabeth Timothy became editor of the weekly *South Carolina Gazette* in Charleston when her husband Lewis died in 1738. Lewis had apprenticed with Benjamin Franklin in Philadelphia, and in 1731 Franklin sponsored the beginning of the *Gazette*. "I was to receive one-third of the profits of the business, paying one-third of the expenses," Franklin wrote in his *Autobiography*. Because he paid part of the publishing costs for the paper, Franklin could be considered the owner of America's first newspaper chain.

Lewis became editor of the *Gazette* two years later, with his oldest son Peter as his apprentice. Lewis and Franklin agreed that Peter would succeed Lewis, but then Lewis died unexpectedly when Peter was only 13. Elizabeth Timothy published her first edition on January 4, 1737, under her son's name. Her first editorial appealed to the community to continue to support the "poor afflicted Widow and six small Children."

Timothy proved to be a good businesswoman, and Franklin used her as an example in favor of the education of women. "She not only sent me as clear a

The first editorial cartoon, Benjamin Franklin's "Join, or Die" snake (1754), appeared in Franklin's *Pennsylvania Gazette* as an appeal to the colonists to unite against the British.

statement as she could find of the transactions past," he wrote in his *Autobiography*, "but continued to account with the greatest regularity and exactness every quarter afterwards." Mother and son ran the paper together until 1746, when she bought out Franklin and Peter formally took over the business.[6]

## The Revolutionary Partisan Press

As dissatisfaction with British rule grew in the colonies, newspapers — which until this time had concentrated primarily on news events — became political tools, essential outlets for revolutionary ideology. Revolutionary newspapers fostered the debate that eventually led to the colonies' independence.

By 1750, 14 weekly newspapers were being published in the colonies.[7] The first editorial cartoon appeared in Benjamin Franklin's *Pennsylvania Gazette* in 1754. This picture of a snake cut into eight parts and the caption "Join, or Die" appealed to the colonists to unite against the British. The head represented New England; the seven other parts stood for New York, New Jersey,

The tombstone edition of the *Pennsylvania Journal* mocked the British Stamp Act by publishing a skull and crossbones in the lower right-hand corner where the official stamp would have appeared.

Pennsylvania, Maryland, Virginia, North Carolina, and South Carolina. The cartoon, a big hit, was quickly reprinted in the New York and Boston papers.

**The Stamp Act.** The snake appeared next in 1765 as a symbol of opposition to the British Stamp Act, which signaled the beginning of the revolutionary period. The Stamp Act taxed publishers a halfpenny for each issue that was a half sheet or less and one penny for a full sheet. Each advertisement was taxed two shillings. All the colonial newspapers, even those loyal to the crown, fought the Act.

Many newspapers threatened to stop publication, but only a few of them did. Most editors published editions that mocked the tax. William Bradford III issued the famous tombstone edition of the *Pennsylvania Journal* on October 31, 1765. The front page, bordered in black, was printed with a skull and crossbones where the official stamp should have been. The *Maryland Gazette* issued a "Doom's-Day Number" with a similar skull and crossbones stamp and a bold black headline, "The Times are Dreadful, Dismal, Doleful, Dolorous, and Dollarless."[8]

The Stamp Act Congress met in New York in October 1765 and adopted the now-familiar slogan "No taxation without representation." Parliament, facing united opposition from all the colonial publishers, repealed the Stamp Act on March 18, 1766.

A decade later, the lack of supplies killed some newspapers during the Revolutionary War, but a hunger for war news supported others. By war's end, only 20 of the 35 newspapers being published at the beginning of the war survived.[9]

America's first *daily* newspaper was the *Pennsylvania Evening Post*, begun in 1783. Alexander Hamilton sponsored the *Gazette of the United States* in 1789 in New York to support adoption of the Constitution, and two years later Thomas Jefferson began Philadelphia's *National Gazette* to oppose whatever Hamilton supported, defining the role of newspapers as partisan outlets for opinion.

Partisan political debates often turned into personal attacks. Benjamin Franklin's grandson, Benjamin Franklin Bache, attacked George Washington in Bache's paper the *General Advertiser*. Trying to discredit the new government, Bache wrote: "If ever a nation was debauched by a man, the American nation has been debauched by Washington."[10] Bache, who was nicknamed "Lightning Rod Junior," had learned how to use his newspaper to play politics.

**The Alien and Sedition Laws.** The Alien and Sedition Laws, passed by Congress in 1798, were the federal government's first attempt to control its critics. Congress said that anyone who "shall write, print, utter, or publish . . . false, scandalous and malicious writing or writings against the government of the United States, or either house of the Congress of the United States, or the President of the United States" could be fined up to $2,000 and jailed for two years.

Several people went to jail. A Boston publisher spent 30 days in jail for libeling the Massachusetts legislature. A New York editor was fined $100 and jailed for four months. Benjamin Franklin Bache also was sued under the Laws, but he died from yellow fever before the case was tried. By 1800, the angry rhetoric had dissipated. The Alien and Sedition Laws expired after two years and were not renewed. However, throughout American press history, the tradition of an independent press, established by James Franklin in 1721, continued to confront the government's desire to restrain criticism.

# Early 1800s: Newspapers Diversify as Their Audiences Grow

HE TECHNOLOGICAL advances of the 19th century—such as cheaper newsprint, mechanized printing, and the telegraph—meant that newspapers could reach a wider audience faster than ever before. Improved manufacturing lowered the cost of newsprint, which meant that newspapers could carry more pages per issue. Printing presses, which once were expensive and immobile, became more affordable and less cumbersome, making it easier for publishers to start newspapers. And the invention of the telegraph meant that news could travel faster and more economically. This, in turn, meant that the newspaper business became an attractive investment. Writes media scholar Anthony Smith,

*It became apparent that great fortunes could be made by turning the medium into a universal one, rather than restricting it to the special groups who needed a regular diet of material drawn from the worlds of politics and finance. . . . These new needs were met by transforming the newspaper, or certain examples of it, into a medium of entertainment and thus attracting so large an audience that publishers could promise the advertisers access to virtually every home.* [11]

By the 19th century, newspaper publishers had changed their opinion about their audience. Confined to Eastern cities and highly educated urban audiences during the 1700s, newspaper publishers in the 1800s sought new readers—from the frontier, from among the nation's growing number of immigrants, and from within the shrinking Native American population. This expansion resulted in four additions to American newspapers: frontier journalism, ethnic and cultural newspapers, the alternative press, and the penny press. Another innovation of the period was the beginning of cooperative news gathering.

## Frontier Journalism

Gold, silver, and adventure lured people west, and when the people arrived they needed newspapers. The *Indiana Gazette*, the *Texas Gazette*, the *Oregon Spectator*, the *Weekly Arizonian*, and Colorado's *Rocky Mountain News* met that need, aided by the telegraph, which moved news easily from coast to coast.

Frontier journalists learned to improvise. This press operation, assembled to publish New Mexico's first newspaper, was set up under a juniper tree near Kingston, New Mexico.

The wide-open land beckoned many journalists. The most celebrated journalist to chronicle the frontier was Samuel Clemens, who traveled to Nevada in 1861 prospecting for silver. Clemens didn't find any silver, but a year later the Virginia City *Territorial Enterprise* — the area's largest paper — hired him for $25 a week. Clemens first signed his name Mark Twain on a humorous travel letter written for the *Enterprise*.

## Ethnic and Native American Newspapers

English-language newspapers did not satisfy everyone's needs. In the first half of the 19th century, many newspapers sought to succeed by catering to ethnic and cultural interests. In the early 1800s, Spanish-speaking people in Georgia could read *El Misisipi*. Herman Ridder's German newspaper *New Yorker Staats-Zeitung*, founded in 1845, was the most successful foreign-language newspaper. It formed the financial basis for today's Knight-Ridder chain.

Elias Boudinot published the first Native American newspaper, the *Cherokee Phoenix*, from 1828 to 1832.

People outside of the mainstream of society, such as Spanish and German immigrants, used newspapers to create a sense of community and ethnic identity. In the 1800s, Native Americans who had been displaced by the settlers also felt a need to voice their complaints. On February 21, 1828, the nation's first Native American newspaper appeared.

The *Cherokee Phoenix* was edited by Elias Boudinot, a Native American who had been educated at a Northern seminary. The Cherokee nation held exclusive control over the four-page paper, which was printed half in English and half in an 86-character alphabet that represented the Cherokee language. (Authorities shut down the press in 1832 because they felt that Boudinot was arousing antigovernment sentiment.)

## Dissident Voices: The Alternative Press

Two strong social movements, emancipation and women's suffrage, brought new voices to the American press. This **alternative press** movement signaled the beginning of a significant American journalistic tradition. Newspapers became an outlet for the voices of social protest, a tradition that continues today.

Five early advocates of domestic change who used the press to advance their causes — the abolition of slavery and suffrage for women — were John B. Russwurm, the Reverend Samuel Cornish, Frederick Douglass, Jane Grey Swisshelm, and Ida B. Wells.

Russwurm and Cornish, who were African-American, started *Freedom's Journal* in 1827 with very little money in New York City to respond to racist attacks in several local newspapers. "We wish to plead our cause," they wrote in their first issue. "Too long have others spoken for us. Too long has the public been deceived by misrepresentations in the things that concern us dearly."[12] *Freedom's Journal* lasted for two years and reached only a few readers, but it was the beginning of an African-American press tradition that eventually created more than 2,700 newspapers, magazines, and quarterly journals.[13]

What has often been called the most important African-American pre-Civil War newspaper was Frederick Douglass' weekly *North Star*. "Right is of no Sex — Truth is of no Color — God is the Father of us all, and we are all Brethren" read the masthead. Beginning in 1847, Douglass struggled to support the *North Star* by giving lectures. The newspaper eventually reached 3,000 subscribers in the United States and abroad with its emancipation message. Douglass also included social and foreign news for his readers.

In 1851, Douglass merged the *North Star* with another newspaper to try to get more readers, but by 1864 he realized that he could not continue as a weekly. The weekly became a monthly in the mid-1860s and stopped three years later. Douglass worked for the Washington weekly *New Era* beginning in 1870 and invested more than $10,000 of his own money before the magazine stopped in 1875. Douglass died in 1895 at age 78.

Like Douglass, Jane Grey Swisshelm campaigned for civil rights. Her first byline appeared in 1844 in the *Spirit of Liberty*, published in Pittsburgh. Four years later she began her own abolitionist publication, the *Pittsburgh Saturday Visiter*, which also promoted women's rights.

As a correspondent for Horace Greeley's *New York Tribune* in Washington, D.C., Swisshelm convinced Vice President Millard Fillmore to let her report from the Senate press gallery. The gallery had been open to male journalists for 55 years, and on May 21, 1850, Swisshelm became the first female journalist to sit in the gallery.

She founded a newspaper in Minnesota, often working as both printer and writer, using women assistants as typesetters. After she sold the paper to her nephew, she worked for the War Department, edited a newspaper in Washington, D.C., and then wrote her autobiography at her family home in Swissvale, Pennsylvania, where she died in 1884 at age 69.

Ida B. Wells, part-owner of the Memphis *Free Speech and Headlight*, who wrote under the pseudonym Iola.

Ida B. Wells didn't start out to be a journalist, but the cause of emancipation drew her to the profession. She was born to slave parents during the Civil War. When the war was over, Ida's parents were freed and the family moved to Mississippi, where her mother worked as a cook and her father as a carpenter.

In 1878, both of Wells' parents and her infant sister died in a yellow fever epidemic, and 16-year-old Wells took responsibility for her six brothers and sisters, attended Rust College, and then moved the family to Memphis and became a teacher.

A Baptist minister who was an editor of the Negro Press Association hired her to write for his paper. She wrote under the pseudonym Iola. Soon she became part-owner of the Memphis *Free Speech and Headlight*. She traveled throughout the Delta soliciting subscriptions, and circulation rose from 1,500 to 4,000 under her management.[14]

In 1892, Wells wrote a story about three African-American men who had been kidnapped from a Memphis jail and killed. "The city of Memphis has demonstrated that neither character nor standing avails the Negro, if he dares to protect himself against the white man or become his rival," she wrote. "We are out-numbered and without arms."[15] While in New York, she read in the *New York Sun* that a mob had sacked the *Free Speech* office.

Wells decided not to return to Memphis. She worked in New York and lectured in Europe and then settled in Chicago, where she married lawyer

Ferdinand Lee Barnett. Ida Wells-Barnett and her husband actively campaigned for African-American rights in Chicago, and she continued to write until she died at age 69 in 1931.

These pioneers — Russwurm, Cornish, Douglass, Swisshelm, and Wells — had used newspapers to lobby for social change. These dissident newspapers offered a forum for protest, which is an important cultural role for an independent press.

## Toward Mass Readership: The Penny Press

The voices of social protest reached a limited, committed audience, but most people could not afford to subscribe to a daily newspaper. Newspapers were sold by advance yearly subscription for $6 to $10 at a time when most skilled workers earned less than $750 annually. Then, in 1833, Benjamin Day demonstrated that he could profitably appeal to a mass audience by dropping the price of a newspaper to a penny and selling the paper on the street every day.

Day's *New York Sun* published sensational news and feature stories to interest the working class. He was able to lower the price to a penny by filling the paper with advertising and by hiring newsboys to sell the paper on street corners. This first successful **penny paper** reported local gossip, sensationalized police news, and carried a page and a half of advertising in a four-page paper. Newsboys bought 100 papers for 67 cents and tried to sell them all each day to make a profit. After a year, the *Sun*, using the slogan "It Shines for ALL," was selling 10,000 copies a day, twice as many as its nearest rival.

Day's penny paper was followed by similar papers in Boston, Philadelphia, and Baltimore. In New York, Horace Greeley introduced the *New York Tribune* as a penny paper to compete with the *Sun*. Even *The New York Times*, founded by Henry J. Raymond in 1851, was a penny paper when it began. The legacy of the penny press continues in today's gossip columns and crime stories that newspapers and broadcast stations report in an effort to attract an audience.

## Cooperative and For-Profit News Gathering

The invention of the telegraph by Samuel F. B. Morse in 1844 meant that news that once took weeks to reach publication could be transmitted in minutes. In 1848, six newspapers in New York City decided to share the costs of gathering foreign news by telegraph from Boston. Henry Raymond drew up the agreement among the papers to pay $100 for 3,000 words of telegraphic news.[16]

Soon known as the New York Associated Press, this organization was the country's first **cooperative news gathering** association. This meant that the member newspapers shared the expenses to get the news, returning any profits to the members. Today's Associated Press is the result of this early partnership, as newspapers joined together in a cooperative, with several members sharing the cost of gathering the news, domestic and foreign.

A different way of sharing information was devised by the United Press, founded in 1882 to compete with the Associated Press. United Press was established not as a cooperative but as a privately owned, for-profit wire service. (Today, these wire services are called news services.) The original United Press, which went bankrupt, was revived by E. W. Scripps in 1897.

Scripps set fees for the wire service that would make him a profit. Unlike the Associated Press, which limited who could join, United Press allowed anyone to buy its service. (Eventually United Press merged with William Randolph Hearst's International News Service to form United Press International in 1958. In 1982, Scripps Howard sold UPI.)

# The Civil War Years: Accreditation and Photojournalism

I N T H E 1860s interest in the emotional issues of the Civil War sent many reporters to the battlefront. Hundreds of correspondents roamed freely among the soldiers, reporting for the North and the South. Two important results of Civil War reporting were the accreditation of reporters and the introduction of photographs to enhance written reports.

## Government Accreditation of Journalists

The issue of government interests versus press freedom surfaced early in the Civil War. In 1861, Union General Winfield Scott forbade telegraph companies to transmit military information because he was afraid that some stories would help the South.

This photograph, from the Mathew Brady collection, shows Civil War journalists gathered outside the battlefield headquarters for the *New York Herald*.

At the Battle of Bull Run in July 1861, *New York Times* editor Henry Raymond, reporting the war from the front, mistakenly telegraphed a story that said the North had won. When he followed up with the correct story, military censors blocked the news, arguing that the information should be kept secret.

Then General William T. Sherman ordered *New York Herald* correspondent Thomas E. Knox arrested and held as a spy for sending sensitive military information. President Lincoln intervened to compromise the needs of the press with the needs of the nation through a process called **accreditation**. This meant that members of the press would be certified by the government to cover the war. Accredited journalists were required to carry press passes, issued by the military.

The practice of accreditation continues to be the government's method of certifying war-reporting journalists. Press pools during wartime are a recent refinement of this practice: A select number of journalists are chosen to represent their colleagues, and the reports from the press pool are shared with all journalists covering the same story. (See Chapter 13 for a further discussion of the press in wartime.)

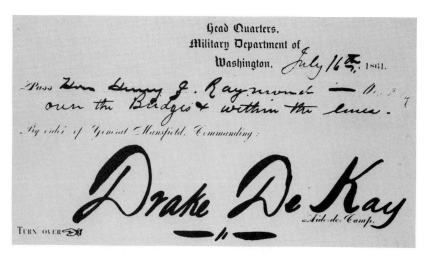

This press pass, for *New York Times* editor Henry Raymond, is an early example of press accreditation by the federal government.

## The Birth of Photojournalism

Also at the Battle of Bull Run was photographer Mathew Brady, who convinced Lincoln that a complete photographic record of the war should be made. Brady photographed the battles of Antietam and Fredericksburg and sent photographic teams to record the war's other events. He financed the ambitious project himself.

The photographic teams traveled anywhere they wanted, carrying their equipment in primitive black covered wagons and camping alongside the troops. To soldiers, the black wagon's ominous arrival signaled that a battle would soon follow. Newspapers did not yet have a method to reproduce the photographs, but the pictures were published in magazines, and Brady became the nation's first news photographer. His 3,500 photographs provide an invaluable mirror of Americans at war with one another.

Brady's wartime experiment demonstrated the practicality and effectiveness of news photography. Until this time, photography had been confined primarily to studio portraits because of the cumbersome equipment and slow chemical processing. Still, news photography did not become widespread until after the turn of the century. In 1906, news photographers documented the San Francisco earthquake and fire, and in 1907, the first photograph was transmitted by wire, which eventually meant that immediate images could flow from the site of a story to several newspapers at once. The marriage of photographs and text to tell a better story than either could tell alone formed the beginnings of today's concept of **photojournalism**, which uses photographs to help report a news story.

# The Heyday of Newspapers

**F**OR THE first 20 years of the 20th century — before radio and television — newspapers dominated the country. Newspapers were the nation's single source of daily dialogue about political, cultural, and social issues. This was also the era of greatest newspaper competition.

Many newspapers born in the 1800s eventually would be among the nation's most notable 20th-century papers: *The New York Times*, the *Baltimore Sun*, the *Boston Globe*, the *Philadelphia Inquirer*, William Allen White's *Emporia* (Kansas) *Gazette, The Wall Street Journal,* the *Los Angeles Times*, the *Chicago Tribune*, and the *Washington Post*.

Most of the country's newspaper titans, such as Joseph Pulitzer, William Randolph Hearst, and the *Los Angeles Times'* Harrison Gray Otis, were in place. The story of Adolph S. Ochs and *The New York Times* is a good example of how many newspaper empires began. It is difficult to believe today, but in the early 1890s, the *Times* was near bankruptcy.

The *Times*, dwarfed by the circulations of its competitors, was struggling to keep its 9,000 paid subscribers (compared to 20,000 at Pulitzer's New York *World*). Capitalizing on the paper's vulnerability, Ochs invested $75,000 in the paper in 1896 with an agreement from the paper's other investors that he would win control if he could get more people to buy the paper.

Ochs gave his readers a quality paper that emphasized foreign, government, and business news. Mocking the competition's cheap efforts to lure readers, he advertised with a slogan "It Does Not Soil the Breakfast Cloth," which he eventually changed to "All the News That's Fit to Print."

Circulation went up to 25,000, but that wasn't enough for Ochs, so in 1898 he dropped the price to a penny — compared to 2 cents for Hearst's New York *Journal* and 3 cents for the *World*. *Times* circulation jumped to 75,000, Ochs gained control of the paper, and popular support for what is often called America's greatest newspaper was established.

Joseph Pulitzer (left) and William Randolph Hearst (right), whose New York newspaper war spawned the term *yellow journalism*.

## Competition Breeds Sensationalism

In large cities like New York, as many as ten newspapers competed for readers at once, so the publishers looked for new ways to expand their audience. Two New York publishers — Pulitzer and Hearst — revived and refined the penny-press sensationalism that had begun in 1833 with Benjamin Day's *New York Sun*. Like Day, Pulitzer and Hearst proved that newspapers could reap enormous fortunes for their owners. They also demonstrated that credible, serious reporting is not all that people want in a newspaper. Pulitzer and Hearst promoted giveaways and fabricated stories. Hearst is even blamed for starting the Spanish-American War.

Joseph Pulitzer, a Hungarian immigrant, started his newspaper career by spending $2,500 at a sheriff's sale to buy the bankrupt *St. Louis Post*. He used the profits from that paper (which became the *Post-Dispatch*) to buy the New York *World* in 1883. An ambitious man who knew how to grab his readers' interest, Pulitzer published the first newspaper comics and sponsored journalist Nellie Bly on an around-the-world balloon trip to try to beat the fictional record in the popular book *Around the World in 80 Days*.

To promote his newspaper, The New York *World*, Joseph Pulitzer sent journalist Nellie Bly (her real name was Elizabeth Cochran) around the world. Readers were invited to follow her progress on a game card printed in the paper.

Bly cabled back stories, and the *World* published a game so readers could guess her progress. Bly finished the trip in 72 days, 6 hours, and 11 minutes, and the stunt brought Pulitzer the circulation he craved.

In San Francisco, young William Randolph Hearst, the new editor of the *San Francisco Examiner*, sent a reporter to cover Bly's arrival.[17] Hearst, the only son of wealthy parents, had worked a year for Pulitzer after being expelled from Harvard. Then in 1887 he convinced his father, who owned the *Examiner*, to let him run the paper, which had already lost $250,000.

Hearst tagged the *Examiner* "The Monarch of the Dailies," added a lovelorn column, and attacked several of his father's influential friends in the newspaper.

He spent money wildly, buying talent from competing papers and staging showy promotional events. Eventually, after his father spent another $750,000, circulation climbed. Then Hearst bought the New York *Journal* in 1896 to compete head-on with Pulitzer.

# Yellow Journalism and the Spanish-American War

In New York, Hearst hired Pulitzer's entire Sunday staff and cut the *Journal*'s price to a penny, so Pulitzer dropped his price to match it. Hearst bought a color press and printed color comics. Then he stole Pulitzer's popular comic "Hogan's Alley," which included a character named the Yellow Kid. Pulitzer continued to publish the comic with a new artist.

Hearst relished the battle, as the *Journal* screamed attention-grabbing headlines like "Thigh of the Body Found" and the paper offered $1,000 for information that would convict the murderer. Critics named this sensationalism **yellow journalism** after the Yellow Kid, an epithet still bestowed on highly emotional, exaggerated, or inaccurate reporting that emphasizes crime, sex, and violence.

By 1900, about one-third of the metropolitan dailies were following the trend toward yellow journalism.[18] Hearst's circulation, up 150,000 in one year, challenged Pulitzer's, but beginning in 1898, the Spanish-American War provided the battlefield for Pulitzer and Hearst to truly act out their newspaper war. For three years, the two newspapers unrelentingly overplayed events in the Cuban struggle for independence from Spain, each trying to beat the other with irresponsible, exaggerated stories, many of them manufactured.

The overplaying of events that resulted from the sensational competition between Pulitzer and Hearst showed that newspapers could have a significant effect on political attitudes. The Spanish-American War followed the sinking of the U.S. battleship *Maine* in Havana harbor, killing 266 men. Hearst dubbed the event "the *Journal*'s War," but in fact Hearst and Pulitzer shared responsibility, because both men had inflamed the public unnecessarily about events in Cuba.

During the Spanish-American War, Hearst and Pulitzer irresponsibly manufactured public excitement over events to boost their own profits. The serious consequences of their yellow journalism directly demonstrated the importance of press responsibility. After the war, Pulitzer renounced yellow journalism. His health declined, and when he died in 1915, Pulitzer endowed the Pulitzer Prizes to reward excellence in journalism. Hearst eventually expanded his media empire to 27,000 employees at newspapers and radio stations throughout the country.

**Left:** To promote circulation, William Randolph Hearst's New York *Journal* featured articles about sensational crimes. The *Journal* offered a reward in this issue for information leading to the murderer, whose victim's thigh was illustrated on the front page. **Right:** This 1928 photo of Ruth Snyder's execution exemplifies the screaming headlines and large photographs that typified jazz journalism.

## Jazz Journalism

The journalistic legacy of Day, Pulitzer, and Hearst surfaced again in the **tabloid journalism** of the 1920s, often called **jazz journalism**. In 1919, the publishers of the *New York Daily News* sponsored a beauty contest to inaugurate the nation's first tabloid. A tabloid is a small-format newspaper, usually 11 inches by 14 inches, featuring illustrations and sensational stories.

The *Daily News* merged pictures and screaming headlines with reports about sex and violence to exceed anything that had appeared before. It ran full-page pictures with short, punchy text. Love affairs soon became big news, and so did murders. In the ultimate example of tabloid journalism, a *Daily News* reporter strapped a camera to his ankle in 1928 and took a picture of Ruth

Snyder, who had conspired to kill her husband, as she was electrocuted at Sing Sing. The picture covered the front page, and the caption stated "This is perhaps the most remarkable exclusive picture in the history of criminology." Photojournalism had taken a sensational turn, very different from what Mathew Brady had envisioned when he documented the Civil War.

Daily circulation of the newspaper had by this time reached more than 1 million. Imitators followed, but no jazz journalism tabloid ever matched the *Daily News'* success. Jazz journalism's successors today are the supermarket tabloids, such as the *National Enquirer*, which feature large photographs and stories about sex, violence, and celebrity romances.

# Reporters' Evolving Role

**b**ESIDES THE New York City newspaper war, the first half of the 20th century brought two very different events in the evolving role of American reporters: unionization and war censorship. Unionization standardized reporters' wages at many of the nation's largest newspapers, and war censorship revived the debate over press freedom versus press responsibility.

## Unionization Encourages Professionalism

Labor unions were first established at newspapers in 1800, and the International Typographical Union went national in the mid-1850s. Other unions formed to represent production workers at newspapers: the International Stereotypers and Electrotypers' Union, the International Photo-Engravers' Union, and the International Printing Pressmen and Assistants' Union. But reporters didn't have a union until 1933, when *New York World-Telegram* reporter Heywood Broun called on his colleagues to organize.

In his regular newspaper column, Broun announced a meeting, saying, ". . . The fact that newspaper editors and owners are genial folk should hardly stand in the way of the organization of a newspaper writers' union. There

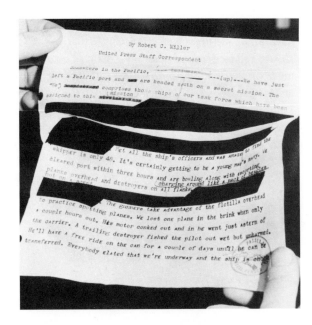

All war stories passed through the Office of War Information, such as this communiqué by United Press correspondent Robert C. Miller, showing parts that were removed by the OWI in 1942. The stamp in the lower right-hand corner verifies OWI scrutiny.

should be one. Beginning at nine o'clock in the morning of October 1, I am going to do the best I can in helping get one up."[19]

The Newspaper Guild held its first meeting four months later and elected Broun its president. Broun remained president until he died in 1939 at age 51. The Guild continues today to cover employees at many of America's larger newspapers. Unions represent roughly one in five newspaper employees.

With the rise of unions, employee contracts, which once had been negotiated in private, became public agreements. In general, salaries for reporters at union newspapers rose, and eventually this led to a sense of professionalism, including codes of ethics.

# War Reporting: Press Freedom Versus National Interest

With news photographers and the news services well established, reporting in both world wars and the Korean War excelled. Some newspapers — *The New York Times*, the *Chicago Tribune*, and the *Christian Science Monitor* — established permanent overseas bureaus, but most papers depended on the news services to report major events or they sent correspondents to cover specific breaking stories.

War reporting matured amid a constant tug-of-war between the issues of freedom of the press and protecting America's self-interest. " Correspondents seek to tell as much as possible as soon as possible," says Phillip Knightley in his book *The First Casualty*. "The military seeks to tell as little as possible as late as possible." (The title *The First Casualty* comes from Senator Hiram Johnson, who in 1917 said, "The first casualty when war comes is truth.")[20]

Still, some brilliant newspaper stories reached the American public from such journalists as Dorothy Thompson, Marguerite Higgins, William L.

## Ernie Pyle: The War Correspondent Who Hated War

Ernie Pyle worked for Scripps Howard. This reflection on his work was written by **Dan Thomasson**, the editor of Scripps Howard News Service, to accompany a collection of Pyle's dispatches that was published in 1986. The Pyle story about Captain Waskow cited here is a fine example of war correspondence.

THE OTHER day while going through some old files in our library, I came upon a yellowed and tattered dispatch.

It made me cry.

It told about the death of a Capt. Waskow during the Italian campaign of 1944. And it probably is the most powerful treatise on war and death and the human spirit I have ever read.

I took it out and had it treated and framed and I hung it in the office in a prominent position where now and then one of the younger reporters will come by and read it and try to hide the inevitable tear.

The man who wrote it, Ernest Taylor Pyle, is but a memory as distant as the war he covered so eloquently and ultimately died in.

But unlike so many who perished beside him, Pyle's contribution to what Studs Terkel calls "the last good war" remains with us in his work —

thousands of words that will forever memorialize brave men and debunk the "glory" of war.

The column that says it best perhaps is the one drafted for the end of the fighting in Europe. It was found in his pocket by the foot soldiers who had risked their lives to retrieve his body on the Japanese island of Ie Shima in 1945.

"Those who are gone would not wish themselves to be a millstone of gloom around our necks.

"But there are many of the

Shirer, and Ernie Pyle. In World War II alone, 37 American correspondents died and 112 were wounded.[21]

Among the dead was 45-year-old Ernie Pyle, a legendary journalistic figure during the war. Pyle's talent was his ability to ignore the war's larger political arguments and focus instead on war's effects on each individual soldier. His stories were the most widely read, most widely quoted examples of reportage from the soldier's point of view. (See Impact/Profile, Ernie Pyle: The War Correspondent Who Hated War.)

War correspondent Ernie Pyle (1900–1945) died during the last days of World War II on the Japanese island of Ie Shima.

living who have burned into their brains forever the unnatural sight of cold dead men scattered over the hillsides and in the ditches along the high rows of hedge throughout the world.

"Dead men by mass production — in one country after another — month after month and year after year. Dead men in winter and dead men in summer.

"Dead men in such familiar promiscuity that they become monotonous.

"Dead men in such monstrous infinity that you come almost to hate them."

. . . When I was a kid starting out in this business, the trade magazines were full of job-seeking ads by those who claimed they could "write like Ernie Pyle." This was 10 years after his death and he was still everyone's model. . . .

Here is some of what he wrote about the death of Capt. Waskow. One needs to read no further to understand why he has withstood the decades when others have not, and why 41 years later [in 1986] a collection of his dispatches would be a Book-of-the-Month Club selection.

"Then a soldier came and stood beside the officer [a captain], and bent over, and he too spoke to his dead captain, not in a whisper but awfully tenderly, and he said:

"'I sure am sorry, sir.'

"Then the first man squatted down, and he reached down and took the dead hand, and he sat there for a full five minutes, holding the dead hand in his own and looking intently into the dead face and he never uttered a sound all the time he sat there.

"And finally he put the hand down, and then reached up and gently straightened the points of the captain's shirt collar, and then he sort of rearranged the tattered edges of his uniform around the wound. And then he got up and walked away down the road in the moonlight, all alone."

―――――――――――――

*"Why They Still Write Ernie Pyle Books,"* Honolulu Advertiser, *June 20, 1986, p. A-11.*

In the 1991 Gulf War, war reporting came from a selected press pool of reporters and photographers, who represented news services, newspapers, television, and radio.

# Newspapers in the Television Era

THE ADVENT of television dramatically affected the newspaper industry. Newspaper publishers already had learned how to live with the only other 20th-century news industry — radio. In the 1920s, when radio had first become popular, newspapers had refused to carry advertising or time logs for the programs, but eventually newspapers conceded the space to radio.

But television was a larger threat; television offered moving images of the news in addition to entertainment. The spread of television demonstrated how interrelated the media are. The newspaper industry relinquished its supremacy as the major news medium, forced to share the audience for news with broadcasting. And over time, television's influence changed both the look and the content of many newspapers.

In 1947, newspaper readership was at its peak. New Yorkers bought more than 6 million newspapers during the week and more than 10 million every Sunday.[22] Beginning in the 1950s, television posed a very large threat. If people could see the news every night for free, why should they buy a newspaper? And why should advertisers invest in newspaper space when they could buy TV time instead?

Newspaper readership dropped substantially in the 1950s, but the introduction of television was not the only reason. The Depression had killed a lot of newspapers, as fewer businesses advertised and fewer people had money to buy newspapers. As newspapers failed, companies with money to invest bought out their competitors, and some newspapers just stopped publishing. The result was a consolidation of the newspaper industry in the 1950s.

## The Revival of the Dissident Press

The social movements of the 1960s briefly revived one portion of the newspaper industry — the alternative press. Like their 1800s predecessors in the abolitionist and emancipation movements, people who supported the alternative press in the 1960s felt that the mainstream press was avoiding important issues, such as the anti-Vietnam War movement and the civil rights movement.

In 1955, journalist I. F. Stone anticipated the trend that created 1960s alternative newspapers. As an articulate critic of the government, Stone began *I. F. Stone's Weekly*, which he researched, wrote, and published virtually by himself. Filled with valuable insider information about the federal government that only Stone seemed to know, *I. F. Stone's Weekly* outlasted many of the weeklies created by the social protest movements of the 1960s. (Citing poor health, Stone stopped his *Weekly* — which had by then become biweekly — in 1972.)

In 1964, as a way to pass along news about the antiwar movement, the *Los Angeles Free Press* became the first underground paper to publish regularly. The *Barb* in Berkeley, *Kaleidoscope* in Chicago, and *Quicksilver Times* in Washington, D.C., soon followed.

In his book *Uncovering the Sixties: The Life and Times of the Underground Press*, Abe Peck describes the alternative voice:

*Mainstream newspapers ran crime news and arts reviews and Dick Tracy. Underground papers ran demonstration news and rock reviews and the* Fabulous Furry Freak

Brothers, *a comic about three amiable "heads" Tracy would have busted for their rampant pot-smoking.*

Cornell University professor Theodore J. Lowi, who calls the '60s activists "extreme reformists," says that one reason the alternative press declined is that the causes these newspapers espoused became part of the mainstream. In 1971, for example, the *Los Angeles Times* editorialized against the Vietnam War, and the *Boston Globe* followed a year later. These reformists

*used radical action to gain attention, but their demands and hopes were for the present society to live by its own ideals. . . . And the Sixties movement succeeded to a large extent. Universities reorganized themselves; there is more public access to agencies; there have been civil rights advances; there is more pacifism. Success is one reason for the decline of the movement.*[23]

What the 1960s underground press did prove had been proved in the nineteenth century — that in America, causes need a voice, and if those voices are not represented in the mainstream press, publications emerge to support alternative views.

# A Declining Readership

Since the 1970s, the overall number of newspapers has declined. Many afternoon papers died when TV took over the evening news. Other afternoon papers changed to mornings. Then newspaper publishers realized that television could provide the news headlines, but newspapers could offer the background that television news could not.

Newspaper publishers also began to see that they could play on the popularity of television personalities, who became news items. Eventually, advertisers realized that viewers cannot clip coupons out of their television sets or retrieve copies of yesterday's TV ads, so advertisers began to use newspapers to complement television advertising campaigns.

Today, the majority of small dailies are part of a chain. As shown in Figure 2.1, competition between local papers has declined dramatically because most cities have only one newspaper. And in an attempt to match television's visual displays, newspapers have introduced advanced graphics and vivid color. (See Impact/Perspective, The New Storytellers.) The newspaper industry still earns more every year than any other medium.

**2.1 ➤**

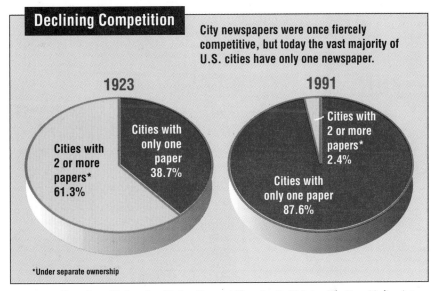

**Declining Competition**

City newspapers were once fiercely competitive, but today the vast majority of U.S. cities have only one newspaper.

**1923**

Cities with 2 or more papers* 61.3%

Cities with only one paper 38.7%

**1991**

Cities with 2 or more papers* 2.4%

Cities with only one paper 87.6%

*Under separate ownership

SOURCE: Data from Christopher H. Sterling and Timothy R. Haight, *The Mass Media: Aspen Institute Guide to Communication Industry Trends* (New York/London: Praeger, 1977) and American Newspaper Publishers Association, Washington, D.C., Joseph Lorfano, personal communication, December 13, 1991.

# How Newspapers Work

MANY COLONIAL publishers handled all the tasks of putting out a newspaper singlehandedly, but today's typical newspaper operation is organized into two separate departments: the editorial side and the business side. The *editorial* side handles everything that you read in the paper — the news and feature stories, editorials, cartoons, and photographs. The *business* side handles everything else — production, advertising, distribution, and administration.

On the editorial side at a medium-size daily, different *editors* — a news editor, a sports editor, a features editor, and a business editor, for example — handle different parts of the paper. The managing editor oversees these news departments. A copy editor checks the reporters' stories before they are set in type, and a layout editor positions the stories. Editorial writers and cartoonists

# The New Storytellers

One sign of television's influence on newspapers is the increasing emphasis on using pictures and graphics to tell a news story. This article by **Scott Aiges** describes the growing role of a new professional specialist — the graphics reporter.

I T USED to be that when an editor wanted a story, he or she sent a writer to get it. Eventually, photographers went too. Now, at several papers, graphic artists have joined the team. When a story breaks, papers send a writer, a photographer, *and* an artist — and on business cards across the country the title "graphics reporter" is popping up.

The reason is simple: publishers have read the market surveys; they believe that to prevent a further defection of readers to television they must make their product visually attractive. Thanks to recent improvements in computer technology, news artists can produce colorful, informative graphics fast. According to

surveys, "information graphics" are often the first — and sometimes the only — part of a story that gets read.

"Tradition had pigeonholed the art department as a service department, so the art department would sit around and wait for the editor or reporter to come in and request a specific map or cartoon or logo of a company to be drawn," says Wendy Govier, projects editor of the Knight-Ridder Graphics Network. "They were missing all the opportunities for the insight and creativity of the artist to become part of the project."

"What a graphics reporter looks for in a story is totally different from what a reporter is out there doing and what a photographer is out there doing," says Carol Zuber-Mallison, a news graphics de-

signer at *The Dallas Morning News*. At a plane-crash site, for example, a reporter may be looking for survivors to interview and a photographer for scenes of human suffering or physical destruction. A graphics reporter, meanwhile, will look for the details (did the plane skid 800 feet or 2,000 feet?) needed for an accurate scale drawing.

The new field was in effect legitimized in 1989 when staff designer and graphics coordinator Karen Blessen, then of *The Dallas Morning News*, was awarded a Pulitzer Prize (along with reporter David Hanners and photographer William Snyder) in explanatory journalism for her part in a special report on airplane-crash investigations.

While some editors view

IMPACT/
PERSPECIVE

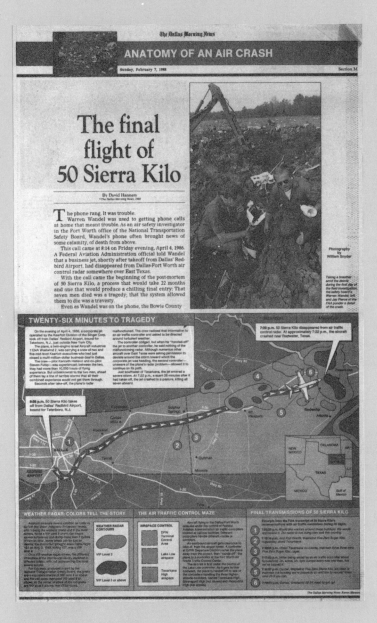

This example from the *Dallas MorningNews* shows how graphics reporter Karen Blessen created a story that merged words, graphics, and photographs to win her the first Pulitzer Prize in explanatory journalism awarded to a graphic designer. She worked as part of a reporting team that included reporter David Hanners and photographer William Snyder.

graphic artwork as mere window dressing, others have welcomed new ways of presenting news, in many cases without an accompanying article. On the whole, artists say, resistance to the trend toward using artists as journalists is diminishing. Govier of the Knight-Ridder Graphics Network predicts the emergence of "a new type of story" that integrates words and visuals — "where it's all one, so as you're moving through the text you see what is being described."

*From* Columbia Journalism Review *xxiv, no. 6 (March/April 1991): 36.*

IMPACT/
PERSPECTIVE

usually work for an editorial page editor. All of these people report to the *editor-in-chief* or the *publisher* or both.

A *business manager* and his or her staff runs the business side of the paper: getting the paper out to subscribers, selling advertising, and making sure the paper gets printed every day. These people also ultimately report to the editor-in-chief or the publisher. Sometimes the publisher is also the owner of the paper. If a corporation owns the paper, the publisher reports to its board of directors.

Technology has strongly affected the way newspapers are published. The history of newspapers, like that of all media, is the history of technological advances. In their book *The Press and America*, Edwin and Michael Emery describe the clumsiness of colonial printing:

*The bed of the press is rolled out by means of a wheel and pulley arrangement. The type, all set by hand, is locked tight in the form and is placed on the bed. A young apprentice, or "devil," applies the homemade ink to the type, using a doeskin dauber on a stick for this purpose.*

*The paper is then moistened in a trough so that it will take a better impression. It is placed carefully over the type. The bed is rolled back under the press.*

*The "platen," or upper pressure plate, is then pressed against the type by means of a screw or lever device. The platen is released; the bed is wheeled out; the sheet is hung on a wire to dry before it is ready for its second "run" for the reverse side.*[24]

In today's newsroom, reporters type their stories on computer terminals. In the composing room, people lay out the newspaper on a video screen, joining copy with ads. The final version, created by directions to the computer, is transferred to film from which copies of the paper are made. Nobody touches a piece of metal type. The efficiency of this *offset* method, compared to the complicated process of Franklin's day, was not possible even 35 years ago.

# The Newspaper Industry Today

 S THEY reach for the 21st century, newspapers sell 62 million copies daily, and six out of ten adults read a newspaper every day. Big-city newspapers are losing readers as people move to the suburbs, and suburban newspapers are growing, as are suburban editions of big-city papers.

*USA Today*'s use of strong graphics and eyecatching display boxes have transformed the newspaper industry.

Newspapers depend primarily on advertising for support. Subscriptions and newsstand sales account for only a small percentage of newspaper income. (For an overview of the newspaper industry today, see the Industry Snapshot, p. 70.)

Newspaper companies in the 1980s, looking for new ways to make money, rediscovered and expanded on some old ideas. Gannett introduced a new national newspaper. The news services streamlined their operations. And more newspaper organizations joined the syndication business.

# National Newspapers

Of all the nation's group owners, the Gannett newspaper chain has been the biggest gambler. In 1982, Gannett created *USA Today*, which it calls "The Nation's Newspaper," to compete with the country's only other major national

# Newspapers

## Industry Snapshot

Newspapers are still the leading segment of the media industry in overall revenue. Key trends in the industry today: the concentration of ownership in fewer hands and efforts to halt the decline in newspaper readership, especially among the young.

① **The Chains' Share of Daily Circulation**

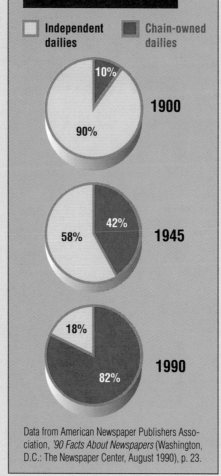

Independent dailies

Chain-owned dailies

10%
90%
**1900**

42%
58%
**1945**

18%
82%
**1990**

Data from American Newspaper Publishers Association, *'90 Facts About Newspapers* (Washington, D.C.: The Newspaper Center, August 1990), p. 23.

**Concentration of ownership:** In 1900, most U.S. dailies were independently owned, but today chains account for more than four-fifths of daily newspaper circulation.

Although newspaper circulation is holding steady, daily readership is declining —especially among younger adults.

② **Losing the Habit?**

Percentage of people who say they read a newspaper every day

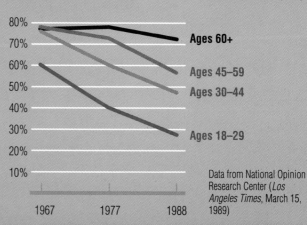

Ages 60+

Ages 45–59

Ages 30–44

Ages 18–29

80%
70%
60%
50%
40%
30%
20%
10%

1967    1977    1988

Data from National Opinion Research Center (*Los Angeles Times*, March 15, 1989)

## The Top Ten U.S. Newspapers and Who Owns Them

| | Newspaper | Daily Circulation in 1990 | Owner |
|---|---|---|---|
| 1 | The Wall Street Journal | 1,936,000 | Dow Jones Co. |
| 2 | USA Today | 1,387,000 | Gannett Co. |
| 3 | Los Angeles Times | 1,210,000 | Times Mirror Co. |
| 4 | New York Daily News | 1,180,000 | Tribune Co. |
| 5 | The New York Times | 1,150,000 | New York Times Co. |
| 6 | Washington Post | 824,000 | Washington Post Co. |
| 7 | Chicago Tribune | 741,000 | Tribune Co. |
| 8 | Newsday | 711,000 | Times Mirror Co. |
| 9 | Detroit Free Press | 640,000 | Knight-Ridder Newspapers |
| 10 | San Francisco Chronicle | 569,000 | Chronicle Publishing |

Data from American Newspaper Publishers Association, *'90 Facts About Newspapers* (Washington, D.C.: The Newspaper Center, August 1990), p.16.

A huge gamble when it was founded in 1982, *USA Today* is now the nation's second largest daily.

**3** Chains own the top nine U.S. newspapers, including the trend-setting *USA Today*.

**4** Competition with television and the need to attract younger readers are changing the look of American newspapers.

newspaper, *The Wall Street Journal.* Dubbing it "McPaper" with only "Mc-Nuggets" of news, critics said the slim publication was the fast-food approach to newspapers. It features expensive color graphics, a detailed national weather report, comprehensive sports coverage, and news stories that rarely run longer than 600 words.

*USA Today* went after a different audience from the *Journal* — people who don't want to spend a lot of time reading but who like to know the headlines. Someone in an airport or someone who wants something to read on a coffee break, Gannett argued, may not need a paper the size of *The Wall Street Journal* or a large metropolitan daily. Gannett's innovations also have influenced many other newspapers, which have added graphics and color and shortened the average length of stories.

*USA Today* and the *Journal* both publish regional editions by satellite so that a local bank, for example, can place an ad. Each area's regional edition is distributed in a defined geographic area, so a local advertiser (like the bank) pays a lower price than someone who advertises nationwide.

In 1990, *USA Today* was in second place in circulation, half a million behind the *Journal*, which had nearly 2 million readers. Circulation doesn't necessarily mean profit because newspapers survive on their advertising, and by 1990, *USA Today* still had not yet gathered enough advertisers to make a profit. Yet, not even Pulitzer or Hearst ever matched *USA Today*'s record of growth.

# News Services

Using satellites and computer terminals instead of the original telegraph machines, cooperative and for-profit news gathering has grown faster and more efficient. Today the wire services prefer to be called **news services**. Two out of three American newspapers subscribe to one news service — either United Press International or Associated Press — and some papers use both services. Many other news services send stories and broadcasts worldwide: Agence France-Presse (France), Reuters (Great Britain), Tass (Soviet Union), Agenzia Nationale Stampa Associate (Italy), Deutsche Presse Agentur (Germany), and Xinhua (China).

The news services especially help small newspapers (and broadcast stations) that can't afford an overseas correspondent. Large dailies with their own correspondents around the world still rely on the news services when they can't get to a story quickly.

The Associated Press is still a cooperative, as it was when it began in New York in 1848. Scripps Howard sold the financially struggling UPI in 1982, and since then UPI has had several owners and continues to struggle financially.

Some newspaper organizations in the United States — *The New York Times*, the *Washington Post*, the *Los Angeles Times*, and Knight-Ridder — have started their own news services. Newspapers that subscribe can publish the news service stories. For many newspapers, these stories fill space at a relatively low cost, because the newspaper doesn't need a staff reporter.

## Syndicates

Newspapers also can add to their content without sending their own reporters to stories by using **syndicates**, which are agencies that sell articles for publication in a number of newspapers simultaneously. The first syndicated column was a fashion letter distributed in 1857. Today more newspapers are syndicating their columns and features to try to add income. Syndicates mainly provide columnists and comics — William F. Buckley, Ellen Goodman, and William Raspberry, as well as "Doonesbury" and "Peanuts," for example. The price of syndicated copy for each newspaper is calculated on the newspaper's circulation. A large newspaper pays more for "Doonesbury" than a small newspaper.

## Facing the Future

Since their colonial beginnings, newspapers have shown their ability to appeal to changing audiences, adapt to growing competition, and continue to attract advertisers. The American Newspaper Publishers Association and other newspaper analysts project these advances in the future:

• *Reporters in the field will be sending more stories from portable computers through cellular telephones in their cars, without needing a telephone line for their computer hookup. Photographers will be using video and digital cameras. Their pictures will be sent to the newsroom electronically. Several manufacturers have developed systems that can reproduce still pictures for newspapers from video images.*

• *Newspapers will expand profits by selling more of the information they gather. Once a story is in a computer, the information can be sold to people who want that information: lawyers, researchers, and home computer users.*

• *Satellite publishing will bring more customized newspapers in regional editions, and advertisers will be able to choose their audiences more selectively. Cheaper production methods could mean that the cost of starting a newspaper will decrease, which could increase the number of alternative and small community newspapers.*

*• Lower costs for information systems will mean that more newspapers will be able to afford more computer technology.*

*• The offset process may be replaced by a new system called* flexography, *which uses less paper and replaces expensive, toxic oil-based inks with water-based inks.*

Three other emerging trends that will affect the future of the newspaper industry are the growing challenges by publishers to newspaper unions; as in all media, the intensifying concentration of ownership; and the changing newspaper audience.

**Newspaper Unions.** The new technology means that machines are doing work formerly done by people. For newspaper unions, this has meant a consistent effort among newspaper owners to challenge union representation.

Before 1970, newspapers needed typographers to hand-set metal type, and labor unions represented most of these typographers. With the introduction of photocomposition, newspaper management slowly moved to eliminate the typographers' jobs. The unions fought the transition, and many newspaper workers went on strike — notably at the *Washington Post* in 1975, at *The Sacramento Bee* in 1978, at the *Philadelphia Inquirer* in 1985 (when 4,500 employees walked out), and at the *New York Daily News* in 1990.

With the threat of technology eliminating even more jobs in the future, newspaper unions are understandably worried. Membership in the Newspaper Guild (which covers reporters) has remained steady, but most of the other unions have lost members, especially the International Typographers Union, whose membership is half what it was before photocomposition.[25] Forecasts are that union influence at newspapers with circulations above 50,000 will remain strong, but that the effort to diffuse union influence at smaller newspapers will continue.

**Concentration of Ownership.** Newspapers are economically healthy, but overall newspaper circulation remains static. Instead of editors competing locally within a community, like Hearst battling Pulitzer, national chains now compete with one another. Today, chains own three-fourths of America's daily newspapers (see Figures 2.2 and 2.3).

This doesn't mean that every newspaper in a chain speaks with the voice of the chain owner. Chains can supply money to improve a newspaper's printing plant and to add more reporters. But critics say the tendency to form chains can consolidate and limit the sources of information for readers.

According to media scholar Anthony Smith, "It is obvious that in some of the chains . . . there are clear editorial lines to which editors normally adhere." The majority of Scripps Howard papers, says Smith, "print the editorials

**2.2 ➤**

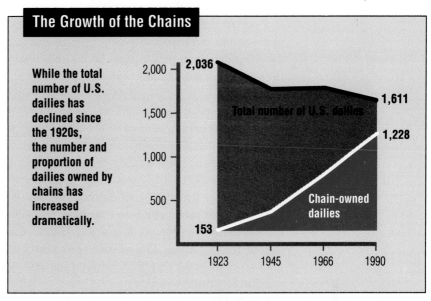

## The Growth of the Chains

While the total number of U.S. dailies has declined since the 1920s, the number and proportion of dailies owned by chains has increased dramatically.

Total number of U.S. dailies

2,036

1,611

1,228

Chain-owned dailies

153

2,000 — 1,500 — 1,000 — 500 —

1923    1945    1966    1990

SOURCE: Data from Christopher H. Sterling and Timothy R. Haight, *The Mass Media: Aspen Institute Guide to Communication Industry Trends* (New York/London: Praeger, 1977) and American Newspaper Publishers Association, *'91 Facts About Newspapers*, Washington, D.C., April 1991, p. 23; *Newspaper Newsletter*, Morton Research, January 31, 1991.

**2.3 ➤**

## The Top Ten U.S. Newspaper Chains

|   |   | Daily circulation (millions) | Number of dailies |
|---|---|---|---|
| 1 | Gannett Company, Inc. | 6.0 | 82 |
| 2 | Knight-Ridder Inc. | 3.7 | 28 |
| 3 | Newhouse Newspapers | 2.9 | 26 |
| 4 | Times Mirror Co. | 2.62 | 8 |
| 5 | Tribune Company | 2.60 | 9 |
| 6 | Dow Jones & Company, Inc. | 2.4 | 24 |
| 7 | Thomson Newspapers Inc. | 2.1 | 124 |
| 8 | The New York Times Co. | 1.9 | 27 |
| 9 | Scripps Howard Newspapers | 1.5 | 21 |
| 10 | Cox Enterprises Inc. | 1.2 | 18 |

SOURCE: Data from American Newspaper Publishers Association, *'90 Facts About Newspapers* (Washington, D.C.: The Newspaper Center, August 1990), p. 17; Standard and Poor's Industry Surveys, February 7, 1991, p. 19.

sent out to them from the chain's Washington bureau on subjects affecting national and international policy."[26] Critics fear that chain ownership may mean less debate on public issues because editorial policy for all newspapers in the same chain will become uniform. (See Chapter 11 for further discussion of this issue.)

Today's newspapers often are seen as acquisitions in a corporate game plan. Most newspapers are very profitable, or buyers wouldn't be competing so vigorously to acquire them. For example, from 1973 to 1986, Gannett acquired 40 papers, many of them big investments. Gannett paid $300 million for the *Louisville Courier-Journal* and *Times* newspapers in Kentucky; $717 million for the Evening News Association, which publishes the *Detroit News* and four other newspapers and operates two television stations; and $200 million for the Des Moines Register & Tribune Company, with holdings that include the *Des Moines Register.* Gannett's yearly earnings in 1990 were more than 16 times what they were 17 years before — $377 million in 1990 compared to $23 million in 1973.[27]

Chains also make money by selling newspaper companies, as they shift position in the market. Rupert Murdoch began his American media empire with the *San Antonio Express* in 1973. Murdoch aggressively bought more newspapers, including the *Chicago Sun-Times* in 1984. Two and a half years later, he sold the *Sun-Times* for $145 million, a $45 million profit.

According to Anthony Smith, profitability is only one reason newspapers are so attractive. The second reason is that, through their advertising, newspapers

*preside over the total spending power of a whole community without any comparable medium threatening to undercut the rate at which space is sold.*

*The newspaper has competitors in radio and television in respect to editorial content and competition for the reader's time, but a newspaper that can get its advertisements into the vast majority of homes within a given geographical area holds great power over every enterprise attempting to sell goods within that region.*[28]

**Changing Readership.** Although newspapers still hold power for advertisers, recent studies reveal that younger readers are deserting the medium. Daily newspaper readership among people aged 30 to 44 in 1972 was close to 75 percent. By 1989, that percentage had dropped to less than 50 percent.[29] "It dawned on us that if we don't start luring teenagers into the paper and start them reading us now, they may not subscribe in the future," according to Grant Podelco, arts editor of the Syracuse (New York) *Herald-Journal.*[30]

To stop the slide among young readers, many newspapers have added inserts directed to, and sometimes written by, teenagers. *The Wall Street Journal* introduced a high school classroom edition. At the *Chicago Tribune*, five teenage film reviewers appear in the newspaper every Friday with their choices, and a "Preps Plus" section covers high school sports. *The Dallas Morning News* runs a half-sheet called "The Mini Page," subtitled "Especially for Kids and Their Families," which carries puzzles, explanatory stories about current issues, and a teacher's guide.

Newspaper executives often blame television for the declining audience, but others say that people's reading habits also reflect changing uses of family time. "That time has been lost to working moms, aerobic classes, and of course TV," according to Jean Gaddy Wilson, executive director of New Directions for News, an independent research group at the University of Missouri School of Journalism. "Many kids today don't even see a paper at home these days. At best, a paper is in a mix of entertainment and news media."[31]

Newspapers are competing to maintain their audience because audiences attract advertisers — and profits. The average daily newspaper is about two-thirds advertising, and in some newspapers advertising runs as high as 70 percent. National advertisers (such as Procter & Gamble) buy television time as much as they buy newspaper space, but for local businesses, nothing works so well as the local newspaper. Seventy cents of each local advertising dollar goes to newspapers. There may be fewer newspaper owners in the country, but as long as newspapers can maintain their profitability, the survivors will continue comfortably.

**IN FOCUS**

**The Newspaper Industry**

• The issue of government control of newspapers surfaced early in colonial America when the authorities stopped *Publick Occurrences* in 1690 after a single issue because the paper angered local officials.

• James Franklin published the first newspaper without the heading "By Authority," which began the tradition of an independent press in this country.

• The John Peter Zenger case established an important legal precedent: If what a newspaper reports is true, the paper cannot be successfully sued for libel.

• As dissatisfaction grew over British rule, newspapers became essential political tools in the effort to spread revolutionary ideas, including opposition to the British Stamp Act and to the Alien and Sedition Laws.

• The technological advances of the 19th century, such as cheaper newsprint, mechanized printing, and the telegraph, meant that newspapers could reach a wider audience faster than ever before. This also lowered production costs, which made newspapers attractive investments.

• Newspapers spread their reach in the 1800s to include people on the frontier, the growing number of immigrants, and the Native American population. The penny press made newspapers affordable for virtually every American.

• The emancipation and suffrage movements found a voice in the dissident press, which marks the beginning of newspapers as a tool for social protest.

• Cooperative news gathering began in 1848 with the formation of the New York Associated Press. The United Press followed. AP is a cooperative; UPI is a for-profit company.

• Government interests confronted the issue of press freedom during the Civil War, when the government decided to certify journalists to cover the war through a process called accreditation. This practice continues today.

• Mathew Brady's careful documentation of the Civil War demonstrated that news photography can be practical and effective. This documentary record is the first example of what today is called photojournalism.

• Intense competition bred yellow journalism, which nurtured the sensational coverage of the Spanish-American War in 1898. This newspaper war underscored the importance of press responsibility.

• Unionization at newspapers standardized wages for reporters and increased professionalism.

• Censorship during World War II again highlighted the difference between the goal of government, which is to fight a war effectively, and the goal of the press, which is to keep the public informed about wartime events.

• Television contributed to a decline in newspaper readership in the 1950s, although the social causes of the 1960s briefly revived the dissident press.

• Although individually owned newspapers still exist in some cities, today chains and conglomerates publish three-fourths of American daily newspapers.

• Newspapers still hold power for advertisers, but recent studies reveal that younger readers are deserting the medium faster than any other age group. To stop the slide, newspapers have introduced features and sections targeted for teenagers.

• The future success of newspapers depends on their ability to appeal to a shifting audience, meet growing competition, and continue to attract advertisers.

*By the early 1950s, magazine mogul Henry Luce's* Time

*and* Fortune *were well established. He often traveled*

*with his wife, Ambassador Clare Boothe Luce, and instead of asking Henry Luce*

*questions of international importance, many of the people he met overseas wanted to*

*talk with him about sports.*

*"Luce knew nothing about sports," says* Los Angeles Times *sports columnist Jim*

*Murray, who in the early 1950s was writing sports for*

*Time magazine. "But every place he'd go, all over the*

**The Magazine Industry**

Today's magazine publishers try to appeal to different specialized audiences. These magazines are all published by Condé Nast.

world, the conversation would veer to the World Cup or the British Open or whatever.

"He got fascinated and irritated, I guess, and finally said, 'Why this all-consuming interest in games?' We said, 'Well, that's the way the world is, Harry.' He said, 'Well, maybe we ought to start a sports magazine.'"[1] The result, of course, was *Sports Illustrated*, which today boasts a circulation of 3.5 million and is ranked among the nation's most profitable magazines.

*Sports Illustrated* was one of the earliest magazines to anticipate today's trend in magazines. Successful magazines today cater to specialized audiences. You probably have seen a copy of *Sports Illustrated* recently, or perhaps you have read *Glamour, PC Magazine,* or *Muscle & Fitness*. All these publications are ranked among the country's top 100 magazines. They give their readers information that they can't find anywhere else, and the number of people who read *Glamour, PC Magazine,* and *Muscle & Fitness* might surprise you.

*Glamour* reaches more than 2 million readers every month, and is ranked among the nation's top ten women's magazines. Published by Advance Publications, *Glamour* earns nearly $150 million a year from subscriptions and newsstand sales.

*PC Magazine*, the nation's fastest growing computer magazine, caters primarily to small business and home computer users. Less than a million people read the magazine every month, but the magazine's readership is very attractive to advertisers, who paid $147 million in 1990 to reach *PC Magazine*'s audience. Subscribers and newsstand sales add another $36 million, so *PC Magazine*'s total 1990 earnings ($183 million) were higher than *Glamour* with half as many subscribers. The company that publishes *PC Magazine*, Ziff Communications, also publishes several other computer magazines.

*Muscle & Fitness*, following the national fight against flab, is published in Woodland Hills, California, by Brute Enterprises. *Muscle & Fitness* advertises products such as exercise equipment and bodybuilding formulas to nearly half a million subscribers. Advertisers pay $21 million a year to reach this audience, and newsstand and subscriber sales add $26 million, for total annual earnings of $47 million.[2]

These examples highlight a significant fact about the history of the magazine industry: *Magazines reflect the surrounding culture and the demographics of the society.* As readers' needs and lifestyles change, so do magazines. The trend toward specialty magazines is only the latest chapter in this evolution.

# Colonial Competitors

i N 1741, more than 50 years after the birth of the colonies' first newspaper, magazines entered the American media marketplace. Newspapers covered daily crises for local readers, but magazines could reach beyond the parochial concerns of small communities to carry their cultural, political, and social ideas and foster their identity as part of a nation. Until the 1920s, magazines were the only medium in the United States that could reach a national audience. For this reason, from 1741 until the 1920s magazines, more than newspapers, often provoked as

Ben Franklin continued his publishing war with Andrew Bradford by issuing his *General Magazine* to compete with Bradford's *American Magazine*.

well as reflected the nation's more widespread cultural, social, and political changes.

American magazine publishing celebrated its 250th birthday in 1991. Of the 12,000 different magazines published in America today, the top 300 alone collect about $16 billion annually from advertisers and subscribers. This is quite different from 1741 in Philadelphia, when Benjamin Franklin and Andrew Bradford rekindled the publishing rivalry that began when they both published newspapers, as they raced each other to become America's first magazine publisher.

Bradford won, but he didn't play fair. Franklin originated the idea of starting the first American magazine, and he asked a lawyer friend to be his editor. The lawyer told Bradford, and then Bradford hired the lawyer and issued his *American Magazine* first, on February 13, 1741. Franklin's *General Magazine* came out three days later.

Like most of the 100 American magazines that began in the 18th century, *American Magazine* and *General Magazine* recycled articles from British newspapers and magazines. (International copyright laws weren't enacted until the late 19th century.) The magazines had no subscribers or advertisers. Franklin, whose magazine was twice the size of Bradford's, also published local government news for the colonies.

Because he was Philadelphia's postmaster, Franklin was able to get some revenge against Bradford. Philadelphia's postriders carried Franklin's *General Magazine*, but Franklin wouldn't let them distribute his rival's publication. Neither magazine lasted very long — Bradford published three issues and Franklin six — but they initiated a rich tradition.

Because they didn't carry advertising, early magazines were expensive and their circulations remained very small, but like colonial newspapers, early magazines provided a means for political expression. In the late 18th century, revolutionary magazines published the political messages of important political figures like Thomas Paine, John Hancock, and Samuel Adams.

# The First National Mass Medium

NEWSPAPERS FLOODED the larger cities by the early 1800s, but they circulated only within the cities' boundaries, so national news spread slowly. Colleges were limited to the wealthy, and books were expensive. Magazines became America's only *national* medium, and subscribers depended on them for news, culture, and entertainment. Magazines became the country's teachers. The magazine that first reached a large public was *The Saturday Evening Post*.

For a nickel, starting in 1821, you could buy a magazine that the editors claimed was started by Benjamin Franklin in 1728, which wasn't true. The editors, Charles Alexander and Samuel Coate Atkinson, printed the magazine in the same building where Franklin founded the *Pennsylvania Gazette*, but Franklin, who died in 1790, had no connection with the *Post*.

The *Post* (published every Saturday at a time when there were no Sunday papers) featured news, fiction, poetry, essays, theater reviews, and a column called "The Lady's Friend." The early *Post*s were only four pages, with no illustrations, and one-fourth of the magazine was advertising. The *Post* published stories by Edgar Allan Poe, Harriet Beecher Stowe, and Nathaniel Hawthorne, and for 40 years it was one of America's most important weeklies. By 1855, it had 90,000 subscribers.

# Reaching New Readers

**M**AGAZINES LIKE *The Saturday Evening Post* reached a wide readership with their general-interest content. But many other audiences were available to 19th-century publishers, and they spent the century locating their readership. Four enduring subjects that expanded the magazine audience in the 1800s were women's issues, social crusades, literature and the arts, and politics.

## Women's Issues

Because women were a sizable potential audience, magazines were more open to female contributors than newspapers. Many early magazines published poetry and stories by women. Although some women wrote under men's names, most used their true names. Two central figures in the history of women's magazines in America were Sarah Josepha Hale and Edward Bok.

In 1830, Louis A. Godey was the first publisher to capitalize on an audience that the *Post* had identified with "The Lady's Friend" column. Women, most of whom had not attended school, sought out *Godey's Lady's Book* and its gifted editor Sarah Josepha Hale for advice on morals, manners, literature, fashion, diet, and taste. Hale was self-educated in a time when colleges in America didn't admit women, and she had worked as a teacher before she married.

When her husband died in 1822, Hale sought work to support herself and her five children. She was first editor of *Ladies Magazine* in Boston. Then as the editor of *Godey's* for 40 years beginning in 1837, she fervently supported higher education and property rights for women until she retired from the magazine when she was 89, a year before she died.

Although Hale's name may not be familiar, a poem she wrote for her children is universally known: "Mary Had a Little Lamb." She also wrote the first novel by a woman published in the United States, *Northwood: A New England Tale*, about the divisions among families during the Civil War.[3] In *Godey's*, Hale published distinguished American writers such as Horace Greeley, Washington Irving, Henry Wadsworth Longfellow, and Mary Virginia Terhune. By

A sample of 1875 fashions displayed in *Godey's Lady's Book*, edited by Sarah Josepha Hale.

1860, *Godey's* had 150,000 subscribers.[4] According to magazine historian Frank Luther Mott, under Hale's editorship *Godey's* was "transformed from a mediocre miscellany to a literary magazine of great importance."[5]

## Social Crusades

Magazines also became important instruments for social change. Cyrus Curtis, editor of *The Ladies' Home Journal*, is credited with leading a crusade against dangerous medicines. Many of the ads in women's magazines in the 1800s were for patent medicines like Faber's Golden Female Pills ("successfully used by prominent ladies for female irregularities") and Ben-Yan, which promised to cure "all nervous debilities."

*The Ladies' Home Journal* was the first magazine to refuse patent medicine ads. Founded in 1887 by Cyrus Curtis, the *Journal* launched several crusades. It offered columns about women's issues, published popular fiction, and even printed sheet music.

Editor Edward Bok began his crusade against patent medicines in 1892 after he learned that many of them contained more than 40 percent alcohol. He reprinted a magazine ad that said that women with health problems could write to the woman who was pictured in the ad working in her laboratory. Next to the reprinted ad, Bok showed a photograph of her headstone. She had died 20 years earlier.

Next Bok revealed that a medicine sold to soothe noisy babies contained morphine. Other magazines joined the fight against dangerous ads and, partly because of Bok's crusading investigations, Congress passed the Pure Food and Drug Act of 1906.

The most notable Bok crusade began in 1906, when he published an editorial about venereal disease. Believing that women should know about the disease's threat, he continued articles about the subject even after 75,000 subscribers canceled. Bok clearly knew how to attract an audience — and how to lose one — but said he felt that "the time had come when women should learn the truth, and that, so far as it lay in his power, he intended to see that they did know."[6] Eventually, the readers returned and Bok's crusading made *The Ladies' Home Journal* even more popular.

## Fostering a Literary Tradition

In the mid-1800s, American magazines began to seek a literary audience by promoting the nation's writers. For example, almost everything Edgar Allan Poe wrote — short stories, literary criticism, and verse — appeared first in magazines. Many other major American literary figures used magazines to expand their reputations and to make some money as well.

Two of today's most important literary magazines — *Harper's* and *The Atlantic Monthly* — began more than a century ago. *Harper's New Monthly Magazine*, known today as *Harper's*, was a contemporary of *Godey's*. The first issue appeared in 1850. As a monthly, *Harper's* didn't try to compete for the *Post's* general audience or for Sarah Hale's readers. The magazine earned an early reputation for literate attention to science, biography, travel, and fiction. Henry J. Raymond, who later established *The New York Times*, was *Harper's* first editor.

Mark Twain (Samuel Clemens) was one of *Harper's* magazine's early contributors.

Raymond marked America's literary independence from Great Britain, as he encouraged America's best writers to contribute to his magazine. He published stories by Mark Twain, Willa Cather, Joseph Conrad, and Stephen Crane. By the Civil War, *Harper's* circulation was 200,000.[7]

Pictures from Mathew Brady's traveling photo wagons appeared in *Harper's*. So did the drawings and cartoons of the great Thomas Nast, who worked for *Harper's* for 25 years.

Nast's most damaging political cartoons depicted New York's Boss Tweed as a money-hungry opportunist. Tweed, a politician who defrauded New York City out of $30 million, reacted to Nast by saying, "I don't care so much what the papers write about me — my constituents can't read; but, damn it, they can see pictures!"[8] *Harper's* today continues to publish essentially the same mix of articles that made it so popular in the 1800s.

The American literary showcase grew when *The Atlantic Monthly* appeared in 1857 in Boston. With James Russell Lowell as editor, *The Atlantic Monthly* paid Henry David Thoreau $198 for "Chesuncook," 33 pages at $6 a page. This was the most Thoreau had ever been paid for his writing.[9]

In 1909, *Atlantic* editor Ellery Sedgwick said the magazine's purpose was "to inoculate the few who influence the many." That formula continues today, with *The Atlantic* still provoking literary and political debate.

# Political Commentary

With more time (usually a month between issues) and space than newspapers had to reflect on the country's problems, political magazines provided a forum for public arguments by scholars and critical observers. Three of the nation's progressive political magazines that began in the 19th and early 20th centuries have endured: *The Nation, The New Republic,* and *The Crisis*. The *National Review*, which offers conservative political opinion, began in the 1950s to respond to its liberal predecessors.

*The Nation*, founded in 1865, is the oldest continuously published opinion journal in the United States, offering critical literary essays and arguments for progressive change. This weekly magazine has survived a succession of owners and financial hardship.

One editor described the magazine's purpose best when he said, "This magazine has been and will continue to be frankly partisan. Our hearts and our columns are on the side of the worker, of the minority group, of the underprivileged generally. We side with the intellectual and political noncon-formist in his clear constitutional right to refuse to conform."[10]

Another outspoken publication, which began challenging the establishment in the early 1900s, is *The New Republic*, founded in 1914. The weekly's circulation has rarely reached 40,000, but its readers enjoy the role it plays in regularly criticizing political leaders. Through a succession of owners and support from sympathetic patrons, the original concept of the magazine has remained, as one of its early editors put it, to start "little insurrections."

*The New Republic* often is seen as a companion of *The Nation* because of its similar social and political outlook. Both magazines have been consistent 20th-century voices for reform.

An organization that needed a voice at the beginning of the century was the National Association for the Advancement of Colored People (NAACP). For 24 years, beginning in 1910, that voice was W. E. B. Du Bois, who founded and edited the organization's monthly magazine, *The Crisis*.

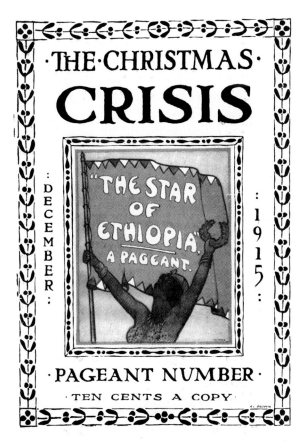

Du Bois graduated from Harvard in 1895 with a Ph.D. in history, and he began *The Crisis* as the official monthly magazine of the NAACP. Du Bois attacked discrimination against African-American soldiers during World War I, exposed Ku Klux Klan activities, and argued for African-American voting and housing rights. By 1919, circulation was more than 100,000.

Fiercely independent, Du Bois often criticized the organization in its own magazine. Disagreements with some NAACP leaders caused Du Bois to leave in 1934, when he joined the faculty at Atlanta University. Du Bois left America in 1961 to live in Ghana, where he died two years later at age 95. *The Crisis* continues today to publish monthly.

In 1954, William F. Buckley began the *National Review* as a conservative alternative to *The Nation* and *The New Republic*. Aided by his iconoclastic image and weekly appearances on public television, Buckley has maintained the *National Review* as a showplace for conservative ideology. According to one observer, "The truly distinguishing thing about *National Review* writers is the gaiety with which they accept their mission of confounding the Liberals and making all things 'debatable again.'"[11]

## The Postal Act's Effects

Passage of the Postal Act of 1879 encouraged the growth of magazines. Before passage of the Act, newspapers traveled free while magazines had to pay postage. Arguing for special treatment for magazines, Representative H. D. Money called magazines the nation's "highest educators."[12]

With the Postal Act of 1879, Congress gave magazines second-class mailing privileges. Congress then instituted a rate of a penny a pound for newspapers and magazines. This meant quick, reasonably priced distribution for magazines, and today magazines still travel on a preferential rate. Magazine publishers also expanded the space allotted for advertising to hold down magazine prices.

Aided by cheaper postal rates, the number of monthly magazines grew from 180 in 1860 to over 1,800 by the turn of the century. However, because magazines travel through the mail, they are vulnerable to censorship (see Chapter 13).

# The Muckrakers: Magazine Journalists Campaign for Change

"a STRONG EDITOR, even a strongly wrongheaded editor, has usually meant a strong and influential magazine," wrote magazine historian James Playsted Wood, "whereas intelligent editors of moderate views and no firm opinions have often produced colorless and comparatively ineffective magazines."[13] Wood's observation certainly applies to the colorful, campaigning journalists just before the turn of the century who became known as **muckrakers**. The strongest editor in the first ten years of the 20th century was legendary magazine publisher Samuel S. McClure, who founded *McClure's Magazine* in 1893.

McClure and his magazine were very important to the Progressive era in American politics, which called for an end to the close relationship between government and big business. To reach a large readership, McClure priced his new monthly magazine at 15 cents an issue, while most other magazines sold for 25 or 35 cents. *McClure's Magazine* began as a literary showcase for American writers. The November 1896 issue contained the first chapter of *Captains Courageous* by Rudyard Kipling (which was continued in the next issue); a poem by Hamlin Garland; reprints of rare pictures of Daniel Webster, James Fenimore Cooper, and Oliver Wendell Holmes; and an article (part of a series) by Ida M. Tarbell about the 1860 nomination of presidential candidate Abraham Lincoln.

McClure first met Tarbell when she was in Paris, submitting articles to his syndicate. Tarbell had graduated with a degree in biology as the only woman in her class at Pennsylvania's Allegheny College. She wanted to see Europe, so she supported herself as a freelancer in Paris, where she attended the Sorbonne and wrote for *McClure's*, the Pittsburgh *Dispatch*, the Cincinnati *Times-Star*, and the *Chicago Tribune*.

She joined *McClure's* in 1894 as associate editor. After her series about Lincoln boosted circulation to 370,000, Tarbell and McClure came up with an idea for a more ambitious project. Tarbell would tackle Standard Oil. (See Impact/Profile, Ida Tarbell Uncovers John D. Rockefeller.)

Tarbell peeled away the veneer of the country's biggest oil trust. Her 19-part series began running in *McClure's* in 1904. Eventually the series became a two-volume book, *History of the Standard Oil Company*, which established Tarbell's reputation as a muckraker.

The muckrakers' targets were big business and corrupt government. President Theodore Roosevelt coined the word *muckraker* in 1906 when he compared reformers like Tarbell to the "Man with the Muckrake" who busily dredged up the dirt in John Bunyan's *Pilgrim's Progress*. Tarbell hated the description; she thought of herself as a dedicated researcher. Standard Oil founder John D. Rockefeller called her "that misguided woman."

An important colleague of Tarbell's at *McClure's* was another muckraker, Lincoln Steffens. His special interest was politics, and for *McClure's* Steffens wrote *Shame of the Cities*, a series about political corruption in St. Louis, Minneapolis, Pittsburgh, Philadelphia, and Chicago. Advertisers scrambled for space in the courageous magazine. The June 1901 issue carried 104 pages of ads.

Other magazines, such as *Everybody's, Munsey's,* and *Cosmopolitan*, attempted similar ambitious investigations, but *McClure's* embodied muckraking at its best. By 1910, many of the reforms sought by the muckrakers had been adopted, and this particular type of magazine journalism declined. But on May 15, 1911, the U.S. Supreme Court verified Tarbell's findings when it declared Standard Oil of New Jersey a monopoly in restraint of trade and ordered the holding company dissolved. Today, Standard Oil is still separated into independent companies that run the parent firm's operations in each state. The muckrakers often are cited as America's original investigative journalists.

# Ida Tarbell Uncovers John D. Rockefeller

Ida Tarbell's investigation of Standard Oil's owner, John D. Rockefeller, is significant in the history of magazine journalism because it demonstrates how a well-researched, carefully documented examination of an influential business can bring the public's attention to a need for change.

**W**HEN JOHN D. Rockefeller refused to talk with her, Ida Tarbell sat at the back of the room and watched him deliver a Sunday-school sermon. In her autobiography, *All in the Day's Work*, written when she was 80, Tarbell described some of her experiences as she investigated the Standard Oil Company:

"The impression of power deepened when Mr. Rockefeller took off his coat and hat, put on a skullcap, and took a seat commanding the entire room, his back to the wall. It was the head which riveted attention. It was big, great breadth from back to front, high broad forehead, big bumps behind the ears, not a shiny head but with a wet look. The skin was as fresh as that of any healthy man about us. The thin sharp nose was like a thorn. There were no lips; the mouth looked as if the teeth were all shut hard. Deep

In 1904, muckraker Ida Tarbell targeted oil magnate John D. Rockefeller who called her "that misguided woman."

furrows ran down each side of the mouth from the nose. There were puffs under the little colorless eyes with creases running from them.

"Wonder over the head was almost at once diverted to wonder over the man's uneasiness. His eyes were never quiet but darted from face to face, even peering around the jog at the audience close to the wall. . . .

"My two hours' study of Mr. Rockefeller aroused a feeling I had not expected, which time has intensified. I was sorry for him. I know no companion so terrible as fear. Mr. Rockefeller, for all the conscious power written in face and voice and figure, was afraid, I told myself, afraid of his own kind. . . ."[14]

# Magazines in the First Half of the 20th Century

MAGAZINES IN the first half of the 20th century matured and adapted to absorb first, the invention of radio and then, television. As with magazines today, magazine publishers had two basic choices: (1) publishers could seek a *definable, targeted loyal audience,* or (2) publishers could seek a *broad, general readership*. These two different types of American publishers in the first half of the 20th century are best exemplified by a very unlikely twosome: the disheveled, absent-minded Harold Ross, founding editor of *The New Yorker*, and the worldly, bombastic Henry Luce, who started Time Inc.

## Harold Ross and *The New Yorker*

Harold Ross' *New Yorker* magazine launched the wittiest group of writers that ever gathered around a table at New York's Algonquin Hotel. The "witcrackers," who met there regularly for lunch throughout the 1920s, included Heywood Broun, Robert Benchley, Dorothy Parker, Alexander Woollcott, James Thurber, and Harpo Marx. Because they sat at a large round table in the dining room, the group came to be known as the Algonquin Round Table. When they weren't meeting at the Algonquin, they were playing poker in Harold Ross' apartment; he often lost.

Ross, who never attended college, met some of the people who first wrote for his magazine when he was in the service. Some of Ross' writers, such as Benchley, had written for the *Harvard Lampoon*. Dorothy Parker had worked for the original *Life*, which was a humor magazine before Henry Luce bought it. Parker became the most celebrated of the Round Table's wits, and her wisecracks were legendary. (When she learned that placid President Calvin Coolidge had died, she said, "How can they tell?")

Ross persuaded Raoul Fleischmann, whose family money came from the yeast company, to invest half a million dollars in *The New Yorker* before the magazine began making money in 1928, three years after its launch.

The first issue of *The New Yorker* featured a sophisticated New York gentleman discovering a whimsical butterfly, representing the upscale audience the magazine hoped to attract.

Ross published some of the country's great commentary, fiction, and humor, sprinkled with cartoons that gave *The New Yorker* its charm. Ross edited the magazine until he died in 1951, when he was succeeded by William Shawn.

*The men and women of* The New Yorker *have long existed on a plane apart from workers at other magazines. The intellectual standing of their magazine, the generous pay, the university-like tenure, the absence of deadlines for many staffers, the respect accorded their work (it's always the "artists" at the magazine, never "the cartoonists"), and above all, the magnanimous, moral, nurturing figure of the editor, William Shawn,* Mister *Shawn — all this [made]* The New Yorker *a self-enclosed universe, unique in American journalism.* [15]

After one owner — the Fleischmann family — and only two editors in 60 years, *The New Yorker* was sold in 1985 to Advance Publications, owned by the Newhouse family, for more than $150 million. In 1985 Newhouse also owned 29 newspapers, Random House, *Parade* magazine, and the Condé Nast magazines, which include *Vogue, GQ, Mademoiselle, House and Garden,* and *Self.*

*Time* founder Henry Luce and his wife, Ambassador Clare Boothe Luce

William Shawn retired in 1987 and was replaced by Newhouse-appointed Robert Gottlieb. *The New Yorker* today still continues to be the primary showcase for American writers and artists.

# Henry Luce's Empire

A contemporary of Harold Ross, Henry Luce is the singular giant of 20th-century magazine publishing. Unlike Ross, who sought a sophisticated, wealthy audience, Luce wanted to reach the largest possible audience. "He was a big man," writes David Halberstam. "Little ideas and little concepts and little men did not interest him; he was always in search of giants. He was ever restless, ever dissatisfied, he was not a man of inner peace."[16]

Luce's first creation was *Time* magazine, which he founded in 1923 with his Yale classmate Briton Hadden. Luce and Hadden paid themselves $30 a week and recruited their friends to write for the magazine. The nation's first news magazine's purpose was "to summarize the week's news in the shortest possible space."

The first issue of *Time* covered the week's events in 28 pages, minus six pages of advertising — half an hour's reading. "It was of course not for people who really wanted to be informed," wrote Luce's biographer W. A. Swanberg. "It was for people willing to spend a half-hour to avoid being entirely uninformed."[17]

Margaret Bourke-White (1906–1971), pictured here photographing New York City from 61 stories up, photographed *Life's* first cover.

The magazine developed around a new system of reporting. *Time* correspondents sent their reports to desk people in New York, who would do what Luce described as "write for space." The best of the field reports were condensed into unsigned articles, written in a distinctive style.

Hadden's ambition had been to make a million dollars before he was 30. When he died suddenly in 1929 at age 31, he left *Time* stock worth more than $1.1 million. The brash news magazine became the foundation of a Luce empire that now publishes *Time, Fortune, Life, Sports Illustrated, Money,* and *People Weekly.*

*Fortune,* founded in 1930 shortly after the stock market crash, was making money by 1933. Now that Luce was reaching a wide audience with *Time,* he used that success to underwrite *Fortune,* targeted at wealthy readers. *Fortune* used fancy color graphics and elaborate advertising; its name reflected the preoccupation of its audience.

In 1936 Luce paid $85,000 to use the name *Life,* which was originally the name of a humor magazine without pictures, founded in 1885. After six

*Life* magazine spawned lookalike imitations, including *Ebony* and *Look*.

months in print, *Life* was selling a million copies a week, featuring photo essays by some of the world's best photographers, including Margaret Bourke-White. In an era before television, Luce cultivated the photo essay and nurtured and expanded the concept of photojournalism first introduced by Mathew Brady (see Chapter 2).

Bourke-White was the first *Fortune* photographer, hired by Luce after he saw some of her pictures in a Midwestern newspaper. She became America's first woman photojournalist for a national magazine. Six years after her *Fortune* debut, Bourke-White took the pictures for the first *Life* cover. With her camera, she galloped on horseback across the Soviet Union, photographed the concentration camp at Buchenwald in World War II, climbed onto a gargoyle 61 stories above New York City to take a photograph, and survived a torpedo attack in the Atlantic and military missions in Korea. She died in 1971, after suffering from Parkinson's disease for nearly 20 years.

*Money* (a popularized version of *Fortune*) and *People Weekly* (a personality feature magazine) were founded after Luce died in 1967. Today Time Inc. is the largest magazine publisher in the United States, but the magazines are only part of the giant company Time Warner that includes television stations, book publishing companies, and Home Box Office.

Luce left an enduring legacy for American magazines. More than any other 20th-century publisher, he knew how to follow an audience and to adapt the magazine medium to effectively reach the readers his advertisers wanted.

Many of Luce's magazines fostered lookalikes. *Look* magazine mimicked *Life*. So did *Ebony*, an African-American magazine introduced by the Johnson chain in the 1940s. John H. Johnson, the magazine's publisher, also launched *Jet* magazine. By the 1980s, *Ebony* and *Jet* had a combined readership of 12 million.

# The Second Half of the 20th Century: Specialized Magazines

IN THE 1950s, television began to offer Americans some of the same type of general-interest features that magazines provided. General-interest magazines collapsed. *The Saturday Evening Post*, with a circulation of 3 million during the Depression, stopped publication in the 1960s, and then restarted. (Its present readership is less than half a million.) *Look* died, and *Life*, which had been a weekly, stopped publication in 1972 and reemerged in 1978 as a monthly.

Gradually, readers began to buy magazines for specialized information that they could not get from other sources. These new specialized magazines segmented the market, which meant that more magazines got fewer readers.

Hugh Hefner launched *Playboy* in 1953 to shock America's postwar readers with a nude Marilyn Monroe. The nudity in *Playboy* challenged the limits of magazine respectability, but the magazine also challenged social conventions. Was nudity acceptable in a general circulation magazine?

A different kind of shock had come one year earlier when *Mad* magazine began. *Mad* was directed at a young audience, and it mocked traditional social and political values. Like *Playboy, Mad* sought to extend the boundaries of magazine journalism.

*Playboy*'s success led to a number of imitators, including *Penthouse* and, later, *Playgirl*. *Mad* magazine and *Playboy* and its imitators typify how, beginning in the 1950s, magazine publishing sought new audiences in an environment that was becoming more crowded with other types of media.

Very few general-interest magazines survive today. The trend, since television expanded the media marketplace, is for magazines to find a specific audience interested in the information that magazines can deliver. This is called *targeting an audience*, which magazines can do more effectively today than any other media.

# Types of Magazines

Today's magazines can be divided into three types: (1) consumer publications; (2) trade, technical, and professional publications; and (3) company publications.

You probably are most familiar with **consumer magazines**, which are popularly marketed: *Time, Glamour,* and *Esquire*, for example. *PC World* and *Muscle & Fitness* also are considered consumer magazines. In the magazine business, *consumer* magazines are not just those that give buying advice. This term refers to all magazines sold by subscription or at newsstands, supermarkets, and bookstores. As a group, consumer magazines make the most money because they have the most readers and carry the most advertising.

*Trade, technical, and professional magazines* are read by people in a particular industry to learn more about their business. *Veterinary Practice Management*, for example, is a trade magazine, published as "a business guide for small animal practitioners." So are the *Columbia Journalism Review* (published by Columbia University) and *American Medical News* (published by the American Medical Association). These magazines are issued by media companies for their subscribers (such as *Veterinary Practice Management*, published by Whittle Communications, which also owns TV properties); universities or university-connected organizations for their subscribers (such as the *Columbia Journalism Review*); or by professional associations for their members (such as *American Medical News*). Most trade, technical, and professional magazines carry advertising directed at the professions they serve.

*Company magazines* are produced by businesses for their employees, customers, and stockholders. These magazines usually don't carry advertising. Their main purpose is to promote the company. Chevron, for instance, publishes a company magazine called *Chevron USA Odyssey*.

# How Magazines Work

**m**AGAZINE EMPLOYEES work in one of five divisions: (1) editorial; (2) circulation sales; (3) advertising sales; (4) administration; (5) manufacturing and distribution.

The articles and photographs that appear in a magazine are the responsibility of the *editorial department. Circulation* takes care of the subscribers. *Advertising* sells the ads that surround the copy. *Administration* runs the office — paying the editor's restaurant bill, for example. *Manufacturing* and *distribution* actually publish the magazine and get it to the newsstand or to the mailing house that sends it out to subscribers.

Because advertisers provide nearly half of a magazine's income, tension often develops between a magazine's advertising staff and its editorial staff. The advertising staff may lobby the editor for favorable stories about potential advertisers, but the editor is responsible to the audience of the magazine. The advertising department might argue with the editor, for example, that a local restaurant will not want to advertise in a magazine that publishes an unfavorable review of the restaurant. If the restaurant is a big advertiser, the editor must decide how to best maintain the magazine's integrity.

Circulation figures for member magazines are verified and published by the Audit Bureau of Circulations, an agency of print media market research. Advertisers use ABC figures to help them decide which magazines to use to reach their audience.

As you can see in Figure 3.1, putting the magazine together and selling it (circulation, advertising, administration, manufacturing, and distribution) cost more than organizing the articles and photographs that appear in the magazine (editorial). Often a managing editor coordinates all five departments.

The magazine editor's job is to keep the content interesting so people will continue to read the magazine. Good magazine editors — by carefully choosing the best articles for the magazine's audience and ensuring that they are well-written — can create a distinctive, useful product.

Many articles are written by full-time magazine staffers, such as a food editor who creates recipes or a columnist who writes commentary. Nearly half of the country's 12,000 magazines, however, use articles by **freelancers**. Freelancers do not receive a salary from the magazine; instead, they are paid

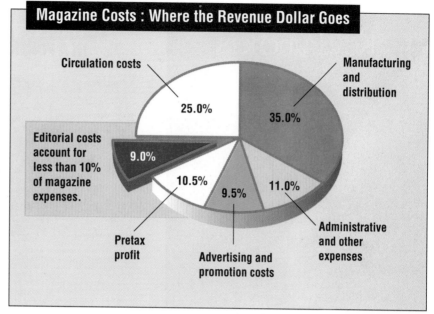

**3.1 ➤**

**Magazine Costs : Where the Revenue Dollar Goes**

Circulation costs — 25.0%

Manufacturing and distribution — 35.0%

Editorial costs account for less than 10% of magazine expenses. — 9.0%

Pretax profit — 10.5%

Advertising and promotion costs — 9.5%

Administrative and other expenses — 11.0%

SOURCE: Data from Magazine Publishers Association, Inc., 1990.

for each of their articles published in the magazine. Many freelancers write for several magazines simultaneously. Some freelancers specialize — just writing travel articles, for example. Other freelancers work just as the tradition of their name implies — they have a pen for hire, and they can write about any subject a magazine editor wants.

# The Magazine Industry Today

**t**ODAY, TRENDS in magazine publishing continue to reflect social and demographic changes, but magazines no longer play the cutting-edge social, political, and cultural role they played in the past. Instead, most magazines are seeking a specific audience, and many more magazines are competing for the same readers. *Newsweek* and *U.S. News & World Report* compete with *Time* to serve the reader who wants a weekly news roundup. *Fortune* is no longer alone; it has

**Left:** *Smithsonian* promotes its upscale audience to advertisers. **Right:** SpanAmerica publishes Hispanic magazines, targeting this segment of the audience for advertisers.

been joined by magazines like *Business Week, Forbes,* and *Nation's Business.* Some of the counterculture magazines of the 1960s, such as *Rolling Stone* and *Mother Earth News,* survive, but they face competition for an audience that has grown older and today reads *PC World, Smithsonian,* and *Architectural Digest.*

Women continue to be the single most lucrative audience for magazines. *Family Circle* and *Woman's Day,* called point-of-purchase magazines because they are sold only at the checkout stands in supermarkets, are only one part of the women's market. *Vogue, Glamour,* and *Cosmopolitan* cater to the fashion-conscious, and women's magazines have matured to include the working women's audience with *Savvy, Self,* and *Working Woman,* for example. The market is divided still further by magazines like *Essence,* aimed at professional African-American women, and the specifically targeted *Today's Chicago Woman* for female executives who live in Chicago. Today more than 300 different periodicals compete for the women's market.[18]

The two newest segments of the magazine audience to be targeted by special-interest magazines are owners of personal computers and videocassette recorders. Titles like *PC, PC World,* and *Popular Computing* already are among the nation's top 400 magazines, and so are *Video* and *Video Review.*

This tendency to specialize has not reached the level suggested by one magazine publisher, who joked that soon there might be magazines called *Working Grandmother, Lefthanded Tennis,* and *Colonial Homes in Western Vermont.* But magazine publishers are seeking readers with a targeted interest and then selling those readers to the advertisers who want to reach that specific audience — skiers, condominium owners, motorcyclists, toy collectors. (See Industry Snapshot, page 104.)

Besides targeting a special audience, such as gourmets or golfers, magazines today also can divide their audience further with regional and special editions that offer articles for specific geographic areas along with regional advertising. The news weeklies, for example, can insert advertising for a local bank or a local TV station next to national ads. This gives the local advertiser the prestige of a national magazine, at a lower cost.

Today's newest specialization success is *Modern Maturity*, published by the American Association of Retired Persons (AARP). With over 22 million readers, *Modern Maturity* provides articles on investments, careers, and personal relationships for readers 50 years and older. *Modern Maturity* boasts more readers than any other American monthly magazine.

*Modern Maturity*'s success story is a comment on the current state of the magazine industry. The audience for magazines, as for newspapers, is growing older. Younger readers are less likely to read magazines than their parents. In 1990, for the first time, the number of magazines published in the United States stopped growing. There were about the same number of magazines (12,000) being published at the beginning of the year as there were at the end. And, because 500 new magazines began publishing in 1990, that meant that the same number of magazines went out of business.

Most new magazines "started each year are modest publications, probably designed on someone's kitchen table, produced on a laptop computer and financed by loyal relatives or friends. But the choices of subject often mirror those coming out of the boardrooms of the giant media companies."[19] Sex is the favorite category for new magazines, followed by lifestyle, sports, media personalities, and home subjects.

But very few new magazines succeed. Today, only one in three new magazines will survive more than five years.[20] The reason most magazines fail is that the companies do not have the money to keep publishing long enough so that they can refine the editorial content, sell advertisers on the idea, and gather subscribers: in other words, until the magazine can make a profit.

# Magazines

## Industry Snapshot

General-interest consumer magazines still command a large share of total magazine circulation. Increasingly, however, U.S. magazines are targeting specific audiences because of the audience's appeal for advertisers.

**1** More than 12,000 periodicals are published in the United States—most of them targeted at specific audiences.

**2** Several of the top ten U.S. magazines are directed at women—traditionally the leading consumers of magazines. But the nation's largest magazine targets a specific, and growing, *age group*—people over 50.

## The Ten Largest U.S. Magazines

June 1990 circulation (millions)

| |  |  |
|---|---|---|
| 1 | *Modern Maturity* | 22.4 |
| 2 | *Reader's Digest* | 16.3 |
| 3 | *TV Guide* | 15.8 |
| 4 | *National Geographic* | 10.1 |
| 5 | *Better Homes and Gardens* | 8.0 |
| 6 | *Family Circle* | 5.1 |
| 7 | *Good Housekeeping* | 5.1 |
| 8 | *Ladies' Home Journal* | 5.0 |
| 9 | *McCall's* | 5.0 |
| 10 | *Woman's Day* | 4.6 |

Data from *Advertising Age*, 61, No. 34 (August 20, 1990): 42.

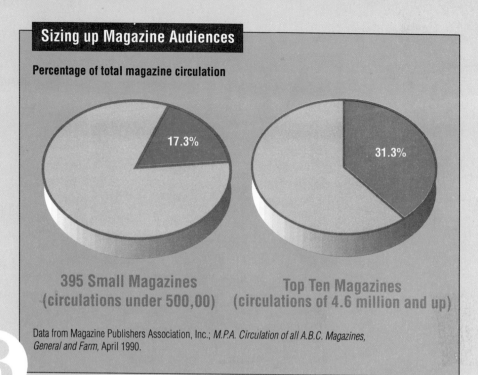

## Sizing up Magazine Audiences

**Percentage of total magazine circulation**

17.3%

31.3%

**395 Small Magazines**
**(circulations under 500,00)**

**Top Ten Magazines**
**(circulations of 4.6 million and up)**

Data from Magazine Publishers Association, Inc.; *M.P.A. Circulation of all A.B.C. Magazines, General and Farm,* April 1990.

**3**

**The vast majority of U.S. magazines have relatively small circulations, compared with the huge circulations of the leading consumer magazines.**

**4**

**The nation's largest magazines have millions of readers, but magazines with comparatively small circulations can earn substantial revenues by attracting advertisers who want to reach a specific audience.**

## Small Magazines that Earn Big Dollars

| Ten U.S. magazines with paid circulations less than 100,000 and total revenues over $15 million | 1990 paid circulation | 1990 revenue (millions) |
|---|---|---|
| 1 **PC Week** | 0* | $100.4 |
| 2 **Travel Weekly** | 40,000 | $53.4 |
| 3 **HFD—The Weekly (Home Furnishings)** | 26,000 | $48.4 |
| 4 **Advertising Age** | 90,000 | $35.1 |
| 5 **Billboard** | 48,000 | $30.5 |
| 6 **Nature** | 50,000 | $26.7 |
| 7 **Supermarket News** | 53,000 | $21.1 |
| 8 **Chronicle of Higher Education** | 89,000 | $21.1 |
| 9 **Automotive News** | 79,000 | $19.9 |
| 10 **Medical Economics** | 21,000 | $17.6 |

*Distributed free to a controlled readership

Data from *Advertising Age,* June 24, 1991.

The nation's number one monthly magazine targets the nation's growing audience of readers over age 50.

The number of magazines people buy each year remains static, but revenues are increasing. Although magazines once were very inexpensive and advertising paid most of the cost of production, publishers gradually have been charging more, and subscribers are willing to pay more for the magazines they want (see Figure 3.2).

The average magazine reader graduated from high school, is married, owns a home, and works full-time, with an average household income of nearly $31,000.[21] This is a very attractive audience for advertisers. Advertisers also like magazines because people often refer to an ad weeks after they first see it.

Many readers say they read the magazine as much for the ads as they do for the articles. This, of course, is also very appealing to advertisers. The Magazine Publishers Association reports that people keep a magazine an average of 17 weeks and that each magazine has at least four adult readers. This magazine sharing is called **pass-along readership**.

**3.2 ➤**

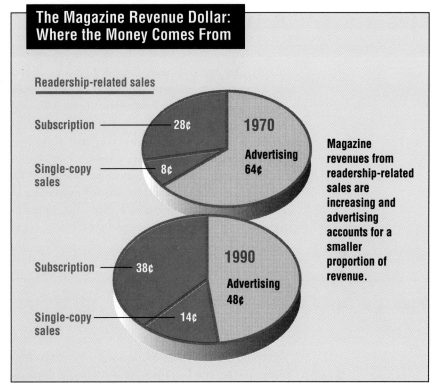

**The Magazine Revenue Dollar:
Where the Money Comes From**

Readership-related sales

**1970**

Subscription ——— 28¢

Single-copy ——— 8¢
sales

Advertising
64¢

**Magazine revenues from readership-related sales are increasing and advertising accounts for a smaller proportion of revenue.**

**1990**

Subscription ——— 38¢

Single-copy ——— 14¢
sales

Advertising
48¢

SOURCE: Data from Magazine Publishers Association, Inc., 1990.

All magazines, however, are vulnerable to trends in the economy. At one time, computer ads were 35 percent of *Business Week*'s ad pages. But when consumers bought fewer computers, as they did in 1986, computer manufacturers spent less for advertising, so 1986 ad pages at *Business Week* fell 15 percent.

And not all advertisers want the affluent audience that magazines tend to deliver. Liquor and cigarette companies are two pillars of magazine advertising, partly because these companies do not advertise on television. Today liquor and tobacco sales are down, so advertising budgets are tighter. For example, when R. J. Reynolds discovered that its advertising mix was reaching a disproportionate number of what Director of Media Dan Parsons called "heavy readers," Reynolds added advertising in the *National Enquirer* and the *Star* and reduced advertising in the news weeklies and business magazines.[22]

## Magazines Join Big Business

In 1984, for the first time, the price paid for individual magazine companies and groups of magazines bought and sold in one year reached $1 billion. *U.S. News & World Report* sold for $100 million. *Billboard* sold for $40 million. CBS bought a group of consumer magazines for $362.5 million, and Rupert Murdoch bought a group of business magazines and *New Woman* for $370 million.

Condé Nast paid $24 million for *Gourmet*; Capital Cities paid $72 million for *Institutional Investor*; the Newhouse chain paid $25.5 million for 17 percent of *The New Yorker*, which the company eventually bought for more than $150 million.[23] Like other media industries, magazines are being gathered together under large umbrella organizations.

## Facing the Future

The trend toward more refined audience targeting by magazines is likely to continue. As the audience becomes more segmented, magazine publishers envision a time when they will deliver to each reader exactly what he or she wants to read. This means an infinitely defined readership, so that advertisers can reach only the people they want.

The editors of *Folio:*, the magazine for people who publish magazines, asked industry executives to predict the future. Here are some of their conclusions:

• *More editors will review the final copy on a screen and transmit the full-color product by satellite directly to remote printing plants located for the quickest distribution to subscribers, newsstands, supermarkets, bookstores, and other outlets.*

• *Advertisers will be able to target their audience better because magazines will be able to divide their audience not only by geography, income, and interest but also by zip code.*

• *Subscribers may be asked to pay as much as half the cost of producing each magazine. If subscription prices rise substantially, fewer people will be able to afford to buy magazines, thus decreasing the potential audience.*

• *Desktop publishing will expand the number of small publishers. Using a personal computer and a laser printer, desktop operations can do everything to get a magazine ready for production except print the pictures.*

Magazines survive because they complement the other media and they have their own special benefits. Wayne Warner, president of Judd's Inc., which prints more than 77 American magazines as diverse as *The New Republic, Modern Plastics,* and *Newsweek*, best described the advantages of magazines as a medium: "With magazines, we can read *what* we want, *when* we want, and *where* we want. And we can read them again and again at our pace, fold them, spindle them, mutilate them, tear out coupons, ads, or articles that interest us and, in short, do what we damn well please to them because they are 'our' magazines."[24]

• American magazines began in 1741 when Andrew Bradford published *American Magazine* and Benjamin Franklin published *General Magazine*. Like colonial newspapers, early magazines provided a means for political expression.

• *The Saturday Evening Post*, first published in 1821, was the nation's first general-interest magazine.

• Magazines widened their audience in the 1800s by catering to women, tackling social crusades, becoming a literary showcase for American writers, and encouraging political debate.

• The Postal Act of 1879 encouraged the growth of magazines because it ensured quick, reasonably priced distribution for magazines; today magazines still travel on a preferential rate.

• American investigative reporting was pioneered by *McClure's Magazine* at the turn of the century. *McClure's* published the stories of Lincoln Steffens and Ida Tarbell that were critical of public officials and American industrialists.

• Magazines in the first half of the 20th century adapted to absorb the invention of radio and television. To adapt, some publishers sought a defined, targeted audience; others tried to attract the widest audience possible. *The New Yorker* and *Time* magazine are media empires that began during this period.

• Magazines in the second half of the 20th century have survived by targeting readers' special interests. This segments an audience for advertisers, making magazines the most specific buy an advertiser can make.

• Magazines can be divided into three types: (1) consumer publications; (2) trade, technical, and professional publications; and (3) company publications.

• Women continue to be the single most lucrative audience for magazines.

• Very few general-interest magazines survive today. Most magazines target a very specific readership.

• The audience for magazines, as for newspapers, is growing older. In 1990, for the first time, the number of magazines published in the country stopped growing.

• Magazine prices will probably rise as each subscriber is asked to pay as much as half the cost of producing each magazine. This rise in prices may mean that the audience for magazines will become smaller than it is today.

*Imagine that the date is September 8, 1940. War has*

*begun its second year in Europe. You do not have a*

*television set. You are sitting at home in the United States, listening to your radio.*

*CBS announces a special bulletin from journalist Edward R. Murrow, reporting the*

*first bombing of London: 625 German bombers have pounded the city, leaving more*

*than 1,000 people dead and 2,000 people injured.*

*You and your family listen intently in your front room*

*as Murrow describes:*

**The Radio Industry**

*men with white scarves around their necks instead of collars . . .*

*dull-eyed, empty-faced women. . . . Most of them carried little cheap cardboard suitcases and sometimes bulging paper shopping bags. That was all they had left. . . .*

*A row of automobiles with stretchers racked on the roofs like skis, standing outside of bombed buildings. A man pinned under wreckage where a broken gas main sears his arms and face . . .*

*the courage of the people; the flash and roar of the guns rolling down streets . . .*

*the stench of air-raid shelters in the poor districts.* [1]

*This* was radio reporting at its best. And for 26 years, from 1921 until the advent of television news in 1947, broadcast reporters like Murrow painted pictures with words. Radio reporters described Prohibition and its repeal, the stock market crash, the Depression, the election of Franklin D. Roosevelt, the New Deal, the bombings of London and Pearl Harbor, the Normandy invasion, Roosevelt's funeral, and the signing of the armistice that ended World War II.

Our memory today of events that happened in the quarter-century beginning in 1921 is keenly tied to radio. Newspapers offered next-day reports and occasional extras, movie theaters offered weekly newsreels, magazines offered long-term perspectives. But radio gave its listeners an immediate record at a time when world events demanded attention.

Radio also gave people entertainment: big bands, Jack Benny, George Burns and Gracie Allen, Jimmy Durante, Red Skelton, Abbott and Costello, Bob Hope, and the Shadow ("The weed of crime bears bitter fruit. Crime does not pay! The Shadow knows!")

Radio was America's second national medium, after magazines. Radio transformed national politics by transmitting the voices of public debate, as well as the words, to the audience. Radio also expanded Americans' access to popular, as well as classical, culture: Opera played on the same dial as slapstick comedy.

The legacy of news and music remains on radio today, but the medium that was once the center of attention in everyone's front room has moved into the bedroom, the car, even the shower. Radio wakes you up and puts you to sleep. Radio goes with you when you run on the trail or sit on the beach. Consider these industry statistics about radio today:

• *58 percent of America's bedrooms have radios and 60 percent of all homes have clock radios.*

• *43 percent of Americans listen to the radio sometime between midnight and 6 A.M.*

• *17 percent of America's bathrooms have radios.*

• *95 percent of America's cars have radios, and radio reaches three out of four adults in their cars at least once each week.* [2]

Using perhaps the first version of today's Walkman, a couple on Guglielmo Marconi's yacht *Electra* do the foxtrot while sailing to Albany, New York, in 1922.

Although radio is more accessible today, what you hear is not the same as what your parents or grandparents heard. Advertisers, who once sought radio as the only broadcast access to an audience, have many more choices today. For audiences, radio has become an everyday accessory rather than a necessity. No one envisioned radio's place in today's media mix when radio's founders began tinkering just before the turn of the century. All they wanted to do was send information along a wire, not through the air.

# America's Second National Medium: How Radio Began

WE ARE SO accustomed to sending and receiving messages instantaneously today that it is hard to imagine a time when information took more than a week to travel from place to place. In the early 1800s, if you wanted to send a message across the country or even into the next town, you hired a messenger. The pony express took ten and a half days to go from St. Joseph, Missouri, to San Francisco, California. Stage coaches needed 44 hours to bring news from New York to Washington.[3]

With the technological advances of the 20th century came rapid changes in how quickly information could move throughout the country. First came the invention of the telegraph and the telephone, which depend on electrical lines to deliver their messages, and then wireless telegraphy, which delivers radio signals through the air. As early as 1826, Harrison Grey Dyar operated a telegraph line on Long Island. Two Englishmen, Charles Wheatstone and Sir William Cooke, patented a telegraph instrument in Great Britain in 1837.

In America, Samuel F. B. Morse first demonstrated his electromagnetic telegraph system in 1835. In 1843, he asked Congress to give him $30,000 to string four telegraph lines along the Baltimore & Ohio Railroad right-of-way from Baltimore to Washington. The first official message — "What hath God wrought?" — was sent from Baltimore to Washington, D.C., on May 24, 1844, by the daughter of the commissioner of patents. Morse received the message in the U.S. Supreme Court chamber.

Telegraph lines followed the railroads, and for more than 30 years Americans depended on Morse's coded messages printed on tape, sent from one railroad station to another. Then on March 10, 1876, Alexander Graham Bell sent a message by his new invention, the telephone, to his associate Thomas A. Watson in an adjoining room of their Boston laboratory: "Mr. Watson, come here. I want you."

Both Morse's telegraph and Bell's telephone used wires to carry messages. Then in Germany in 1887, the physicist Heinrich Hertz began experimenting with radio waves, which became known as Hertzian waves — the first discovery in a series of refinements that led to the development of radio broadcasting.

## Radio's Pioneers

Broadcasting was truly a revolutionary media development. Imagine a society where the only way you can hear music or enjoy a comedy is at a live performance or by listening to tinny noises on a record machine. The only way you can hear a speech is to be in the audience. Movies show action but no sound. Without the inventions of broadcasting's early pioneers such as Heinrich Hertz you could still be living without the sounds of media that you have come to take for granted.

Broadcasting has been defined as the "transmission of music, speech, and/or pictures in forms that the general public can understand, on a regular and announced schedule, on a frequency band for which the general public has receivers, by a station licensed by the government for that purpose (if licensing was then required)."[4] Four pioneers besides Hertz are credited with advancing radio broadcasting in America: Guglielmo Marconi, Reginald Aubrey Fessenden, Lee de Forest, and David Sarnoff.

**Guglielmo Marconi.** Twenty-year-old Marconi, the son of wealthy Italian parents, used the results of the three discoveries by Morse, Bell, and Hertz to expand his idea that messages should be able to travel across space without a wire. Marconi became obsessed with the idea, refusing food and working in his locked upstairs room.

Soon Marconi could ring a bell across the room or downstairs without using a wire. His father became intrigued and sponsored Guglielmo and his mother on a trip to England, where Marconi showed the invention to the chief telegraph engineer in the British Post Office. Their first messages traveled 100 yards. Eventually Marconi was able to broadcast over a distance of nine miles. "The calm of my life ended then," Marconi said later.[5]

The Wireless Telegraph and Signal Company formed in 1897 to promote and sell Marconi's invention. Marconi, now 23, received half of the company's stock and 15,000 British pounds. The company, which became known as British Marconi, was organized primarily to provide ship-to-shore communications.

The *New York Herald* invited Marconi to America to report the America's Cup Race in October 1899. Marconi reported "by wireless!" the *Columbia*'s victory over the *Shamrock*. American business people, intrigued by the military potential of Marconi's invention, invested $10 million to form American Marconi.[6] Amateur radio operators created clubs to experiment with the new discovery. Two experimenters, Reginald Aubrey Fessenden and Lee de Forest, advanced the Marconi discovery to create today's radio.

**Reginald Aubrey Fessenden.** Fessenden, a Canadian, began wireless experiments in the United States in 1900 when he set up his National Electric Signaling Company to attempt sending voices by radio waves. On Christmas Eve 1906, "ship wireless operators over a wide area of the Atlantic, sitting with earphones to head, alert to the crackling of distant dots and dashes, were startled to hear a woman singing; then a violin playing; then a man reading passages from Luke. It was considered uncanny; wireless rooms were soon crowded with the curious."[7] The noises were coming from Fessenden's experimental station at Brant Rock, Massachusetts. Fessenden's experiment in 1906 is considered the world's first voice and music broadcast.

Guglielmo Marconi (right) and David Sarnoff, two of broadcasting's pioneers.

Fessenden eventually manufactured "crystal detectors" that could capture radio waves. But he went bankrupt after a few years, and Westinghouse acquired his patents.

**Lee de Forest.** De Forest is often called the father of radio because in 1907 he perfected a glass bulb called the Audion that could detect radio waves. "Unwittingly then," wrote de Forest, "had I discovered an invisible Empire of the Air."[8]

Besides being an inventor, de Forest was a good publicist. He began what he called "broadcasts" from New York and then from the Eiffel Tower. In 1910 he broadcast Enrico Caruso singing at the Metropolitan Opera House. Later his mother broadcast an appeal to give women the vote. De Forest made some sales to the navy, but most of the people who listened to his early programs used home-constructed variations on Fessenden's crystal set rather than the Audion. De Forest's invention worked much better, but it was too expensive. Eventually facing bankruptcy, de Forest sold most of his patents to the American Telephone & Telegraph Company. Gradually the Audion became the foundation of modern broadcasting.

**David Sarnoff.** In 1912, 21-year-old wireless operator David Sarnoff relayed news from Nantucket Island, Massachusetts, that he had received a distress call from the *Titanic* on his Marconi Wireless. Four years later, when Sarnoff was working for the Marconi Company in New York, he wrote a visionary memo that predicted radio's future, although in 1916 his ideas were widely ignored:

> *I have in mind a plan of development which would make radio a household utility. The idea is to bring music into the home by wireless. The receiver can be designed in the form of a simple "radio music box," and arranged for several different wave lengths which should be changeable with the throwing of a single switch or the pressing of a single button. The same principle can be extended to numerous other fields, as for example, receiving lectures at home which would be perfectly audible. Also, events of national importance can be simultaneously announced and received. Baseball scores can be transmitted in the air. This proposition would be especially interesting to farmers and others living in outlying districts.*[9]

Eventually, as commercial manager and then president of RCA, Sarnoff would watch his early vision for radio come true.

## Government Becomes Involved

The federal government decided to regulate broadcasting almost as soon as it was invented. This separated the broadcast media, which were regulated early, from the print media, which are not regulated directly by any federal government agency.

As amateurs competed with the military for the airwaves, Congress passed the Radio Act of 1912 to license people who wanted to broadcast or receive messages. Just before World War I, more than 8,500 people were licensed to transmit on radio in the United States,[10] almost all of whom had built their own equipment.

The federal government decided to license people to transmit signals because the airwaves are *limited*: *There are only a certain number of frequencies available to carry a broadcast signal.* Many amateurs, trying to send signals on the same frequency, were knocking each other off the air. The government therefore intervened to try to keep the operators out of each other's way.

Then, during World War I, the federal government ordered all amateurs off the air and took control of all privately owned stations, and the military took over radio broadcasting. After the war, with the freeze lifted, the navy argued that it should maintain the monopoly over the airwaves it had enjoyed during the war. In 1918, hearings began on legislation that would have given the navy sole control over radio. "It is my profound conviction . . . that it must be a monopoly," testified U.S. Secretary of the Navy Josephus Daniels. "It is up to the Congress to say whether it is a monopoly for the government or a monopoly for a company."[11]

Faced with strong arguments by the amateurs that they should be able to return to the airwaves, Congress decided against a navy monopoly. Instead, the government sanctioned a private monopoly formed by General Electric, Westinghouse, AT&T, Western Electric Company, and United Fruit Company. General Electric bought out American Marconi and its patents, and in 1919 these five sympathetic interests pooled the 2,000 electronic patents they controlled to form Radio Corporation of America (RCA).

Each company owned a percentage of RCA and the right to membership on the RCA board. David Sarnoff became RCA's general manager in 1921. Because of this early monopoly, RCA dominated early radio development, but eventually smaller operations formed all over the country as radio fever spread from coast to coast.

# Independent Entrepreneurs

A plaque in San Jose, California, celebrates the 1909 founding of experimental station FN. "On this site in 1909, Charles D. Herrold founded a voice radio station which opened the door to electronic mass communication. He conceived the idea of 'broadcasting' to the public, and his station, the world's first, has now served Northern California for half a century." Today that station is San Francisco's KCBS.

Various other stations claim that they were among the earliest radio pioneers. Station 9XM broadcast music and weather reports from Madison, Wisconsin; 6ADZ broadcast concerts from Hollywood; 4XD sent phonograph music from a chicken coop in Charlotte, North Carolina; and 8MK in Detroit, operated by *Detroit News* publisher William E. Scripps, transmitted election returns.

These radio operators broadcast messages to each other and their friends, but not to the general public. "The practitioners themselves had woven a mystique around their activity," says media scholar Erik Barnouw, "and surrounded it with arcane terminology. During the war the subject had become even more remote, mysterious, and legendary."[12]

These amateur radio operators were early examples of broadcast entrepreneurs. They were tinkerers, fascinated with an invention that could carry sounds through the air. One of these tinkerers, Frank Conrad, is credited with creating the beginnings of the nation's first commercial radio station.

# The Birth of Commercial Broadcasting

An ad in the September 29, 1920, *Pittsburgh Sun* changed broadcasting from an exclusive hobby to an easy-to-use medium that soon was available to everyone. The ad described a 20-minute evening concert broadcast from the home of Frank Conrad. "Mr. Conrad is a wireless enthusiast and 'puts on' the wireless concerts periodically for the entertainment of the many people in this district who have wireless sets. Amateur Wireless Sets, made by the maker of the Set which is in operation in our store, are on sale here $10.00 up."[13]

Frank Conrad worked for Westinghouse, and he often broadcast concerts from his garage on his station 8XK. But when the ad for receivers appeared, Conrad's boss at Westinghouse, Harry P. Davis, had an idea. Why not improve the broadcasts so more people would want to buy radios? The next day he talked Conrad into setting up a more powerful transmitter at the Westinghouse plant by November 2 so Conrad could broadcast election returns. Westinghouse began to manufacture receivers that sold for $60, not including headsets or loudspeakers.[14]

Conrad directed construction of a 100-watt transmitter, and the *Pittsburgh Post* agreed to telephone election returns to the station. On October 27, 1920, using the powers of the 1912 Radio Act, the U.S. Department of Commerce licensed station KDKA as the nation's first *commercial* station. The broadcast began at 8 P.M. November 2, 1920, and continued past midnight, reporting that Warren G. Harding was the nation's next president. KDKA immediately began a daily 1-hour evening schedule, 8:30–9:30 P.M.

Observed broadcast historian Erik Barnouw:

*This called for much improvisation, which was sometimes bizarre. A Westinghouse band was presented by wire from a hall, but the reverberation was unendurable on the air, so the next musical group was presented from the roof, where the acoustics were splendid. Rainy weather came, so a tent was built on the roof; the acoustics were still good. Then the tent blew down, and it was necessary to move indoors again. The acoustical problem was now solved by erecting the tent indoors. In time this arrangement gave way to studios hung with burlap — which often had a tent-like look.*[15]

Pittsburgh's KDKA was licensed in 1920 as the nation's
first commercial radio station.

## Expansion and Regulation

The crude KDKA broadcasts proved that regular programming could attract
a loyal audience. KDKA was just the beginning of what eventually became
radio networks. Westinghouse transmitters soon sprouted at WJZ in Newark,
WBZ in Springfield, Massachusetts, and KYW in Chicago. At first General
Electric was stunned by Westinghouse's network idea, but then GE moved
quickly to establish WGY in Schenectady, New York, KGO in San Franscisco,
and KOA in Denver. RCA initiated WJY in Jersey City and WRC in Washington, D.C.[16]

After KDKA's success, David Sarnoff easily convinced his allies at Westinghouse and General Electric that RCA should sell the sets that Westinghouse
and GE manufactured. AT&T agreed to sell the transmitters.

The radio craze led almost immediately to a period of rapid expansion as
entrepreneurs and advertisers began to grasp the potential of the new medium.
Almost as quickly, government was compelled to step in to expand its regulation of radio broadcasting.

In 1922, Americans spent $60 million on receivers, of which $11 million
went to RCA. Amateurs built the remaining sets. Amateurs also dashed to put
stations on the air—more than 500 stations began broadcasting in 1922.[17]

Radio's potential as a moneymaker for its owners incited competition for the airwaves. Three important developments for radio's future were: the blanket licensing agreement, the decision that radio would accept commercial sponsors, and the Radio Act of 1927.

**Blanket Licensing.** At first stations played phonograph records; then they invited artists to perform live in their studios. Some stations even did remote broadcasts of church services, and KDKA broadcast the World Series. The novelty of radio attracted some of the nation's best talent, who sought the publicity radio could give them. But eventually the performers asked to be paid.

In 1923, the American Society of Composers, Authors and Publishers (ASCAP) sued several stations for payment, claiming that broadcasting ASCAP-licensed music on the radio meant that people would buy less sheet music. Station owners argued that playing the songs on their stations would make more people want to buy the sheet music.

Eventually the stations agreed to pay ASCAP royalties through a **blanket licensing agreement**, which meant that the stations paid ASCAP a fee ($250 a year at first). In exchange, the stations could use all ASCAP-licensed music on the air. (ASCAP licenses its music to stations the same way today. Eventually another licensing organization, Broadcast Music Inc., would also collect broadcast royalties; see page 249.)

**Commercial Sponsorship.** Once station owners conceded that they would have to pay for their programs, they had to figure out where they would get the money. *Radio Broadcast* magazine ran a contest for the best idea. Some of the suggestions:

• *Private endowments should pay for the broadcasts.*

• *Local governments could underwrite radio the same way they paid for schools and libraries.*

• *Each set could be taxed when it was sold; the money would go into a central broadcasting fund that would disburse money to the stations.* [18]

AT&T had the answer in an idea they pioneered at their station WEAF in New York. WEAF inaugurated the policy of selling time. Its first sponsored program cost $100 for ten minutes. At 5 P.M. on August 28, 1922, H. M. Blackwell from the Queensboro Corporation talked about why WEAF's listeners should buy an apartment in Jackson Heights, Long Island.

Advertisers didn't rush to WEAF at first. The total revenue for August and September 1922 was $500. [19] In October, AT&T used its long-distance telephone lines from Chicago to hook up WEAF to broadcast a Princeton–University of Chicago football game, and in November they programmed the Harvard–Yale game.

Then came Christmas, and Macy's bought time. In January, a cosmetics company sponsored actress Marion Davies to talk about "How I Make Up for the Movies." Davies offered a free autographed picture to listeners who wrote in. Hundreds of letters arrived, which convinced advertisers like Lucky Strike, B. F. Goodrich, and Eveready to try this new medium.

The success of commercial sponsorship as a way to support radio settled the issue of who would pay the cost of airing the programs. Advertisers would pay for the programs through their advertising; the American public would pay for the programs indirectly by supporting the advertisers who supported radio.

**Congress Regulates Radio.** As more stations began to crowd the air, their signals interfered with one another. With only so many good frequencies available, the provisions of the Radio Act of 1912 (see page 117) began to seem inadequate. Asking for congressional action, President Coolidge froze station licenses on December 8, 1926.

Congress passed the Radio Act of 1927, which formed the Federal Radio Commission under the jurisdiction of the Department of Commerce. The commission's five members were appointed by the president, with the approval of the Senate.

The limitations on air space required that broadcasting in the United States would operate under a type of government regulation unknown to newspaper and magazine publishers. Stations were licensed for three years and were required by the commission to operate "as a public convenience, interest or necessity requires. . . ." Before assigning call letters, the commission required that the station waive "any claim to the use of any particular frequency or wavelength."

The commission, created to protect the stations by allocating frequencies, also became the license holder. The stations could operate only with the government's approval, and stations could be sold or transferred only if the commission approved. This 1927 law became the foundation for all broadcast regulation in the United States.

In 1934, Congress used the 1927 law as a model when it established the Federal Communications Commission (FCC) to regulate the expanding wireless medium, making the FCC a separate agency of government, no longer a part of the Department of Commerce. The FCC would govern all the services "which rely on wires, cables, or radio as a medium of transmission."[20]

The role of government regulation in broadcasting is covered in Chapter 13, but it is important to remember that the commission's original purpose was to allocate the spectrum so that station broadcasts would not interfere with one another. The FCC was not originally envisioned to oversee what the stations broadcast.

Beginning in 1927, when the Federal Radio Commission was formed, several challenges and court cases reaffirmed that the commission would not act as a censor. The commission would exert its power only at license-renewal time, not day to day.

The FCC began work on July 11, 1934, with seven commissioners appointed by the president, with Senate approval. This same basic structure and purpose govern the commission's actions today, but now there are only five commissioners. The establishment of the FCC in 1934 also set the precedent for the later regulation of television.

# The Nation Tunes In

BY 1924, MANY radio program lineups included entertainment with names like the Ipana Troubadours, the Schrafft's Tearoom Orchestra, and the Wanamaker Organ Concert. The sponsors — Ipana toothpaste, Schrafft's candy, and Wanamaker's Department Store — didn't simply pay for commercial time on the shows. They produced the programs themselves and gave them to the radio stations. "Sponsors were, in effect, being encouraged to take charge of the air."[21]

Most stations mixed entertainment, culture, and public service. On September 12, 1924, you could choose from these evening programs on AT&T station WEAF, New York:

| | |
|---|---|
| 4 P.M. | *John Burnham, concert pianist* |
| 6 P.M. | *Dinner music from the Rose Room of the Waldorf-Astoria* |
| 7:55 P.M. | *Rosella Sheiner, 10-year-old violinist* |
| 8:05 P.M. | *Isabel Duff "Scotty" Wood singing a program of Scotch songs* |
| 8:20 P.M. | *Henry Jentes, jazz pianist* |
| 9–10 P.M. | *B. Fischer & Company Astor Coffee Dance Orchestra* |

Early radio receivers could be found just about anywhere, including this one with a makeshift antenna.

| | |
|---|---|
| *10 P.M.* | *Joseph White, tenor* |
| *10:15–11:00 P.M.* | *Speeches on National Defense Test Day, direct from Washington, D.C.* [22] |

Radio producer Irving Settel observed:

*The impact of radio in this country was so great that it had become one of the most influential forces in American life, stimulating every phase of activity. New stars were born, new expressions were popularized as new program formats were being offered. Radio was penetrating every third home in the country, and tenement house roofs were covered with forests of antennae.* [23]

Radio permitted a new kind of collective national experience. Since the days of George Washington, only those few thousand people who were actually present at a presidential inauguration could hear the oath of office administered and the president-elect's address. But when Calvin Coolidge was reelected president, radio covered his inauguration on March 4, 1925, and the audience was estimated at 15 million. [24]

# Radio's Golden Age

Radio in the 1930s and 1940s became a powerful cultural and political force. Radio gave multitudes of people a new, inexpensive source of information and entertainment. The commercialization of American broadcasting also gave advertisers access to this audience at home. Radio's massive audience sat enraptured with sponsored programming of many types: comedy, music, serials, drama, and news. Eventually, all of these types of programming migrated to television.

**Comedy and Music.** At NBC, Freeman Gosden and Charles Correll played the African-American characters Amos 'n' Andy. Gosden and Correll, both white, wrote each day's program themselves and at first played all the show's characters, which eventually numbered 550. A 1930 survey reported that more than half of all the radios in America tuned in to *Amos 'n' Andy* every night.[25]

The 1930s also was the decade of comedians George Burns and Gracie Allen, Jack Benny, Will Rogers, Groucho Marx, Bob Hope, singers Bing Crosby and Kate Smith, and host Ed Sullivan.

**Serials and Drama.** The soap opera *Helen Trent* began in 1933, followed by other sudsy sagas such as *When a Girl Marries, Road to Life, The Guiding Light,* and *Stella Dallas.* This was also the era of *Lux Radio Theatre* on CBS, which began presenting radio dramas in 1936 and featured such talents as Helen Hayes, Tyrone Power, and Barbara Stanwyck. CBS reached for prestige with programs like *Lux Radio Theatre* and *The Columbia Workshop*, which featured experimental radio that was broadcast without a sponsor.

CBS also introduced the *Mercury Theater on the Air* in July 1938. This hour-long program, produced by members of New York's Mercury Theater, notably Orson Welles, soon brought CBS a type of notoriety that the network did not need.

On Halloween Eve, October 30, 1938, the *Mercury Theater on the Air* broadcast a play based on the H. G. Wells story "War of the Worlds." The live 8 P.M. broadcast played opposite the very popular Edgar Bergen program on NBC and rarely had 4 percent of the audience. Very few people heard the announcement at the beginning of the program that the Mercury Theater was performing a version of the Wells story.

The program began with the announcer introducing some band music. A second voice then said, "Ladies and gentlemen, we interrupt our program of

Sound effects on the set formed an important part of early radio dramas.

dance music to bring you a special bulletin. At 20 minutes before 8 o'clock Central Time, Professor Farrell of Mount Jennings Observatory, Chicago, reports observing several explosions of incandescent gas occurring at regular intervals on the planet Mars."

More dance music followed, and then more bulletins about the Martians, with the startling news that 1,500 people near Princeton, New Jersey, had died when they were hit by a meteor. Then the announcer said it was not a meteor but a spaceship carrying Martians armed with death rays.

Two professors from the Princeton geology department actually set out to locate the "meteors." In Newark, more than 20 families rushed out of their homes, covering their faces with wet handkerchiefs to protect themselves from the "gas."

After a burst of horrified calls, CBS began repeating the announcement that the program was just a play. The episode demonstrated how easily alarming information could be innocently misinterpreted, especially because the listeners had no other source to check the reliability of what they were hearing. Radio listeners truly were a captive audience.

President Franklin D. Roosevelt detailed his economic policies to the nation in a 1942 Fireside Chat. Roosevelt was the first president to use broadcasting to gather public support for his programs.

**News.** Radio allowed listeners to evaluate public officials in a way they never could before. President Franklin D. Roosevelt understood the political power offered by access to a mass audience. Instead of using radio broadcasts just for speeches and campaigns, Roosevelt talked intimately with the American public about his antidotes for the Depression beginning with his first Fireside Chat, broadcast on March 12, 1933, to 50 million listeners.

*It was as if a wise and kindly father had sat down to talk sympathetically and patiently and affectionately with his worried and anxious children, and had given them straightforward things that they had to do to help him along as the father of the family. That speech of the President's over the air humanized radio in a great governmental, national sense as it had never before been humanized.* [26]

During World War II, radio news blossomed. FDR drew the nation's first military draft number on the air, and Edward R. Murrow broadcast the emotion of the bombing of London. When the Japanese attacked Pearl Harbor, radio carried the news. The next day, Roosevelt's declaration of war on the Japanese was broadcast from Congress live on radio.

In June 1944, all commercial programming stopped for the live broadcast of the Normandy invasion. From April 12–15, 1945, all commercial stations stopped their programming once again to cover FDR's funeral. News broadcasters John Daly, Eric Sevareid, Gabriel Heatter, Charles Collingwood, and H.V. Kaltenborn became as prominent in America as the news they read on the air. (See Impact/Profile, H.V. Kaltenborn.) World War II's legacy to radio was to make radio as important to its audience for news and information as it was for entertainment.

# H. V. Kaltenborn (1878–1965)

The following profile by **Alice Goldfarb Marquis** describes the career of H. V. Kaltenborn, who is often credited with defining the purpose of radio commentary and the role of radio commentators.

t

HE DEAN of them all was H. V. Kaltenborn, a mature journalist who had been freelancing as a commentator since the early '20s. Born in Wisconsin, where friends called him "Spiderlegs Kalty," he had left school at the age of 14 and served as a 20-year-old volunteer in the Spanish-American War. He took a degree at Harvard and was the classmate of John Reed, Maxwell Perkins, and Walter Lippmann. By 1910 he had landed a $40-per-week job as an editor at the Brooklyn *Eagle*; in 1917 he became its war editor when he was rejected as a volunteer in the Allied Expeditionary Force because his uncle, Hans von Kaltenborn-Stachau, had been German minister of war during the 1890s. . . .

When the Munich crisis [with Hitler claiming that Great Britain and France could avoid war by allowing Germany to take over Czechoslovakia] broke on September 12, [1938,] both networks were ready for live coverage at a level never before attempted.

# The Growth of Radio Networks

The formation of the networks as a source of programming and revenue is a crucial development in the history of American radio. As the networks stretched across the country, they provided a dependable source of programming. Most stations found it easier to affiliate with a network and receive its programming than to develop local programs.

**NBC.** NBC grew out of the government's original agreement with RCA. RCA, GE, and Westinghouse formed the National Broadcasting Company in

**H. V. Kaltenborn**

Within the next 18 days, they spent $200,000, more than had ever been paid for coverage of any single sequence of events. CBS carried 151 short-wave pickups and NBC 147 — at an average cost of $500 each. This time listeners not only heard directly from observers in various capitals, they also eavesdropped on spontaneous, continuing conversations among all of them as they questioned each other and commented ad lib.

The hero of those 20 tense days was H. V. Kaltenborn, as even the rival NBC news director Abel Schechter conceded. During the long crisis the 60-year-old commentator lived in Studio 9 at CBS, napping on a cot between bulletins, flashes, running stories, and commentaries. He made 102 broadcasts ranging from two minutes to two hours in length. So habituated did Kaltenborn become to instant analysis that when the Archbishop of Canterbury broadcast a prayer for peace, he analyzed that too. "I drew on everything I had learned during my entire lifetime," he wrote, "my travels, my interviews, my knowledge of languages, my close association with current events. . . ."

The effects of radio coverage during these days were profound. Kaltenborn went from one or two broadcasts per week, at $100 each, to a weekly income of thousands of dollars. For the first time in radio history, news drew more listeners than entertainment.

*From "Radio Grows Up,"* American Heritage 34, no. 5 (August/September 1983): 77–78.

1926, with AT&T leasing the wires for the broadcasts to NBC, which used equipment manufactured by Western Electric. For the first year, the chain spanning the 15 cities covered by RCA would pay AT&T $800,000. AT&T, in turn, sold station WEAF to RCA for $1 million—the first major radio station sale in the country's history.[27]

By January 1927, NBC had formed two networks: the Red network (fed from WEAF) and the Blue network (originating from station WJZ in Newark). Station engineers drew the planned hookups of the two networks with red and blue colored pencils—hence their names.

Anticipating criticism about their broad control over the airwaves, RCA advertised that "The Radio Corporation of America is not in any sense seeking a monopoly of the air. . . . If others will engage in this business, the RC of A will welcome their action, whether it be cooperative or competitive."[28] RCA, however, continued as the world's largest distributor of radios, which were made by Westinghouse and General Electric.

**CBS.** Twenty-six-year-old William S. Paley, heir to a tobacco fortune, bought the financially struggling Columbia Phonograph Company in 1929 for about half a million dollars when he learned that his family's cigar company had advertised very successfully on a Columbia station. He changed the name to Columbia Broadcasting System and sold the company's record division (CBS bought back the record company in 1938). He put the CBS network on the air with 25 stations. Programming originated from WABC in New York.

Paley, who originally planned to run the network part-time while still directing his parents' cigar business, soon found himself working in New York full-time just to keep the company solvent in the face of competition from NBC. "The key to CBS's survival was salesmanship, the art of convincing potential sponsors to buy time. If they believed broadcast advertising would sell their products, they would, Paley believed, pay handsomely for the privilege of using CBS's vast chain of affiliates to spread their message."[29]

Paley succeeded handsomely. In 1932, the second full year of the Depression, CBS collected $16 million in advertising. The Commerce Department estimated 14 million radio sets were in operation, with an average audience of four people per set.[30] Paley became the nemesis of NBC, now controlled by David Sarnoff, and this early competition between Sarnoff and Paley shaped the development of American broadcasting.

**ABC.** In 1941, the FCC ordered RCA to divest itself of one of its networks. In 1943, RCA sold NBC-Blue to Edward J. Noble (who had made his fortune as head of the company that produced LifeSavers). Noble paid $8 million for the network that became the American Broadcasting Company, giving the country a three-network system.

Radio networks prospered until the 1980s, when NBC sold its radio network and CBS and ABC (who also own television properties) gave more attention to their television holdings.

# Radio in the TV Age

INITIALLY, IT seemed that television would cause the death of radio. As soon as television proved itself, advertisers abandoned radio, said comedian Fred Allen, "like the bones at a barbeque."[31] The talent fled, too—Bob Hope, Milton Berle, Jackie Gleason, even Burns and Allen. Public affairs programs like *Meet the Press* made the move to TV, as did Edward R. Murrow's *Hear It Now,* which became *See It Now.*

When World War II ended, fewer than 1,000 AM stations were on the air. By 1953, there were 2,391, slicing an ever-shrinking pie into more parts.[32] The radio networks, which at first tried to compete with television, eventually lost most of the big-name shows. Affiliate owners watched as new local independent radio stations gained local advertisers, and many affiliates left the networks. As the depleted radio networks grew weaker, local radio was left to test whether radio and television could live together.

*Radio jokes abounded in the early 1950s: one cartoon showed a young boy dusting off a radio in the attic and asking his daddy, "What's that?" Americans had seen icemen put out of work, ice chests discarded for refrigerators, and silent pictures give way to talkies. It was against memories like these — recent memories — that many people gauged radio's chances against television.*[33]

Four developments in the 1940s and 1950s changed the medium of radio and guaranteed its survival alongside television: the FCC's licensing of FM; a new source of recorded music for broadcast; the introduction of radio formats; and the introduction of reliable clock and car radios.

## The FCC Recognizes FM

After working more than a decade to eliminate static from radio broadcasts, engineer Edwin H. Armstrong applied to the FCC in 1936 to broadcast using his new technique, frequency modulation (FM). Because of the way FM signals travel through the air, FM offered truer transmission with much less static. Armstrong faced difficult opposition from David Sarnoff, who had been an early Armstrong sponsor. Armstrong needed the upper frequencies for FM, but so did Sarnoff, who wanted to use them to develop television. At the time, only experimental radio sets could receive FM; commercial sets were built for AM only.

Armstrong stubbornly persisted, and the FCC gave him a 50,000-watt station in Alpine, New Jersey. The FCC removed channel 1 from the TV band and gave it to radio. Then the FCC mandated that television must use the FM signal to broadcast its sound. Armstrong seemed destined to win recognition. The FCC received 150 applications for FM licenses in 1939 but then froze licensing during World War II.

After the war, Armstrong again faced Sarnoff, and this time Armstrong lost. The FCC assigned FM new higher frequencies to allow space for TV signals. RCA, which was using Armstrong's frequency modulation in its TV and FM sets, refused to pay him royalties. Armstrong sued RCA.

RCA fought the suit for four years, saying that RCA had been among the early developers of FM, citing RCA's sponsorship of Armstrong's beginning experiments. In 1953, Armstrong became ill and suffered a stroke.

*One day, neatly dressed, he stepped out of a window of his thirteenth-floor East Side apartment. He was found on a third-floor extension. Shortly afterward, RCA made a million-dollar settlement with the estate. Litigation with other companies continued for thirteen years. All suits were won by the Armstrong estate.*[34]

Armstrong's hopes were fulfilled 20 years after his death when the sounds of quadraphonic music sought the clear broadcast of the FM spectrum. FM eventually became the spectrum of choice for music lovers, far surpassing the broadcast quality of AM.

# BMI Licenses Recordings

Early radio station owners avoided playing records because they would have to pay royalties. The FCC also required stations that played records to remind their audiences every half-hour that they were listening to recorded music, not a live orchestra. This discouraged record-spinning.

In 1935, newscaster Martin Block at New York's independent station WNEW began playing records in between his newscasts, and then he started a program called *Make Believe Ballroom*. He is generally considered America's first disc jockey. But he didn't have many followers until 1940, when the FCC ruled that once stations bought a record, they could play it on the air whenever they liked, without the half-hour announcements.

To counteract ASCAP's insistence on royalties, broadcasters formed a cooperative music licensing organization called Broadcast Music Inc. Most rhythm and blues, country, and rock 'n' roll artists eventually signed with BMI, which charged stations less for its music than ASCAP. With an inexpensive source of music available, a new media personality was created — the DJ.

# Formats Revolutionize Programming

How would the stations know which mix of records to use? The answer came from Gordon McLendon, the father of format radio. McLendon first became known as a play-by-play baseball announcer on KLIF in Dallas in 1948. He recreated major league games from running reports he received by telegraph. "For Boston games, he had crowd sounds with a Boston accent. . . . For some games, as McLendon did the play-by-play, he would have a staff member broadcast through an echo chamber announcements such as 'Will the driver of New Jersey license number . . .'."[35]

McLendon outfitted KLIF news cars to search for local news. He targeted local people for interviews on national subjects. He beat television, which was burdened with heavy camera equipment. KLIF's innovative news coverage gave rise to McLendon's first idea for a successful format: all-news radio.

Then McLendon combined music and news in a predictable rotation of 20-minute segments, and eventually KLIF grew very popular. Next he refined the music by creating the Top 40 format. Top 40 played the top-selling hits continually, interrupted only by a disc jockey or a newscast.

By 1959, McLendon had identified another segment of the radio market when he started the beautiful-music format at KABL in San Francisco. In 1964, McLendon used a 24-hour news format for Chicago's WNUS, using three news vans with a "telesign" that showed news on the roof in lights as the van drove around town. One key to the networks' success before McLendon's innovation with formats was that the networks could provide high-quality programming for their affiliates. But formats meant that stations could now share standardized programs that stations previously had to produce individually. Eventually, the idea of formatted programming spread, making network programming and the networks themselves less important to individual stations.

# Clock and Car Radios

Two technological innovations helped ensure radio's survival by making it an everyday accessory. Transistor radios, first sold in 1948 for $40, were more reliable and cheaper than tube radios. Clock radios woke people up and caused them to rely on radio for the first news of the day.

The car radio was invented in 1928 by William Lear, who designed the Lear jet. Early car radios were enormous, with spotty reception, but technology developed during World War II helped refine them. In 1946, 9 million cars had car radios. By 1963, the number was 50 million.[36] *Drive-time audiences* (who listened 6–9 A.M. and 4–7 P.M.) were born when radio station owner Gerald Bartell coined the term in 1957.

A Columbia University report, commissioned by NBC in 1954, defined radio's new role. "Radio was the one medium that could accompany almost every type of activity. . . . Where radio once had been a leisure-time 'reward' after a day's work, television was now occupying that role. Radio had come to be viewed less as a treat than as a kind of 'companion' to some other activity."[37] Like magazines, radio survived in part because the medium adapted to fill a different need for its audience.

# Payola

The rise of rock 'n' roll coincided with the development of transistor and portable radios, which meant that radio played a central role in the rock revolution. "Rock and radio were made for each other. The relationship between record companies and radio stations became mutually beneficial. By providing the latest hits, record companies kept stations' operating costs low. The stations, in turn, provided the record companies with the equivalent of free advertising."[38]

This relationship eventually would prove too close. On February 8, 1960, Congress began hearings into charges that disc jockeys and program directors had accepted cash to play specific records on the air. The term **payola** was coined to describe this practice, combining payoff and Victrola (the name of a popular record player).

"The fee was based on how often the song was played and on the size of the market. In the earliest days record companies would present deejays with gifts simply as 'favors.' As the play lists grew more restricted and the competition among record companies more intense, cash payments developed."[39] Several disc jockeys admitted in the hearings that they had accepted money to play records.

Early car radios required complicated equipment. These radio operators on the road were attempting to pick up a signal in 1923.

In May 1960, the Manhattan grand jury charged eight men with commercial bribery for accepting more than $100,000 in payoffs for playing records. The most prominent among them was Alan Freed, who had worked in Cleveland (where he was credited with coining the term *rock 'n' roll*) and at New York's WABC. He was charged with 26 counts of accepting payoffs when he went on trial in February 1962. He pleaded guilty to two counts, paid a $300 fine, and received six months' probation. Then Freed was found guilty of income tax evasion. He died in 1965 while awaiting trial, at age 43. In September 1960, Congress amended the Federal Communications Act to prohibit the payment of cash or gifts in exchange for air play.[40] (For a discussion of recent payola investigations, see Chapter 7.)

# How Radio Works

**m**ORE THAN 10,800 radio stations were broadcasting in the United States in 1991. Of these, about 5,000 were commercial AMs, about 4,400 were commercial FMs, and the rest were noncommercial FMs.[41]

Network programming plays a much smaller role in radio today than when radio began. NBC sold all of its network-owned radio stations to a company called Westwood One. CBS and ABC still own radio stations, as does the Mutual Radio Network. Westwood One (under the name NBC Radio Network), CBS, ABC, and Mutual Radio still provide news and programming to their affiliates.

Most stations today, however, combine local personalities with different types of programming from companies that call themselves program services. These companies can provide satellite as well as formatted programming.

Some stations are part of a *group*, which means they are owned by a company that owns more than one station in more than one broadcast market. Other stations are part of a *combination AM/FM* (a "combo"), which means that one company owns both an AM and an FM station in the same market. And many stations remain family-owned, single operations that run just like any other small business.

The *general manager* runs the radio station. The *program manager* oversees what goes on the air, including the news programs, the station's format, and any on-air people. *Salespeople* sell the advertising for the programs.

*Traffic* people schedule the commercials, make sure they run correctly, and bill the clients. *Production* people help with local programming and produce commercials for the station. *Engineers* keep the station on the air. And *administrative* people pay the bills, answer the phones, and order the paper clips. At a small station, as few as five people will handle all these jobs.

# The Radio Industry Today

INSTEAD OF dying after the spread of television, radio has managed to thrive by adapting to an audience that seeks the portability and immediacy that radio offers. Today's radio programming is very different from the wide range offered to audiences in the 1930s and 1940s. Nothing can beat radio for quick news bulletins or the latest hits. Radio also delivers a targeted audience much better than television because the radio station you prefer defines you to an advertiser much better than the television station you watch.

The advertising potential of an intimate medium like radio is attracting entrepreneurs who have never owned a station and group owners who want to expand their holdings, given the FCC's deregulation. When you listen to your radio in your car or through earphones while you jog, for instance, radio is not competing with any other medium for your attention. Advertisers like this exclusive access to an audience. (See Industry Snapshot, page 140.)

Four important issues for radio people today are: the rise of FM over AM, deregulation, ratings, and formats.

# FM and AM

AM stations (AM stands for amplitude modulation) send sounds differently from FMs. The way that FM signals travel makes them better carriers for stereo sound than AM, and when the FCC began licensing FM in 1961, it authorized stereo for FM to give it an advantage over AM. In 1985, the FCC approved stereo for AM, and some AM stations broadcast in stereo today, but most people don't yet have radios that can receive the new AM signals. The AM signal also carries less fidelity than the FM signal, so today in most markets FM is more attractive to advertisers than AM.

"Although radio is prospering, AM stations are losing listeners at an alarming rate," reports *The Wall Street Journal*. In 1970, two out of three listeners regularly tuned to AM. By 1990, FM had captured 77 percent of the audience[42] (see Figure 4.1).

AM typically fares best with news, sports, local information, and call-in shows. This type of programming attracts a more loyal audience than the audience for music, which tends to be fickle, switching the dial to hear favorite songs. But the cost of local programming is high compared with prepackaged music formats.

As predicted by the 1954 NBC study (see page 134), radio today has receded into the background, but radio still generates enough money to make it an attractive investment. In 1990, more than 1,000 AM and FM stations, with a total value of nearly $1 billion, were sold.[43]

# Deregulation

The FCC once limited the number of stations that one owner could hold to seven AMs and seven FMs. Today one owner can own 12 AMs and 12 FMs. The Federal Communications Commission also no longer requires that a station owner keep a station a minimum of three years before selling. Radio stations can be bought and sold whenever the owner chooses (see Figure 4.2).

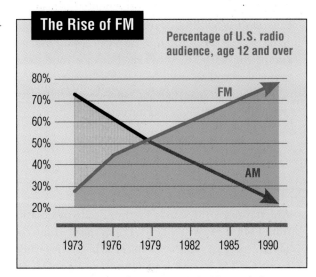

**The Rise of FM**

Percentage of U.S. radio audience, age 12 and over

SOURCE: Data from *Radar Data*, Statistical Research, Inc.

The loosening of restrictions on broadcast ownership is just one way the government in the 1980s deregulated the broadcast industry. That is, many regulations that had been approved by members of the FCC before 1980 were removed in the 1980s under the Reagan administration. The result of this deregulation was that more radio (and television) stations were sold in the 1980s than at any other time in broadcasting history.

# Ratings

Radio station owners depend on ratings to set advertising rates, and the stations with the most listeners command the highest ad rates. Radio ratings began in 1930 when Archibald Crossley organized a ratings service for the Association of National Advertisers. These ratings, called the Crossleys, were based on a random sample of telephone calls. Listeners were simply asked to state what they had been listening to over the past several hours.

C. E. Hooper introduced "Hooperatings" in 1934, which used essentially the same method. By the late 1940s, Hooper and a second group, which published the *Pulse* based on home interviews in person, were the major radio ratings services.

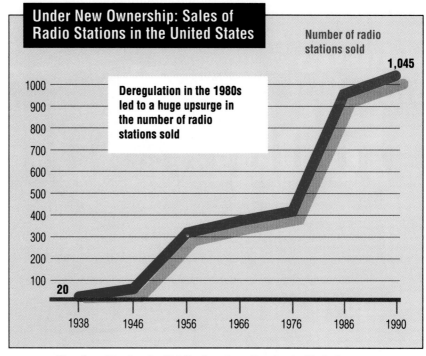

**Under New Ownership: Sales of Radio Stations in the United States**

Number of radio stations sold

1,045

Deregulation in the 1980s led to a huge upsurge in the number of radio stations sold

1000
900
800
700
600
500
400
300
200
100
20

1938    1946    1956    1966    1976    1986    1990

SOURCE: Data from Broadcasting Publications, Inc., *Broadcasting Yearbook*, 1991.

As the ratings grew more important to owners and to advertisers, audience measurement grew more controversial. Critics claimed that telephone surveys didn't reach the rich (who typically have unlisted numbers) or the poor (who might not have telephones). In-home interviewers, critics said, could influence the interviewees. And although Hooper had begun surveying drive-time audiences, the surveys depended on information gathered after the person left the car. How could the ratings be accurate?

In 1963, a congressional committee began an investigation into the ratings services after some television quiz show contestants admitted they had been given the answers to questions by the shows' sponsors to increase the audience ratings (see page 165). The findings of this ratings services investigation affected radio as well as television.

In 1965, the committee issued a report, *Broadcast Ratings: The Methodology, Accuracy and Use of Ratings in Broadcasting*, which made two major criticisms. "The committee found that in some instances ratings services were inept, with ill-designed, sloppily executed research. In other cases the services were accused of misrepresenting their findings."[44]

# Radio

## Industry Snapshot

Radio today sells itself as the "go-anywhere" medium that reaches listeners while they drive, work, shop, and jog. As with magazines, advertisers like radio's ability to reach targeted audiences.

## The Go-Anywhere Medium: Where People Listen

Percentage of total listening time

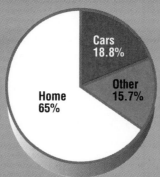

Cars 18.8%
Other 15.7%
Home 65%

**Teens 12–17**

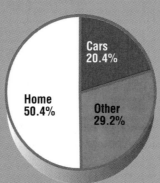

Cars 20.4%
Home 50.4%
Other 29.2%

**Women 18 and over**

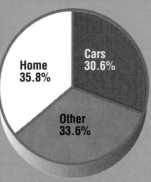

Home 35.8%
Cars 30.6%
Other 33.6%

**Men 18 and over**

Data from Radio Advertising Bureau, Inc., *Radio Facts for Advertisers*, 1990.

**1** Home radio audiences have been declining for years, but this trend is largely offset by an increase in radio listening away from home. Among women, at-home listening now accounts for only about half of total listening time.

**2** Like car radios, take-along radios have helped the industry to find a new niche —but radio still must compete for listening time with cassette and CD "take-alongs."

## Radio's Reach: Who Listens

| | Percent who listen each day | Average time spent listening per day (hr:min) |
|---|---|---|
| Teens 12–17 | 84.7% | 2:20 |
| Men 18 and over | 79.4% | 3:06 |
| Women 18 and over | 75.4% | 3:01 |

Data from Radio Advertising Bureau, Inc., *Radio Facts for Advertisers*, 1990.

**3** **Although radio still holds a significant audience, listening time today is less than the average of 4 hours daily that people listened to radio in the pre-television era.**

**4** **Formats have become an economical way for radio stations to target specific kinds of audiences—and to fine-tune their pitch to advertisers.**

## Formats: What People Are Listening To

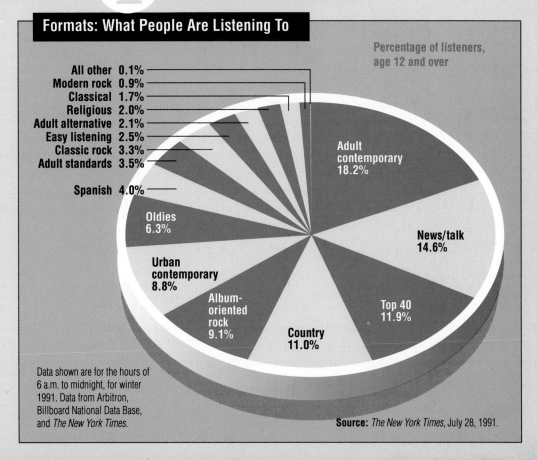

Percentage of listeners, age 12 and over

All other 0.1%
Modern rock 0.9%
Classical 1.7%
Religious 2.0%
Adult alternative 2.1%
Easy listening 2.5%
Classic rock 3.3%
Adult standards 3.5%

Spanish 4.0%

Oldies 6.3%

Urban contemporary 8.8%

Album-oriented rock 9.1%

Country 11.0%

Top 40 11.9%

News/talk 14.6%

Adult contemporary 18.2%

Data shown are for the hours of 6 a.m. to midnight, for winter 1991. Data from Arbitron, Billboard National Data Base, and *The New York Times*.

**Source:** *The New York Times*, July 28, 1991.

As a result, the broadcast industry (radio and television) decided to accredit ratings services and even established a research study to analyze how the ratings should be done. The American Research Bureau, formed in 1949, proposed that listeners fill in diaries and mail them back, which eliminated phone calls. Hooper and the *Pulse* eventually went out of business. Control Data Corporation bought the American Research Bureau and changed its name to Arbitron. Today Arbitron provides the radio business with its ratings.

Arbitron uses four measures of radio listening: average quarter-hour, "cume," rating, and share.

1. Average quarter-hour *means the average number of people listening to a station in any given 15-minute period.*

2. "Cume" *stands for the cumulative audience — the estimated number of people listening to a station for 5 minutes or more in any given time period.*

3. Rating *is the percentage of the* total population *that a station is reaching.*

4. Share *stands for the percentage of* people listening *to radio that a station is reaching.*

Like its predecessors, Arbitron is criticized because minorities, non-English-speaking listeners, and people age 18 to 24 don't return the diaries in the same proportion as other people who are surveyed. Arbitron acknowledges the problems and has tried filling out diaries for people over the phone and adding bilingual interviewers. Still, questions persist.

"Arbitron critics contend that its ratings hurt the different rock and ethnic formats, while aiding the middle-of-the-road, news, and talk formats, whose audiences are both older and more responsive to the diaries."[45] Yet no other major competing radio ratings service exists, and stations are very dependent on ratings to set their rates for advertising. A larger audience means higher ratings, which can be translated into higher advertising rates. Certain groups of people (affluent women 24–30, for example) might be more appealing to advertisers than others, and so stations can also use their programming to target particular types of audiences.

# Formats: Gordon McLendon's Legacy

Today's radio station owner looking for an audience can use one of several ready-made formats. By adjusting their formats, radio station managers can test the market until they find a formula that works to deliver their audience to

California radio stations often use billboards on the freeway to try to capture listeners.

advertisers. If you were a radio station manager today and you wanted to program your station, you could choose from several widely used formats, ranked by the number of stations using them:

**Country and Western.** The Grand Ole Opry first broadcast country music on WSM in Nashville in 1925, and this radio format is the most popular, aimed at 25-to-45-year-olds in urban as well as rural areas. About 2,400 stations use this format.

**Adult Contemporary.** Plays adult rock and light rock music by artists such as Kenny G and Anita Baker. Aims to reach 25-to-40-year-olds in all types of markets. About 2,300 stations use this format.

**Top 40.** Playing songs on *Billboard*'s current hits list, a Top 40 station closely follows trends among listeners, especially teenagers. About 1,000 stations use this format.

**Religious.** "Here's the news of today and the promise of tomorrow," began one station with religious programming. Although some denominations own stations and broadcast their points of view, many stations have adopted religious programming purely as a way to make a profit. These stations offer inspirational music, news, weather, sports, and drama. About 900 stations broadcast a religious format.

**Middle of the Road (MOR).** "Not too hard, not too soft" is the phrase most often used to describe this format. You could also add "not too loud, not too fast, not too slow, not too lush, not too new." The audience is 25 to 35 years old, and the music may include the Beatles, James Taylor, the Supremes, and Stevie Wonder. About 700 stations use this format.

**Album-Oriented Rock (AOR).** Directed toward 18-to-24-year-olds, this format delivers contemporary hits, like Top 40, but with songs from a longer span of time — from within the last two years, for example, instead of the last month. About 500 stations broadcast AOR.

**Talk.** A station with this format devotes most of its air time to different types of talk shows, which can include call-in features, where listeners question on-the-air guests. Its typical audience is 35 and older, and you can hear this format on about 400 stations nationwide.

**News.** It is difficult for a radio station to survive on news alone, hence most news stations are in big cities. The news station with the largest total weekly audience in the country, WINS in New York, advertises that it gives "all the news all the time." Seventy times an hour, for example, WINS tells listeners what time it is. About 385 stations broadcast all-news.

**Spanish.** Spanish stations are the fastest-growing foreign language format, as radio owners target the nation's expanding Hispanic population. Spanish-language radio usually features news, music, and talk. Most Spanish-language stations are AMs that recently have been converted from less-profitable formats. About 200 U.S. stations offer Spanish-language programming.

Stations can divide these traditional formats into even more subcategories: AOR is splitting into modern rock and oldies; some adult contemporary stations play only love songs. The use of taped program formats means that a station can specialize its programming simply by changing the tapes or discs.

This makes disc jockeys as "personalities" much less important than they once were. Many stations operate without disc jockeys altogether, or limit personality programming to morning and evening drive-time. The rest of the day and evening these stations can rely on an engineer and an announcer to carry the programming. (Some stations have reacted to packaged formats by returning to independent programming. See Impact/Perspective, Free-Form Radio Fights Static Formats.)

Networks, which once dominated radio programming (and now include Mutual Radio and Westwood One), today mainly provide national news to their affiliates. Station managers can program their own stations, mixing local news, music, and announcements. Stations also can get programming from syndicated and satellite program services. Syndicaters provide taped program formats. Satellites make program distribution easier; satellite networks, such as Satellite Music Network, promise the broadcaster original, up-to-date programming without a large local staff.

# Facing the Future

The most significant trend in radio is the move toward more and more segmentation of the audience, similar to the division of audiences in the magazine industry. Identifying a specific audience segment and programming for it is called **narrowcasting**. "With narrowcasting, advertising efficiency goes way up as overall costs go down. . . . We are approaching the unstated goal of all radio programmers: to create a station aimed so perfectly that the listener will no longer have to wait, ever, for the song that he wants to hear."[46]

**Demand Programming.** Demand programming is a new term that describes radio's future possibilities. In the ultimate form of narrowcasting, a listener would be able to order up any particular selection at any time — do-it-yourself request radio.

In an *Esquire* magazine article "Radio Lives!" Eric Zorn predicted:

*Listeners of the future, instead of having access to just 30 or 40 stations (many playing the same music and aimed at the same mainstream audiences), will be able to hook into hundreds of channels — blues stations, business-news stations, Czech-language stations, even full-time stations for the blind, anything you can't hear now because the audience for it is too small and scattered for even the biggest cities to support.*[47]

**Digital Audio Broadcast.** Zorn's prediction may become possible before the next century begins through a new technology known as **digital**

# Free-Form Radio Fights Static Formats

In this *Wall Street Journal* article, **Kevin Goldman** says that, in some markets, the free-form radio that was popular in the 1960s is making a comeback.

ON A recent Sunday evening, listeners of radio station WXRK-FM here [New York] heard an unreleased song by Ned Sublette and the Persuasions, "Ever-Widening Circle of Remorse."

Vin Scelsa, the disk jockey on duty, liked it so much he immediately played it again. And again. During the record's third go-around, Mr. Scelsa talked over the song and interrupted it to comment on various lyrics that caught his interest.

Clearly, this isn't cookie-cutter radio.

Mr. Scelsa is an oddity in an era when most radio is dominated by carefully researched, risk-averse formats that live by computer-generated playlists. He is a throwback to the free-form radio of the late 1960s, when progressive rock first hit the airwaves and disk jockeys enjoyed wide freedom to play whatever they wanted.

But Mr. Scelsa may also be the forerunner of a new wave of disk jockeys who are being put on the air for their musical knowledge: Free-form programming, which had dwindled to as few as five stations around the country in the mid-1980s, appears to be making a modest comeback.

To be sure, most free-form stations give disk jockeys less freedom these days than they did in the '60s, when listeners may have been assaulted by a half-hour of sitar music or 18-minute album cuts with seven-minute guitar solos. But the number of stations whose playlists go beyond the staples of album-oriented rock, such as

Led Zeppelin and the Who, has jumped nearly eightfold in the past several years to 39, says Robert Unmacht, president and managing editor of M Street Journal, a Washington-based weekly publication that chronicles format changes.

Free-form radio is re-emerging because it serves as a way for stations to carve distinct identities in a cluttered market. KDHT-FM in Denver adopted a progressive format in June [1990] to stand out from the roughly 40 other radio stations in its metropolitan area. WTKX-AM in Pensacola, Fla., went free-form in December [1989] because it "distinguishes [us] from the rest of the pack," says Matt Shane, program director.

Radio programmers say the format may draw baby boomers, whom advertisers covet, because many grew up listening to it in its heyday. Free-form could also lure college students because free-form dominates college radio stations. . . .

Mr. Scelsa, a short, balding and bespectacled 42-year-old, proudly eschews computer-selected album selections from such rock artists as Tom Petty and the Rolling Stones. On Mr. Scelsa's show, listeners may hear country-music legend Hank Williams Jr. and raunchy rocker Prince back-to-back. Then Clark Gable singing "Putting on the Ritz," followed by They Might Be Giants, an avant-garde rock group.

Nor does Mr. Scelsa confine himself to rock. . . . He hosted Michael Smith, the composer from the Broadway play based on "The Grapes of Wrath," accompanied by actor Ron Crawford and musician L.J. Slavin. They performed a one-hour original piece combining what Mr. Smith calls "eclectic, free-form" music with the text of the John Steinbeck novel.

His weekly four-hour show, "Idiot's Delight," is named for a Robert Sherwood play and a card game. "Idiot's delight is a form of solitaire," he says, "and I'm playing this game alone on the radio."

WXRK, owned by Infinity Broadcasting Corp. and a formatted station during most of the week, limits him to Sundays at 8 p.m., "when I can do little damage," he says. "It's doubtful whether they would ever put me on full time." Mr. Scelsa has trouble holding to a schedule anyway. Most Sundays, he blithely runs well past his scheduled midnight sign-off, playing on as much as an hour longer, "until [the show] reaches a logical conclusion."

Mr. Scelsa concedes that radio consultants and their careful research will continue to set the agenda for most FM rock stations. But "the consultants can only control that which is easy to put into a computer," says Mr. Scelsa. "I can't be controlled."

---

The Wall Street Journal, *May 18, 1990, pp. B-1, B-3.*

audio broadcast (DAB). Digital audio can send music and information in the form of zeros and ones, as in a computer code. This eliminates all of the static and hiss of current broadcast signals, and could mean infinite program choices for consumers.

Discussions have even begun about global radio, using DAB as the standard, combining transmission from satellites and land-based towers on a single radio digital dial that would no longer distinguish among AM, FM, satellite, or other programming. You would simply dial up a number for the signal and the receiver would translate the programming using digital codes.

As radio technology grows more complex, and new formats and different program delivery systems are tested, the competition for your ear expands the choices advertisers can make to reach you. The more stations there are competing for customers, the harder every station must compete for each advertising dollar. This means less revenue for each station because each station's potential audience becomes smaller. In the 1950s, radio learned how to compete with television. Now it must learn how to compete with itself.

## IN FOCUS

### The Radio Industry

• Radio was America's second national medium, after magazines. Radio transformed national politics and also expanded Americans' access to popular, as well as classical, culture.

• Radio technology began with Samuel F. B. Morse's invention of the telegraph, first demonstrated in 1835; Alexander Graham Bell's invention of the telephone, demonstrated in 1876; and Heinrich Hertz's description of radio waves in 1887.

• Guglielmo Marconi's promotion of wireless radio wave transmission began in 1897 through the Wireless Telegraph and Signal Company. Reginald Fessenden advanced wireless technology, but Lee de Forest is called the father of radio because he invented the Audion tube to detect radio waves.

• The federal government intervened to regulate broadcasting almost as soon as it was invented. This early regulation separated the broadcast media from the print media, which are not regulated directly by the federal government.

• Two important developments in the 1920s were blanket licensing and commercial sponsorship. Blanket licensing meant that radio owners could use recorded music inexpensively. Commercial sponsorship established the practice of advertisers underwriting the cost of American broadcasting.

• The Radio Act of 1927 established the concept that the government would regulate broadcasting "as a public convenience, interest or necessity requires."

The 1927 act is the foundation for all broadcast regulation in the United States, including the establishment of the Federal Communications Commission in 1934.

• Radio in the 1930s and 1940s became a powerful cultural and political force. Radio programming expanded to include comedy, music, serials, drama, and news. Radio also indirectly created a collective national experience that had not existed before.

• "War of the Worlds" demonstrated the vulnerability of a captive audience.

• Originally, the three radio networks (NBC, CBS, and ABC) provided most radio programming. Today most stations program themselves using a variety of sources.

• Clock and car radios expanded radio's audience, but radio's role changed once TV could offer visual entertainment and news.

• Today, FM stations are three times as popular as AM stations. Arbitron is the primary ratings service for radio. Ratings are used by stations to set their rates for advertising.

• The most significant trend in radio today is the move toward more and more segmentation of the audience, similar to the division of audiences in the magazine industry.

• Demand programming and digital audio broadcast may soon offer even more program choices for listeners, another challenge to the radio industry's growing competition within itself.

**5**

*"Television is the pervasive American pastime,"* writes

*media observer Jeff Greenfield. "Cutting through geo-*

*graphic, ethnic, class, and cultural diversity, it is the single binding thread of this*

*country, the one experience that touches young and old, rich and poor, learned and*

*illiterate. A country too big for homogeneity, filled by people from all over the globe,*

*without any set of core values, America never had a central unifying bond. Now we*

*do. Now it is possible to answer the question, 'What*

*does America do?' We watch television."*[1]

**The Television Industry**

Americans, on average, watch four hours of television a day, according to the A.C. Nielsen Company, which monitors television usage for advertisers. Even though *you* may not watch TV this much, the percentage of the population that watches television more than four hours counterbalances the time that you spend with your television set.

It's not surprising that the effects of such a pervasive medium have attracted so much attention from parents, educators, social scientists, religious leaders, public officials, and anyone else who is concerned with society's habits and values. TV has been blamed for everything from declines in literacy to rises in violent crime to the trivialization of national politics. And every once in a while it is praised, too, for giving viewers instant access to world events and uniting audiences in times of national crisis.

An industry with this much presence in American life is bound to affect the way we live. Someone who is watching television is not doing other things: playing basketball, visiting a museum, or looking through a telescope at the stars, for instance. Television, however, can bring you to a museum you might never visit, or to a basketball game you cannot attend, or closer to the solar system than you could ever see through a telescope.

The technology of television, adding the reach of pictures to the sounds of radio, truly transformed Americans' living and learning patterns. And the word *television*, which once meant programs delivered by antennas through over-the-air signals, now means television screen, where a variety of delivery systems brings viewers a diversity of programs.

The programs Americans watch today are delivered by antennas, cables, and satellites, but they all appear on the same television screen, and, as a viewer, you can't tell how the program arrived at your television set and probably don't care. What you do know is that television gives you access to all types of programs — drama, comedy, sports, news, game shows, and talk shows. You can see all kinds of people — murderers, public officials, foreign leaders, reporters, soldiers, entertainers, athletes, detectives, doctors. The television screen is truly, as scholar Erik Barnouw observed, a "tube of plenty."

About 1,500 television stations operate in the United States. Three out of four of these are commercial stations and the others are noncommercial stations. More than half of the commercial stations are affiliated with a network.

Commentator Jeff Greenfield writes,

*The most common misconception most people have about television concerns its product. To the viewer, the product is the programming. To the television executive, the product is the* audience.

*Strictly speaking, television networks and stations do not make any money by producing a program that audiences want to watch. The money comes from selling*

Television's "tube of plenty" means that cable programmers like MTV can target specific audience segments. This ad, aimed at potential MTV advertisers, boasts about the size and age group of the MTV audience.

*advertisers the right to broadcast a message to that audience. The programs exist to capture the biggest possible audiences.* [2]

To understand why we get the programming we do, it is important to remember that *commercial television exists primarily as an advertising medium.* Programming surrounds the advertising, but it is the advertising that is being delivered to the audience. Commercial television, from its inception, was created to deliver audiences to advertisers.

Because television can deliver a larger audience faster than any other medium, television can charge the highest rates of any medium for its advertising — which makes TV stations rich investments. A 30-second ad during a network television program, for example, costs an average of $120,000, but during a widely watched program like the Super Bowl (with an estimated audience of half the U.S. population), a 30-second ad costs nearly $1 million.

Today even the smallest television station is a multimillion-dollar operation. The television era began much more humbly, and with very little excitement, near the turn of the century.

# How Television Began

THE WORD *television* first appeared in the June 1907 issue of *Scientific American*.[3] Before then, experiments in image transmission had been called "visual wireless," "visual radio," and "electric vision."

Alexander Graham Bell's telephone and Samuel F. B. Morse's telegraph contributed to the idea of sending electrical impulses over long distances. The first major technological discovery to suggest that pictures also could travel was the *Nipkow disk*. Twenty-four-year-old Paul Nipkow patented his "electrical telescope" in Germany in 1884. This disk, which formed the basis for television's development through the 1920s, was about the size of a phonograph record, perforated with a spiral of tiny holes.

"A beam of light shining through these perforations, as the disk revolved, caused pinpoints of light to perform a rapid 'scanning' movement, like the movement of eyes back and forth across a printed page," explains Erik Barnouw. "The device was at once seen as a way of transmitting pictures by wire, in the form of a series of dots of varying intensity."[4] Nipkow didn't have enough money to retain the patent on his electrical telescope, however, so he let it lapse. Still, he is generally viewed as the inventor of this mechanical system to reproduce pictures of moving objects.[5]

Also crucial in television's (and radio's) development were Guglielmo Marconi (see page 115) and Lee de Forest (see page 116). Marconi eliminated sound's dependence on wires and put sound on airwaves. De Forest contributed the Audion tube, which amplified radio waves so people could hear the sound clearly.

# Television's Pioneers

In 1927, Secretary of Commerce Herbert Hoover appeared on a 2-inch screen by wire in an experimental AT&T broadcast. On September 11, 1928, General Electric broadcast the first dramatic production, *The Queen's Messenger* — the sound came over station WGY, Schenectady, and the picture came from experimental television station W2XAD. All the pictures were close-ups, and their quality could best be described as primitive.

Two researchers, one working for a company and one working alone, brought television into the electronic age. Then the same man who was responsible for radio's original popularity, RCA's David Sarnoff, became television's biggest promoter.

Vladimir Zworykin was working for Westinghouse when he developed an all-electronic system to transform a visual image into an electronic signal. Zworykin's electronic signal traveled through the air. When the signal reached the television receiver, the signal was transformed again into a visual image for the viewer.

Philo T. Farnsworth, working alone in California, developed the cathode ray tube (which he called a dissector tube). Farnsworth's cathode ray used an electronic scanner to reproduce the electronic image much more clearly than Nipkow's earlier mechanical scanning device. In 1930, 24-year-old Farnsworth patented his electronic scanner.

In 1931, Zworykin, now working for RCA, traveled to California to see Farnsworth's invention. Zworykin "appeared impressed but was quoted as saying there wasn't anything RCA would need," says Barnouw.

*Then Sarnoff came; RCA would not need anything young Farnsworth had done, said Sarnoff. But apparently RCA already felt it would have to negotiate with Philo Farnsworth.*

*Farnsworth was ready to license RCA on a royalty basis. But RCA had a policy: What it needed, it bought outright. It didn't pay royalties; it collected them. However, in due time it came to terms with Philo Farnsworth. The RCA attorney is said to have had tears in his eyes as he signed the contract.*[6]

William S. Paley, founder of CBS.

In April 1935, David Sarnoff dramatically announced that RCA would spend $1 million for television demonstrations. NBC television's commercial debut was at the 1939 World's Fair in New York City at the Hall of Television. On April 30, 1939, President Franklin D. Roosevelt formally opened the fair and became the first president to appear on television. Sarnoff also spoke, and RCA displayed its 5-inch and 9-inch sets, priced from $199.50 to $600.[7]

Throughout the fair, RCA broadcast programs from Studio 3H in New York's Radio City. RCA also used a mobile unit, which broadcast something new every day, including a game at Ebbets Field between the Brooklyn Dodgers and the Cincinnati Reds. William Paley's CBS and experimenter Allen B. Dumont also were telecasting from New York in 1939.

World War II put television on hold, and many TV stations folded, but technological advances continued. Zworykin perfected the image-orthicon tube, which gave a much more realistic picture (early TV actors used purple and green makeup to give their faces contrast for the screen). The FCC also authorized FM to carry the sound signals for television.

As explained in Chapter 4, in 1943 NBC sold its Blue network, which became ABC (see page 130). ABC labored from its earliest days to equal the other two networks, but didn't have as many affiliates as NBC and CBS. The two leading networks already had secured the more powerful, well-established broadcast outlets for themselves. Sarnoff and Paley controlled the network game.

# Replacing Radio

WHEN THE FCC resumed television licensing in 1945, ten television stations were on the air in the United States.

*By the late 1940s, television began its conquest of America. In 1949, the year began with radio drawing 81 percent of all broadcast audiences. By the year's end, television was grabbing 41 percent of the broadcast market. When audiences began experiencing the heady thrill of actually seeing as well as hearing events as they occurred, the superiority of television was established beyond doubt.*[8]

Early television was black and white. RCA and CBS both had experimented with color, and CBS persuaded the FCC in 1950 to license CBS's color delivery system. But CBS could not build a good TV set to receive the signal, so CBS's attempt to corner the color television market failed. Black and white became the standard.

RCA, which had attempted to stop CBS's entry into the color television market, pushed ahead with its plans, and the FCC approved the RCA color system in 1953. By this time, however, monochrome (black and white) was entrenched. According to broadcast historians Christopher Sterling and John M. Kittross, "The industry had no reason to consider color until the vast market for monochrome sets became saturated, and the cost was too high — $1,000 and up per set — and there were too few color programs for the public to buy many of the complicated RCA sets."[9]

Television replaced radio so quickly as the nation's major advertising medium that it would be easy to believe that television erupted suddenly in a surprise move to kill radio. But remember that the two major corporate

This early RCA Victor television set (left) sold for about $200. The 5-inch screen sat in a console approximately 4 feet high. This 5-inch television set today (right) costs about the same and can travel in the palm of someone's hand.

executives who developed television — Sarnoff and Paley — also held the country's largest interest in radio. They used their profits from radio to develop television, foreseeing that television eventually would expand their audience and their income.

# Television News

Broadcast news, pioneered by radio, adapted awkwardly at first to the new broadcast medium — television. According to David Brinkley, a broadcast news pioneer who began at NBC,

*When television came along in about 1947–48, the bigtime newsmen of that day — H. V. Kaltenborn, Lowell Thomas — did not want to do television. It was a lot of work, they weren't used to it, they were doing very well in radio, making lots of money. They didn't want to fool with it. So I was told to do it by the news manager. I was a young kid and, as I say, the older, more established people didn't want to do it. Somebody had to.* [10]

As early as 1945, NBC's Sarnoff had assigned a newsreel camera operator to experiment with creating news for television. Then NBC signed an agreement with Movietone News, which produced theater newsreels, to provide news film for television. CBS contracted with the newsreel company Telenews.

In 1947, CBS initiated *Television News with Douglas Edwards* and NBC broadcast *Camel News Caravan* (sponsored by Camel cigarettes) with John Cameron Swayze. Eventually, David Brinkley joined Swayze for NBC's 15-minute national newscast. He recalls:

*The first broadcasts were extremely primitive by today's standards. It was mainly just sitting at a desk and talking. We didn't have any pictures at first. Later we began to get a little simple news film, but it wasn't much.*

*In the beginning, people would call after a program and say in tones of amazement that they had seen you. "I'm out here in Bethesda, and the picture's wonderful." They weren't interested in anything you said. They were just interested in the fact that you had been on their screen in their house.* [11]

The first network TV news reached only the East Coast because the necessary web of national hookups wasn't in place to deliver television across the country. By 1948, AT&T's coaxial cable linked Philadelphia with New York and Washington. The 1948 political conventions were held in Philadelphia and broadcast to the 13 Eastern states. When the 1952 conventions were broadcast, AT&T's national coaxial hookups joined 108 stations across the country.

CBS had developed a strong group of radio reporters during World War II, and by 1950 many of them had moved to the new medium. CBS News also made a practice, more than the other networks, of using the same reporters for radio and television. The major early news figure at CBS was Edward R. Murrow who, along with David Brinkley, created the early standards for broadcast news. (See Impact/Profile, Edward R. Murrow.)

Murrow's first television broadcast was at 3:30 Sunday afternoon November 18, 1951. The program was a television version of his radio program *Hear It Now*, renamed *See It Now*. "From the opening seconds, it was clear that *See It Now* would be more than televised newsreels or radio with pictures," writes Murrow's biographer A. M. Sperber.

*Images and voices came at the viewers in a shifting kaleidoscope of sight and sound; cue channel talk let the audience in on preparations — San Francisco calling in; Murrow talking with San Francisco — music up again, and they were on.*

*Murrow looked into the camera, no longer a disembodied voice: "This is an old team, trying to learn a new trade." He was speaking, as the announcer said, from the control room of Studio 41; behind him, in full view of the camera, were the very tools of telecasting — the controls; monitors; cameras one and two.* [12]

# Edward R. Murrow (1908–1965)

Edward R. Murrow had established a reputation for excellence as a CBS radio news broadcaster when he migrated to television news in 1951. In this profile, veteran journalist **Theodore H. White** outlines Murrow's broadcast career and its impact on television audiences.

I T IS so difficult to recapture the real Ed Murrow from the haze that now shrouds the mythical Ed Murrow of history.

Where other men may baffle friends with the infinite complexity of their natures, Ed was baffling otherwise. He was so straightforward, he would completely baffle the writers who now unravel the neuroses of today's demigods of television. When Ed was angry, he bristled; when he gave friendship, it came without withholding.

He could walk with prime ministers and movie stars, GIs and generals, as natural in rumpled GI suntans as in his diplomatic homburg. But jaunty or somber, to those of us who knew him he was just plain old Ed. In his shabby office at CBS cluttered with awards, you could loosen your necktie, put your feet up and yarn away. The dark, overhanging eyebrows would arch as he punctured pretension with a jab, the mouth would twist quizzically as he questioned. And then there were his poker games, as Ed sat master of the table, a cigarette dangling always from his lips — he smoked 60 or 70 a day — and called the bets.

Then — I can hear him now — there was the voice. Ed's deep and rhythmic voice was compelling, not only for its range, halfway between bass and baritone, but for the words that rolled from it. He wrote for the ear — with a cadence of pauses and clipped, full sentences. His was an aural art but, in Ed, the art was natural — his inner ear composed a picture and, long before TV, the imagination of his listeners caught the sound and made with it their own picture.

We remember the voice. But there was so much more to Ed. He had not only a sense of the news but a sense of how the news fit into history. And this sense of the relation of news to history is what, in retrospect, made him the great pioneer of television journalism. His exploration of television's new range was so powerful in its impact on our dreams and lives that in American journalism only Horace Greeley and Walter Lippmann matched him in shaping our history. . . .

Television was a giant step in the power of the electronic media — and its magic tantalized Ed. In the fall of 1951, the engineers of AT&T had just completed their hookup of microwave towers and coaxial cables that linked the country coast to coast. Ed tested it. On Sunday afternoon, Nov. 18, 1951, on *See It Now*'s first broadcast, he sat in a CBS

Edward R. Murrow

studio in New York's Grand Central Terminal building and invited America to look at itself. He swiveled his chair and showed two monitors — on the one was the Brooklyn Bridge in New York, on the other the Golden Gate in San Francisco: both live and simultaneous. The country was now one continental arena. You could see it now — a moment equivalent to Leland Stanford driving the Golden Spike to link the nation's railways at Promontory Point, Utah, in 1869. . . .

Ed was never reluctant to use the power of the tube — and when he used it, he could rouse thunder. By 1954, he had had enough of Joe McCarthy, that alcoholic and reckless political terrorist who perverted Ameri-

can loathing of communism into a witch hunt of innocents.* Murrow took to the air. On the night of March 9, in an immaculate broadcast devoid of any denunciation, Murrow displayed the senator from Wisconsin at his wheezing, halting, tormenting best — which, of course, was his worst. When Ed had finished, McCarthy's career was finished, too. . . .

By the late 1950s, Ed was suffering from burnout — a psychological affliction of television's personalities akin to silicosis among miners. He was no longer content to observe and report; he wanted to be part of the action itself — history was his calling, news only his trade. So he joined the administration of John F. Kennedy and, as director of the U.S. Information Agency, insisted on a voice in policy. He was wiser than either Kennedy's Secretary of Defense or Secretary of State. But he had not long to go. The ever-dangling cigarette had ravaged his

*The 1954 See It Now broadcast exposed Senator Joseph R. McCarthy for the tactics he was using during hearings before a U.S. Senate subcommittee that was investigating subversive activities. A similar committee, under a different chairman, questioned the Hollywood Ten (see pages 215–218).

health. One lung was removed on Oct. 6, 1963, and so he was in his bed the day Kennedy was shot. But he was alert to the tube, and when I called him that weekend, he was savoring the technical wizardry of the funeral ceremonies.

Ed was not to last long after that. The cancer spread to a tumor near the brain and, when I last saw him, his head was swathed in white bandages. I thought this would be a solemn and mournful visit to a friend I cherished, but Ed opened the conversation by saying, "Say, Buster, how do you like my new haircut?" And we went on to happy reminiscence.

He died shortly after that — at 57, so young that it now seems that fate itself had decided to cut short his honors.

He is very large now, for it was he who set the news system of television on its tracks, holding it, and his descendants, to the sense of history that give it still, in the schlock-storm of today, its sense of honor. Of Ed Murrow it may be said that he made all of us who clung to him, and cling to his memory still, feel larger than we really were.

"When He Used the Power of TV, He Could Rouse Thunder," TV Guide 34, no. 3 (Jan. 18, 1986): 13–14.

IMPACT/
PROFILE

Chet Huntley (left) and David Brinkley broadcast the nation's most successful early newscast, *The Huntley-Brinkley Report*, every weekday from 6:45 to 7:00 P.M. E.S.T.

Public affairs programs like *See It Now* continued to grow along with network news, and in 1956 NBC teamed David Brinkley with Chet Huntley to cover the political conventions. The chemistry worked, and after the convention NBC put Huntley and Brinkley together to do the evening news, *The Huntley-Brinkley Report*. Brinkley often called himself "the other side of the hyphen."

## Entertainment Programming

Early television was like late radio with pictures: It offered variety shows, situation comedies, drama, Westerns, detective stories, Hollywood movies, soap operas, and quiz shows. The only type of show that television offered that radio did not (besides movies, of course) was the talk show. (Ironically, today's radio has created call-in programs, its own version of the talk show.)

**Variety Shows.** The best radio stars jumped to the new medium. Three big variety-show successes were Milton Berle's *Texaco Star Theater*, *The Admiral Broadway Revue* (later *Your Show of Shows*) with Imogene Coca and Sid Caesar, and Ed Sullivan's *Toast of the Town* (later *The Ed Sullivan Show*). These weekly shows featured comedy sketches and appearances by popular entertainers. *The Ed Sullivan Show,* for example, is where most Americans got their first glimpse of Elvis Presley and the Beatles. All of the shows were done live.

The time slot in which these programs were broadcast, 7–11 P.M., is known as **prime time**. Prime time simply means that more people watch television during this period than any other, so advertising during this period costs more. Berle's 8 P.M. program during prime time on Tuesday nights often gathered 85 percent of the audience. *Texaco Star Theater* became so popular that one laundromat installed a TV set and advertised "Watch Berle while your clothes twirl."

The Sullivan show survived for 23 years, but by 1956, Berle's program was gone. *Your Show of Shows* left the air in 1957. Television demanded a lot from its performers. "These outsize talents were burned out by television," says Jeff Greenfield. "It was almost as if they could not survive the expending of so much sheer energy."[13] They were replaced by Jack Benny (whose programs lasted for 15 years) and Red Skelton (on television for 20 years). In the late 1960s, Carol Burnett became an heir to the variety-show format.

The early variety shows originated from New York, where the producers could easily find talent, but two programs originating from California—*I Love Lucy* and *Disneyland*—also became hits. Today, almost all television programs are produced in Southern California.

*Disneyland* premiered on ABC in 1954, giving the new network its first big hit. The show featured the Disney characters and usually showcased Disney's first theme park, which had just been built in Anaheim, California. The arrangement rewarded both the network and Disney—Disney promoted his newly opened amusement park and ABC began to be considered a place where advertisers could find an audience. *Disneyland* spawned *The Mickey Mouse Club*, which by 1956 practically owned the afternoon grade-school audience.

**Situation Comedies.** Along with drama, the **situation comedy** proved to be one of TV's most durable types of programs. The situation comedy (sitcom) established a fixed set of characters in either a home or work situation. *I Love Lucy*, starring Lucille Ball and Desi Arnaz, originated from Los Angeles because the actors wanted to live on the West Coast. In 1951, Ball began a career as a weekly performer on CBS that lasted for 23 years. *The Honeymooners* (starring Jackie Gleason), *The Mary Tyler Moore Show, Cheers*, and *Golden Girls* are examples of situation comedy successes.

**Drama.** *The Loretta Young Show* offered noontime drama—broadcast live—every day in the 1950s. *The Hallmark Hall of Fame* established a tradition for

*I Love Lucy* was one of the first television programs to originate in Southern California. Today, almost all television programs are produced there.

high-quality dramatic, live presentations. For many years, TV dramas were limited to 1- or 2-hour programs. But in the 1970s, encouraged by the success of Alex Haley's *Roots*, which dramatized Haley's search for the story of his African ancestry, television began to broadcast as many as 14 hours of a single drama over several nights. In 1987, ABC spent $40 million to produce *Amerika*, but the ratings were disappointing, and the networks now are less willing to invest so much money in one project.

**Westerns.** TV went Western in 1954, when Jack Warner of Warner Bros. signed an agreement with ABC to provide the network with a program called *Cheyenne*. The outspoken Warner had openly criticized TV's effect on the movie business, but when ABC asked Warner to produce programs for them, Warner Bros. became the first movie company to realize that the studios could profit from television. Other Westerns followed *Cheyenne*'s success: *Maverick, Gunsmoke*, and *Death Valley Days*, as more studios began to produce TV shows. Western serials declined in popularity by the 1970s.

**Detective Stories.** *Dragnet*'s Sergeant Friday was an early TV experiment with detectives. The genre became a TV staple: *Dragnet*'s successors in the 1970s and 1980s were programs like *The Rockford Files, Magnum P.I., Miami Vice*, and *Murder, She Wrote*.

**Movies.** The movie industry at first resisted the competition from TV, but then realized there was money to be made in selling old movies to TV. In 1957, RKO sold 740 pre-1948 movies to television for $25 million. The other studios followed: Warner Bros. collected $21 million; 20th Century-Fox received $30 million; Paramount made a $50 million deal for its films. Through various distribution agreements like these, movie reruns were added to television's program lineup.

**Soap Operas.** Borrowed from radio serials, soap operas filled in morning television programming. Today, game shows and reruns are more popular choices, but programs like *The Young and the Restless* survive. Soap operas have their own magazines, and some newspapers carry weekly summaries of plot development.

**Quiz Shows.** CBS's *$64,000 Question* premiered June 7, 1955, sponsored by Revlon. Contestants answered questions from a glass "isolation booth." Successful contestants returned in succeeding weeks to increase their winnings, and Revlon advertised its Living Lipstick. By September, the program was drawing 85 percent of the audience, and Revlon had substituted an ad for another product: Its factory supply of Living Lipstick had completely sold out.

The *$64,000 Question* engendered imitation: *Treasure Hunt, Giant Step*, and *Twenty-One*. The *$64,000 Question* even spun off a sister program on CBS, *The $64,000 Challenge*. Winnings grew beyond the $64,000 limit; Charles Van Doren won $129,000 on *Twenty-One*. In the fall of 1955, CBS replaced Murrow's *See It Now* with a quiz program.

Many network quiz shows like *The $64,000 Question* were produced by sponsors for the networks, and these programs often carried the sponsor's name. In the 1958–59 quiz show scandals, Revlon was implicated when a congressional subcommittee investigated charges that the quiz shows were rigged to enhance the ratings.

*The first news of something seriously wrong came in August 1958 when* Dotto *was abruptly canceled from its CBS morning slot and its NBC evening position. Several contestants had claimed that the program had been rigged, and one had written to the FCC. Within days, some 20 quiz programs left the air in television's first major*

Charles Van Doren in an "isolation booth" answers a question on *Twenty-One*. Van Doren later testified before Congress that the program was rigged.

*programming scandal. Network officials claimed ignorance of rigging, program produc-*
*ers said that people did not understand commercial television's purposes and practices,*
*and advertisers said nothing.* [14]

Charles Van Doren admitted before the congressional committee that he had been fed the answers by *Twenty-One*'s producer. Staff members from other quiz shows added to Van Doren's testimony.

The scandals caused the networks to reexamine the relationship between advertisers and programs. Before the scandals, one-quarter to one-third of network programming was produced by advertisers and their agencies. The networks began to look to other sources. By the late 1960s, advertisers provided less than 3 percent of network programming, and soon advertisers provided no network shows. The networks programmed themselves. The networks used the newly acquired studio movies to replace the quiz shows, but quiz shows have resurfaced today with *Wheel of Fortune, Family Feud*, and *Jeopardy*.

**The Talk Show.** Sylvester "Pat" Weaver (actress Sigourney Weaver's father) created and produced television's single original contribution to programming: the talk show. Weaver's *Tonight Show* (originally *Jerry Lester's Broadway Open House*) first appeared in 1954. Through a succession of hosts from Lester to Steve Allen to Jack Paar to Johnny Carson and Jay Leno, *The Tonight Show* has lasted longer than any other talk show on television. Imitators Phil Donahue, David Letterman, Oprah Winfrey, and Arsenio Hall followed.

Weaver was also responsible for the first *Today Show*, with its morning news-entertainment format, and for the concept of the TV spectacular. He argued that instead of one sponsor per program, the spectacular would attract multiple sponsors to buy ads, which would take the program away from sponsor control and return it to the network. Weaver booked *Peter Pan* with Mary Martin right after the play's successful run on Broadway, for example, and 65 million people watched the 1960 broadcast. [15]

# Measuring the Audience

After the quiz show scandals, the major criticism of the networks was that they were motivated only by ratings. Ratings provide sponsors with information about the audience they're reaching with their advertising — what advertisers are getting for their money. By the late 1950s, the A. C. Nielsen Company dominated the television ratings business. The national Nielsen ratings describe the audience to advertisers; based on the Nielsens, advertisers pay for the commercial time to reach the audiences that they want.

Nielsen began monitoring television viewing in 1950 with 1,200 meters (called Audimeters), which they attached to TV sets in homes throughout the nation. The Audimeters recorded when the set was turned on, but not who was watching. Nielsen then added 2,200 TV diaries, where families could write down the programs they watched. This sample, claimed Nielsen, reflected the nation's diversity and tastes.

Today Nielsen provides two sets of numbers, known as rating and share. The **rating** is a percentage of the total number of households with television sets. If there are 93 million homes with TV sets (as there were in 1991), the rating shows the percentage of those sets that were tuned in to a specific program.

The **share** (an abbreviation for share-of-audience) compares the audience for one show with the audience for another. Share means the percentage of the audience with TV sets on that is watching each program. If TV sets in 50

**5.1** ➤

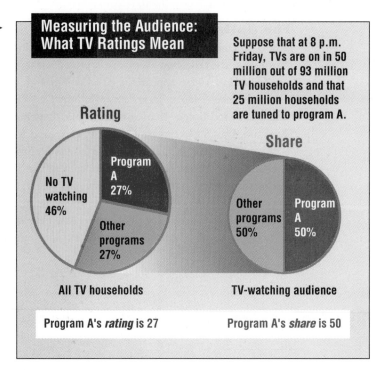

**Measuring the Audience: What TV Ratings Mean**

Suppose that at 8 p.m. Friday, TVs are on in 50 million out of 93 million TV households and that 25 million households are tuned to program A.

**Rating**

No TV watching 46%

Program A 27%

Other programs 27%

All TV households

**Share**

Other programs 50%

Program A 50%

TV-watching audience

Program A's *rating* is 27          Program A's *share* is 50

million homes were turned on at 8 P.M. on Friday night, and 25 million homes were tuned to Program A, the program would have a rating of 27 (25 million divided by 93 million) and a share of 50 (see Figure 5.1).

The most concentrated ratings periods for local stations are "sweeps" months — February, May, and November. (Ratings are taken in July, too, but the numbers are not considered accurate because so many people are on vacation.) The sweeps provide an estimate of the local TV audience, and advertisers use that information when they decide where to place their commercials. **Sweeps** are the months that the ratings services gather their most important ratings, and so the networks and local stations often use these important months to showcase their best programs. This is when you are most likely to see a special 1-hour episode of a popular series, for example, or a very expensively produced made-for-TV movie.

Today's Nielsen ratings work essentially the same as they did in the 1950s, except that the Nielsens now deliver very specific demographic information — age, occupation, and income, for instance. Advertisers use this information to target their most likely consumers — Nike shoes might choose to create a new advertising campaign for the NBA playoffs, for instance, and Nielsen could tell Nike from previous championships all about the people the company will reach with its ads.

# TV Grows Up

t HE 1950s were a trial period for television, as the networks and advertisers tested audience interest in various types of programming. Captured by the miracle that television offered, audiences at first seemed insatiable; they would watch almost anything TV delivered. But in the 1960s, audiences became more discriminating and began to question how well the medium of television was serving the public.

## Newton Minow and TV's Conscience

With television established even in the smaller cities, the medium needed a public conscience. That public conscience was Newton Minow.

An unassuming soothsayer, Minow was named chairman of the FCC in 1961 by newly elected President John F. Kennedy. Minow had received his law degree from Northwestern University in 1950 and went to work as an aide to then-Governor of Illinois Adlai Stevenson. Before he became FCC chairman, he worked in Stevenson's law firm.

On May 9, 1961, speaking to the National Association of Broadcasters in his first public address since his appointment, Minow articulated what he felt were the broadcasters' responsibilities to the public.

*Your license lets you use the public's airwaves as trustees for 180 million Americans. The public is your beneficiary. If you want to stay on as trustees, you must deliver a decent return to the public — not only to your stockholders. . . .*

*Your industry possesses the most powerful voice in America. It has an inescapable duty to make that voice ring with intelligence and with leadership. In a few years this exciting industry has grown from a novelty to an instrument of overwhelming impact on the American people. It should be making ready for the kind of leadership that newspapers and magazines assumed years ago, to make our people aware of their world.*

*Ours has been called the jet age, the atomic age, the space age. It is also, I submit, the television age. And just as history will decide whether the leaders of today's world employed the atom to destroy the world or rebuild it for mankind's benefit, so will history*

Former FCC Chairman Newton Minow coined the phrase "vast wasteland" to describe television.

*decide whether today's broadcasters employed their powerful voice to enrich the people or debase them.* [16]

Minow then asked his audience of broadcast station owners and managers to watch their own programs. He said they would find a "vast wasteland," a phrase that resurfaces today during any critical discussion of television. He was particularly skeptical about the way television executives used the ratings to determine programming.

*I do not accept the idea that the present overall programming is aimed accurately at the public taste. The ratings tell us only that some people have their television sets turned on, and of that number, so many are turned to one channel and so many to another. They don't tell us what the public might watch if they were offered half a dozen additional choices. A rating, at best, is an indication of how many people saw what you gave them. Unfortunately it does not reveal the depth of the penetration, or the intensity of reaction, and it never reveals what the acceptance would have been if what you gave them had been better — if all the forces of art and creativity and daring and imagination had been unleashed. . . .*

Shoe

*My concern with the ratings services is not with their accuracy. Perhaps they are accurate. I really don't know. What, then, is wrong with these ratings? It's not been their accuracy — it's been their use.* [17]

A congressional investigation in 1960–61 turned up some discrepancies in the ratings services' techniques, and in 1963–64, the House Commerce Committee also examined how the ratings were put together. Several industry committees agreed to oversee ratings operations, but criticism about the ratings persists. The main flaw in the ratings today, critics contend, is exactly what Minow predicted in 1961 — the way the ratings are religiously followed and used by the broadcast community to determine programming. See Impact/Profile: A Vaster Wasteland for an update on Minow's view of television.

# A Time of Transition

By 1965, all three networks were broadcasting in color. Television demonstrated its technological sophistication in December 1968 with its live broadcast from the *Apollo* spacecraft while it circled the moon, and seven months later television showed Neil Armstrong stepping onto the moon.

On July 10, 1962, Telstar I sent the first trans-Atlantic satellite broadcast. Before Telstar, copper cable linked the continents, film footage from overseas traveled only by plane, and in most homes a long distance telephone call was a special event.

Telstar I was an experimental satellite operated by the National Aeronautics and Space Administration. Commercial satellites began in 1965, managed by

# A Vaster Wasteland

In 1991, to commemorate the 30th anniversary of his "vast wasteland" speech, Former FCC Commission Chairman **Newton Minow** talked about television's unused potential in a speech delivered at the Gannett Foundation Media Center in New York. Minow is a lawyer and director of the Annenberg Washington program in Communications Policy Studies at Northwestern University.

WHILE SERV-ING as chairman of the Federal Communications Commission during the Kennedy administration, I said that American television was a "vast wasteland." Today, 30 years later, we have expanded television enormously, but we still waste its vast potential.

What happened in 30 years? The number of television sets in American homes increased almost fourfold. Cable expanded from serving 1 million homes in 1961 to serving more than 55 million today. The number of television stations more than doubled. VCRs — unavailable in 1961 — are in more than 58 million American homes.

Cable, broadcast TV and home video offer an almost unlimited variety of programming. If you are a sports fan, a news junkie, a stock market follower, a rock music devotee, a person who speaks Spanish, a nostalgic old-movie buff, a congressional hearing observer, even a weather watcher, you now have your own channel. And you can watch a program when you want to, not just when it's put on the schedule.

Yet, to many of us, this enlarged choice does not satisfy the public interest. There are several reasons.

For one, choice through cable comes at a price not all can afford, and cable is still not available to the entire nation. More choices also may not necessarily mean better choices.

As CBS president Howard Stringer said in a speech at the Royal Institute in London last year, "We see a vast media-jaded audience that wanders restlessly from one channel to another in search of that endangered species — originality."

Another of contemporary television's high icons, Brandon Tartikoff, left NBC last week for Paramount and said in parting that he worries for the future of network television. Well he should. Although NBC became the No. 1 network under his leadership, its ratings were actually 40 percent higher when Tartikoff took over 11 years ago. That's because ABC, CBS and NBC continue to lose audience to the enlarged choices available. Yet each network continues to see the world in terms of only the two other original networks rather than the new universe of cable and independent television, VCRs and satellites.

In 1961 I worried about quiz-show scandals and industry payola. Now I'm faced with a recent study showing that by the time a child is 18, he or she has seen more than 25,000 murders on television. In 1961 I worried that my children would not benefit much from television; today I worry that my grandchildren will actually be harmed by it.

One evening, remote control in hand, I flipped through the channels and saw a man loading a gun on one, a different man aiming a gun on a second and another man shooting a gun on a third.

Can this be changed? My own answer is yes. If we want to, we can provide the American people with meaningful and enriched choices. I reject the view of an FCC chairman in the early 1980s who said that "a television set is merely a toaster with pictures." I reject the ideological view that the marketplace will regulate itself and that free competition will result in perfection. Think of the savings-and-loan industry, the airline industry, the junk-bond market.

Felix Rohatyn, a champion of the marketplace, was on target when he said, "Though I believe that the marketplace knows best most of the time, I am skeptical that it should always be the ultimate arbiter of economic action, and I am more than willing to interfere with it when it becomes a distorting rather than a benign influence.". . .

The television marketplace alone is not enough to fulfill the demands of the public interest. If television is to change, the men and women in television — and those who are charged with regulating it — will have to make it a leading institution in American life rather than merely a reactive mirror of the marketplace. For the record of the last 30 years gives the television marketplace an A + for technology, but only a C for using that technology to serve human and humane goals. A new generation now has the chance to put the vision back into television, and to travel from the wasteland to the promised land.

Los Angeles Times *reprinted in* The Sacramento Bee, *May 13, 1991, B15.*

the Communications Satellite Corporation. INTELSAT II, launched in 1967, brought live satellite television to Hawaii for the first time.

Today, Telstar's 120 descendants orbit at a distance of more than 22,000 miles. A single modern communication satellite can carry 30,000 telephone calls and three television channels. Modern satellites made Ted Turner's Broadcasting System, Rupert Murdoch's Fox Broadcasting, Home Box Office, and Show-Time/The Movie Channel possible.

American society was in transition in the late 1960s, and so was television. None of the top ten programs from the 1968–69 season (including *Laugh-In, Gunsmoke, Gomer Pyle*) remained among the top ten for the 1973–74 season.[18] The protest movements of the late 1960s and early 1970s spawned entertainment programs that challenged the establishment: *All in the Family, Maude, M\*A\*S\*H*. TV even made fun of itself with *The Mary Tyler Moore Show*'s laughable anchorman Ted Baxter.

# Public Television

The concept of educational television has been alive since the 1950s, as a few noncommercial stations succeeded in regularly presenting public service programs without advertisements. But the shows were low-budget and little national programming was done.

The educational network NET (National Educational Television) emerged in 1963 to provide some national programming (about 10 hours a week), sponsored mainly by foundations, with some federal support. Then in 1967, the Ford Foundation agreed to help pay for several hours of live evening programming.

Also in 1967, the Carnegie Commission on Educational Television released its report *Public Television: A Program for Action*, which included a proposal to create the Corporation for Public Broadcasting. CPB would collect money from many sources — including the enhanced federal funds that the Carnegie report suggested — and disburse the money to the stations.

The Johnson administration and several foundations added money to CPB's budget. The Public Broadcasting Service (PBS) was created to distribute programs. The extra money underwrote the creation of programs like *Sesame Street* and *The French Chef*. PBS also began to buy successful British television programs, including *Masterpiece Theatre*, a series of British dramas hosted by Alistair Cooke. PBS programs actually started to show up in the ratings.

Public television's dependence on government grants proved risky. Withdrawal of most of the federal financing in the 1970s and early 1980s forced

PBS to scramble for money. The FCC began "liberalizing" its rules for commercial advertisements on public television in 1981, and the company sponsorship announcements that precede and follow public television programs have begun to sound like ordinary commercials. Public television remains commercial television's stepchild.

# Maturing as a News Medium

Just as radio matured first as an entertainment medium and then expanded to cover important news events, television first established itself with entertainment and then developed a serious news presence. And just as Franklin D. Roosevelt had been the first president to understand and use radio, John F. Kennedy became the country's first television president. Kennedy's predecessors had appeared on television, but he instinctively knew how to *use* television.

Observers credited Kennedy's 1960 presidential victory partly to his success in his televised debates with Richard Nixon. Kennedy was the first president to hold live televised news conferences. In July 1962, he oversaw the launch of the first communications satellite, Telstar I. So it was fitting that he would be the first president to play Cold War brinksmanship on television, when TV grew to become a part of politics, not just a chronicler of political events.

**TV and the Cold War.** President Kennedy asked all three networks to clear him time on Monday, October 22, 1962, at 7 P.M. Eastern time. The president had learned that missile sites were being built in Cuba with Russian help.

Kennedy used television to deliver his ultimatum to dismantle the missile bases. "Using the word 'nuclear' eleven times, Kennedy drew a panorama of devastation enveloping the whole hemisphere. The moves that had made such things possible, said Kennedy, could not be accepted by the United States 'if our courage and our commitments are ever to be trusted again by either friend or foe.'"[19]

Kennedy admonished Russian Premier Nikita Krushchev to stop the ships the Soviet Union was sending to Cuba to help build the missile sites. Faced with such a visible challenge, the Soviet Union turned their ships around in the Atlantic and sent conciliatory messages to reach a settlement. The Cuban missile "crisis" had in fact been a carefully constructed live television drama in which Kennedy performed well.

**United in Mourning.** In 1963, television was forced into an unexpected role as it conveyed a sense of collective national experience following a

President John F. Kennedy at the lectern delivering the nation's first live televised press conference on January 25, 1961. First Lady Jacqueline Kennedy watches from a press booth (left) above.

presidential assassination. For four days beginning at 1:30 P.M. Eastern time on Friday, November 22, 1963, the country witnessed the aftermath of the assassination of President John F. Kennedy. Lyndon Johnson was sworn in as president. On Saturday, TV viewers watched the world's diplomats arrive for the funeral. On Sunday, they watched the first murder ever broadcast live on television, as Jack Ruby killed suspect Lee Harvey Oswald. Then on Monday came the president's funeral.

As many as nine out of ten television sets were turned on during the marathon events surrounding President John Kennedy's funeral. The networks canceled all commercials. "Some television employees had slept as little as six hours in three nights. They went on, almost welcoming the absorption in the task at hand."[20]

They were called television's finest four days. Documentary programming surged as the nation seemed ready to absorb television's reality. Television would twice again meet the challenge of the same sad job—covering the murders of Martin Luther King, Jr., on April 4, 1968, and Robert Kennedy on June 5, 1968. "On the whole, television had won a degree of acceptance that must have exceeded the dreams of Sarnoff," writes Erik Barnouw. "For most people it had become their window on the world. The view it offered seemed to be *the* world. They trusted its validity and completeness.[21]

**The Vietnam War.** Soon after Kennedy's assassination, the longest-running protest program in the nation's history began appearing on television news, as anti-Vietnam War marchers showed up on camera daily. During live coverage of the Chicago Democratic Convention in 1968, demonstrators faced police in a march toward the convention hall. Television covered the resulting violence, which caused injuries to hundreds of protesters and to 21 reporters and photographers.

*When the war in Vietnam began to escalate in 1965, it was the television networks, covering the war with few official restrictions, that brought to American homes pictures of the face of war that had never been shown before: not friendly troops welcomed by the populace, but troops setting fire to villages with cigarette lighters; troops cutting off the ears of dead combat foes; allies spending American tax money for personal gain.[22]*

Candid reporting from the war itself shook viewers as previous war reporting never had.

**Television and National Politics.** Television got credit for uniting the nation, but it also could be blamed for dividing it. President Lyndon Johnson, beleaguered by an unpopular war, used television to announce in 1968 that he would not run for a second term. His successor, President Richard Nixon, had always been uncomfortable with the press and, under the Nixon administration, the press was attacked for presenting perspectives on world affairs that the Nixon administration did not like. Upset with the messages being presented, the Nixon administration battled the messenger, sparking a bitter public debate about the role of a free press (especially television) in a democratic society.

In November 1969, Vice President Spiro Agnew characterized the press as "a small group of men, numbering perhaps no more than a dozen anchormen, commentators, and executive producers, [who] settle upon the twenty minutes or so of film and commentary that's to reach the public [as] a tiny, enclosed fraternity of privileged men elected by no one and enjoying a monopoly sanctioned and licensed by government."[23] Nixon-appointed FCC Chairman Dean Burch said he found Agnew's comments "thoughtful." Agnew had put the media, especially television, on the defensive.

Ironically, television's next live marathon broadcast would chronicle an investigation of the Nixon presidency — Watergate. The Watergate scandal began when burglars broke into the offices of the Democratic party's national headquarters in the Watergate complex in Washington, D.C., on June 17, 1972. Some of the burglars had ties to President Nixon's reelection committee as well as to other questionable activities originating in the White House. In the following months the president and his assistants sought to squelch the resulting investigation. Although Nixon denied knowledge of the break-in and the cover-up, the Senate hearings on the scandal, televised live across the country, created a national sensation.

*Running from May through August 1973, and chaired by North Carolina's crusty Sam Ervin, these hearings were a fascinating live exposition of the political process in America, and were "must" television watching as a parade of witnesses told — or evaded telling — what they knew of the broad conspiracy to assure the reelection of Nixon and then to cover up the conspiracy itself.*[24]

For more than a year the political drama continued to unfold on television's nightly news. Ultimately the Judiciary Committee of the House of Representatives began a televised debate on whether to impeach the president. For the

During the 1991 gulf war, CNN offered unprecedented worldwide access to live coverage of the events of the war (left). Television often carried foreign policy messages from President Bush and Saddam Hussein, as characterized in this editorial cartoon from the (Australian) *Sydney Morning Herald* (above).

first time in its history the nation faced the prospect of seeing a president brought to trial live on national television. On August 8, 1974, President Nixon brought the crisis to an end by announcing his resignation — on television.

In 1987, television repeated its marathon coverage of an important national investigation with the Iran-contra hearings, a congressional investigation of the Reagan administration's role in providing weapons illegally to Nicaraguan rebels, called contras. Unlike the Watergate hearings, however, which were covered live by all the networks daily, the Iran-contra hearings were covered piecemeal by the networks, who cited commercial considerations. Only Cable News Network (CNN) offered gavel-to-gavel coverage.

The Iran-contra hearings gave CNN its first opportunity to show that it could offer more comprehensive news programming than the news operations of the three major networks. The all-news network has grown rapidly in recent years, and in 1991 presented precedent-setting news coverage of another kind with its around-the-clock coverage of the gulf war.

Television news has matured from its early beginnings as a 15-minute newscast to today's access to 24-hour coverage of significant news events. Today, network television news continues to play an important role in setting the agenda for discussion of public issues.

# How Television Works

**a** TYPICAL television station has eight departments: sales, programming (which includes news as well as entertainment), production, engineering, traffic, promotion, public affairs, and administration.

People in the *sales* department sell the commercial slots for the programs. Advertising is divided into *national* and *local* sales. Advertising agencies, usually based on the East Coast, buy national ads for the products they handle.

Ford Motor Company, for instance, may buy time for a TV ad that will run simultaneously all over the country. But the local Ford dealers who want you to shop at their showrooms buy their ads directly from the local station. These ads are called local (or spot) ads. For these sales, salespeople at each station negotiate packages of ads, based on their station's rates. These rates are a direct reflection of that station's position in the ratings.

The *programming* department selects the shows that you will see and develops the station's schedule. Network-owned stations, located in big cities (KNBC in Los Angeles, for example), are called O & O's, which stands for owned-and-operated. Stations that carry network programming but are not owned by the networks are called **affiliates**.

O & O's automatically carry network programming, but affiliates are paid by the network to carry its programming, for which the network sells most of the ads and keeps the money. The affiliate is allowed to insert into the network programming a specific number of local ads, for which the affiliate keeps the money.

Because affiliates can make money on network programming and don't have to pay for it, many stations choose to affiliate themselves with a network. When they aren't running what the network provides, affiliates run their own programs and keep all the advertising money they collect from them.

More than one-third of the nation's commercial TV stations operate as independents. Independent stations must buy and program all their own shows, but independents also can keep all the money they make on advertising. They run some individually produced programs and old movies, but most of their programming consists of reruns of shows that once ran on the networks. Independents buy these reruns from program services called **syndicators**.

Syndicators also sell independently produced programs such as *Donahue*, *The Oprah Winfrey Show*, and *Wheel of Fortune*. These programs are created and sold either by non-network stations or by independent producers. Stations pay for these first-run syndication programs individually; the price is based on the size of the station's market.

One of the largest syndicators, Viacom International, announced in 1989 that *The Cosby Show* reruns sold for a record $320,000 an episode in New York City. The previous record price was $80,000 an episode for the New York syndication rights to *Cheers*.[25]

Local news usually makes up the largest percentage of a station's locally produced programming. In some large markets, local news programming runs as long as 3 hours.

The *production* department manages the programs that the station creates in-house. This department also produces local commercials for the station.

The *engineering* department makes sure that all the technical aspects of a broadcast operation are working: antennas, transmitters, cameras, and any other broadcast equipment.

The *traffic* department integrates the advertising with the programming, making sure that all the ads that are sold are aired when they're supposed to be. Traffic also handles billing for the ads.

The *promotion* department advertises the station — on the station itself, on billboards, on radio, and in the local newspaper. These people also create contests to keep the station visible in the community.

The *public affairs* department often helps organize public events, such as a fun-run to raise money for the local hospital.

*Administration* handles the paperwork for the station — paychecks and expense accounts, for example.

# The TV Industry Today

TODAY'S MOST-WATCHED television programs are situation comedies, sports, and feature movies. More than 50 million households tuned in for the final episode of the dramatic comedy *M*A*S*H* on February 28, 1983, making it the highest-rated television program ever. Super Bowls generally grab nearly half the homes in the United States.

Six developments promise to affect the development of the television industry over the next decade: station ownership; the role of the networks; the growth of independent stations; cable; changing technology; and the accuracy of ratings.

# Station Ownership

Broadcast deregulation (see Chapter 13) now allows one company to own 12 AM radio stations, 12 FM radio stations, and 12 TV stations as long as the group's stations don't reach more than 25 percent of the national audience. Broadcasters also are no longer required, as they once were, to hold onto a station for three years before selling it. Today stations may be sold as soon as they are purchased.

The relaxation of these ownership rules means that the major characteristic of the television business today is changing ownership. Television is *concentrating* ownership, but it is also *shifting* ownership, as stations are bought and sold at an unprecedented rate. This has introduced instability and change to an industry that, as recently as 1980, witnessed very few ownership turnovers.

# The Networks' Role

Advertisers always have been the reason for television's existence, so in 1986 the networks were disturbed to see the first decline in revenues in 15 years. New and continuing developments—such as cable, satellite broadcast, and VCRs—have turned the television set into a smorgasbord of choices (see Industry Snapshot, page 190). The audience, and advertisers, are deserting the networks, and network ratings are declining as a result. Because there are so many new sources of information and entertainment for the audience, advertisers are looking for new ways to capture viewers.

The network share of the prime-time audience has gone from 90 percent in 1978 to 63 percent in 1991—reflecting the continued growth of independent TV stations, syndicated programming, and cable systems. The networks' share of the audience for the evening news also is shrinking.

The story is a familiar one, paralleling radio in the late 1940s as it was supplanted first by television and then began competing with itself. More stations and more sources of programming mean that the networks will have to redefine their audience and give the audience what it cannot get elsewhere.

*Network shares, company cost-cutting, executive-suite maneuvers—or indeed whether the signal comes from a network or a cable system—matter to the audience only when they affect the end product, the program on the screen. . . . When the material is*

*In Living Color*, here featuring Damon Wayans and David Alan Grier in "Men on TV," offers unconventional programming targeted by Fox Broadcasting at an under-30 audience.

*useful or appealing, viewers respond — morning, noon, and night. The real question in the unsettled new world of network television is whether the new managers can produce such programs.* [26]

## Independents

Once TV's second-class citizens, independent stations are seeking their own identity. Ventures like Rupert Murdoch's Fox Broadcasting are helping the nation's 469 independent TV stations to loosely affiliate with a network to deliver their own programming and help the independents compete with the three existing networks. Offering new prime-time programming every night still is too expensive and too risky for the independents, but Fox has successfully offered *The Simpsons* and *In Living Color* as alternatives to programming on the original three networks.

For the 1990–91 season, for example, Fox introduced ten new series. Industry observers call the upstart network "the fox in the henhouse" because of the challenge that Fox is bringing to the traditional network structure.

**5.2** ➤

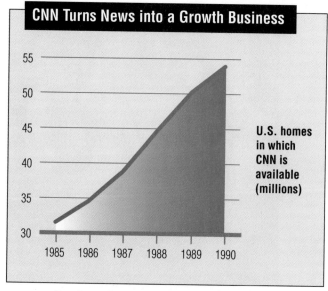

CNN Turns News into a Growth Business

U.S. homes in which CNN is available (millions)

SOURCE: Data from *The Wall Street Journal*, Feb. 1, 1990.

# Cable

Today's cable giants, ESPN (Entertainment & Sports Programming Network) and TNT (Turner Network Television), are descendants of America's first cable TV system, established in Mahoney, Pennsylvania, in 1948. TV reception in Mahoney, a coal-mining town in the Appalachians, was dismal, so TV appliance store owner John Walson built an antenna on a nearby mountain to improve reception.

For $100 Walson would connect each subscriber to his antenna. After that, a subscriber paid $2 a month, and within months Walson had 727 subscribers. Soon this community-antenna television (CATV) system spread to remote areas all over the country where TV reception was poor.

By 1970, there were 2,500 CATV systems in the United States, and commercial broadcasters were getting nervous about what they called wired TV. Cable operators were required by the FCC to carry all local broadcast programming, and programs were often duplicated on several channels. The FCC also limited the programs that cable could carry. One FCC ruling, for example, said that movies on cable had to be at least ten years old.

Believing that cable should be able to offer its own programming, Home Box Office (owned by Time Inc.) started operating in Manhattan in 1972, offering a modest set of programs—a National Hockey League game from

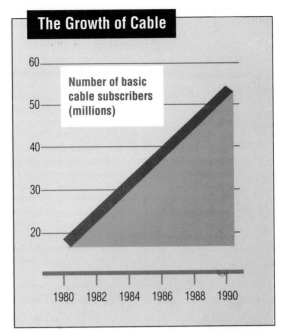

SOURCE: Data from Nielsen Station Index, Nielsen Television Index; Standard & Poor's *Industry Surveys*.

Madison Square Garden and the movie *Sometimes a Great Notion*. HBO's programs were relayed by a microwave antenna atop the Pan Am building to *one* out-of-town cable system in Wilkes-Barre, Pennsylvania. Three more small cable systems followed, but HBO was losing money.

In 1975, HBO leased a channel on one of RCA's domestic-communications satellites. The satellite made nationwide program distribution easier, and by 1977, 262 cable systems across the country were taking HBO. Also in 1977, the FCC lifted its restrictions on cable programming and advertising, and cable began to challenge broadcast television.

Ted Turner's TNT first relayed programs by satellite in 1976, and in 1979 Turner started Cable News Network (CNN) (see Figure 5.2). Today, 100 different program services, ranging from the frantic sounds of Music Television (MTV) to classic 1930s and 1940s movies on Arts & Entertainment (A&E), are available by satellite. Over 53 million households — more than half the homes in America — have basic cable (see Figure 5.3).

Cable television as an alternative to the traditional networks moved to the center of the national news agenda in 1991 when CNN offered 24-hour coverage of the gulf war in Iraq. CNN's fast response to world events underlined the new global role that CNN, and perhaps other companies, will play in future television developments. Reports the *Los Angeles Times*, "By staying on the air 24 hours a day and beaming live coverage of many major news events directly into millions of homes, hotel rooms and government offices world-wide, Atlanta-based CNN has done much to promote the 'global village' long forecast by media visionaries."[27]

**Sports.** Within the last 30 years, the biggest single element of television programming has been sports. In 1964, CBS paid $28 million for television rights to the 1964–65 National Football League (NFL) games. In 1990, the price paid for rights to broadcast NFL football totaled $3.6 billion.[28]

The instant replay, first tried at the Army–Navy football game on New Year's Eve 1964, added to the excitement of watching football on television. Instant replay, coupled with the talented banter between commentators Frank Gifford and Howard Cosell, also helped boost the ratings of ABC's *Monday Night Football*.

Televised sports are television's second biggest moneymaker after prime-time programming, and television fees fund most of the cost of the nation's organized sports. ESPN, the U.S.'s largest cable sports network, was launched in 1979, and in 1990 it contributed $450 million to the fees collected by the NFL. Owned primarily by Capital Cities/ABC, ESPN reaches more than 50 million households and annually offers more than 8,000 hours of televised sports. ESPN's major rival is Turner Network Television (TNT), which matched ESPN's $450 million contribution to the NFL season.

These cable operations have begun to compete heavily for rights to carry sports events because they feel that the primarily male (92 percent for some events), affluent audience is worth the investment.

Televised sports has gone from simple transmission of a football game in 1964 to today's spectacularly complex entertainment packaging, which has turned athletes as well as sports commentators into media stars. The expansion of sports programming to cable channels such as ESPN and TNT means even more sports programming choices for viewers, and more money for American sports teams.

# Rapid Technological Changes

Advances in technology are both a blessing and a bane for television. When technological developments move like a rocket, as they have in the past decade, program production and delivery become easier, but they also can become more expensive. Sophisticated technology also brings more competition.

**Satellite Master Antenna Systems (SMATV).** SMATV brings cable programming to apartment buildings, condominium complexes, private housing developments, and mobile-home parks. The programs come through an earth station aimed at a cable satellite.

**High-Definition Television (HDTV).** A normal television picture scans 525 lines across the screen. High-definition television scans 1,125 lines. CBS first demonstrated HDTV in the United States in 1982. HDTV, which would mean a wider, sharper picture and better sound, is waiting for a practical method to transmit the higher-resolution picture, since it requires more spectrum space than conventional television signals. HDTV is already in use in Japan, and forecasters project that Americans will be using HDTV before 1995.

**Direct Broadcast Satellites (DBS).** The FCC authorized DBS in 1982, making direct-to-home satellite broadcasts possible, but no service is yet available. Extremely powerful earth stations would retransmit signals to small backyard earth stations. So far the enormous financial investment necessary to start such a service has deterred the eight companies that were approved by the FCC from offering DBS service, but this would mean that you could dial up any of the *world's* satellite channels simply by directing your small home receiver. You would pay an access fee for each channel you chose, in the same way people subscribe to cable services today.

**Pay-Per-View.** An adaptation of satellite and cable, pay-per-view was introduced in 1981 for the Sugar Ray Leonard–Thomas Hearns welterweight-championship fight. For the first time, audiences could watch a specific television program only if they paid to see it. The charge was $15 per set, and pay TV collected nearly $8.5 million.[29]

Pay TV offered movie producers another way to profit from the rival medium of television. Movie producers began to look at pay-per-view as a way to distribute their movies directly to the home with a guaranteed audience and income. One pay-TV executive told *The New Yorker* magazine, "The dream has been that the movie would be provided in the home at approximately the same time that it would be released in the theatres. If this came to pass, we would be catering to an entire audience in the home that doesn't want to go out to see movies. The motion-picture industry has realized that the home itself is becoming a theatre."[30]

With pay-per-view, cable operators can increase their income by offering special programs (such as sports events) that are not available to viewers any other way. Pay-per-view collected $610 million in 1990.

**Low-Power Television (LPTV).** The FCC authorized low-power television in 1982. As the name suggests, these stations operate at a fraction of the transmitting power of traditional stations. Designed to deliver local programming to rural areas, their signals seldom reach beyond 15 miles from their transmission tower. Nearly 800 LPTV stations are on the air.

**VCRs.** Both the movie and the television industries are closely watching the growth of videocassette recorders (VCRs), which celebrated their 15th birthday in 1991. More than half of all American households now have a VCR; some homes have two.

The movie industry collects substantial income from videocassette sales. For the television business, the VCR is a threat because someone who tapes a program can fast-forward through ("zap") the commercials, and commercials pay for television programs. The next generation of VCRs may offer built-in editing equipment to make zapping effortless.

VCR owners also can watch what they want when they want, a practice known as **time-shifting**. Cable operators and commercial broadcasters are afraid that if time-shifting spreads, it will create havoc in the ratings system.

# Ratings Accuracy: People Meters

People meters, first used in 1987 by the A. C. Nielsen Company to record television viewing, gather data through a 4-inch by 10-inch box that sits on the television set in metered homes. People meters monitor the nation's Nielsen families (about 4,000 of them), and the results of these recorded viewing patterns (which Nielsen says reflect a cross-section of American viewers) sets the basis for television advertising rates.

Nielsen family members each punch in an assigned button on top of the set when they begin to watch TV. The system's central computer, linked to the home by telephone lines, correlates each viewer's number with information about that person stored in its memory. Network ratings have plunged since people meters were introduced as a ratings system, and the networks have complained that the new measuring device underestimates viewership.

To respond to this criticism, Nielsen announced in 1989 that it will carry the research one step further, to develop a "passive people meter" in conjunction with the David Sarnoff Research Center at Princeton. If successful, this new system would be able to identify precisely who is watching television when, without their having to do anything.

The passive people meter system uses a cameralike device and a computer attached to the top of the TV set in each Nielsen home. Facial images of each member of the family will be programmed into the computer. When someone turns on the TV set, the camera scans the room for the faces it recognizes, and records who is watching. Nielsen predicts that this passive people meter system will be ready for use by 1995.

# Facing the Future

Forecasts for the future of television parallel the forecasts for radio — a menu board of hundreds of programs and services available to viewers at the touch of a remote control button.

**Interactive Video.** In 1991, the FCC was asked to approve a new technology, interactive video, which will let you do something you haven't been able to do before — talk back to your television set. Using interactive television (for a monthly fee) you can, for example, play along with game show contestants by punching in your answers and then comparing your answers to people nationwide who played with you. The service's promoters say that eventually interactive video subscribers will be able to order a pizza or a new bathing suit, learn a foreign language, participate in a national poll, or do their banking and pay their bills without leaving home.

**Fiber Optics.** Fiber optics, which allows the transmission of huge amounts of data using clear glass strands as thin as a human hair, forms the basis for many of today's cable systems, and fiber optics could change television dramatically.

Imagine your television as an artificial reality machine. This machine, says *The Wall Street Journal*, would use "remarkably crisp pictures and sound to 'deliver' a viewer to a pristine tropical beach, to a big football game or to a quiet mountaintop retreat. Japanese researchers envision golfers practicing their swings in front of three-dimensional simulations of courses."[31]

The definition of television today is expanding faster than our ability to chronicle the changes. Lanny Smoot, an executive at Bell Communications Research, calls the future of television a *telepresence*. "This," he says, "is a wave that is not possible to stop."[32]

# Television

## Industry Snapshot

Today's television audience is fragmented with the addition of a fourth network (Fox Television), cable systems, VCRs, and even game systems such as Nintendo. Broadcast station operators are increasingly challenged to hold on to audiences.

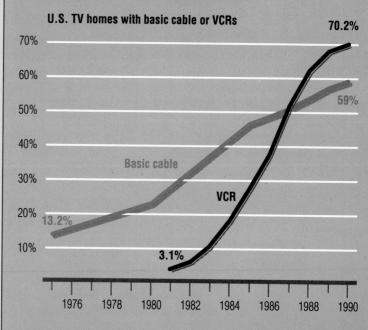

**Viewer's Choice: Cable and VCRs Change the Face of TV**

U.S. TV homes with basic cable or VCRs

- 70.2%
- 59%
- 13.2%
- 3.1%

Basic cable

VCR

70%
60%
50%
40%
30%
20%
10%

1976  1978  1980  1982  1984  1986  1988  1990

Data from Cabletelevision Advertising Bureau (*Advertising Age*, Feb. 11, 1991) and Standard & Poor's *Industry Surveys*, March 14, 1991.

**1** In the last decade, cable and TV technology have greatly expanded audience choices, changing when and how people watch TV.

**2** With hit shows like *In Living Color* and *The Simpsons*, Fox Television has become a fourth network, competing for viewers and advertising dollars with the original big three: NBC, CBS, and ABC.

MATT GROENING

Challenged by competition from cable and independent stations, as well as the success of the Fox network, the original three TV networks are rapidly losing their hold on the prime-time audience.

Not all TV homes have cable, and the cable audience is fragmented by the number of program offerings. As a result, national advertisers still find broadcast TV the most efficient way to reach masses of viewers.

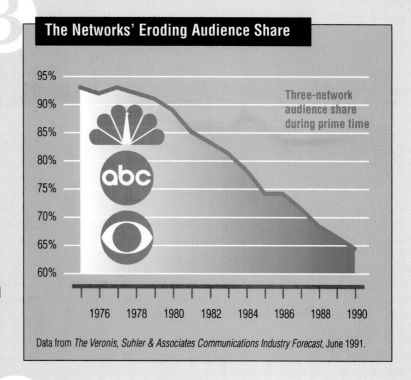

## The Networks' Eroding Audience Share

Three-network audience share during prime time

Data from *The Veronis, Suhler & Associates Communications Industry Forecast,* June 1991.

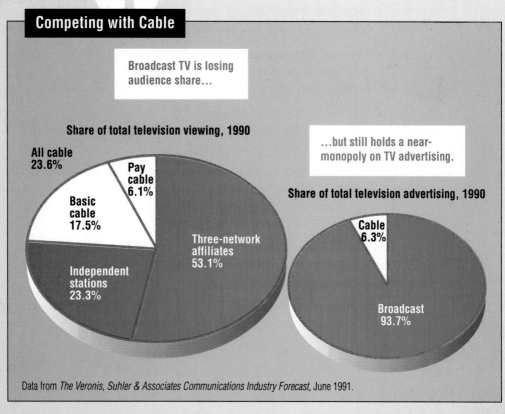

## Competing with Cable

Broadcast TV is losing audience share...

Share of total television viewing, 1990

All cable 23.6%

Pay cable 6.1%

Basic cable 17.5%

Three-network affiliates 53.1%

Independent stations 23.3%

...but still holds a near-monopoly on TV advertising.

Share of total television advertising, 1990

Cable 6.3%

Broadcast 93.7%

Data from *The Veronis, Suhler & Associates Communications Industry Forecast,* June 1991.

• The word *television*, which once meant programs delivered by antennas through over-the-air signals, today means television screen, where a variety of delivery systems brings viewers a diversity of programs.

• About 1,500 television stations operate in the United States. Three out of four of these are commercial stations and more than half of U.S. stations are affiliated with a network.

• More than any other media industry today, commercial television exists primarily as an advertising medium.

• Guglielmo Marconi put sound on airwaves. Lee de Forest invented the Audion tube. Vladimir Zworykin turned an electronic signal into a visual image. Philo T. Farnsworth added the electronic scanner.

• The rivalry between David Sarnoff (RCA) and William S. Paley (CBS) is central to the early history of television. The ABC network was formed when the FCC ordered Sarnoff to sell one of his two networks (Red and Blue). The Blue network became ABC.

• Early television used black and white, although primitive color transmission had been developed by CBS. Color was too expensive to market, however, and so the first television standard became black and white.

• The first television news broadcasts were primitive compared to today's broadcasts. Then, like radio news, television news developed its own standard of excellence, led by news pioneers David Brinkley and Edward R. Murrow.

• Most of television entertainment programming was derived from radio. The only type of program that didn't come from radio was the talk show. The situation comedy proved to be one of television's most durable types of programming.

• The 1950s quiz show scandals caused the networks to eliminate advertiser-produced programming.

• In the 1960s, audiences grew more discriminating and began to question how well the medium of television was serving the public. An influential spokesperson for these views was FCC Chairman Newton Minow, who coined the phrase "vast wasteland" to describe television.

• As TV's news capability matured, it helped create national experiences, but TV also drew criticism for the way it was perceived to influence politics and the dialogue about national issues.

• Many groups are concerned that, because of its pervasiveness, television influences the nation's values, habits, and behavior.

• The Nielsen ratings determine the price that TV advertisers pay to air their commercials. Nielsen introduced people meters in 1987, and promises passive audience measurement before 1995.

• Deregulation, with relaxed ownership rules, means that instability and change have become a major characteristic of television today.

• Today traditional network audiences are shrinking, as more stations are licensed to broadcast and as rapidly changing technology competes for TV audiences.

• Today, more than 100 program services on cable offer alternatives to network programming.

• Televised sports are television's second biggest moneymaker after prime-time programming, and television fees fund most of the cost of the nation's organized sports.

• Interactive video and fiber optics are two examples of developing technologies that will further blur the definition of television as simply a source of news and entertainment. One researcher has defined the new world of television as a telepresence.

**6**

*"In no other business is a single example of product fully created at an investment of millions of dollars with no real assurance that the public will buy it. In no other business does the public 'use' the product and then take away with them . . . merely the memory of it. In the truest sense, it's an industry based on dreams."*[1]

It would be easy to assume that the movie industry is one of the biggest media industries because the publicity surrounding movie celebrities captures a great deal of attention. So it is often

**The Movie Industry**

surprising to find that the movie industry accounts for the smallest amount of media industries income — about 4 percent.

Movies and movie stars need the public's attention because the audience determines whether or not movies succeed. Movies are very costly investments, and most movies lose money. Investors, therefore, often favor "bankable" talent that will bring a following to a movie, rather than new talent that is untested. Yet, even movies featuring established talent can fail; no one in the movie industry can accurately predict which movies will be hits.

Writes film scholar Jason E. Squire,

> *At its simplest, the feature film is the shuffling of light images to win hearts in dark rooms. At its most complex, it is a massive venture of commerce, a vast creative enterprise requiring the logistical discipline of the military, the financial foreshadowing of the Federal Reserve, and the psychological tolerance of the clergy, all harnessed in private hands on behalf of the telling of a story. In the commercial movie industry, the idea is to make movies that attract vast audiences who cumulatively pay enough money for the privilege so that all the costs involved in making that movie are recouped, with enough left over to make more movies. The profit motive is at work here, but the formula that attracts audiences is as elusive as can be.*[2]

Movies mirror the society that creates them. Some movies offer an underlying political message. Other movies reflect changing social values. And still other movies are just good entertainment. All movies need an audience to succeed.

Like other media industries, the movie industry has had to adapt to changing technology. Before the invention of television, movies were the nation's primary form of visual entertainment. Today, the use of special effects — something you can't get from television — is one way the movie industry competes with television for your attention, and your dollars. But special effects don't fit every movie, and they are very expensive. And today, the economics of moviemaking is very important.

# Capturing Motion on Film: How Movies Began

MOVIES WERE invented at a time when American industry welcomed any new gadget, and inventors wildly sought patents on appliances and electrical devices. The motion picture camera and projector were two of the Industrial Revolution's new gadgets.

Movies were not the invention of one person. First a device to photograph moving objects had to be invented and then a device to project those pictures. This process involved six people: Étienne Jules Marey, Eadweard Muybridge, William K. L. Dickson, Auguste and Louis Lumière, and Thomas Edison.

In the late 1870s, Marey and Muybridge worked 8,000 miles apart on separate problems — Marey in Paris and Muybridge in Palo Alto, California. Marey, a scientist, wanted to invent a device to prove Darwin's theory of natural selection; Muybridge wanted to help a wealthy patron win a bet.

Marey sought to record an animal's movement by individual actions — one at a time — to compare one animal to another. He charted a horse's movements on graphs and published the information in a book, *Animal Mechanism*.

Unknown to Marey, Muybridge was hired in America by railroad millionaire and horse breeder Leland Stanford to settle a $25,000 bet. Stanford bet that during a trot, all four of a horse's feet simultaneously leave the ground. Muybridge's first photos in 1872 did not prove Stanford's point, but five years later Stanford read Marey's *Animal Mechanism* and he hired Muybridge again.[3]

This time Muybridge and Stanford built a special track with 12 cameras precisely placed to take pictures of a horse as it moved around the track. The horse tripped a series of equidistant wires as it ran, which in turn tripped the cameras' shutters. Stanford won his $25,000 — one photograph showed that all four of the horse's feet did leave the ground — and the photographic series provided an excellent study of motion.

Muybridge expanded to 24 cameras, photographed other animals, and then took pictures of people moving. He developed a projector that he called a zoopraxiscope to project the images onto a large screen. He traveled throughout Europe showing his photographs, and eventually Muybridge and Marey met.

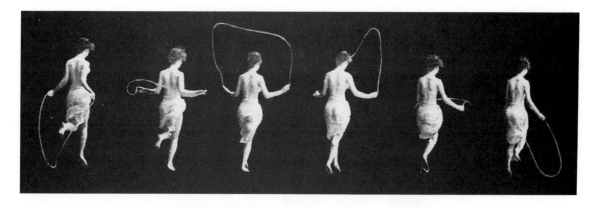

**This woman in motion is one of the early images photographed by Eadweard Muybridge.**

Marey felt that Muybridge's photographs were too imprecise for scientific analysis, and in 1882 Marey perfected a photographic gun camera that could take 12 photographs on one plate — the first motion picture camera.[4]

Edison bought some of Muybridge's pictures in 1888 and showed them to his assistant, William K. L. Dickson. Edison then met with Marey in Europe, where Marey had invented a projector that showed pictures on a continuous strip of film. But the strip film moved unevenly across the projector lens, so the pictures jumped.

Back in America, Dickson perforated the edges of the film so that, as the film moved through the camera, sprockets inside the camera grabbed the perforations and locked the film in place, minimizing the jumps. Dickson looped the strip over a lamp and a magnifying lens in a box 2 feet wide and 4 feet tall. The box stood on the floor with a peephole in the top so people could look inside. Edison named this device the kinetoscope.

On April 11, 1894, America's first kinetoscope parlor opened in New York City with ten kinetoscopes in a former shoe store at 1155 Broadway. For 25 cents, people could see ten different 90-second black-and-white films, including "Trapeze," "Horse Shoeing," "Wrestlers," and "Roosters."

In France, the Lumière brothers, Auguste and Louis, improved on the kinetoscope by developing a projector called the cinematographe, which could show film on a large screen. Then they invented a camera that ran film through at 16 frames a second (instead of Edison's 48), and they took some pictures with their new camera.

The first public Lumière showing was on December 28, 1895: ten short subjects with such riveting titles as "Lunch Hour at the Lumière Factory," which showed workers leaving the building, and "Arrival of a Train at a Station." Admission was 1 franc and the Lumières collected 35 francs.[5]

America's first public motion picture showing in 1896, using Thomas Edison's Vitascope.

## American Movies Premiere

Edison resisted the Lumière approach of showing a movie on a single screen because he was selling his kinetoscopes for $100 each. Theaters also paid Edison rental fees for his film strips. But four months after the Lumière premiere in France, Edison organized the first American motion picture premiere with an improved camera developed by independent inventor Thomas Armat. Edison dubbed the new machine the Vitascope, and America's first public showing of the motion picture was on April 23, 1896, at Koster and Bial's theater in New York. Edison sat in a box seat and Armat ran the projector from the balcony.

At first, movies were a sideshow. Penny arcade owners showed movies behind a black screen at the rear of the arcade for an extra nickel. But soon the movies were more popular than the rest of the attractions, and the arcades were renamed nickelodeons.

In 1900, there were more than 600 nickelodeons in New York City, with more than 300,000 daily admissions.[6] Each show lasted about 20 minutes. The programs ran from noon until late evening, and many theaters blared music outside to bring in business.

By 1907, Edison had contracted with most of the nation's movie producers, as well as the Lumière brothers and the innovative French producer Georges Méliès, to provide movies for the theaters. Licensed Edison theaters used licensed Edison projectors and rented Edison's licensed movies, many of which Edison produced at his own studio.

The important exception to Edison's licensing plan was his rival, the American Biograph and Mutoscope Company, commonly called Biograph. Biograph manufactured a better motion picture camera than Edison's, and Edison was losing business.

Edison sued Biograph, charging that Biograph had stolen his ideas. He lost several appeals, but he threatened to carry his case to the U.S. Supreme Court. The prospect of a costly suit caused Biograph to sign an agreement with Edison, forming the Motion Picture Patents Company (MPPC) in 1908.

The MPPC pooled the major French and American producers and manufacturers, including Biograph, with Eastman Kodak Company, the only American film manufacturer. Licensed producers, using only Eastman Kodak film, distributed their movies only through distributors who used MPPC-licensed films. The distributors rented their films only to exhibitors who used MPPC-licensed equipment.

Licensed exhibitors paid $2 a week to MPPC, and any distributor or exhibitor who violated the agreement by handling independent films was banned from the MPPC. The MPPC collected more than $1 million the first year, with Edison receiving most of the royalties.[7] Thomas Alva Edison thus established the first motion picture trust, a virtual monopoly on the movie business.

# Early Films

Two innovative filmmakers are credited with turning the novelty of movies into art: Georges Méliès and Edwin S. Porter. (All of these early films were black-and-white silents. Sound was not introduced to the movies until the 1920s, and color experiments did not begin until the 1930s.) French filmmaker Georges Méliès added fantasy to the movies. Before Méliès, moviemakers photographed theatrical scenes or events from everyday life. But Méliès, who was a magician and a caricaturist before he became a filmmaker, used camera tricks to make people disappear and reappear and to make characters grow and then shrink. Méliès' 1902 film *A Trip to the Moon* was the first outer space movie adventure, complete with fantasy creatures. When his films, which became known as trick films, were shown in the United States, American moviemakers stole his ideas.

Georges Méliès created these fanciful creatures for his 1902 *A Trip to the Moon*, introducing fantasy to the movies.

Edison hired projectionist/electrician Edwin S. Porter in 1899, and in the next decade Porter became America's most important filmmaker. Until Porter, most American films were trick films or short documentary-style movies that showed newsworthy events (although some filmmakers used titillating subjects such as "Pajama Girl" and "Corset Girl" to cater to men, who were the movies' biggest fans). In 1903 Porter produced *The Great Train Robbery*, an action movie with bandits attacking a speeding train.

Instead of using a single location like most other moviemakers, Porter shot 12 different scenes. He also introduced the use of dissolves between shots, instead of abrupt splices. Porter's film technique — action and changing locations — prefigured the classic storytelling tradition of American movies.

## The Studio System Is Born

None of the players in the early movies was given screen credit, but then fans began to write letters to Biograph star Florence Lawrence addressed "The Biograph Girl." In 1909, Carl Laemmle formed an independent production company, stole Florence Lawrence from Biograph, and gave her screen credit. She became America's first movie star.

Biograph became the first to make movies using the studio system. The studio system meant that a studio hired a stable of stars and production people who were paid a regular salary. These people were then under contract to that studio and could not work for any other studio without their employer's permission.

In 1910, Laemmle lured Mary Pickford away from Biograph by doubling her salary. He discovered, says film scholar Robert Sklar, "that stars sold pictures as nothing else could. As long as theaters changed their programs daily — and the practice persisted in neighborhood theaters and small towns until the early 1920s — building up audience recognition of star names was almost the only effective form of audience publicity."[8]

By 1915, Mary Pickford was making $2,000 a week (the equivalent of $20,000 a week today) plus half the profits from her pictures, and Mutual Film Corporation gave Charlie Chaplin $150,000 just for signing a contract, plus $10,000 a week. Other independent producers followed Laemmle's example, and soon more than a dozen independents were challenging the exclusivity of the Motion Picture Patents Company. Edison was angry that anyone would challenge the MPPC system. The independents formed the Motion Picture Distributing and Sales Company in 1910 as an exclusive distributor for the independents.

When Edison founded the MPPC in 1908, it controlled 100 percent of the film importation and distribution business. Four years later, because of the independents, the MPPC share had fallen to just a little more than 50 percent.[9] In 1915, a federal court declared that the MPPC was an illegal conspiracy in restraint of trade. The MPPC, the first attempt at motion picture monopoly, was dead.

The star system, which promoted popular movie personalities to lure audiences, was nurtured by the independents. This helped broaden the movies' appeal beyond the working class. Movie houses began to show up in the suburbs. In 1914, President Woodrow Wilson and his family were shown a popular movie at the White House. From 1908 to 1914, movie attendance doubled.[10] Then in 1915, the first real titan of the silent movies, director D. W. Griffith, introduced the concept of spectacular entertainment. His movies were so ambitious, so immense, that no one could ignore them.

Most early movies were two reels long, 25 minutes. At first Griffith made two-reelers, but then he expanded his movies to four reels and longer, pioneering the feature-length film. From 1908 to 1913, he directed more than 400 films, but his name didn't appear on them; like the players, directors received no screen credit.

Griffith's best-known epic was as controversial as it was spectacular. In *The Birth of a Nation* (1915), the Southern-born Griffith presented a dramatic view

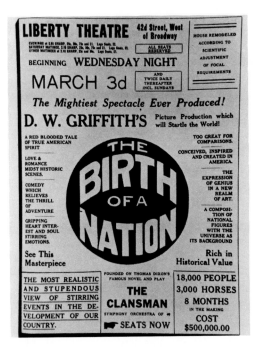

D. W. Griffith's controversial epic *The Birth of a Nation* cost $110,000 to make and eventually earned $18 million. (Film scholars generally accept the $110,000 figure, although Griffith advertised his cost at $500,000.)

of the Civil War and Reconstruction, portraying racial stereotypes and touching on the subject of sexual intermingling of the races. It was an ambitious film on a bitter, controversial topic, shown to an audience that had not reconciled the war's divisions. The movie's cost — about $110,000 — was five times more than that of any American film until that time.[11]

Writes Jack Ellis in *A History of American Film*,

*Though* [The Birth of a Nation] *played in "legitimate" theaters for as much as two dollars a ticket, it has been estimated that the first six months of its national run drew more people than had attended all the performances of all the stage plays in the U.S. during any given five-year period.*

*More than merely a motion picture, it was a cultural phenomenon that everyone felt obliged to witness. Because of its evident racial biases, it created enormous controversy, even riots, and the notoriety attracted still more customers.*[12]

*The Birth of a Nation* eventually earned more than $18 million. With this and his subsequent epics, Griffith showed the potential that movies had as a mass medium for gathering large audiences. He also proved that people would pay more than a nickel or a dime to see a motion picture. Films had moved from the crowded nickelodeon to respectability.

New production companies quickly formed to feed what seemed to be the public's unquenchable desire for movies. (See Impact/Profile, The Lincoln Motion Picture Company.) The biggest companies were First National, Famous Players-Lasky, Metro, Loew's, Fox, and Paramount. In 1918, Paramount, headed by Adolph Zukor, distributed 220 features in one year, more than any single company before or since.[14]

# The Movies Become Big Business

HE MOVIE business was changing quickly. Five important events in the 1920s transformed it: the industry's move to California, the adoption of block booking, the formation of United Artists, the efforts at self-censorship, and the introduction of sound.

## A Change of Scene

During the first decade of the 20th century, the major movie companies were based in New York, the theater capital. Film companies sometimes traveled to Florida or Cuba to chase the sunshine because it was easier to build sets outdoors to take advantage of the light. But this soon changed.

In 1903, Harry Chandler owned the *Los Angeles Times*, but he also was investing in Los Angeles real estate. Chandler and several influential partners bought some rural land in northwest Los Angeles, built a hotel and a rail line to bring prospective buyers, then subdivided the property. The hotel was named the Hollywood Hotel.

Chandler and his friends courted the movie business, offering cheap land, moderate weather, and inexpensive labor. The moviemakers moved, some of them aided by loans from Chandler and from California banker A. P. Giannini, founder of the Bank of Italy, which eventually became Bank of America.

# Block Booking

People who owned theater chains soon decided to make movies, and movie-makers discovered that they could make more money if they owned theaters, so production companies began to build theaters to exhibit their own pictures. Fox Theaters Corporation, for example, announced plans to build 30 first-run movie houses in major cities that would each seat between 4,000 and 5,000 people. [15]

The connection between production, distribution, and exhibition grew, led by Paramount's Adolph Zukor. Zukor controlled the nation's best movie talent. Mary Pickford, Douglas Fairbanks, Gloria Swanson, comedian Fatty Arbuckle, Norma and Constance Talmadge, and directors Cecil B. de Mille and D. W. Griffith worked under contract exclusively for Paramount. Through his First National Exhibitors Circuit, Zukor licensed more than 500 theaters to show only Paramount pictures. To gain even more control, Zukor devised a system called **block booking**.

Block booking meant that a company such as Paramount would sign up one of its licensed theaters for as many as 104 pictures at a time. The movie package contained a few "name" pictures with stars, but the majority of the movies in the block were lightweight features with no stars. Because movie bills changed twice a week, the exhibitors were desperate for something to put on the screen. Often without knowing which movies they were getting in the block, exhibitors accepted the packages and paid the distributors' prices.

# Rebels With a Cause: United Artists

In 1919, the nation's five biggest movie names — cowboy star William S. Hart, Mary Pickford, Charlie Chaplin, Douglas Fairbanks, and D. W. Griffith — decided it was time to rebel against the strict studio system of distribution.

On January 15, 1919, the stars announced:

*A new combination of motion picture stars and producers was formed yesterday, and we, the undersigned, in furtherance of the artistic welfare of the moving picture industry, believing we can better serve the great and growing industry of picture productions, have decided to unite our work into one association, and at the finish of existing contracts, which are now rapidly drawing to a close, to release our combined productions through our own organization.* [16]

# The Lincoln Motion Picture Company

**This profile describes how small, independent moviemakers contributed to the early history of the movies.**

WHILE THE largest movie companies sought more and more of the audience, smaller companies were formed to fill special needs. The Lincoln Motion Picture Company, for example, incorporated on January 20, 1917, to produce pictures starring an all-African-American cast, made specifically for African-American audiences. Through African-American newspapers, the company sold stock at $1 a share, and the company claimed assets of $15,623.68 when it incorporated.

The goal of the Lincoln Motion Picture Company was to counteract the "insulting, humiliating and undignified portrayal of the cheap burlesque slap-stick comedies so universally shown as characteristic of the Afro-American ideals." The Lincoln Motion Picture Company's first two movies, *The Realization of a Negro's Ambition* and *A Trooper of Troop K*, traveled the country. Students and teachers at the Tuskegee Institute saw the movies and another show was sponsored by the Negro Business Men's League in Kansas City.

*The Realization of a Negro's Ambition* was a two-reel movie about a young civil engineer who seeks his fortune out West, where he finds pervasive prejudice. But after he rescues the daughter of a wealthy oilman, the oilman gives the engineer a job. The engineer

# MOVING PICTURES

The Lincoln Motion Picture Co. of Los Angeles, a Negro Firm
presents their first release, entitled

## "The Realization of a Negro's Ambition"

At **Lincoln Electric Park**

20th and Woodland

## MONDAY AND TUESDAY

### AUGUST 14 and 15

The Negro Business Men's League has gone to a big expense to secure
these educational pictures. Positively the last time shown in Kansas City
before going South. Your first opportunity to see a picture owned, written
acted and produced entirely by Negroes. Don't fail to see it.

A Two-reel drama, well acted by an all star Negro cast, featuring No
ble M. Johnson, Universal City's favorite Negro actor and playwright.

**Several Reels of Comedies also will be shown**

Admission 10 cts.　　　Children 5 cts.

The Lincoln Motion Picture Company advertised and exhibited its movie *The Realization of a Negro's Ambition* before selected audiences.

strikes oil and returns home to the love of his childhood sweetheart.

*A Trooper of Troop K* chronicled the heroic actions of African-American troopers of the U.S. 10th Cavalry. The filmmakers advertised that the film "depicts in gripping scenes the unflinching bravery of Negro Troopers under fire and how they, greatly outnumbered, sacrificed their blood and life for their country. Interposed in the picture are scenes of romantic love, comedy and human interest." Several former members of the 10th Cavalry were featured in the movie.

The Lincoln Motion Picture Company charged the organizations a $15 rental fee to show *The Realization of a Negro's Am-* *bition*. Admission was 10 cents for adults and 5 cents for children. After the Tuskegee showing, the Lincoln Motion Picture Company received a letter from the school's principal that said, "You do not know how much pleasure and satisfaction our Institute community received last evening from the showing of your two moving picture productions. . . . The largest attendance which has assembled in the Tuskegee Institute Chapel this year, composed of nearly 1600 students and our 200 teachers, Institute families, and persons from the town of Tuskegee and the village of Greenwood, south of the Institute, greeted the showing of these two pictures."[13]

(Left to right) Douglas Fairbanks, Mary Pickford, Charlie Chaplin, and D. W. Griffith — the founders of United Artists.

Eventually Hart withdrew from the agreement, but the remaining partners formed a company called United Artists. They eliminated block booking and became a distributor for independently produced pictures, including their own.

In its first six years, UA delivered many movies that today are still considered classics: *The Mark of Zorro, The Three Musketeers, Robin Hood,* and *The Gold Rush.* These movies succeeded despite the fact that UA worked outside of the traditional studio system, proving that it was possible to distribute films to audiences without using a major studio.

# Responding to Critics: Self-Regulation

In the 1920s, the movie industry faced two new crises: scandals involving movie stars and criticism that movie content was growing too provocative. Movie industry moguls began a period of self-examination to decide how to respond to the public's reaction. The result was the decision by the moviemakers to regulate themselves.

Comedian Fatty Arbuckle sparked scandal in Hollywood that eventually led to the formation in 1930 of the Motion Picture Production Code.

The star scandals began when comedian Roscoe "Fatty" Arbuckle hosted a marathon party in San Francisco over Labor Day weekend in 1921. As the party was ending, model Virginia Rappe, who had complained that she felt ill, was rushed to the hospital with stomach pains. She died at the hospital, and Arbuckle was charged with murder.

Arbuckle had been alone with Rappe in the bedroom during the party, and newspaper stories alleged that Rappe was pregnant and had come to Arbuckle asking for money for an abortion. The stories also implied that an angry Arbuckle was responsible for Rappe's death. Eventually the cause of death was listed as peritonitis from a ruptured bladder, and the murder charge was reduced to manslaughter. After three trials, two of which resulted in a hung jury, Arbuckle was acquitted.

Then director William Desmond Taylor was found murdered in his home. Mabel Normand, a friend of Arbuckle's, was identified as the last person who had seen Taylor alive. Normand eventually was cleared, but then it was revealed that Taylor was not the director's real name and there were suggestions that he was involved in the drug business.

Hollywood's moguls and business people were aghast. The Catholic Legion of Decency announced a movie boycott. Quick to protect themselves, Los Angeles business leaders met and decided that Hollywood should police itself.

The *Los Angeles Times'* Harry Chandler invited 100 newspaper editors to send reporters to Hollywood at his expense to see that the town was not completely filled with rogues. Then he worked with movie leaders to bring in ex-Postmaster General and former Republican Party Chairman Will Hays to respond to these and other scandals in the movie business. Hays' job was to lead a moral refurbishing of the industry.

In March 1922, Hays became the first president of an organization called the Motion Picture Producers and Distributors Association (MPPDA), at a salary of $100,000 a year. A month later, even though Arbuckle had been acquitted, Hays suspended all of Fatty Arbuckle's films. The estimated cost to Arbuckle and his studio (Famous Players-Lasky) was $1 million.

Besides overseeing the stars' personal behavior, Hays decided that his office also should oversee movie content. The Motion Picture Producers and Distributors Association, called the Hays Office, wrote a code of conduct to govern the industry. As early as 1909, scattered local attempts had been made to control the content of the movies. Chicago passed the first censorship rules in 1909, and from 1909 to 1922, eight states passed some form of censorship legislation.[17] Threatened with more local actions, the industry had to figure out how to monitor itself.

At first, the Hays Office created a Studio Relations Committee, which presented the studios with a list of do's and don'ts. The committee had no enforcement power, and many producers ignored the MPPDA's suggestions. When sound was added to the movies in 1926, it gave the Hays Office even more to worry about — they had to monitor words as well as pictures. So on February 17, 1930, the MPPDA adopted a production code, which began by stating three general principles:

*1. No picture shall be produced which will lower the moral standards of those who see it. Hence the sympathy of the audience shall never be thrown to the side of crime, wrongdoing, evil or sin.*

*2. Correct standards of life, subject only to the requirements of drama and entertainment, shall be presented.*

*3. Laws, natural or human, shall not be ridiculed, nor shall sympathy be created for its violation.*[18]

The code then divided its rules into 12 categories of wrongdoing, including:

• *Murder: "The technique of murder must be presented in a way that will not inspire imitation."*

• *Sex: "Excessive and lustful kissing, lustful embraces, suggestive postures and gestures are not to be shown."*

• *Obscenity:* "*Obscenity in word, gesture, reference, song, joke, or by suggestion (even when likely to be understood only by part of the audience) is forbidden.*"

• *Costumes:* "*Dancing costumes intended to permit undue exposure or indecent movements in the dance are forbidden.*"[19]

In 1935, the MPPDA announced a $25,000 fine for any movie that was distributed without a certificate of approval from the Production Code Administration (PCA), an office of the MPPDA. Movie companies paid the PCA to review story ideas and shooting scripts for every movie, and PCA staff members followed the movie through production.

An acceptable movie displayed a PCA seal of approval in the titles at the beginning of the picture. Producers balked at the interference, but most of them, afraid of censorship from outside the industry, complied with PCA monitoring. Although standards have relaxed, self-regulation of content still operates in the motion picture industry today.

# Sound Comes to the Movies: The Talkies

By the mid-1920s, silent movies were an established part of American entertainment, but technology soon pushed the industry into an even more vibrant era — the era of the talkies. MPPDA President Will Hays was the first person to appear on screen in the public premiere of talking pictures on August 6, 1926, in New York City. Hays congratulated Warner Bros. and Western Electric, which had developed the sound experiment. Then followed seven short subjects, including a concert by the New York Philharmonic and a vaudeville comedy skit. Together the eight short subjects were called *The Vitaphone Preludes.*

The men who created the *Preludes* were the Warner brothers: Sam, Harry, Jack, and Albert. They were upstart, ambitious businessmen who beat their competitors to sound movies by buying Vitaphone and borrowing the money to develop the necessary theater sound system, which they then marketed to theaters.

Other companies resisted sound, but the Warners kept developing sound movies. On October 6, 1927, *The Jazz Singer* starring Al Jolson opened at the Warners' Theater in New York, the first feature-length motion picture with sound. The movie was not an all-talkie, but instead contained two sections with synchronized sound.

The success of *The Jazz Singer* convinced Warners' competitors not to wait any longer to adopt sound. By July 1, 1930, 22 percent of theaters still showed silent films; by 1932, the percentage of silents had dropped to 2.6 percent. By 1933, only 0.5 percent of the movies shown in theaters were silents.[20]

# The Rise of the Moguls:
# The Growth of the Studio System

In the 1930s, the movie business was dominated by the Big Five: Warner Bros., Metro-Goldwyn-Mayer, Paramount, RKO, and 20th Century-Fox. The Big Five produced about half the industry's films (each made 40 to 60 pictures a year[21]) and about three-fourths of the best features, which were called class A movies, so most of the movies that played in the best theaters with top billing were made and distributed by the Big Five. That meant that the Big Five collected more than two-thirds of the nation's box office receipts.

All these studios were vertically integrated — they produced movies, distributed them worldwide, and owned theater chains, which guaranteed their pictures a showing. The studios maintained stables of stars, directors, producers, writers, and technical staff. Film scholar Tino Balio calls the studios at this point in their history a "mature oligopoly" — a group of companies with so much control over an industry that any change in one of the companies directly affected the future of the industry.

Operating in a comfortable relationship with the Big Five were the Little Three: Universal, Columbia, and United Artists. Universal and Columbia had their own studios and provided low-cost pictures to the major studios. United Artists remained solely a distribution company for independent producers.

In the 1930s, Walt Disney became the only major successful Hollywood newcomer. He had released *Steamboat Willie* as "the first animated sound cartoon" in 1928. Disney was 26 years old, and he sold his car to finance the cartoon's sound track.

After some more short-animated-feature successes, Disney announced in 1934 that his studio would produce its first feature-length animated film, *Snow White and the Seven Dwarfs*. The film eventually cost Disney $2.25 million, more than MGM usually spent on a good musical. *Snow White* premiered December 21, 1937, at the Cathay Circle Theater in Hollywood. The film earned $8 million in its first release, and to date has earned Disney more than $40 million.[22]

Products in a store window capitalize on the popularity of the first feature-length animated film, *Snow White and the Seven Dwarfs* (1937).

Box office receipts sagged as the Depression settled into every aspect of America's economy. Facing bankruptcy, several theaters tried to buoy up their profits by adding Bingo games and cut-rate admissions. The one innovation that survived the '30s was the double feature: two movies for the price of one.

The Depression introduced one more factor into motion picture budgets: labor unions. Before the 1930s, most aspects of the movie business were not governed by union agreements. But in 1937, the National Labor Relations Board held an election that designated the Screen Actors Guild to bargain for wages, working conditions, and overtime. The Screen Writers Guild was certified in 1938 and the Screen Directors Guild soon afterward.

Unionization limited the moguls' power over the people who worked for them. The Screen Writers Guild, for instance, gained the authority to arbitrate screen credits. Previously, six or seven people might help write a screenplay only to have full screen credit given to the last writer on the picture. Before the Guild, many writers wrote scenarios for films on speculation. If the studio boss rejected the script, the writer wasn't paid. The Guild contract banned this type of speculative writing.

The studio owners were unhappy with the agreement — Jack Warner had once reportedly called screenwriters "schmucks with Underwoods" (Underwood was the name of a popular typewriter). So the owners tried to convince screenwriters not to certify the Guild. But the union agreements were approved anyway in the late 1930s, as the Depression ended and the studios once again prospered.

# The Golden Age and After

**W**ITH GLAMOROUS stars and exciting screenplays, supported by an eager pool of gifted directors, producers, and technical talent, plus an insatiable audience for its productions, the movie industry reached its apex in the late 1930s and early 1940s. The most successful studio in Hollywood was MGM, which attracted the best writers, directors, and actors. MGM concentrated on blockbusters, such as *The Great Ziegfeld, Mutiny on the Bounty, The Wizard of Oz*, and *Gone with the Wind*. Not only did *Gone with the Wind's* phenomenal success demonstrate the epic character that movies could provide, but the movie also was a technological breakthrough with its magnificent use of color.

As some of the nation's most talented actors, writers, and directors settled in Hollywood, the movies became a showcase for their skills — social drama, such as *Dead End* (1933) with Humphrey Bogart, *The Grapes of Wrath* starring Henry Fonda (1940), *Citizen Kane* created by Orson Welles (1941), and *The Best Years of Our Lives* (1946) starring Myrna Loy, Fredric March, and Dana Andrews; scary spectacles, such as *King Kong* (1933); the great Busby Berkeley musicals, such as *42nd Street* (1933); sophisticated comedies, such as *The Philadelphia Story* (1940), and slapstick ones, such as the "Road Pictures" of the '40s starring Bob Hope and Bing Crosby.

The movie business was so rich that even MGM's dominance didn't scare away the competition.

## The End of an Era

Before television arrived throughout the country in 1948, two other events of the late 1940s helped to reverse the prosperous movie bonanza that began in mid-1930: the hearings of the House Un-American Activities Committee and the 1948 U.S. Supreme Court decision in *United States* v. *Paramount Pictures, Inc., et al.*

*Gone with the Wind* won Academy Awards in 1939 for Best Picture, Best Actress (Vivien Leigh), and Best Supporting Actress (Hattie McDaniel). Clark Gable did not win; the Best Actor award went to Robert Donat in *Goodbye, Mr. Chips.*

**The House Hearings.** In October 1947, America was entering the Cold War. This was an era in which many public officials, government employees, and private citizens seemed preoccupied with the threat of communists and people they identified as "subversives." The House of Representatives' Committee on Un-American Activities, chaired by J. Parnell Thomas, summoned ten "unfriendly" witnesses from Hollywood to testify about their communist connections. (Unfriendly witnesses were people whom the committee classified as having participated at some time in the past in "un-American activities." This usually meant that the witness had been a member of a left-wing organization in the decade before World War II.) These eight screenwriters and two directors came to be known as the Hollywood Ten.

Why these ten were singled out is still debated today. Their 1930s labor activities are cited as one reason. Many of them had been involved in the formation of the Screen Writers Guild. Some of the Ten also had been members

In the late 1930s and early 1940s, spectaculars such as
"The Great Ziegfeld" (above) and "The Wizard of Oz"
(opposite) helped to make MGM the most successful
studio in Hollywood.

of liberal and left-wing political organizations. (See Impact/Profile, Dalton
Trumbo of the Hollywood Ten.) Another reason was that the screenwriters
were visible — an easy target that could quickly send a public message that no
one was exempt from the committee's scrutiny.

   The Ten's strategy was to appear before the committee as a group and to
avoid answering the direct question "Are you now or have you ever been a
member of the Communist party?" Instead, the Ten tried to make statements
that questioned the committee's authority to challenge their political beliefs.
A support committee of Hollywood luminaries, including Lauren Bacall and
Humphrey Bogart, flew to Washington to show their sympathies.

In a rancorous series of hearings, the committee rejected the Ten's testimony; they found themselves facing trial for contempt. All of them were sentenced to jail, and some were fined. By the end of November 1947, all of the Hollywood Ten had lost their jobs. Many more movie people would follow. In an article for the *Hollywood Review*, Hollywood Ten member Adrian Scott reported that 214 movie employees eventually were blacklisted, which meant that many studio owners refused to hire people who were suspected of taking part in subversive activities. The movie people who were not hired because of their political beliefs included 106 writers, 36 actors, and 11 directors.[23] This effectively gutted Hollywood of some of its best talent.

**This profile focuses on Dalton Trumbo, who was one of the most outspoken members of the Hollywood Ten.**

a S A screenwriter at MGM, Dalton Trumbo was earning $75,000 per script when he was called before the House Un-American Activities Committee in October 1947. Trumbo had written some very popular films, including *Thirty Seconds Over Tokyo* and *Kitty Foyle*. When he appeared before Congress, Trumbo represented the feelings of many movie people who felt unfairly singled out for their political activities. In 1948, Trumbo was cited for contempt of Congress. He was tried, convicted, and sentenced to pay a $1,000 fine and spend a year in jail.

When he was released, Trumbo found that the only way he could sell his scripts was to use a pseudonym. He also no longer commanded his previous salary. He wrote a friend: "It simply requires that I work three times as fast for about one-fifth of my former price."[24]

The King Brothers bought Trumbo's scripts. Writing under the name Robert Rich, Trumbo sold the King Brothers a screenplay called *The Boy and the Bull*, which eventually was produced as the movie *The Brave One*. In 1957, Robert Rich won an Academy Award for the screenplay, but at the ceremony no one accepted the prize.

In 1959, 12 years after Trumbo appeared before the committee, and two years after Robert Rich won an Academy Award, Kirk Douglas' production company hired Trumbo to write *Spartacus*, crediting Trumbo with the screenplay. Then Otto Preminger hired Trumbo in 1960 to write *Exodus*. The blacklist was broken, but many of Trumbo's blacklisted friends never worked in the movie industry again

Dalton Trumbo, 1905–1976

after they appeared before the committee. The only other member of the Hollywood Ten to achieve success in movies again was Ring Lardner, Jr., who won an Academy Award in 1970 for the screenplay *M*A*S*H*.

**United States v. Paramount Pictures.** The U.S. Justice Department began another antitrust suit against the studios in 1938, just as the government had sued the Motion Picture Patents Company in 1915. In 1940, the studios came to an agreement with the government, while admitting no guilt. They agreed to:

*1. Limit block booking to five films.*

*2. Stop **blind booking** (the practice of renting out films without showing them to the exhibitors first).*

*3. Stop requiring theaters to rent short films as a condition of acquiring features.*

*4. Stop buying theaters.*

After this agreement, the Justice Department dropped its suit with the stipulation that the department could reinstitute the suit again at any time.

By 1944, the government was still unhappy with studio control over the theaters, so they reactivated the suit. In 1948, *United States* v. *Paramount Pictures* reached the Supreme Court. Associate Justice William O. Douglas argued that although the five major studios—Paramount, Warner Bros., MGM-Loew's, RKO, and 20th Century-Fox—owned only 17 percent of all theaters in the United States, these studios did hold a monopoly over first-run exhibition in the large cities. By 1954, the five major production firms had divested themselves of ownership or control of all their theaters. Production and exhibition were now split. Vertical integration was crumbling.

When the movie companies abandoned the exhibition business, banks grew reluctant to finance film projects because the companies could not guarantee an audience—on paper. The studios had a choice: They could finance their own movies, or they could buy movies from independent producers that the studios would then distribute. Soon the studios decided to leave the production business to the independents and became primarily distributors of other peoples' pictures. The result was the end of the studio system.

# How TV Changed the Movie Industry

In the 1950 Paramount movie *Sunset Boulevard*, aging silent screen star Norma Desmond (played by Gloria Swanson) romances an ambitious young screenwriter (played by William Holden) by promising him Hollywood connections.

"You're Norma Desmond. You used to be in silent pictures. You used to be big," says the screenwriter.

"I *am* big," says Desmond. "It's the pictures that got small."

Desmond could have been talking about the picture business itself, which got much smaller after 1948, when nationwide television began to offer home-delivered entertainment.

The House hearings and the consent decrees in the Paramount case foretold change in the movie business, but television truly transformed Hollywood forever. The number of television sets in the 1950s grew by 400 percent, while the number of people who went to the movies fell by 45 percent.[25]

Theaters tried to make up for the loss by raising their admission prices, but more than 4,000 theaters closed from 1946 to 1956.[26] Attendance has leveled off or risen briefly a few times since the 1950s, but the trend of declining movie attendance continues today. The movie industry has tried several methods to counteract this downward trend.

**Wide-Screen and 3-D Movies.** Stunned by television's popularity, the movie business tried technological gimmicks in the 1950s to lure its audience back. First came 3-D movies. These movies used special effects to create the illusion of three-dimensional action. Rocks, for example, seemed to fly off the screen and into the audience. To see the 3-D movies, people wore special plastic glasses and the novelty was fun, but the 3-D movie plots were weak, and most people didn't come back to see a second 3-D movie.

Next came Cinerama, Cinemascope, VistaVision, and Panavision — wide-screen color movies with stereophonic sound. All of these techniques tried to give the audience a "you are there" feeling — something they couldn't get from television. Songwriter Cole Porter described the way Hollywood tried to attract an audience:

*Today to get the public to attend a picture show*
*It's not enough to advertise a famous star they know.*
*If you want to get the crowd to come around*
*You've got to have glorious Technicolor,*
*Breathtaking CinemaScope, and*
*stereophonic sound.*[27]

The new wide-screen theaters offered extravaganzas, such as *Spartacus* and *Ben-Hur*, and charged hefty admission prices, but the wide-screen theaters survived mainly in large cities. What could the movie people do? A Supreme Court decision prompted one answer.

**Changes in Movie Censorship.** On May 26, 1952, the Supreme Court announced in *Burstyn* v. *Wilson* that motion pictures were "a significant

In the 1950s moviemakers tried every technical trick they could, including 3-D, to lure audiences away from television and back into the theaters.

medium for the communication of ideas," which were designed "to entertain as well as to inform." The effect of this decision was to protect movies under the First Amendment. The result was fewer legal restrictions on what a movie could show. Until this ruling, movies were very tame by today's standards. The word *damn* was rarely uttered, and when married couples were shown in a bedroom, they were fully clothed in cotton pajamas and slept in twin beds. Sex was not a topic that was frankly discussed on the screen. A series of subsequent court decisions said that the only reason a movie could be banned was that it contained obscenity.

In 1953, Otto Preminger challenged the movies' self-regulating agency, the Production Code Administration (PCA). United Artists agreed to release Preminger's movie *The Moon Is Blue*, an adaptation of a successful Broadway play, even though the PCA would not give the movie a certificate of approval because it contained such risqué words as *virgin* and *mistress*. Then in 1956 United Artists released Preminger's *Man with the Golden Arm*, a film about drug addiction, and the PCA restrictions were forever broken.

Buoyed by the *Burstyn* decision and the United Artists test, moviemakers tried sex and violence to attract audiences away from television. In the 1950s, Marilyn Monroe and Jane Russell were generously proportioned examples of the new trend. Foreign films also became popular because some of them offered explicit dialogue and love scenes.

Marilyn Monroe and Jane Russell epitomize Hollywood's preoccupation with sultry beauty in the 1950s.

**Movie Spectactulars.** One by one the studio moguls retired, and they were replaced by a new generation of moviemakers. "They [the second generation] inherited a situation where fewer and fewer pictures were being made, and fewer still made money," says Robert Sklar, "but those that captured the box office earned enormous sums. It was as if the rules of baseball had been changed so that the only hit that mattered was a home run."[28]

Spectaculars like *The Sound of Music* (1965) and *The Godfather* (1971) and its sequels rewarded the rush for big money. But then a few majestic flops taught the studios that nothing can demolish a studio's profits like one big bomb.

**Movie Ratings.** In 1966, Jack Valenti, former presidential adviser to Lyndon Johnson, became president of the Motion Picture Producers Association, renamed the Motion Picture Association of America (MPAA). One of his first acts was to respond to continuing public criticism about shocking movie content.

The MPAA began a rating system modeled on Great Britain's: G for general audiences; M (later changed to PG) for mature audiences; R for restricted (people under 17 admitted only with an adult); and X for no one under 18 admitted. (Valenti still heads the MPAA as the lobbyist for the nation's major studios. The PG-13 — special parental guidance advised for children under 13 — has been added and the X rating has been changed to NC-17X.)

When two X-rated movies, *The Devil in Miss Jones* and *Deep Throat*, became box office hits in 1973, some movie companies responded by producing more X-rated movies. But soon the general public tired of explicit movie sex, and an X on a movie came to mean box office death. From 1968 to 1990, only 4 percent of the movies rated to be shown in U.S. theaters received an X rating.[29]

# The Movie Industry Today

i N TODAY'S system of moviemaking, each of the six major studios (Columbia, Paramount, 20th Century-Fox, MCA/Universal, Time Warner, and Walt Disney) usually makes less than 20 movies a year. The rest come from independent producers, with production, investment, distribution, and exhibition each handled by different companies. Most of these independently produced movies are distributed by one of the six large studios.

Today the dream merchants are aiming at a youthful group of buyers. Unlike the first movie audiences, which were primarily adults, nearly half the people who go to the movies today are under 25. So the biggest box office successes are movies that appeal to this younger audience: *Star Wars, Back to the Future, E. T.,* and *Teenage Mutant Ninja Turtles* were among the biggest successes of the last two decades. Woody Allen's films had wide appeal, and some "serious" feature films such as *Dead Poets Society* and *Dances with Wolves* succeeded, but films that chased the teen audience topped the box office list (see Industry Snapshot, page 228).

Today's movies are created by one group (the writers and producers), funded by another group (the investors), sold by a third group (the distributors), and shown by a fourth group (the exhibitors). No other mass media industry is so fragmented.

# How the Movie Industry Works

IN 1946, the movies' best year, American theaters collected more than 4 billion tickets. Today, although more people watch more movies on videocassettes, the number of theater admissions has dropped to about 1 billion.[30] Exhibitors feel that if they raise their admission prices, they'll lose more of their patrons. This is why exhibitors charge so much for refreshments, which is where they make 10 to 20 percent of their income. (One interesting finding from a theater exhibitor's study: People watching G-rated films spent 27 percent more on refreshments than people watching PG or R films.[31])

With declining audiences and fewer successful movies, the studios complain that they lose money on most of the pictures they underwrite. Producers say that the studios take exorbitant profits on the movies they distribute, which raises the cost of making movies for producers.

People in the movie business seem to make a habit of pointing fingers at each other. Says independent producer David V. Picker,

*The trouble with our business is that nobody trusts anybody in it. The distributor doesn't trust the exhibitor. The exhibitor doesn't trust the distributor. The producer doesn't trust the creator. The creator is sure the distributor is putting in invalid charges against his picture. The financier is positive that the creator has spent forty-five unnecessary days in shooting the picture. Despite all this, somehow or other, we wind up with films that people sometimes go to see.*[32]

Weakened by declining box office and fewer movies, the studios in the 1960s became attractive targets for conglomerates. Gulf + Western bought Paramount. Sony bought Columbia Pictures. Movies, like many other media, became part of corporate ownership, which means that stockholder loyalty comes first. These studios tend to choose safer projects and seek proven audience-pleasing ideas rather than take many risks.

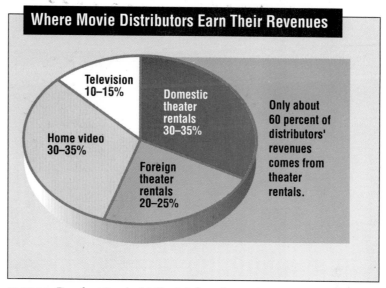

6.1 ▶

**Where Movie Distributors Earn Their Revenues**

Television 10–15%

Domestic theater rentals 30–35%

Home video 30–35%

Foreign theater rentals 20–25%

Only about 60 percent of distributors' revenues comes from theater rentals.

SOURCE: Data from Standard & Poor's *Industry Surveys*, March 14, 1991.

One way the movie industry collects predictable income is to make movies for television. Half of the movies produced every year are made for television and are underwritten by the networks.

Two important factors for the future funding of the movie industry are the sale of ancillary rights and the advances of new technology.

## Ancillary Rights

In 1950, a ticket to a movie cost about 50 cents. Today you can still see a movie for 50 cents if you rent a videocassette for $2.50 and invite four friends to join you at home to watch it. The explosion of videocassette rentals since the videocassette recorder was first marketed in 1976 is having a powerful effect on how the movie business operates today (see Figure 6.1). More than 70 percent of all homes in the United States have a VCR. The sale of movies for videocassettes is part of the **ancillary-rights market**.

The median cost to make a theatrical movie (as opposed to a made-for-television movie) is $30 million,[33] and only two out of ten theatrical movies make money.[34] "Some pictures make a lot of money," says David V. Picker, "and a lot of pictures make no money."[35] Before a theatrical movie starts

Videocassette sales and rentals form an important part of the economics of today's moviemaking.

shooting, the investors want to be sure they'll make their money back. Movie executive Gordon Stulberg describes how ancillary rights work:

> Today, on a picture costing $8 million, a large return on that investment is possible from nontheatrical distribution sources alone from the "ancillary rights." For instance, pay-television rights *can be sold for $850,000, based on 10 cents or more for each of the 8,500,000 or more pay-TV terminals available around the country. . . .* Network television sales . . . *can now pay as much as $10 million or more for two runs.*
>
> Television syndication rights *domestically and around the world have escalated over the years. After the syndicator is paid for selling the picture and residuals are paid to the people in the film, it's possible to produce net revenue against the picture of $300,000 to $800,000.*
>
> Sales to airlines *for showing in-flight can deliver between $60,000 and $150,000 per picture.* Navy sales, *covering one branch of the military, can produce from $25,000 to $60,000 in revenue.* Sixteen-millimeter *sales to colleges can be important, as well.* Little Big Man *grossed over $1 million in college rentals alone.*

Motion picture soundtrack albums and singles *can mean huge revenues. . . . There is also a lot of money to be made in the exploitation of* book-publishing *rights in the form of novelizations of screenplays, picture books, calendars, or reprints.* [36]

Movies also have been getting more commercialized in the sense that they are tied to products. And, products can be "advertised" by being included in a movie. A movie that can be exploited as a package of ancillary rights with commercial appeal is much more attractive to an investor than a movie with limited potential.

Often the only choice for a filmmaker who wants to make a film that doesn't have substantial ancillary-rights potential is to settle for a low budget. Joan Micklin Silver made her first movie, *Hester Street*, for $365,000. Her husband, Raphael D. Silver, a real estate investor who had never financed a film, raised the money.

Once the film was made, the Silvers distributed it themselves, opening in four cities and eventually spreading to 15. Then Carol Kane was nominated for an Academy Award for her role in the movie, and more theaters became interested.

Raphael Silver explains the difficulties of distributing a film outside of the studio distribution system:

*[T]he majors are opening their movies in ever-widening multiples, with more and more theatres sucked into these orbits. For certain peak periods when many movies are released, such as Christmas, Easter, and summer, there are rarely any theaters of quality available for independent product.*

*Majors may open their pictures in 300 to 1,500 theaters during these intense marketing periods. . . . [The theaters] become available to an independent only when a studio picture fails commercially. Even then, the major distributor will attempt to recycle an older picture offered as a fill-in at a very attractive price. The combination of all these factors is making it more difficult for independent films to find those little windows through which they can enter the market and secure public recognition.* [37]

# Technology

Today's technology affects three aspects of the movie business: production, distribution, and exhibition. There are several ways technology affects how movies are made today and how they will be shown in the future.

# Movies

## Industry Snapshot

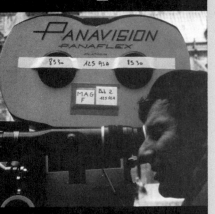

Today's movie-making is a high-stakes business dominated by major studios, which frequently target youthful audiences and capitalize on hit movies with sequels. But box office performance is only the beginning—increasingly, moviemakers depend on other sources of income, including video sales and rentals.

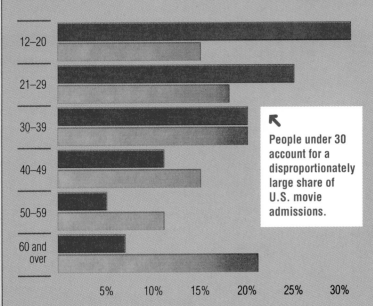

### Who Goes to the Movies?

U.S. movie admissions, by age group (1990)

■ Percentage of movie admissions
■ Percentage of U.S. population

| Age group |
|---|
| 12–20 |
| 21–29 |
| 30–39 |
| 40–49 |
| 50–59 |
| 60 and over |

5%  10%  15%  20%  25%  30%

People under 30 account for a disproportionately large share of U.S. movie admissions.

Data from Motion Picture Association, "Incidence of Motion Picture Attendance among the Adult and Teenage Public," July 1990.

**1** The American moviegoing audience is considerably younger than the population as a whole.

**2** Sequels illustrate a major trend in moviemaking—the studios' search for proven audience-pleasing ideas.

COMING SOON ... SEQUEL II

**③**

This list of movie blockbusters illustrates several trends: (1) all are lavishly produced fantasies that appeal to younger audiences; (2) all were distributed by a major studio; (3) all are relatively recent, reflecting the effects of higher ticket prices; (4) four are sequels; and (5) five were directed or produced by Steven Spielberg.

## What People Go to See: The All-Time Top Ten Moneymakers

Movie rentals* of all-time leading movies through December 1990 (U.S. and Canada)

| | | | |
|---|---|---|---|
| 1 | *E.T., The Extra-Terrestrial* | 1982, Universal | **$229 million** |
| 2 | *Star Wars* | 1977, Fox | **$194 million** |
| 3 | *Return of the Jedi* | 1983, Fox | **$168 million** |
| 4 | *Batman* | 1989, Warner | **$151 million** |
| 5 | *The Empire Strikes Back* | 1980, Fox | **$142 million** |
| 6 | *Ghostbusters* | 1984, Columbia | **$133 million** |
| 7 | *Jaws* | 1975, Universal | **$130 million** |
| 8 | *Raiders of the Lost Ark* | 1981, Paramount | **$116 million** |
| 9 | *Indiana Jones and the Last Crusade* | 1989, Paramount | **$116 million** |
| 10 | *Indiana Jones and the Temple of Doom* | 1984, Paramount | **$109 million** |

*Movie rentals are the share of box office revenues that theater owners pay to distributors.

Data from Standard & Poor's *Industry Surveys*, March 14, 1991.

## The VCR Boom: Bringing the Movies Home

U.S. consumer spending on videocassette sales and rentals versus movie box office receipts (millions of dollars)

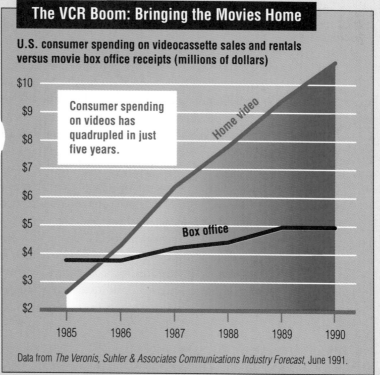

Consumer spending on videos has quadrupled in just five years.

Home video

Box office

Data from *The Veronis, Suhler & Associates Communications Industry Forecast*, June 1991.

**④**

First television, and then the VCR, changed the way Americans watch movies—and the way distributors earn profits. Today consumer spending on video sales and rentals far outstrips box office receipts.

Special effects, such as those used in *Terminator II*, can raise the cost of making a movie, cutting into profits. The budget for *Terminator II* was reported to be more than $50 million.

**Production.** Smaller portable cameras mean that a camera operator can move more easily throughout a crowd. New types of film mean that filmmakers can shoot more scenes at night and in dark places with less artificial lighting.

Most directors now videotape scenes as they film them and immediately play back the videotape to make sure they have the shot they want. Computer technology offers exciting special-effects possibilities. Filmmakers also are experimenting with the holograph, which uses lasers to make a computer-generated three-dimensional image from a flat picture.

In 1986, MGM began "colorizing" several classic black-and-white pre-1950s movies to make them "suitable for television." The 8,000-member Directors Guild condemned colorization as a classic example of unnecessary technological tinkering and a corruption of their art, but colorizing continues. Also, the ability to "digitize" color using computers means that the images in movies can be intensified, adjusted, and even totally transformed after the movie is shot in a way that was impossible even ten years ago.

**Distribution.** Reproducing copies of films to send to theaters and guaranteeing their arrival is one of the costliest aspects of moviemaking. In the future, companies will probably send their movies by satellite to satellite dishes on top of each theater. Live performances, such as a symphony concert or a major sports event, will probably be available regularly by satellite at your local theater.

**Exhibition.** With VCRs stealing the theater audience, theaters may return to creating the picture-palace environment that enchanted moviegoers in the 1930s. "The movie theatre will have to become an arena; a palace to experience the full grandeur and potential of the theatrical motion picture," says futurist and electronic technology consultant Martin Polon.[38]

Theaters may experiment with wraparound screens. They may add seats with vibrators underneath to give you the feeling of motion when movie characters ride a train or fly over the Grand Canyon. Computerized equipment could circulate scents through the theater's ventilation system to help you smell what you're seeing.

The result, says Polon, "would be to experience a motion picture. If the movie has a scene on the docks of London, the seating would move just perceptibly, while the sound supplies suitable creaks. The smell of ocean and a cool touch of water vapor would complete the illusion given by the multi-channel sound and wide picture."[39]

# Facing the Future

Today's movie industry is undergoing two major changes. One recent trend in the movie business is global ownership and global marketing. The second trend is the merging of the movie industry with the television industry.

**Global Influence.** Foreign companies own half of the major studios (Matsushita bought MCA/Universal, Sony owns Columbia Pictures, and Rupert Murdoch's News Corporation owns 20th Century-Fox). These foreign acquisitions all have happened within the last five years. This percentage of foreign ownership is higher in the movie industry than in any other American media business (see Figure 6.2).

Foreign ownership means easier access to foreign markets. American motion pictures are one of America's strongest exports, and income from foreign sales accounts for more than one-third of the movie industry's profits. "If Hollywood has learned anything the past few years," says *Business Week*, "it's that the whole

Academy members often are targeted by filmmakers, who hope to gather votes for their movies. In this ad from *Variety*, the movie community's widely-read publication, The Swiss Film Center invites academy members to special viewings of the Swiss nominee for Best Foreign Film.

## Who's Who in Hollywood

### The Big Six Movie Studios

| Studio | Parent Company | Country | Other Interests | Estimated 1990 Revenues |
|---|---|---|---|---|
| MCA/ Universal | Matsushita | Japan | MCA Records, Universal Studio tours, movie theaters, broadcast equipment | $51 billion |
| Sony Pictures Entertainment * | Sony | Japan | Electronics, CBS Records | $27.1 billion |
| Warner Bros. | Time Warner | U.S. | HBO, cable systems, magazines, records, books | $11.3 billion |
| 20th Century-Fox | News Corp. | Australia | Fox network, TV stations | $6.6 billion |
| Walt Disney | Disney | U.S. | Theme parks, cable network | $5.7 billion |
| Paramount | Paramount Communications | U.S. | TV stations, movie theaters, cable networks | $3.7 billion |

*Formerly Columbia Pictures

SOURCE: Data from *Los Angeles Times*, Nov. 27, 1990, and *The Sacramento Bee*, Oct. 22, 1990.

world is hungry for the latest it has to offer."[40] (See Impact/Perspective, Hollywood Spending Spree Sees Salaries and Budgets Soar.)

**Merging with Television.** Today, people in the television business are buying pieces of the movie business. And people in the movie business want to align themselves with television companies. The Federal Communications Commission prohibits the networks from making and syndicating their own programs. But this could change soon, as the networks look for other sources of revenue and pressure the FCC to let them enter the movie business.

The result *could* be consolidated companies that would finance movies, make movies, and show those movies in their own theaters, on their own television stations, and on videocassette. By controlling all aspects of the business, a company would have a better chance to collect a profit on the movies it makes. Sound familiar? The studios held this type of controlling interest in their movies before the 1948 consent decrees.

The studios' latest hope is that the 1948 consent decrees will be rescinded so they can once again control production, distribution, and exhibition.[41] Reports *The Wall Street Journal*, "The more aggressive players, some industry experts believe, could build concentrations of market power surpassing that enjoyed by the movie studios in the late 1930s and the 1940s — with severe consequences for weaker competitors."[42] Today's major studios are trying to become again what they once were: a mature oligopoly in the business of dreams.

# Hollywood Spending Spree Sees Salaries and Budgets Soar

**In this article, *New York Times* reporter Geraldine Fabrikant says that bidding wars for Hollywood's top talent are transforming the economics of the movie industry.**

WHILE MANY American industries are retrenching in the face of a recession, Hollywood is on a spending spree. The studios are paying unprecedented prices for scripts, stars, directors and other talent required to produce feature films.

The theatrical, video and pay television businesses have exploded abroad, setting off bidding wars among the studios for the handful of talent believed to have the greatest global appeal.

Artists involved in action films, which consistently play well worldwide, have seen the most spectacular increases. And rates like the following are beginning to serve as benchmarks for the entire industry:

• *"The Godfather, Part III,"* which stars Al Pacino, . . . cost Paramount Pictures at least $55 million.

• *Arnold Schwarzenegger was paid $10 million for starring in "Total Recall" and will earn $12 million from Carolco Pictures for "The Terminator II."*

• *Screenwriter Shane Black earned less than $750,000 for "Lethal Weapon," one industry executive said, but he received $1.7 million from Warner Brothers for his latest script, "The Last Boy Scout."*

• *Screenwriter Joe Esterhaus received $3 million for a screenplay*

This latest trend toward consolidation worries veteran filmmaker Mel Brooks:

*As for the future of the business, I see bigger profits on fewer pictures. It's a thrilling business, but it's sad to think that we're making a third of the movies we made 20 years ago. The new home entertainment technology scares me more than anything, because I want an audience to laugh at my movies. I want people to sit in a dark theater, let the silver screen bathe them with images, and have them laugh as a group.*

*It's thrilling to hear a lot of people laughing together. But with the direction of current technology, it seems we'll have tiny little groups at home, or sometimes even one*

for Carolco Pictures' "Basic Instinct," and Irwin Winkler earned $1 million to produce the film, even though both left the project by mutual agreement shortly after production began.

Though there are myriad reasons behind the rise in fees, many Hollywood executives seem to agree that Carolco Pictures, a small Hollywood studio, is partly responsible.

In the last few years, Carolco has carved out a niche making big-budget films with international appeal at a time when foreign markets were growing rapidly. It paid actors like Sylvester Stallone, Schwarzenegger and Mel Gibson enormous fees, recouping its investment by selling the films around the world.

Now, other studios have difficulty hiring these actors for substantially less money, even to appear in films in other genres like comedy that do not travel as well abroad.

And once the fees of actors increase, so do those of the other artists working on their films. Technical experts like cameramen and editors can charge more.

"It is an industry where everyone looks at what everyone else makes," said Tom Hansen, an entertainment lawyer at Hansen, Jacobson & Teller in Los Angeles. "That creates a type of momentum." . . .

As one top executive at a major studio put it: "It's like a herd of elephants going down Main Street with each one's

trunk hooked into the next one's tail. What they don't know is that the lead elephant is blind and has no idea what he's doing." . . .

*New York Times News Source,* Dec. 23, 1990.

IMPACT/
PERSPECTIVE

*skinny person watching a big fat Mel Brooks movie. You can't get a lot of laughs that way. I wasn't born to make one thin person laugh; I was born to make a lot of fat and skinny people sit in the dark together and laugh.* [43]

**IN FOCUS**

**The Movie Industry**

• Eadweard Muybridge and Thomas Edison were the two Americans who contributed the most to the creation of the movies. Muybridge demonstrated how to photograph motion and Edison developed a projector, the kinetoscope. Edison also organized the Motion Picture Patents Company (MPPC) to control movie distribution.

• French filmmaker Georges Méliès envisioned movies as a medium of fantasy. Edwin S. Porter assembled scenes to tell a story. D. W. Griffith mastered the full-length movie.

• The practice of block booking, led by Adolph Zukor, obligated movie houses to accept several movies at once, usually without previewing them first.

• Biograph became the first studio to make movies using what was called the studio system. This system put the studio's stars under exclusive contract, and the contract could not be broken without an employer's permission.

• The formation of United Artists by Mary Pickford, Charlie Chaplin, Douglas Fairbanks, and D. W. Griffith was a rebellion against the big studios because UA distributed films for independent filmmakers.

• In the 1920s the movie industry faced two new crises: scandals involving movie stars and criticism that movie content was growing too explicit. The movie industry responded by forming the Motion Picture Producers and Distributors Association (MPPDA), under the direction of Will Hays.

• As the studio system developed, the five largest Hollywood studios were able to control production, distribution, and exhibition. In the 1930s, labor unions challenged studio control and won some concessions.

• The movies' golden age was the 1930s and the 1940s, supported by the studio system and an eager audience.

• Three factors caused Hollywood's crash in the 1950s: the House Un-American Activities Committee hearings; the U.S. Justice Department's antitrust action against the studios; and television.

• Hollywood tried to lure audiences back with technological gimmicks and sultry starlets, but these efforts did not work very well. Today the number of theatergoers continues to decline, although videocassette sales and rentals have added to movie industry income; nearly half the moviegoers are under 25.

• Today's movie ratings system began in 1966, supervised by the Motion Picture Association of America (MPAA). Very few movies actually receive the most explicit (NC-17X) rating.

• The median cost to make a movie today is $30 million, and two out of ten theatrical movies make money. Most movies are funded in part by ancillary-rights sales. Thus, most movies are sold as packages, with all their potential media outlets underwriting a movie before it goes into production. This makes independent filmmaking difficult.

• Foreign corporations own half of the major movie studios. This is a higher percentage of foreign ownership than in any other media industry.

• American movies are a major U.S. export; foreign sales account for more than one-third of movie industry income.

• In the future, the movie industry and the television industry may align themselves more closely, which eventually would mean that one company could control all aspects of moviemaking.

*"Popular music is like a unicorn,"* writes R. Serge Denisoff *in his book* Solid Gold. *"Everyone knows what it is supposed to look like, but no one has ever seen it."*[1] *More than half the recordings sold every year in the United States are categorized as popular music.*

*If the average person buys four recordings a year, as the Recording Industry Association reports, popular music is recorded on two of them. Other types of music — country, gospel, classical, show tunes, jazz, and children's recordings — make up the other half, but most of the big*

**The Recording Industry**

A 1913 recording session of Indian songs.

profits and losses in the recording business result from the mercurial fury of popular music.

Like the radio and television industries, the recording industry is challenged by rapidly changing technology. And, like the movie industry during the first half of this century, the recording industry is at the center of recent debates over the protection of free artistic expression versus the industry's perceived effect on moral values.

# Edison's Amazing Talking Machine: How Records Began

TODAY'S RECORDING industry would not exist without Thomas Edison's invention more than a century ago of what he called a phonograph (which means "sound writer"). In 1877, *Scientific American* reported Thomas Edison's first demonstration of his phonograph. Edison's chief mechanic had constructed the machine from an Edison sketch that came with a note reading "Build this."

An early ad shows a phonograph, complete with a case that contained cylinders and a picture of Thomas Edison.

*When the machine was brought to Edison, the inventor wrapped a piece of tinfoil around the cylinder, adjusted the recording diaphragm, turned the crank, and shouted against the diaphragm the nursery rhyme "Mary Had a Little Lamb." He then reversed the cylinder until it moved back to its starting point, adjusted the reproducing diaphragm, and turned the crank again.*

*To everyone's utter astonishment, so the story goes, the words spoken by Edison came back with clearness and fidelity. Even Edison, who had every reason to expect this result, later wrote, "I was never so taken aback in my life. I was always afraid of things that worked the first time."*[2]

In 1887, Emile Berliner developed the gramophone, which replaced Edison's cylinder with flat discs. Berliner and Eldrige Johnson formed the Victor Talking Machine Company (later to become RCA Victor) and sold recordings of opera star Enrico Caruso. Edison and Victor proposed competing technologies as the standard for the industry, and eventually the Victor disc won. Early players required large horns to amplify the sound. Later the horn was housed in a cabinet below the actual player, which made the machine a large piece of furniture.

In 1925, Joseph Maxfield perfected the equipment to eliminate the tinny sound of early recordings. The first jukeboxes were manufactured in 1927 and brought music into restaurants and nightclubs.

By the end of World War II, 78 rpm (revolutions per minute) records were standard. Each song was on a separate recording, and "albums" in today's sense did not exist. An album in the 1940s consisted of a bound set of ten envelopes about the size of a photo album. Each record, with one song recorded on each side, fit in one envelope. (This is how today's collected recordings got the title "album" even though they are no longer assembled in this cumbersome way.) These recordings featured the era's popular musicians, opera stars, and orchestras. Each shellac hard disc recording ran 3 minutes. Peter Goldmark, working for Columbia Records (which was owned by CBS), changed that.

In 1947, Goldmark was listening with friends to Brahms' Second Piano Concerto played by pianist Vladimir Horowitz and led by the world-famous conductor Arturo Toscanini. The lengthy concerto had been recorded on six records, 12 sides. Goldmark hated the interruptions in the music every time a record had to be turned over. He also winced at the eight sound defects he detected.

"He asked his friends to play the records again," reports Robert Metz in his book *CBS: Reflections in a Bloodshot Eye*, "and while they did so, he sat gritting his teeth and racking his brain. Finally he produced a ruler and started calculating, counting 80 grooves to the inch, and he began pondering the principle of the phonograph. . . . He concluded that he could get more mileage by slowing the turntable speed while crowding significantly more grooves onto a disk."[3] The result, after several refinements and the approval of CBS's William Paley, was the long-playing (LP) record, which could play for 23 minutes.

Paley realized, however, that he was taking a big risk by introducing this product when most people didn't own a record player that could play the bigger 33⅓ rpm LP records at the slower speed. While the LP record was being developed, Paley decided to call RCA executive David Sarnoff, since RCA made record players, to convince Sarnoff to form a partnership with CBS to manufacture LPs.

Sarnoff arrived in Paley's office accompanied by eight engineers. Peter Goldmark explained what happened next:

*Paley stepped forward and smoothly explained that I [Goldmark] would first be playing an ordinary seventy-eight and then I would follow it with the CBS invention. I could see Sarnoff stiffen and become attentive. I played the seventy-eight for about fifteen seconds and then switched over to the new record.*

*With the first few bars Sarnoff was out of his chair. I played it for ten seconds and then switched back to the seventy-eight. The effect was electrifying, as we knew it would be. I never saw eight engineers look so much like carbon copies of tight-lipped gloom. Turning to Paley, Sarnoff said loudly and with some emotion: "I want to congratulate you and your people, Bill. It is very good."*

In the 1940s and 1950s consumers faced confusing choices between David Sarnoff's 45 rpm records and William Paley's 33⅓ rpm records. These two types of records required different players.

*. . . I later learned what happened after the group returned to RCA headquarters. Sarnoff, who had been so affable and congratulatory, had gone into what could only be described as an executive tantrum. How could little CBS, with a two-by-four labora-tory, beat RCA? . . . A few days later, Sarnoff phoned Paley to say that he had decided not to come in with us on the record.*[4]

Sarnoff was angry because RCA already had decided to manufacture 7-inch 45 rpm records, which played for 4 minutes. Stubbornly, Sarnoff introduced his new record in 1948. Forty-fives had a quarter-size hole in the middle and required a different record player, which RCA started to manufacture.

Forty-fives were a perfect size for jukeboxes, but record sales slowed as the public tried to figure out what was happening. "General Sarnoff was foolish to refuse Paley's offer of a license [to manufacture LPs]," says Robert Metz. "When Sarnoff decided to fight against Columbia's superior system he was guilty — and not for the first time — of allowing pride to triumph over good sense."[5]

Eventually Toscanini convinced Sarnoff to manufacture LPs and to include the 33⅓ speed on RCA record players to accommodate classical-length recordings. CBS, in turn, agreed to use 45s for its popular songs. Later, players were developed that could play all three speeds (33⅓, 45, and 78 rpm).

# Hi-Fi and Stereo Rock In

**a**S DISCUSSED in Chapter 4, the introduction of rock 'n' roll redefined the concept of popular music in the 1950s. Contributing to the success of popular entertainers like Elvis Presley were the improvements in recorded sound quality that originated with the recording industry. First came *high fidelity*, developed by London Records, a subsidiary of Decca.

*The new "hi-fi" recordings also created a new type of record collector, one interested in precise and authentic sound reproduction.*

*To serve that new collector, an entirely new industry arose to engineer turntables without rumbles, amplifiers without noise, and speakers with a fuller, more realistic sound range. The hi-fi collector preferred good recordings of boat whistles, passing trains, or even geese in flight to the muddy music of the old 78s.[6]*

Tape recorders grew out of German experiments during World War II. European radio stations were playing recorded tapes as early as 1941. Ampex Corporation built a high-quality tape recorder, and Minnesota Mining and Manufacturing (3M) perfected the plastic tape. Tape meant that recordings could be edited and refined, something that couldn't be done on discs.

Stereo arrived in 1956, and soon afterward came groups like the Supremes with the Motown sound, which featured the music of African-American blues and rock 'n' roll artists. At the same time, the FCC approved "multiplex" radio broadcasts so that monaural and stereo could be heard on the same stations. The development of condenser microphones helped bring truer sound.

In the 1960s, miniaturization resulted from the transistor. Eventually the market was overwhelmed with tape players smaller than a deck of playing

Improvements in recorded sound quality in the 1950s contributed to the success of rock 'n' roll entertainers like Elvis Presley.

cards. Quadraphonic (four-track) and eight-track tapes seemed ready to become the standard in the 1970s, but cassette tapes proved more adaptable and less expensive. In 1979, Sony introduced the Walkman as a personal stereo. (Although the company is Japanese, the name Sony comes from the Latin *sonus* for sound and *sunny* for optimism.) Walkmans were an ironic throwback to the early radio crystal sets, which also required earphones.

Today's compact discs promise crystal sound, transforming music into digital code on a 4.7-inch plastic-and-aluminum disc read by lasers. When introduced in 1982, players sold for $1,000 and discs cost $20, but today the players cost less than $150, and the discs have dropped to $10.

Discs last longer than records and cassettes, and they can play for as long as 74 minutes, twice the playing time for LPs. Disc sales approached $3 billion in 1990. "It took VCRs seven years to get to the point where we got in just two years," said Leslie Rosen, executive director of the Compact Disc Group.[7] Music videos and the cable TV music channel MTV expanded the audience and the potential income for featured artists.

# How the Recording Industry Works

**R**ECORDINGS, LIKE books, are supported primarily by direct purchases. But a recording company involves five separate levels of responsibility before the public hears a sound: artists and repertoire, operations, marketing and promotion, distribution, and administration.

*Artists and repertoire*, or A & R, functions like a book editor — to develop and coordinate talent. Employees of this division are the true talent scouts.

*Operations* manages the technical aspects of the recording, overseeing the sound technicians, musicians, even the people who copy the discs. This work centers on creating the master recording, from which all other recordings are made. Before stereophonic recording was developed in 1956, a recording session meant gathering all the musicians in one room, setting up a group of microphones, and recording a song in one take. Today, artists on the same song — vocals, drums, bass, horns, guitars — are recorded individually, and then the separate performances are *mixed* for the best sound.

The producer, who works within the operations group, can be on the staff of a recording company or an independent freelancer. Producers coordinate the artist with the music, the arrangement, and the engineers.

*Marketing and promotion* decides the best way to sell the record. These employees oversee the cover design and the copy on the cover (jacket or sleeve). They also organize giveaways to retailers and to reviewers to find an audience for their product. Marketing and promotion might decide that the artist should tour or that the record needs a music video to succeed. Recording companies often use promoters to help guarantee radio play for their artists. This has led to abuses (see Payola, pages 134, 251, and 252–253).

*Distribution* gets the record in the stores. There are two kinds of distributors: independents and branches. Independents contract separately with different companies to deliver their recordings. But independents, usually responsible for discovering a record that is outside of the mainstream, are disappearing as the big studios handle distribution through their own companies, called branches. Because branches are connected with the major companies, they typically can offer the retailer better discounts.

*Administration*, as in all industries, handles the bills. Accounting tracks sales and royalties. Legal departments handle wrangles over contracts.

All of these steps are important in the creation of a recording, but if no one hears the recording, no one will buy it. This makes record promotion particularly important. RCA, for example, stuffed flyers in the Eurythmics' second album for a $1 refund on the group's first record. To promote Jefferson Starship's album *Nuclear Furniture*, RCA organized a contest that featured the winner in Starship's next music video. *Nuclear Furniture* went gold.[8]

To recoup investments, record companies often promote unknown acts heavily. To encourage air play for "See You in Hell" by Grim Reaper, RCA ran ads offering consumers cardboard discs with a 5-minute cut from the record. "For the fledgling band Autograph," reported *The Wall Street Journal*, "RCA teamed up with the Paper Mate division of Gillette Company. Paper Mate furnished RCA with thousands of its new Sharpwriter pencils to hand out at concerts and paid $60,000 to produce the music video *Sign In Please*. In return, the pencil was accorded a starring role in the video."[9]

# The Recording Industry Today

ABOUT 5,000 companies in the United States produce records and tapes. These companies ship about 800 million records, cassettes, and compact discs each year and collect over $7 billion. The biggest recording-industry profits are divided among the six major labels: Sony (formerly CBS Records), Time Warner, Phillips (Polygram), Thorn/EMI, Bertelsmann (RCA), and Matsushita (MCA) (see Figure 7.1). The main recording centers are Los Angeles, New York, and Nashville, but most large cities have at least one recording studio to handle local productions.

The recording industry, primarily concentrated in large corporations, generally chooses to record what has succeeded before. "Increasingly, the big record companies are concentrating their resources behind fewer acts," reports *The Wall Street Journal*, "believing that it is easier to succeed with a handful of blockbuster hits than with a slew of moderate sellers. One result is that fewer records are produced."[10]

Most radio formats today depend on popular music, and these recordings depend on radio to succeed. The main measurement of what is popular is

## The Music Industry's Big Six

| | Company | Country | Leading Artists | 1990 Worldwide Music Sales* |
|---|---|---|---|---|
| 1 | Sony | Japan | New Kids on the Block, Michael Jackson, Bruce Springsteen | $3.6 billion |
| 2 | Philip's (Polygram) | Netherlands | Def Leppard, John Bon Jovi, Janet Jackson | $3.1 billion |
| 3 | Time Warner | United States | Phil Collins, Mötley Crüe, Tracy Chapman | $2.9 billion |
| 4 | Bertelsmann (RCA) | Germany | Whitney Houston, Kenny G, Taylor Dayne | $2.1 billion |
| 5 | Thorn/EMI | United Kingdom | M.C. Hammer, Vanilla Ice, Pink Floyd | $2.0 billion |
| 6 | Matsushita (MCA) | Japan | Guns N' Roses, Bell Biv DeVoe, Bobby Brown | $550 million |

*Some totals include music publishing and contributions from other areas, such as videos.

SOURCE: Data from Standard & Poor's *Industry Surveys*, March 14, 1991.

*Billboard*, the music industry's leading trade magazine. *Billboard* began printing a list of the most popular vaudeville songs and the best-selling sheet music in 1913. In 1940, the magazine began publishing a list of the country's top-selling records.

Today, *Billboard* offers more than two dozen charts that measure, for example, air play and album sales as well as the sale of singles. Elvis Presley has had 149 records on the charts, and 20 Beatles hits reached No. 1. Since 1955, only four singles stayed at No. 1 for ten weeks or more ("Don't Be Cruel" and "Hound Dog," a double-sided hit by Elvis Presley; "Singing the Blues" by Guy Mitchell; Olivia Newton-John's "Physical"; and "You Light Up My Life" by

Debby Boone).[11] Radio, governed by ratings and what the public demands, tends to play proven artists. For an overview of the recording industry today, see Industry Snapshot, page 258.

## Money Matters

The industry collects income from direct sales and from music licensing.

**Direct Sales.** The promotional tour once was the major way a company sold records. But in the 1980s, music videos became very visible promotion for an artist. This shift changed the industry's economics. Paula Abdul and Janet Jackson are attractive to record companies because they are recording artists who also can perform well in videos.

*It is now virtually impossible for an LP to succeed without the exposure that a video can generate. So promoting a record these days requires not only the extra expense of producing a video but also the complications of battling others for air time on the cable channel Music Television (MTV) and on other video-oriented programs over network and cable TV.*[12]

**Music Licensing.** For the first 30 years of commercial radio, one of the reasons broadcasters used live entertainment was to avoid paying royalties to the record companies. Today two licensing agencies handle the rights to play music for broadcast: the American Society of Composers, Authors and Publishers (ASCAP) and Broadcast Music Inc. (BMI).

ASCAP, founded in 1914, was the first licensing organization. As noted in Chapter 4, in the 1920s ASCAP sued radio stations that were playing recorded music. Eventually some radio stations agreed to pay ASCAP royalties through a blanket licensing agreement, which meant that each station that paid ASCAP's fee could play any music that ASCAP licensed.

Throughout the 1930s, ASCAP fees increased. In 1930, ASCAP collected $800,000; in 1937, $2.7 million; and in 1939, $4.15 million.[13] Most stations refused to pay ASCAP because the stations didn't have any money. These stations agreed to explore the idea of forming a separate organization so they could license the music themselves.

In 1939, the broadcasters came together to establish a $1.5 million fund to build their own music collection through BMI (see page 133). ASCAP and BMI became competitors — ASCAP as a privately owned organization and BMI as an industry-approved cooperative. BMI used the same blanket licensing

The public and private lives of recording artists like Madonna focus attention on the recording industry.

agreement, collecting payments from broadcasters and dividing royalties among its artists. ASCAP licensed the majority of older hits, but rhythm and blues and rock 'n' roll gravitated toward BMI.

Today, most broadcasters subscribe to both BMI and ASCAP. They also agree to play only licensed artists, which makes getting on the air more difficult for new talent. ASCAP collects 67 percent of royalties and BMI collects 32 percent of the total royalties paid each year.[14] (Six smaller music licensing groups collect the remaining 1 percent.) BMI and ASCAP in turn pay the authors, recording artists, producers, sometimes even the recording companies — whoever owns the rights to use the music.

Recording industry income has received a boost from the higher prices consumers pay for CDs; prices of cassettes also have been edging upward. Growth in the actual number of recordings sold is much slower. (For industry sales income, see Figure 7.2.)

7.2 ➤

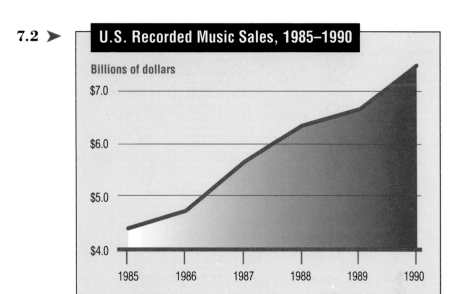

**U.S. Recorded Music Sales, 1985–1990**

Billions of dollars

SOURCE: Data from *The Veronis, Suhler & Associates Communications Industry Forecast*, June 1991.

## Moral Matters

Four major issues face today's recording industry: piracy, payola, attempts to control the content of recordings, and the authenticity of artists' performances.

**Piracy.** The recording industry loses substantial income when people make their own tapes. The Japan Phonograph Record Association estimates that cassette-recorder owners make 8 billion illegal copies of records and CDs every year.[15] To counteract this practice, recording companies have proposed that the federal government tax blank cassettes to fund royalties for artists.

A more threatening type of piracy for the industry is overseas copying of prerecorded cassettes that are then sold in the United States. Pirates control 18 percent of tape and album sales; the recording industry estimates this represents $1.5 billion a year in lost royalties.[16]

**Payola.** In 1960, congressional hearings into charges of payola centered on disc jockeys who collected fees and favors to play certain records (the word *payola* is a contraction of *pay* and *Victrola*, the trademark of the Victor Talking Machine Company). In 1974, payola allegations against rhythm and blues disc jockeys caused several radio station employees to resign. The issue surfaced

# The Roots of Payola

In this excerpt from his 1990 book *Hit Men*, author **Fredric Dannen** says that payola in the music business began as early as the 1940s. Enforcement of laws against payola, he says, was "fairly toothless."

"PAYOLA" IS a word the record industry has bestowed on the English language. The term's familiarity has led to a common perception — unfortunately true — that the business is full of sharpies and opportunists and crooks. But as crimes go, payola is no big deal if the government's enforcement effort is an indication. After [Alan] Freed's commercial bribery bust in 1960 [see page 135] and congressional hearings on payola the same year, Congress passed a statute making payola a misdemeanor offense punishable by a maximum fine of $10,000 and one year in prison. To date, no one has ever served a day in jail on payola charges. The law is hardly a strong deterrent. . . .

Even the commercial bribery laws were fairly toothless. . . . The legions of radio people and record executives called before the congressional payola hearings of 1960 made a mockery of the law's ambiguity. Unless it could be shown that they took money to play specific records, there was no illegality. So no one disputed receiving cash and gifts, just what the boodle was for. It magically turned into thank-you money. Thanks for giving my little ol' record a spin, pal — even though I never asked you to.

The men who presided over the hearings were not bowled over by the logic of this explanation. It drove some of them to sarcasm. One congressman demanded of a record executive, "Is it not a fact that these payments were payola up until the time that this investigation started? Then suddenly they became appreciation payments or listening fees or something else?"

Rock historians like to gripe that the hearings were an attack on rock and roll. Maybe they were. But the congressmen heard expert testimony that payola could be traced back at least to 1947, when the record business began to take off. It even existed in the Big Band era. "It was customary for the song plugger to walk up to a [band leader] and slip him an envelope with some money in it," one witness testified. No doubt some politicians believed that were it not for payola, radio would be playing Frank Sinatra and Dinah Shore. . . . "Do you think without payola that a lot of this so-called junk music, rock and roll stuff, which appeals to teenagers would not be played?" one congressman demanded of a disc jockey. "Never get on the air," came the solemn reply. . . .

*From* Hit Men *(New York: Times Books, 1990), pp. 44–46.*

again in 1984, when a congressional committee investigated charges of payola, but the committee said they could find no abuses. (See Impact/Perspective, The Roots of Payola.)

In 1985, a new set of payola charges arose. *The New York Times* reported,

*According to sources in the music and broadcasting industries, record manufacturers are paying more than $50 million a year to a small group of freelance record promoters around the country to get public exposure for their records and have them listed among the top hits of the week on trade newspaper charts.*

*Much of the $50 million is spent legitimately, according to radio and record industry sources, but a sizable portion — nobody knows how much — goes for under-the-table payments to program directors and other executives at key radio stations in some cities.*[17]

The accusations centered on independent promoters, not people on record company payrolls. These promoters concentrated primarily on Top 40 stations, because those playlists are limited to 40 or fewer current songs, which are played several times a day. The cost of ethically promoting one top-20 hit today ranges from $150,000 to $250,000.[18] In 1986, the six major record companies reported that they had suspended several independent promoters. Payola allegations again surfaced in 1990, but no arrests were made.

**Content of Recordings.** In 1985, the Parents Music Resource Center (PMRC) called for recording companies to label their records for explicit content. The new group was made up primarily of the wives of several national political leaders, notably Susan Baker, wife of Treasury Secretary James A. Baker III, and Tipper Gore, wife of Senator Albert Gore of Tennessee.

Saying that records come under the umbrella of consumer protection, the PMRC approached the National Association of Broadcasters and the Federal Communications Commission with their complaints. "After equating rock music with the evils of 'broken homes' and 'abusive parents,' and labeling it a 'contributing factor' in teen pregnancy and suicide, they single[d] out Madonna, Michael Jackson, Motley Crue, Prince, Sheena Easton, Twisted Sister, and Cyndi Lauper for their 'destructive influence' on children," reported Louis P. Sheinfeld, who teaches journalism law at New York University.[19] (See Impact/Perspective, Do Rock Lyrics Affect You?)

The result was that beginning in January 1986, the Recording Industry Association (whose member record companies account for 80 percent of U.S. record sales) officially urged its members to provide either a warning label or to print lyrics on record albums with potentially offensive content. Cassettes and CDs must carry the words "See LP for Lyrics." Like the movie industry when it adopted its own ratings system (see page 222), the recording industry favored self-regulation rather than government intervention.

# Do Rock Lyrics Affect You?

This article by **Randy Lewis**, which originally appeared in the *Los Angeles Times*, describes the current debate over the lyrical content of today's recordings.

THE GOOD news for parents is that song lyrics about sex, drugs, violence and Satanism have little impact on the vast majority of teenagers.

The bad news for educators is that most teenagers cannot accurately describe their favorite songs, suggesting that they are seriously lacking in literary skills to understand and interpret metaphors and symbolism.

Those are the conclusions reached by two California State University, Fullerton, researchers who surveyed nearly 300 Southern California junior high and high school students.

Preliminary results from a 40-page questionnaire administered . . . in four Southern California public and private schools are contained in a paper titled "Sex, Violence and Rock 'n' Roll: Youths' Perceptions of Popular Music."

"One thing that struck us with all the hearings in Congress and media attention on lyrics is that nobody asked teenagers what they think," said Lorraine Prinsky, a Cal State sociology professor who conducted the study with Jill Rosenbaum, an assistant professor of criminal justice.

In the questionnaire, teens were asked to name three favorite songs and give a brief description of what each is about.

Among the key findings:

• *Of 662 songs students listed as their favorites, only 7 percent were perceived by those students as being about sex, violence, drugs or Satanism.*

• The most popular single topic was love — at *26 percent — while the "other" category, which included songs about politics, growing up, life's struggles and other subjects, accounted for 34 percent of the songs described.*

• Students were unable to explain *37 percent of the songs they named as their favorites.*

"Even with the songs they are exposed to the most and listen to the most, they do not automatically pick up on all the messages," Rosenbaum said.

Led Zeppelin's "Stairway to Heaven," for instance, was often interpreted literally as being about "climbing stairs on the way to heaven."

(Other more widely accepted interpretations are that it is a drug or sex song — the stairway being the chemical or sexual "rush.")

Those who named Bruce Springsteen's "Born in the U.S.A." as one of their favorite songs offered interpretations ranging from "It's about life in the U.S.A." to the belief that it refers to "the town Bruce Springsteen lives in."

("Born in the U.S.A." is a blue-collar look at America — of being swept along with the tide with little or no control over your life. If you're born poor, you stay poor; not much

of a chance for kids from small industrial towns to ever make good.)

Some even listed instrumental movie themes among their favorite songs and wrote descriptions of the film's plot.

"What we found is that specific lyrics seem to be of little consequence to most kids," Prinsky said. Instead, the study concludes, "the musical beat or overall sound of a recording is of greater interest to teenagers."

That conclusion is disputed by the Parents Music Resource Center, the organization whose campaign against controversial lyrics resulted . . . in an agreement with the record industry for a voluntary record labeling plan. . . .

[Parents Music Resource Center] administrative assistant Jennifer Norwood said, "It's ridiculous to say that music does not have an effect on human behavior.

"In 'Eat Me Alive,' a Judas Priest song, that title is repeated 18 times in three minutes. In Kiss' 'Lick It Up,' that phrase is repeated 30 times in four minutes. I can't believe it's not getting through. It's getting into the subconscious, even if they can't recite the lyrics."

But Prinsky rejected the idea that lyrics reach the lis-

tener on a subliminal level, saying, "Good data on the subconscious indicate that it just doesn't work that way."

Students were also asked to rate 35 heavy metal, punk, R&B and mainstream rock performers on whether their songs involved sex, violence, drugs, the devil, love-feelings or other subjects. Most students answered that they did not know which category the various groups' songs belonged in.

Based on the responses, Prinsky estimated that "in our sample maybe 2 percent or 3 percent" of all teenagers devote their full attention to lyrics when listening to music. Most simply use rock 'n' roll as "background noise."

---

*"Rock Lyrics: Who's Listening?" Los Angeles Times News Service, reprinted in* Honolulu Advertiser, *June 16, 1986, p. B-2.*

The issue of the recording industry's right to free expression surfaced in 1990 when a Florida record store owner was arrested for selling the album "As Nasty as They Wanna Be" by 2 Live Crew. Three members of 2 Live Crew (on right) and one from Poison Clan (left) are pictured here at a news conference.

In 1990, the nation's two largest record retailers ordered all of their outlets to stop stocking and selling sexually explicit recordings by the controversial rap group 2 Live Crew. A Florida judge ruled that the group's album *As Nasty as They Wanna Be* was obscene, even though the album carried a warning about explicit lyrics. The Luke Skywalker record label that produced the album said that the controversy increased sales, but the ban meant that more than 1,000 stores nationwide refused to sell the record, continuing the debate over the government's role in protecting free expression versus protecting public morals.

**Authenticity of Performances.** In 1990, a new controversy arose in the recording industry when the Grammy-winning duo Milli Vanilli admitted that they did not sing a note on the album that won them the award. (The album had sold more than 10 million copies worldwide.) The National Academy of Recording Arts and Sciences, which awards the Grammys, asked the group to return the prize. No artist in the Grammys' history had been charged with similar allegations.

The two Milli Vanilli singers (Robert Pilatus and Fab Morvan) were hired as front men for the actual singers, to appear on the album cover and in promotional materials and to lip-synchronize for music videos.

"Technology is helping a growing number of performers expand truth as it never has been expanded before," wrote *Los Angeles Times* columnist Robert Epstein. Epstein described recent technological changes in the industry that contributed to the problem: (1) singers use body microphones, which amplify their voices; (2) recordings — pop and classical — are dubbed and enhanced to a degree "only dreamed of by mere human performers"; (3) most of the video industry seems based on lip-synchronized and computer-engineered performances.[20]

Record industry executives claimed that the incident was an isolated event, but ironically, the technology that contributed to the quality of today's recordings also made the Milli Vanilli hoax possible.

# Facing the Future

From the beginning, profits in the recording industry have been tied to technology. Ever since William Paley and David Sarnoff decided to produce LPs and 45s, the consumer has tracked the equipment manufacturers, looking for better, more convenient sound.

As LP sales declined to only 5 percent of sales, a new technology threatened compact discs. **Digital audiotape (DAT)** recorders are being sold in Japan to replace current cassette equipment. The digital technology reproduces sound more accurately and eliminates the hiss on current cassettes.

DAT manufacturers, to combat owners who planned to use the new machines to copy discs or cassettes, approved "spoiler" chips that will prevent people who use DAT players from recording compact-disc music directly. This means that people who use DAT players must buy prerecorded DAT tapes.

Further research could interfere with DAT's success even before the recorders reach the American market. Promising projects include: recordable compact discs; compact discs that provide both audio and visual information and that store computer information; digital television; and even a credit-card-shaped disc.[21]

When Thomas Edison demonstrated his phonograph for the editors of *Scientific American* in 1877, the magazine reported that

*Mr. Thomas Edison recently came into this office, placed a little machine on our desk, turned a crank, and the machine inquired as to our health, asked how we liked the phonograph, informed us that* it *was very well, and bid us a cordial good night. These*

# Recordings

## Industry Snapshot

From cylinders to vinyl discs to CDs and music videos, the recording industry has always been a volatile, technology-driven business. And it's not only the format that changes—consumers' tastes change, too, with each new wave of youthful listeners.

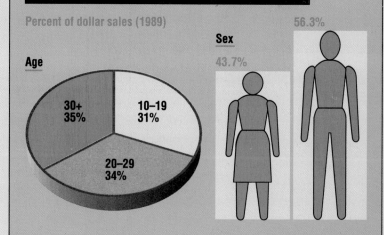

### The Recording Industry's Youthful Market

Percent of dollar sales (1989)

**Age**

- 30+ 35%
- 10–19 31%
- 20–29 34%

**Sex**

- 43.7%
- 56.3%

Data from Recording Industry Association of America, Inc., *Inside the Recording Industry: A Statistical Overview, Update 1990.*

**1** The recording industry's average consumer is younger than in any other media industry. People under 30 account for nearly two-thirds of the industry's sales revenues.

**2** The industry's youthful market is reflected in the music consumers buy. In dollar volume, recorded rock far outstrips all other kinds of music.

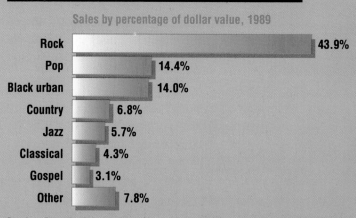

### What People Buy: Types of Music Purchased

Sales by percentage of dollar value, 1989

- Rock — 43.9%
- Pop — 14.4%
- Black urban — 14.0%
- Country — 6.8%
- Jazz — 5.7%
- Classical — 4.3%
- Gospel — 3.1%
- Other — 7.8%

Data from Recording Industry of America, Inc., *Inside the Recording Industry: A Statistical Overview, Update 1990.*

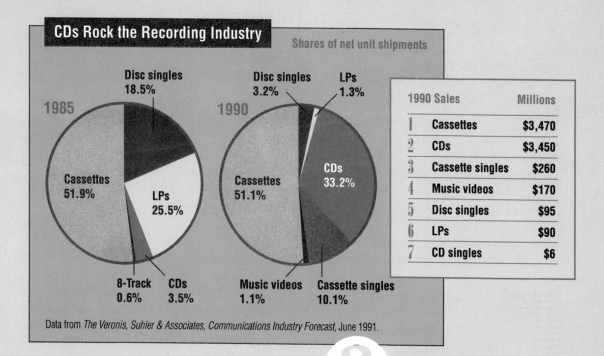

## CDs Rock the Recording Industry

Shares of net unit shipments

**1985**

Disc singles 18.5%
Cassettes 51.9%
LPs 25.5%
8-Track 0.6%
CDs 3.5%

**1990**

Disc singles 3.2%
LPs 1.3%
CDs 33.2%
Cassettes 51.1%
Music videos 1.1%
Cassette singles 10.1%

| 1990 Sales | Millions |
|---|---|
| 1 Cassettes | $3,470 |
| 2 CDs | $3,450 |
| 3 Cassette singles | $260 |
| 4 Music videos | $170 |
| 5 Disc singles | $95 |
| 6 LPs | $90 |
| 7 CD singles | $6 |

Data from *The Veronis, Suhler & Associates, Communications Industry Forecast*, June 1991.

**3** Compact discs have mushroomed from an insignificant part of the recording industry to the second-leading format. Because CDs cost more, they are rapidly overtaking cassettes as the industry's sales leader in dollar volume.

**4** A media hybrid, music videos are the latest innovation in an industry driven by technological changes.

*remarks were not only perfectly audible to ourselves, but to a dozen or more persons gathered around.* [22]

None of the discoveries by Edison's successors has been a new invention, only a refinement. Berliner flattened the cylinder; Goldmark and Sarnoff slowed down the speed; hi-fi, stereo, and quadraphonic sound increased the fidelity; and cassettes, compact discs, and digital recorders refined the sound further. But the basic discovery remains Edison's.

Reflecting on the movie version of Edison's life, Robert Metz discusses the importance of Edison's development of the phonograph:

*[A] tinkerer employed in the Edison labs . . . was shown playing with a makeshift device consisting of a rotating piece of metal with a pointed piece of metal scratching its surface. The device was full of sound and fury—and signified a great deal. Edison seized upon the idea and labored to construct a better device. Eventually he was seen speaking into a metal diaphragm whose vibrations in turn wiggled a needle pressed against a rotating cylinder of wax. And thus, supposedly through idle play, came the first permanent "record" of ephemeral sound. By any measure, it was an invention of genius.* [23]

## IN FOCUS

### The Recording Industry

- Rapidly changing technology affects the recording industry quicker than some media industries.

- Thomas Edison first demonstrated his phonograph in 1877. Emile Berliner developed the gramophone in 1887. Berliner and Eldrige Johnson formed the Victor Talking Machine Company (later RCA Victor) to sell recordings. Joseph Maxfield perfected recording equipment to eliminate the tinny sound.

- The first standard records were 78 rpm. The long-playing record ($33\frac{1}{3}$ rpm) was developed by Peter Goldmark, working for William Paley. The 45 rpm record was David Sarnoff's idea. Eventually, record players were sold that could play all three record speeds.

- High fidelity became popular in the early 1950s, and eventually stereo and quadraphonic sound followed.

- The recording industry efforts to improve recorded sound quality contributed to the success of rock 'n' roll entertainers like Elvis Presley.

- A recording company is divided into artists and repertoire, operations, marketing and promotion, distribution, and administration.

- About 5,000 companies produce records and tapes in the United States. These companies sell about 800 million records, cassettes, and compact discs a year. The industry collects income from direct sales, music licensing, and music videos, but recording industry income today is flat.

• The four major issues facing today's recording industry are: piracy, payola, attempts to control the content of recordings, and the authenticity of artists' performances.

• The recording industry, like the movie industry, responded to threats of government regulation of music lyrics by adopting its own standards for record labeling.

• Technology is changing the industry very quickly. Advances in recording technology contributed to the possibility of unauthentic performances being sold as authentic. Digital audiotape (DAT) recorders will replace today's current technologies, but even more advanced compact disc technology soon could replace DAT.

**8**

*"I'm not sure I can explain how to write a book,"* said

*essayist and author* E. B. White, *who wrote 19 of them,*

*including* Charlotte's Web. *"First, you have to* want *to write one very much. Then,*

*you have to know of something that you want to write about. Then, you have to begin.*

*And, once you have started, you have to keep going. That's really all I know about*

*how to write a book."*[1]

*The process of writing a book is a little more complex*

*than White suggests, but every year in the United States,*

**The Book
Publishing
Industry**

Non-fiction books, such as those on the subject of architecture, outsell fiction books, such as mysteries, by a margin of about 4 to 1.

publishers produce about 40,000 individual titles.[2] This includes revised editions of already published books, but most of these titles are new.

The Association of American Publishers says that the definition of a book includes:

• *All hardcover volumes that are not magazines regardless of how long they are.*

• *All juvenile titles, hardbound or softbound, regardless of how long they are, except coloring books.*

• *All softbound volumes that are not magazines and are more than 48 pages long. (A softbound volume that is less than 48 pages long is called a pamphlet, unless it is a text-related workbook.)*

The publishing industry always has been tugged by what publishing scholars Lewis A. Coser, Charles Kadushin, and Walter W. Powell call "the culture and commerce of publishing" — the desire to preserve the country's intellectual ideas versus the desire to make money. But a publisher who doesn't make a profit cannot continue to publish books.

Coser and his colleagues describe the four characteristics of book publishing in America today:

*1. The industry sells its products — like any commodity — in a market that, in contrast to that for many other products, is fickle and often uncertain.*

*2. The industry is decentralized among a number of sectors whose operations bear little resemblance to each other.*

*3. These operations are characterized by a mixture of modern mass-production methods and craftlike procedures.*

*4. The industry remains perilously poised between the requirements and restraints of commerce and the responsibilities and obligations that it must bear as a prime guardian of the symbolic culture of the nation.*[3]

Many new owners of publishing houses try to bring some predictability to the market. Says Coser, "Publishers attempt to reduce . . . uncertainty . . . through concentrating on 'sure-fire' blockbusters, through large-scale promotion campaigns, or through control over distribution, as in the marketing of paperbacks. In the end, however, publishers rely on sales estimates that may be as unreliable as weather forecasts in Maine."[4]

# Colonial Days: How American Book Publishing Began

ODAY THE book publishing industry divides responsibilities among many people. But when Americans first started publishing books, one person often did all the work.

Aboard the *Mayflower* in 1620 were two dogs and 70 adults but very few books. The Pilgrims were very practical. They brought a map of Virginia and John Smith's *Description of New England*, but the main books they carried were their Bibles.

The first books in the United States were imports, brought by the new settlers or ordered from England after the settlers arrived. When he died in 1638, settler John Harvard had accumulated 300 books — all imports — which he bequeathed to Newtowne College. The colonists were so grateful that they renamed the college for him. His books were the first volumes in the Harvard College library.

Also in 1638, the colonists set up a press at Cambridge, Massachusetts, and in 1640 they printed America's first book: *The Bay Psalm Book*. As the only book, it became an instant best-seller. There were only about 3,500 families in the colonies at the time, and the book's first printing of 1,750 sold out.[5]

By 1680, Boston had 17 booksellers, but most of the books still came from England. Between 1682 and 1685, Boston's leading bookseller, John Usher, bought 3,421 books. More than half of them were religious books — sermons, catechisms, and Bibles. Many of them were textbooks, but another sign of the colonists' tastes was that Usher also ordered 162 romance novels.

In 1731, Benjamin Franklin decided that Philadelphia needed a library. So he asked 50 subscribers to pay 40 shillings each to a Library Company. The company imported 84 books, which circulated among the subscribers. This circulating library was America's first.

The year after he established the circulating library, Franklin published *Poor Richard's Almanack* (see Chapter 2). Unlike most printers, who waited for someone to come to them with a manuscript, Franklin wrote his own books. The typical author sought a patron to pay for the book's printing and then sold the book at the printshop where it was published.

# Reaching a Wider Audience

To EXPAND readership, early publishers sold political pamphlets, novels, poetry, and humor. In addition, three events of the 19th century ensured that the book publishing industry would prosper in the 20th century: passage of the International Copyright Law; formation of publishing houses; and establishment of compulsory education.

Thomas Paine (1737–1809),
author of *Common Sense*

## Political Pamphlets

The big seller of the 1700s was Thomas Paine's revolutionary pamphlet *Common Sense*, which argued for independence from Great Britain. From January to March 1776, colonial presses published 100,000 copies of Paine's persuasive political argument — one copy for every 25 people in the colonies — a true best-seller.

In the autumn of the same year, as George Washington complained of fatigue, Paine published his second pamphlet, *The American Crisis*, with its famous line, "These are the times that try men's souls." Washington read the pamphlet to his troops before they made the fateful crossing of the Delaware. Throughout the Revolutionary War, Paine was America's best-read author.

## Novels

Political pamphlets became much less important after the new nation was established, and printers turned their attention to other popular reading, especially fiction. Benjamin Franklin is credited with selling *Pamela* by Samuel

Richardson in 1744, the first novel published in the United States, although it was a British import that had first appeared in England in 1740.

Like other media industries, book publishing has always faced moral criticism. Novels, for example, didn't start out with a good reputation. One critic said the novel "pollutes the imaginations." In England, an article appeared titled "Novel Reading a Cause of Female Depravity," and it was widely reprinted in America.

Women wrote one-third of all the early American novels,[6] and women also bought most of them. Novels often were melodramatic, and one writer suggested a formula for a successful novel: "Remember to mix a sufficient quantity of sighs, tears, swooning hysterics, and all the moving expression of heart-rending woe. . . . Be sure you contrive a duel; and, if convenient, a suicide might not be amiss."[7]

Because there was no international copyright law, colonial printers freely reprinted British novels like *Pamela* and sold them. It was cheaper than publishing American authors, who could demand royalties.

James Fenimore Cooper's *Last of the Mohicans* and Washington Irving's stories ("Rip Van Winkle" and "The Legend of Sleepy Hollow") were the most popular reading of the first half of the 19th century. Although the 1850s saw the publication of American writers like Hawthorne, Melville, Thoreau, and Whitman, the sale of all of these books together did not equal the sale of what were called women's novels. The main characters of these novels were women who triumphed over one tragedy after another.

"America is now wholly given over to a d--d mob of scribbling women," wrote Hawthorne, "and I should have no chance of success while the public taste is occupied with their trash."[8]

An author with the unlikely name of Fanny Fern sold 180,000 books in 1855. Other successful women authors were Louisa May Alcott (author of *Little Men* and *Little Women*), Mary Jane Holmes (who eventually sold 2 million copies of her series of novels), and Sarah Josepha Hale (see Chapter 3).

Especially popular after the Civil War and before the turn of century were dime novels, America's earliest paperbacks. Eventually most of them cost only a nickel, but some early paperbacks were as expensive as 20 cents. They were quick adventures, such as *The Indian Wife of the White Hunter* by Ann Sophia Stephens, the first dime novel. Many of the characters were real-life American heroes: Kit Carson, Buffalo Bill, Davy Crockett, and General Custer. The titles favored strong main characters: *Double Dan, the Dastard* and *Roaring Ralph Rockwood, the Reckless Ranger*.

Harriet Beecher Stowe's realistic story about slave life in the South, *Uncle Tom's Cabin*, appeared first in the antislavery journal *National Era* before being published in two volumes in 1852. The book sold 20,000 copies in three

Harriet Beecher Stowe (1811–1896).

135,000 SETS, 270,000 VOLUMES SOLD.

# UNCLE TOM'S CABIN

## FOR SALE HERE.

AN EDITION FOR THE MILLION, COMPLETE IN 1 Vol., PRICE 37 1-2 CENTS.
"      "      IN GERMAN, IN 1 Vol., PRICE 50 CENTS.
"      "      IN 2 Vols., CLOTH, 6 PLATES, PRICE $1.50.
SUPERB ILLUSTRATED EDITION, IN 1 Vol., WITH 153 ENGRAVINGS,
**PRICES FROM $2.50 TO $5.00.**

## The Greatest Book of the Age.

Like many early best-sellers, the Civil War novel *Uncle Tom's Cabin* was written by a woman, Harriet Beecher Stowe.

weeks and 300,000 copies the first year. Perhaps the first example of subsidiary marketing occurred when a manufacturer came out with an Uncle Tom and Little Eva parlor game, based on characters in the book.

## Poetry

Poetry generally has been difficult to sell, and it is correspondingly difficult for poets to get published. Although he never sold nearly as many copies of his books as Harriet Beecher Stowe, Henry Wadsworth Longfellow managed to support himself with his writing — the first American poet to do so. He sold to magazines and newspapers, and some of his poems became expensive gift books. "The Song of Hiawatha," his most popular work, sold 300 copies a day at its peak. John Greenleaf Whittier accumulated $100,000 in royalties for "Snow-Bound." Literary scholar James D. Hart says that although poetry was never as popular as prose, the mid-1800s were "the great era of poetry. . . . It was more widely read in those years than it has been since."[9]

## Humor

Humor has been a durable category in book publishing since the days of humorist Mark Twain. Made famous by his *Celebrated Jumping Frog of Calaveras County*, Twain became a one-man publishing enterprise. One reason his books sold well was that he was the first American author to recognize the importance of advance publicity.

Before his books were published, Twain traveled throughout the country giving lectures based on stories in his books — an early version of today's author's tour. His first serious book, *The Innocents Abroad*, sold 100,000 copies within two years of publication, and the publisher, American Publishing, then offered Twain a lucrative royalty contract.

After writing three more books for American Publishing, Twain decided to distribute his own books. He paid a company named James Osgood to print his next book, gave the company a small royalty, and then sold it himself. The bittersweet humorous tales of *Huckleberry Finn* sold 50,000 copies within a few weeks. After *Huck Finn's* success, Twain formed his own publishing company.

Twain hired people to sell his books the way many books were sold in his day — door to door. Sales agents took advance orders before the books were published so publishers could estimate how many to print. More than three-fourths of the popular books sold in America before 1900 were sold door to door.[10]

## International Copyright Law of 1891

Before 1891, publishers were legally required to pay royalties to American authors, but not to foreign authors. As noted previously, this hurt American authors.

After the passage of the International Copyright Law of 1891, all authors — foreign and American — had to give permission to publish their works. For the

The publishing house of Charles Scribner ran a bookstore in the ground floor of the same building that held the main offices. Here, the entire building is decorated to welcome Theodore Roosevelt home from Africa (1910).

first time, American authors cost publishing houses the same amount as foreign authors. This motivated publishers to look for more American writers. After 1894, of the novels published in the United States, more were by American writers than by foreign writers.[11]

## Publishing Houses

Many publishing houses that began in the late 18th and throughout the 19th centuries continued into the 20th century. Nineteenth-century book publishing houses were just that — book publishing houses. They were nothing like today's multimedia corporations. These pioneering companies housed all aspects of publishing under one roof: They sought out authors, reviewed and edited copy, printed and then sold the books. Some representative houses and the dates they were founded: J. B. Lippincott (1792), Harper & Row (1817), Houghton Mifflin (1832), Charles Scribner (1850), Rand McNally (1856), and Doubleday (1897).

## Compulsory Education

By 1900, 31 states had passed compulsory education laws. This was important to book publishing because schools buy textbooks, and also because education created more readers. The standard textbook before the turn of the century was the *McGuffey Reader*, which sold 107 million copies. Widespread public education meant that schools broadened their choices and textbook publishing flourished. Expanded public support for education also meant more money for libraries — more good news for the publishing industry.

# The Twentieth Century: Creating a Mass Market

THE FIRST quarter of the 20th century brought still more publishing houses to meet the public's needs: McGraw-Hill (1909), Prentice-Hall (1913), Simon & Schuster (1924), and Random House (1925). Publishers that specialized in paperbacks started in the 1930s and 1940s: Pocket Books (1939), Bantam Books (1946), and New American Library (1948). [12]

As the newspaper industry learned at the beginning of the 20th century with the penny press, if you drop a product's price drastically, sales can explode. That's exactly what happened with the introduction of book clubs and paperbacks.

## Book Clubs

Book clubs replaced the door-to-door sales agent as a way to reach people who otherwise wouldn't buy books. Book-of-the-Month Club was founded in 1926, Literary Guild in 1927. By 1946, there were 50 clubs in America as diverse as the Aero and Marine Book Club, the Scientific Book Club, and the Catholic Children's Book Club. At first, publishers balked, worried that the book clubs would steal buyers from booksellers, but they soon learned that book clubs expanded their audience. People who had never bought books before began to buy them from clubs. By 1946, the Book-of-the-Month Club was selling nearly 12 million copies a year.[13] Book-of-the-Month Club and Literary Guild are still the nation's two largest book clubs.

# Paperbacking America

In 1939, Robert de Graff introduced America's first series of paperback best-sellers, called Pocket Books. Unlike the paperbacks published after the Civil War, which appeared only in paperback, Pocket Books issued titles that had already succeeded as hardbound books. They were inexpensive, and they fit in a pocket or purse. "Suddenly, a book could reach not hundreds or thousands of readers but millions, many of whom had never owned a book before. Universally priced at 25 cents in its early years, the paperback democratized reading in America."[14]

De Graff announced in 1939 that his newly formed company would publish ten paperback titles, all of them proven best-sellers. He mixed how-tos with classics and current popular hardbound books. The first paperbacks, about an inch smaller than today's mass-market paperbacks, carried the announcement on the cover that the book was "complete and unabridged" so buyers would know they were getting the entire book, not an edited copy.

De Graff sold Pocket Books on newsstands, in drugstores, and at department stores. The first day the books were offered for sale, Macy's alone sold 695 copies. Two months later, *Publishers Weekly*, the magazine of the book publishing industry, reported that Pocket Books had sold 325,000 copies. Booksellers' orders averaged 12,000 to 15,000 copies daily.[15]

Other publishers joined Pocket Books: New American Library (NAL), Avon, Popular Library, Signet, and Dell. British publisher Penguin Books, which successfully introduced paperbacks in England before de Graff's Pocket Books hit America, joined the American market with British titles. NAL distinguished itself by being the first mass-market reprinter willing to publish serious books by African-American writers—Richard Wright's *Native Son*, Lillian Smith's *Strange Fruit*, and Ralph Ellison's *Invisible Man*. Signet's unexpected hit was J. D. Salinger's novel *Catcher in the Rye*.

But some critics questioned the quality of reading that paperbacks provided. Writing in *The Nation* magazine in 1951, Harvey Swados summarized some of the public's objections:

Book prices have surged from the day when editions like these were offered for as little as 19 cents a copy.

*Last year, the stupefying total of 214,000,000 paperbound books was published in this country, as compared with 3,000,000 in 1939. Most of them were sold and the probability is that a larger proportion of them was read than of hard-cover books, many of which are bought as unwanted gifts or as book-club prestige items for the coffee table. Whether this revolution in the reading habits of the American public means that we are inundated by a flood of trash which will debase farther the popular taste, or that we shall now have available cheap editions of an ever-increasing list of classics, is a question of basic importance to our social and cultural development.* [16]

The 1950s brought paperback auctions, as best-selling hardcover authors sought more money for paperback rights to their books. In 1946, for example, when Pocket Books published Dr. Spock's *Baby and Child Care*, Spock received no advance royalties and only one-half cent for each copy sold. [17]

Authors and agents grew more savvy, and paperback rights to best-sellers began going for $15,000 to $30,000. James Jones' paperback publisher paid $102,000 for the rights to his war novel *From Here to Eternity*, setting a record for paperback reprint rights.[18] To cover their costs, publishers began to raise the price of paperbacks, first to 35 cents and then 50 cents. Paperback sales surpassed trade hardback sales for the first time in 1960.[19]

## Testing Censorship

Book publishers have always resisted any attempts by the government to limit freedom of expression. One of the first publishers to test those limits was Grove Press.

In 1959 Grove published the sexually explicit *Lady Chatterley's Lover* by D. H. Lawrence (originally published in 1928) and in 1961 published *Tropic of Cancer* by Henry Miller (originally published in Paris in 1934). Both books had been banned as obscene. The legal fees to defend Miller's book against charges of pornography cost Grove more than $250,000, but eventually the U.S. Supreme Court cleared the book in 1964.[20]

The publisher again challenged conventional publishing in 1965 when it issued the controversial *Autobiography of Malcolm X,* the story of the leader of the African-American nationalist movement, in hardback. "Grove was often outrageous, daring, avant-garde, and disrespectful of authority," writes paperback scholar Kenneth C. Davis. According to Davis, Grove's owner Barney Rosset "had made his name and reputation by taking chances on writers that others were not willing to risk."[21]

# How Book Publishing Works

WHEN AUTHORS get together, they often tell stories about mistakes publishers have made — about manuscripts 20 or 30 publishers turned down that some bright-eyed editor eventually discovered and published. The books, of course, then become best-sellers. Some of the stories are true.

But the best publishing decisions are less haphazard. They are made deliberately, to deliver an awaited book to an eager market. Successful publishing companies must consistently anticipate both their competitors and the market.

Books must not only be written, they must be printed and they must be sold. This whole process usually takes at least 18 months from the time a book is signed by an editor until the book is published, so publishers are always working ahead. The classic publisher's question is, "Will someone pay $25 (or $5 or $10 — whatever the projected price of the book is) for this book 18 months from when I sign the author?"

Publishers acquire books in many ways. Some authors submit manuscripts "over the transom," which means they send an unsolicited manuscript to a publishing house, hoping the publisher will be interested. Many of the nation's larger publishers refuse to read unsolicited manuscripts, however, and only accept books that are submitted by agents.

Agents who represent authors collect fees from the authors they represent. Typically, an agent's fee is 10 to 15 percent of the author's royalty, and a typical author's royalty contract can run anywhere from 10 to 15 percent of the *cover price* of the book. If a publisher prices a book at $20, for example, the author would receive from $2 to $3 per book, depending on the author's agreement with the publisher; the agent would then receive 20 to 45 cents of the author's $2 to $3, depending on the agent's agreement with the author.

Today the author is only one part of publishing a book. Departments at the publishing house called aquisitions, production, design, manufacturing, marketing, and fulfillment all participate in the process. At a small publishing house, these jobs are divided among editors who are responsible for all the steps.

The *author* proposes a book to the acquisitions editor, usually with an outline and some sample chapters. Sometimes an agent negotiates the contract for the book, but most authors negotiate their own contracts.

The *acquisitions editor* looks for potential authors and projects and works out an agreement with the author. The acquisitions editor's most important role is to be a liaison among the author, the publishing company, and the book's audience. Acquisitions editors also may represent the company at book auctions and negotiate sales of **subsidiary rights**, which are the rights to market a book for other uses — to make a movie, for example, or to print a character from the book on T-shirts (see page 283).

The *production editor* manages all the steps that turn a double-spaced typewritten manuscript into a book. After the manuscript comes in, the production editor sets up a schedule and makes sure that all the work gets done on time.

The *designer* decides what a book will look like, inside and out. The designer chooses the typefaces for the book and determines how the pictures, boxes,

Book designers now use computers to help them create a book's interior and exterior appearance.

heads, and subheads will look and where to use color. The designer also creates a concept — sometimes more than one — for the book's cover.

The *manufacturing supervisor* buys the typesetting, paper, and printing for the book. The book usually is sent outside the company to be manufactured.

*Marketing*, often the most expensive part of creating a book, is handled by several different departments. *Advertising* designs ads for the book. *Promotion* sends the book to reviewers. *Sales representatives* visit bookstores and college campuses to tell book buyers and potential adopters about the book.

*Fulfillment* makes sure that the books get to the bookstores on time. This department watches inventory so that if the publisher's stock gets low, more books can be printed.

# The Publishing Industry Today

t WENTY THOUSAND American companies call themselves book publishers today, but only about 2,200 publishing houses produce more than three titles a year. Most publishing houses are small: 80 percent of all book publishing companies have fewer than 20 employees. [22]

Nonfiction beats fiction more than 4 to 1 in the number of titles published each year. Of all the books published in the United States annually, about 17 percent of them are categorized as fiction, literature, poetry, and drama. (See Figure 8.1.) The rest are in nonfiction categories, such as biography, economics, and science.

The number of new books and new editions has stabilized, but the per-copy price is going up. Paperbacks and hardbacks today cost nearly three times what they cost in 1977. For an overview of today's book publishing industry, see Industry Snapshot, page 286.

# Types of Books

Books fall into six major categories. These classifications once described the publishing houses that produced different types of books — someone who was called a textbook publisher produced only textbooks, for example. Today, many houses publish several different kinds of books, although they may have several divisions for different types of books and markets.

*Trade Books.* These are books designed for the general public and usually are sold through bookstores and to libraries. Trade books include hardbound books and trade (or "quality") paperbound books for adults and children.

Typical trade books include hardcover fiction, current nonfiction, biography, literary classics, cookbooks, travel books, art books, books on sports, music, poetry, and drama. Many college classes use trade books as well as textbooks. Juvenile trade books can be anything from a picture book for children who can't yet read to novels for young adults.

*Religious Books.* Hymnals, Bibles, and prayer books fall into this category. Recently, religious publishers have begun to issue books about social issues from a religious point of view, but these books are considered trade books, not religious books.

*Professional Books.* These are directed to professional people, specifically related to their work. These fall into three subcategories. *Technical and science books* include the subjects of biological and earth sciences as well as technology. *Medical books* are designed for doctors and nurses. *Business and other professional books* are addressed to business people, librarians, lawyers, and other professionals not covered in the first two categories.

*Mass-Market Paperbacks.* Here definitions get tricky. These books are defined not by their subjects but by where they are sold. Although they can also be found in bookstores, mass-market paperbacks are mainly distributed through "mass" channels — newsstands, chain stores, drugstores, and super-

## American Book Title Production by Category

| Category | Percentage (%) | Category | Percentage (%) |
|----------|----------------|----------|----------------|
| Agriculture | 0.5 | Literature | 4 |
| Art | 3 | Medicine | 9 |
| Biography | 4 | Music | 0.5 |
| Business | 3 | Philosophy, Psychology | 4 |
| Education | 2 | Poetry, Drama | 2 |
| Fiction | 11 | Religion | 5 |
| General works | 4 | Science | 6 |
| History | 5 | Sociology, Economics | 15 |
| Home economics | 2 | Sports, Recreation | 2 |
| Juveniles | 10 | Technology | 5 |
| Language | 0.5 | Travel | 0.5 |
| Law | 2 | *Total* | *100* |

SOURCE: Data from *Publishers Weekly*, March 8, 1991, p. 36.

markets — and usually are "rack-sized." Many are reprints of hardcover trade books; others are originally published as mass-market paperbacks. Generally they're made from cheaper paper and cost less than trade paperbacks.

*Textbooks.* These books are published for elementary and secondary students (called the "elhi" market) as well as for college students. Most college texts are paid for by the students but chosen by their professors.

Very little difference exists between some college texts and trade books. The only real difference between many textbooks and trade books is that texts include what publishers call *apparatus* — for example, test questions and summaries. If the difference is difficult to discern, the Association of American Publishers classifies these two types of books according to where thay are sold the most. A book that is mainly sold through college bookstores, for example, is called a text.

*University Press Books.* A small proportion of books are published every year by university presses. These books are defined solely by who publishes them — a university press book is one that is published by a university press. Most university presses are nonprofit and are connected to a university, museum, or research institution. These presses produce mainly scholarly materials in hardcover and softcover. Most university press books are sold through the mail and in college bookstores.

# Book Publishing Consolidates

Forecasts for growing profits in book publishing in the 1960s made the industry attractive to corporations looking for new places to invest. Before the 1960s, the book publishing industry was mostly composed of independent companies whose only business was books. Then rising school and college attendance from the post–World War II baby boom made some areas of publishing, especially textbooks, lucrative investments. Beginning in the 1960s, publishing companies began to consolidate. Says publishing expert John P. Dessauer: "Publishing stocks, particularly those of educational companies, became glamour holdings. And conglomerates began to woo every independent publisher whose future promised to throw off even a modest share of the forecast earnings."[23]

The list of the acquisitions and mergers included the following transactions: RCA bought Random House after absorbing Knopf and Pantheon Books; Holt, Rinehart & Winston became a subsidiary of CBS; Times Mirror bought New American Library and Harry N. Abrams; Xerox took over R. R. Bowker; and Time Inc. acquired Little, Brown.

Between 1965 and 1969, at least 23 publishing mergers took place each year. The peak years were 1968 (with 47 mergers) and 1969 (44).[24] Other publishers raised money for expansion by going public — selling stock in their companies on the New York Stock Exchange.

Dessauer acknowledges that the new owners often brought a businesslike approach to an industry that was known for its lack of attention to the bottom line. But, according to Dessauer, another consequence of these large-scale acquisitions was that "in many cases they also placed the power of ultimate decision and policymaking in the hands of people unfamiliar with books, their peculiarities and the markets."[25]

The same pace of acquisitions continues today. In 1986, Harcourt Brace Jovanovich bought CBS's book-publishing operations for $500 million. In that same year, Time Inc. paid $520 million to acquire textbook publisher Scott, Foresman & Company, publishers of elementary texts such as the Dick and Jane series. In 1988, Times Mirror (owners of eight newspapers including the *Los Angeles Times*) bought the college textbook company Richard D. Irwin Inc.

for $135 million. And Bantam, Doubleday, and Dell, which once were independent companies, are now all joined as the Bantam Doubleday Dell Publishing Group Inc.

# Demand for Higher Profits

The result of all of this consolidation is that the giants in today's publishing industry are demanding increasingly higher profits. The companies look for extra income in three ways: subsidiary rights, blockbuster books, and chain bookstore marketing.

**Subsidiary Rights.** Trade and mass-market publishers are especially interested in and will pay more for books with the potential for subsidiary-rights sales. The rights to make a movie from a book, for example, are subsidiary rights. The same rights govern whether a book character becomes a star on the front of a T-shirt. "In the nineteenth century, a hardcover trade book's profit was determined by the number of copies sold to individual readers. Today, it is usually determined by the sale of subsidiary rights to movie companies, book clubs, foreign publishers, or paperback reprint houses."[26] For some houses, subsidiary-rights sales are the difference between making a profit and going out of business.

**Blockbusters.** Selling many copies of one book is easier and cheaper than selling a few copies of several books. This is the concept behind publishers' eager search for blockbuster books. Publishers are attracted to best-selling authors because they are usually easy to market. There is a "brand loyalty" among many readers that draws them to buy every book by a favorite author, and so publishers try to capitalize on an author's readership in the same way movie producers seek out stars who have made successful films.

Judith Krantz, who received $3.2 million for her sex-filled *Princess Daisy*, explained the benefits of being a blockbuster author: "I'm no Joan Didion — there are no intelligent, unhappy people in my books. I want to be known as a writer of good, entertaining narrative. I'm not trying to be taken seriously by the East Coast literary establishment. But I'm taken very seriously by the bankers."[27]

Some recent amounts that publishers paid for blockbusters:

• *The Hearst Corporation's William Morrow & Company set a bidding record when it paid $5 million for* Whirlwind, *an adventure novel about Iran by James Clavell.*

Books often provide material for popular movies. *The Doctor* was based on the book *A Taste of My Own Medicine*, written by Ed Rosenbaum, M.D. *Doc Hollywood* was created from a book by another doctor, *What? Dead Again?* by Neil B. Shulman, M.D.

*Clavell is the author of* Shogun, *which had been made into a very successful TV miniseries, but* Whirlwind *did not sell enough copies to recover its large advance.*

• *Viking paid $800,000 for the right to publish* The Satanic Verses. *(See Impact/ Profile, Furor over* The Satanic Verses.*)*

• *Harper & Row paid $1 million for* paperback *rights alone to* Billy Bathgate *by popular novelist E. L. Doctorow.*

• *Warner books paid $500,000 to New York developer Donald Trump for* paperback *rights only to* Trump: The Art of the Deal. *Trump subsequently faced the possibility of bankruptcy, which discouraged book sales.*

Only the big publishing houses can afford such a bidding game. Some publishers have even developed computer models to suggest how high to bid for a book, but these high-priced properties are a very small part of book publishing, perhaps 1 percent. The majority of editors and writers rarely get involved in an argument over seven-figure amounts. Many authors would be pleased to see five figures on a contract.

# Furor over *The Satanic Verses*

Many independent booksellers resist any attempt to stop the sale of controversial books, but *The Satanic Verses* conflict demonstrated the broad power of the nation's book chains over a book's distribution. In spite of this power, however, *The Satanic Verses* eventually reached its audience.

I N 1989, Iran's Ayatollah Ruhollah Khomeini called for the death of Salman Rushdie, author of the novel *The Satanic Verses*, because Khomeini said the book blasphemed the Moslem faith. In the United States, a bomb threat caused the evacuation of the building that housed the book's publisher, Viking Penguin, but no bomb was found.

The nation's two largest book chains, B. Dalton and Waldenbooks, pulled the book from their shelves immediately after Khomeini issued his threat. B. Dalton and Waldenbooks together account for about one-third of the nation's book sales.

Independent booksellers, publishers, and authors' groups quickly chastised the chains for yanking the book. Most independent booksellers continued to sell the book, and three major publishers' groups placed an ad in *The New York Times* promising that the book would be available.

"We're inviting other groups to try to impose such threats," said Edward Morrow, president of the American Booksellers' Association and owner of the Northshire Bookstore in Manchester, Vermont. Morrow told *The Wall Street Journal*, "If they see it works once, then others are going to say, 'Aha! We can get away with that!'"

The chains said they stopped selling the book because they feared for their employees' safety. But Stuart Brent, the 75-year-old owner of Stuart Brent Books, in Chicago, told the *Journal* that the chains' concerns about safety were "meaningless drool on every level."

Salman Rushdie went into hiding in Europe, and eventu-

Salman Rushdie, author of *The Satanic Verses*, seen here at the Whitbread Book of the Year awards in London, January 1989.

ally the chains decided to restock the book. By mid-1989, *The Satanic Verses* had reached No. 1 on *The New York Times* hardback best-seller list.

Some critics feel that what has been called a blockbuster complex among publishing houses hurts authors who aren't included in the bidding. One Harper & Row editor told *The Wall Street Journal* that seven-figure advances "divert money away from authors who really need it and center attention on commercial books instead of less-commercial books that may nonetheless be better. God help poetry or criticism."[28]

**Chain Bookstores.** The most significant change in book marketing in the last 30 years has been the growth of book chains. The two largest chains, B. Dalton and Waldenbooks (owned by K mart Corp.), account for half the bookstore sales of trade books. B. Dalton (with about 800 stores) and Waldenbooks (with about 1,000) have brought mass-marketing techniques to the book industry, offering book buyers an environment that is less like the traditional cozy atmosphere of a one-owner bookstore and more like a department store.

"The large chains are the power behind book publishing today," says Joan M. Ripley, a former president of the American Booksellers Association. "Blockbusters are going to be published anyway, but with a marginal book, like a volume of poetry, a chain's decision about whether to order it can sometimes determine whether the book is published."[29]

Discount chains such as Crown Books are another factor in book marketing. The discount chains buy in huge volume, and they buy books only from publishers who will grant them big discounts. Books that are published by smaller publishing houses, which usually cannot afford these large discounts, never reach the discount chain buyer. But for the blockbusters, issued by bigger houses, the discount chain is just one more outlet.

Like the resistance to book clubs when they were first introduced, the skepticism among book publishers about chain bookstores has changed into an understanding that chain stores in shopping malls have expanded the book market to people who didn't buy very many books before. But a major unknown factor is what happens when the distribution of an industry's products is controlled by so few companies.

# Small Presses

The nation's large publishing houses (those with 100 or more employees) publish 80 percent of the books sold each year. But many of the nation's publishers are small operations with fewer than ten employees. These publishers

Small press publishers can offer titles targeted at narrower audiences than the wider audiences often sought by large corporate publishing companies.

are called **small presses**, and they counterbalance the corporate world of large advances and multimedia subsidiary rights.

Small presses do not have the budgets of the large houses, but their size means that they can specialize in specific topics, such as the environment or bicycling, for example, or specific types of writing that are unattractive to large publishers, such as poetry.

Small presses are, by definition, alternative. Many of them are clustered together in locations outside of the New York City orbit, such as Santa Fe, New Mexico, and Santa Barbara, California. And the book titles they publish probably are not familiar: *Bicycle Technology: Technical Aspects of the Modern Bicycle* by Rob Van der Plas, published by Bicycle Books; *Nine-in-One, Grr! Grr!*, a Hmong folktale by Blia Xiong and Cathy Spagnoli, published by Children's Book Press; *Warning! Dating May Be Hazardous to Your Health* by Claudette McShane, published by Mother Courage Press; or *48 Instant Letters You Can Send to Save the Earth* by Write for Action, published by Conari Press.

Still, some small presses and some small press books are quite successful. One example of a recent small press success is *The Lemon Book* by Ralph Nader

# Book Publishing

## Industry Snapshot

Like moviemakers, many trade book publishers seek blockbuster projects and try to capitalize on the name recognition of their stars—best-selling authors. But this type of publishing is only one aspect of a complex industry.

## Who Reads Books?

Index of avid book reading in U.S. households. (100 = U.S. average)

Age of head of household

| Age | Index |
|-----|-------|
| 18–24 | 70 |
| 25–34 | 88 |
| 35–44 | 106 |
| 45–54 | 108 |
| 55–64 | 109 |
| 65 and up | 103 |

20  40  60  80  100  120

Data from Standard Rate & Data Service, *The Lifestyle Market Analyst*, 1990.

**1**

Unlike most kinds of media consumption, avid book reading tends to be more common among older, better-educated and more affluent adults.

**2**

Huge chains like B. Dalton, Waldenbooks, and Crown Books have become the main distribution channels for trade books, perhaps contributing to a "blockbuster" syndrome among publishers.

**3**

Best-selling authors represent the glamor of the book industry—and much of trade publishers' profits.

## Some Best-Selling Authors

Estimated net hardcover American sales per book for authors who have repeatedly written best-sellers

| Author | Publisher | Average sales (copies) |
|---|---|---|
| Tom Clancy | Putnam | 1,300,000 |
| Stephen King | Viking | 1,200,000 |
| Danielle Steel | Delacorte | 1,100,000 |
| James Michener | Random House | 850,000 |
| Sidney Sheldon | Morrow | 850,000 |
| Robert Ludlum | Random House | 750,000 |
| Judith Krantz | Crown | 500,000 |
| Jackie Collins | Simon & Schuster | 475,000 |
| John Le Carré | Knopf | 450,000 |
| Ken Follett | Dell | 330,000 |
| Jeffrey Archer | HarperCollins | 250,000 |

Source: The *New York Times*.

**4**

While trade books are the most visible type of publishing, the industry includes several segments serving different markets. Educational books (college and elementary/high school textbooks) generate nearly as many sales dollars as trade books.

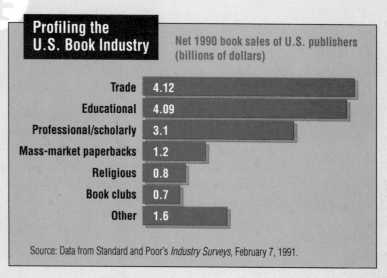

## Profiling the U.S. Book Industry

Net 1990 book sales of U.S. publishers (billions of dollars)

| | |
|---|---|
| Trade | 4.12 |
| Educational | 4.09 |
| Professional/scholarly | 3.1 |
| Mass-market paperbacks | 1.2 |
| Religious | 0.8 |
| Book clubs | 0.7 |
| Other | 1.6 |

Source: Data from Standard and Poor's *Industry Surveys*, February 7, 1991.

and Clarence Ditlow. This step-by-step guide to buying a car and what to do if you get a bad one grabbed the attention of the *Larry King Show, Good Morning America*, and more than 50 other local TV and radio programs. The book sold 42,000 copies in its first year, and the publisher, Moyer Bell, is planning a *Lemon* annual, which will list each year's auto rejects.

As *The Lemon Book* demonstrates, specialization and targeted marketing are the most important elements of small press success.

# Facing the Future

Technology will be a factor in most of the future changes in book publishing. (See Impact/Perspective, The Electronic Novel.) Because books cost so much to publish, any advances that lower production costs benefit the industry. Several changes are coming:

*1. Computers already can more closely monitor inventories so that publishers can order a new printing of a book that is running low in stock.*

*2. Book publishing is becoming an on-screen industry. Publishers can now receive manuscripts from authors by computer modem over phone lines. These manuscripts are edited on a computer screen and then sent into production by computer, the same process now used at many newspapers.*

*3. Electronic graphics will make books more interesting to look at. As technology lowers the cost of color printing, more textbooks will be published with color throughout, instead of just on the cover.*

*4. Desktop publishing will lower the cost of book production. The result should be more small presses being created to publish specialized books for targeted audiences.*

*5. Writers' organizations in the United States are lobbying for an authors' lending royalty — a computer-assisted system of payment to authors every time someone borrows a book from a library. Lending royalties already are paid to writers in ten countries, including Great Britain. Every time someone checks out a book from a library, the author's account is credited. The money, which would come from federal taxes, would be paid to the author yearly.*

*6. Although the larger publishers are buying one another, the number of small publishers who issue less than 20 books a year is increasing. New York is still the center of book*

# The Electronic Novel

This article by **David Lehman** describes the potential of computer technology as a way to expand the markets for books.

**Y**OU WAKE up stark naked in your Manhattan hotel room. You go to the mirror expecting yourself to have blond hair, a mustache, blue eyes. Wrong on all counts: you're cleanshaven, dark, brown-eyed. The hotel accountant on the phone calls you "Mr. Cameron," so that must be your name — though it comes as news to you. The maid at the door reminds you that you'd better put on some clothes, but there aren't any in the room. It seems there's a lady who expects you to marry her in the chapel downstairs. And the police are after you for crimes you may or may not have committed. You can't remember anything; that's your predicament. Now what are you going to do about it? Think fast. Choose unwisely and you may end up facing a firing squad. Choose well and further adventures await you on the streets of Manhattan. Welcome to Tom Disch's "Amnesia."

Or enter the fictional universe of Robert Pinsky's "Mindwheel." Once again you are cast in the unlikely role of hero, player and creator of your own destiny — only here you must travel through the minds of four world historical individuals preserved in "matrix immortality": a rock star, a poet, a military dictator and a female Einstein ("Eva Fein"). . . .

Written in conjunction with computer programmers and published as formatted discs, Disch's "Amnesia" and Pinsky's "Mindwheel" aren't novels, at least in any ordinary sense. Reading them is rather like playing chess with your computer. Nor are they games pure and simple. They tell not one story but many, as each move you make alters the narrative. What's certain is that Pinsky and Disch have given a new spin to that highly suspect term "computer literacy." They have fused the computer game and the novel into a hybrid rich in literary possibilities. Call it what you will — "interactive text adventure," "computer fiction," "electronic novel," even "participastory" have all been tried — a new art form is waiting to be christened. . . .

The form itself incorporates a multiple-choice principle into the proceedings. It's you who determines which scenario gets played out, and it's this participatory dimension that makes "Mindwheel" exhilarating and "Amnesia" unforgettable. . . .

"For the player, it's really a direct intellectual engagement with the author," says the tall, bewhiskered Disch.

"*You Are What You Read.*" Newsweek. Jan. 12. 1987. p. 67.

Drawing by M. Stevens; © 1991 The New Yorker Magazine, Inc.

*"I'd rather not talk about my pain right now,
Linda—I'd rather talk about my book."*

*publishing, but the number of houses based in the East is declining. Seven percent of the country's book publishers are now in California, and that percentage is increasing.*[30]

Because book publishing is America's oldest mass medium, the contrast between its simple beginnings and its complicated corporate life today is especially stark. This may be because Americans maintain a mistaken romantic idea about book publishing's early days:

*The myth is widespread that book publishing in the nineteenth and twentieth centuries was a gentlemanly trade in which an editor catered to an author's every whim, whereas commercialism and hucksterism have taken over in our day. It is a useful myth, to be sure, for it permits authors to point to a golden past and allows publishers to fashion for themselves a fine pedigree going back to a time when their profession was not sullied by the crass requirements of the marketplace. There once may have been more gentlemen in publishing than there are now, but there were surely sharp operators, hucksters, and pirates galore. In publishing, as in many other spheres of social life, there is very little that is new.*[31]

• The book publishing industry has always been divided by what publishing scholars call the culture versus the commerce of publishing — the desire to preserve the nation's intellectual ideas versus the desire to make money.

• America's first book was *The Bay Psalm Book*, printed in 1640.

• Early publishers widened their audience by publishing political pamphlets, novels, poetry, and humor.

• Many of the nation's major publishing houses were founded in the nineteenth century; these pioneering companies housed all aspects of publishing under one roof.

• The International Copyright Law of 1891 expanded royalty protection to American writers. The formation of publishing houses centralized the process of producing books.

• Compulsory education throughout the United States was good for book publishing because schools buy textbooks and education creates more readers. Expanded support for education also meant more money for libraries.

• Book clubs and the introduction of paperbacks made books available to more people at a lower cost. Book-of-the-Month Club, founded in 1926, was the first book club.

• One of the first publishers to resist government limits on freedom of expression was Grove Press.

• The process of publishing a book usually takes at least 18 months from the time an author is signed until the book is published.

• The six departments at a publishing house are called acquisitions, production, design, manufacturing, marketing, and fulfillment.

• American book publishers produce about 40,000 new titles every year. Most of these are nonfiction. The number of new books has stabilized.

• Books are divided into six categories: trade books, religious books, professional books, mass-market paperbacks, textbooks, and university press books.

• Before the 1960s, the book publishing industry was composed mostly of independent companies whose only business was books. The peak of publishing company consolidation occurred in the 1960s, as some publishing companies merged and others raised money by selling stock. This pattern of consolidation continues today.

• To reduce their risks, many publishers look for blockbuster books (and authors), sold through large-scale promotion campaigns. Publishers are especially interested in books with subsidiary-rights potential.

• One significant change in book marketing in the last 30 years has been the growth of book chains. *The Satanic Verses* controversy demonstrated the control of book chains over book distribution.

• Most of the nation's books are published by the large publishing houses, but many of the nation's specialized books are issued by small presses. Small presses are, by definition, alternative.

• Computer technology and desktop publishing are changing the way books are published, lowering the cost and streamlining the process.

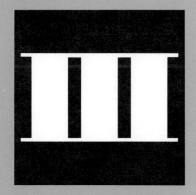

Support
Industries

**9** The American Marketing Association defines advertis-

ing *as "any paid form of nonpersonal presentation and*

*promotion of ideas, goods, or services by an identified sponsor." American consumers*

*pay for most of their media (newspapers, magazines, radio, and television) by watch-*

*ing, listening to, and reading advertisements.*

*You pay directly for books, movies, and recordings, although these media use*

*advertising to sell their products. But the broadcast pro-*

**Advertising**

*grams you want to hear and see and the articles you want*

to read are surrounded by advertisements placed by advertising people who want to sell you products.

# Paying for Our Pleasures: Advertising and the Media

**a**DVERTISING IS not a medium. Advertising carries the messages that come to you from the people who pay for the American media. The price for all types of advertising in America (including billboards and direct mail, as well as print and broadcast advertising) is more than $130 billion a year (see Figure 9.1).

## How Ads Began

Americans were not the first consumers. In 1200 B.C., the Phoenicians painted messages on stones near the paths where people often walked. In the sixth century B.C., ships that came into port sent criers around town with signboards to announce their arrival. In the 13th century A.D., the British began requiring trademarks to protect buyers and to identify faulty products. The first printed advertisement was prepared by printer William Caxton in England in 1478 to sell one of his books.

Advertising became part of the American experience even before the settlers arrived. "Never was there a more outrageous or more unscrupulous or more ill-informed advertising campaign than that by which the promoters for the American colonies brought settlers here," writes historian Daniel Boorstin.

*Brochures published in England in the seventeenth century, some even earlier, were full of hopeful overstatements, half-truths, and downright lies, along with some facts which nowadays surely would be the basis for a restraining order from the Federal Trade Commission. Gold and silver, fountains of youth, plenty of fish, venison without limit, all these were promised, and of course some of them were found.* [1]

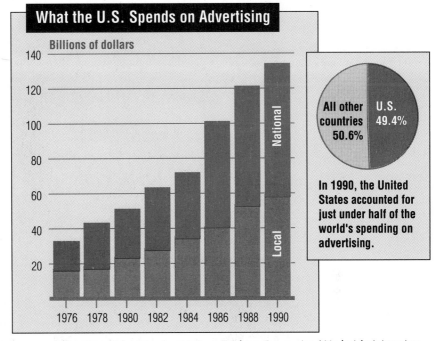

**What the U.S. Spends on Advertising**

**Billions of dollars**

*(Bar chart showing National and Local advertising spending from 1976 to 1990, with values rising from about 35 billion in 1976 to about 135 billion in 1990)*

In 1990, the United States accounted for just under half of the world's spending on advertising.

All other countries 50.6%

U.S. 49.4%

SOURCE: Data from *Advertising Age*; McCann-Erickson; International Trade Administration; Standard & Poor's *Industry Surveys*, Feb. 7. 1991.

# Newspaper Advertising

The nation's first newspaper advertisement appeared in *The Boston News-Letter*'s first issue in 1704 when the newspaper's editor included an ad for his own newspaper. The penny press of the 1800s counted on advertising to underwrite its costs. In 1833, the *New York Sun* candidly stated in its first issue: "The object of this paper is to lay before the public, at a price within the means of everyone, all the news of the day, and at the same time afford an advantageous medium for advertising."[2]

Three years later, the *Philadelphia Public Ledger* said that "advertising is our revenue, and in a paper involving so many expenses as a penny paper, and especially our own, the only source of revenue."[3] Because they were so dependent on advertisers, newspapers in the 1800s accepted any ads they could get. Eventually they got complaints from customers, especially about the patent medicines that promised cures and often delivered hangovers (many of these medicines were mostly alcohol).

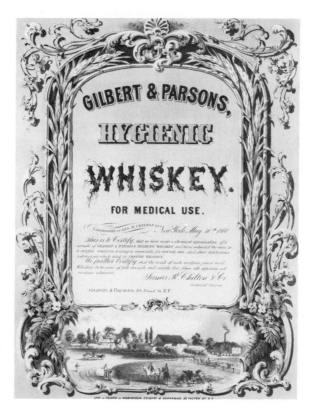

Publishers did not scrutinize early ads, such as these for whiskey and for something called Wizard Oil (opposite), which carried unchallenged claims that they were healthy products.

Products like Anti-Corpulene pills claimed they would help someone lose 15 pounds a month. "They cause no sickness, contain no poison and never fail."[4] Dr. T. Felix Couraud's Oriental Cream guaranteed that it would "remove tan, pimples, freckles, moth patches, rash and skin diseases and every blemish on beauty."[5]

The newspaper publishers' response to complaints was to develop an open advertising policy, which allowed the publishers to continue accepting the ads. Then publishers criticized ads on their editorial pages. The *Public Ledger*'s policy was that "Our advertising columns are open to the 'public, the whole public, and nothing but the public.' We admit any advertisement of any thing or any opinion, from any persons who will pay the price, excepting what is forbidden by the laws of the land, or what, in the opinion of all, is offensive to decency and morals."[6] But some editors did move their ads, which had been mingled with the copy, to a separate section.

Advertising historian Stephen Fox writes:

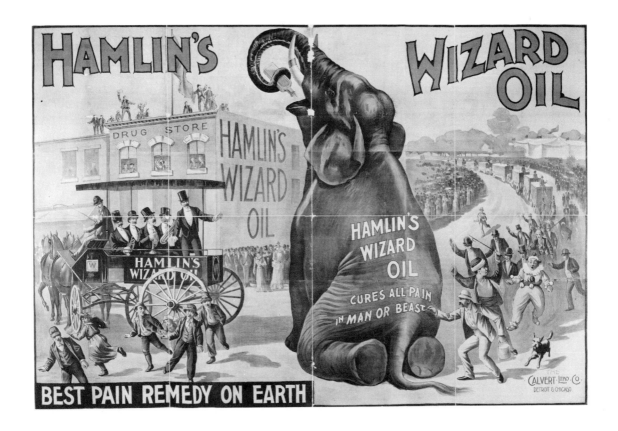

*Advertising was considered an embarrassment . . . the wastrel relative, the unruly servant kept backstairs and never allowed into the front parlor. . . . A firm risked its credit rating by advertising; banks might take it as a confession of financial weakness.*

*Everyone deplored advertising. Nobody — advertiser, agent, or medium — took responsibility for it. The advertiser only served as an errand boy, passing the advertiser's message along to the publisher; the medium printed it, but surely would not question the right of free speech by making a judgment on the veracity of the advertiser.*[7]

## Magazine Advertising

Until the 1880s, magazines remained wary of advertising. But Cyrus H. K. Curtis, who founded *The Ladies' Home Journal* in 1887, promoted advertising as the way for magazines to succeed. Once when he was asked what made him successful, he answered, "Advertising. That's what made me whatever I am. . . . I use up my days trying to find men who can write an effective advertisement."[8]

When Curtis hired Edward Bok as editor, Bok began a campaign against patent medicine ads and joined with *Collier's* and the American Medical Association to seek government restraints. Congress created the Federal Trade Commission in 1914, and part of its job was to monitor deceptive advertising. The FTC continues today to be the major government watchdog over advertising (see page 319).

# Radio Advertising

WEAF in New York broadcast its first advertising in 1922, selling apartments in New Jersey. B. F. Goodrich, Palmolive, and Eveready commercials followed. In September 1928, the Lucky Strike Dance Orchestra premiered on NBC, and Lucky Strike sales went up 47 percent. More cigarette companies moved to radio, and Camel cigarettes sponsored weekly, then daily programs.

Sir Walter Raleigh cigarettes sponsored the Sir Walter Raleigh Revue. In one hour, the sponsor squeezed in 70 references to the product.

*The theme song ("rally round Sir Walter Raleigh") introduced the Raleigh Revue in the Raleigh Theater with the Raleigh Orchestra and the Raleigh Rovers; then would follow the adventures of Sir Walter in Virginia and at Queen Elizabeth's court, with ample mention of his cigarettes and smoking tobacco.[9]*

In 1938, for the first time, radio collected more money from advertising than magazines.

# Television Advertising

Television began as an advertising medium. Never questioning how television would be financed, the networks assumed they would attract commercial support. They were right. In 1949, television advertisers totaled $12.3 million. In 1950, the total was $40.8 million. In 1951, advertisers spent $128 million on television.[10]

In a practice adopted from radio, television programs usually carried **direct sponsorship**. Many shows, such as *Camel News Caravan*, carried the sponsor's name in the title and advertised a product. Advertising agencies became television's programmers. "Given one advertiser and a show title often bearing its name, viewers associated a favorite show with its sponsor and — because of a 'gratitude factor' — would buy the products."[11]

Alfred Hitchcock became legendary for leading into his show's commercials with wry remarks about the sponsor: "Oh dear, I see the actors won't be ready for another sixty seconds. However, thanks to our sponsor's remarkable foresight, we have a message that will fill in here nicely."[12] But Hitchcock's sarcasm was the exception, and most programs welcomed advertising support without comment.

A sponsor also could profit from a program's integrity. Alcoa continued to sponsor Edward R. Murrow's *See It Now* even after he grilled Senator Joseph R. McCarthy (see Chapter 5). "We don't think it's proper for a sponsor to influence the news," said an Alcoa representative. "It's Mr. Murrow's show. We buy what he has to offer. We expect him to attract an audience — and the kind of audience — before which we want to present our commercials."[13] One year after the McCarthy show, however, Alcoa dropped its sponsorship.[14] The issues on the program had made Alcoa nervous, but the sponsor waited until the controversy passed before withdrawing from the show. For this reason, and because of disputes over the content of subsequent programs, CBS canceled the show in 1956. This incident and the TV quiz show scandals (see page 165) point up the vulnerability of the media to commercial sponsorship.

# How Advertisements Work

t HE WORD *advertise* originally meant to take note or to consider. By the 1700s, that meaning had changed. To advertise meant to persuade. "If we consider democracy not just a political system," says Daniel J. Boorstin, "but as a set of institutions which do aim to make everything available to everybody, it would not be an overstatement to describe advertising as the characteristic rhetoric of democracy."[15]

Sixty years after this ad for luxury transportation appeared in the May 1931 issue of *Fortune* magazine, the May 1991 issue of *Fortune* magazine still carried a similar upscale appeal (opposite) targeting the same audience.

## Common Characteristics

Boorstin says that advertising in America shares three characteristics: repetition, style, and ubiquity.

**Repetition.** When Robert Bonner bought the *New York Ledger* in 1851, he wanted to advertise his newspaper in the competing *New York Herald*, owned by James Gordon Bennett. Bennett limited all his advertisers to the same size typeface, so Bonner paid for an entire page of the *Herald*, across which he repeated the message "Bring home the *New York Ledger* tonight."

**We're accused of being obsessed with perfection, precision and meticulous attention to every detail. Thank you.**

The little things on a flight tell you a lot about an airline. So you'll notice that at Lufthansa, your drink and meal arrive at the same time. And that your electronic headset is free even in Economy Class. Or if you don't want to eat, drink or watch movies, you can get a "Do Not Disturb" sign. Of course, the way our crew works together also adds to your flight. Things like these show our passion to make your flight enjoyable. One you feel in everyone at Lufthansa. From the wine steward who inspects every bottle to the pilot who gets you there on time. A passion for perfection that ensures you the best flying experience possible.

A passion for perfection.℠

**⊙ Lufthansa**

Lufthansa is a participant in the mileage programs of United, Delta, USAir and Continental/Eastern. See your Travel Agent for details.

This is an early example of the widespread practice of repeating a simple message for effect.

**An Advertising Style.** At first, advertising adopted a plain, direct style. Advertising pioneer Claude Hopkins, says Boorstin, claimed that "Brilliant writing has no place in advertising. A unique style takes attention from the subject. . . . One should be natural and simple . . . in fishing for buyers, as in fishing for bass, one should not reveal the hook."[16]

The plain-talk tradition is a foundation of what advertisers call modern advertising. But advertising today often adopts a style of hyperbole, making large claims for products. Boorstin calls this "tall talk."

The tall-talk ad is in the P. T. Barnum tradition of advertising. Barnum was a carnival barker and later impresario who lured customers to his circus acts with fantastic claims. You may recognize this approach in some of the furniture and car ads on television, as an announcer screams at you that you have only a few days left until all the chairs or all the cars will be gone.

Both plain talk and tall talk combine, Boorstin says, to create advertising's *new myth*:

*This is the world of the neither true nor false — of the statement that 60 percent of the physicians who expressed a choice said that our brand of aspirin would be more effective in curing a simple headache than any other brand. . . . It is not untrue, and yet, in its connotation it is not exactly true."*[17]

**Ubiquity.** In America, advertising can be and is everywhere. Advertisers are always looking for new places to catch consumers' attention. Ads appear on shopping carts, on video screens at sports stadiums, atop parking meters.

*The ubiquity of advertising is, of course, just another effect of our uninhibited efforts to use all the media to get all sorts of information to everybody everywhere. Since the places to be filled are everywhere, the amount of advertising is not determined by the needs of advertising, but by the opportunities for advertising, which become unlimited.*[18]

But in some cases this ubiquity works to advertising's disadvantage. Many advertisers shy away from radio and TV because the ads are grouped so closely together. In 1986, in an attempt to attract more advertisers, TV began selling the "split-30" ad, which fits two 15-second ads into a 30-second spot. Even 10-second ads are available. Wherever these shorter commercials are sold, the station runs twice as many ads for different products, crowding the commercial time even more.

# Grabbing Attention

To sell you products, advertisers must catch your eye or your ear or your heart (preferably all three). A study by the Harvard Graduate School of Business Administration reported that the average American is exposed to 500 ads a day. With so many ads competing for your attention, the advertiser must first get you to read, listen to, or watch one ad instead of another. "The immediate goal of advertising [is to] tug at our psychological shirt sleeves and slow us down long enough for a word or two about whatever is being sold."[19]

Which of the 15 advertising appeals listed on pages 305–307 can you identify in this 1939 billboard ad?

# The Psychology of Ads

You make your buying decisions based on several other sources of information besides advertising: friends, family, and your own experience, for example. To influence your choices, the advertising message must appeal to you for some reason, as you sift through the ads to make judgments and choose products. Humanities and human sciences professor Jib Fowles in his book *Mass Advertising as Social Forecast* enumerated 15 appeals, which he calls an "inventory of human motives" that advertisers commonly use in their commercials:

*1.* Need for sex. *Surprisingly, Fowles found that only 2 percent of the television ads he surveyed used this appeal. It may be too blatant, he concluded, and often detracts from the product.*

*2.* Need for affiliation. *The largest number of ads uses this approach: You are looking for friendship. Advertisers can also use this negatively, to make you worry that you'll lose friends if you don't use a certain product.*

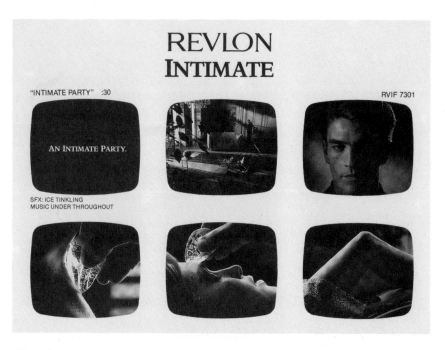

The advertising agency Hill, Holliday, Connors, Cosmopulos created this series of ads for Revlon. These "ice ads" became the subject of stories in every newspaper and many local news reports. Reported *Adweek*, "The commercial already has succeeded in doing what it's supposed to do: get attention."

3. Need to nurture. *Every time you see a puppy or a kitten or a child, the appeal is to your maternal or paternal instincts.*

4. Need for guidance. *A father or mother figure can appeal to your desire for someone to care for you, so you won't have to worry. Betty Crocker is a good example.*

5. Need to aggress. *We all have had a desire to get even, and some ads give you this satisfaction.*

6. Need to achieve. *The ability to accomplish something difficult and succeed identifies the product with winning. Sports figures as spokespersons project this image.*

7. Need to dominate. *The power we lack is what we can look for in a commercial: "Master the possibilities."*

8. Need for prominence. *We want to be admired and respected, to have high social status. Tasteful china and classic diamonds offer this potential.*

9. Need for attention. *We want people to notice us; we want to be looked at. Cosmetics are a natural for this approach.*

*10.* Need for autonomy. *Within a crowded environment, we want to be singled out, to be "a breed apart." This can also be used negatively: You may be left out if you don't use a particular product.*

*11.* Need to escape. *Flight is very appealing; you can imagine adventures you cannot have. The idea of escape is pleasurable.*

*12.* Need to feel safe. *To be free from threats, to be secure is the appeal of many insurance and bank ads.*

*13.* Need for aesthetic sensations. *Beauty attracts us, and classic art or dance makes us feel creative, enhanced.*

*14.* Need to satisfy curiosity. *Facts support our belief that information is quantifiable and numbers and diagrams make our choices seem scientific.*

*15.* Physiological needs. *Fowles defines sex (#1) as a biological need, and so he catalogues our need to sleep, eat, and drink in this category. Advertisements for juicy pizza are especially appealing late at night.* [20]

# Criticism of Advertising

The study of advertising provokes three main criticisms, according to Louis C. Kaufman, author of *Essentials of Advertising*:

*1.* Advertising adds to the cost of products. *Critics of advertising maintain that advertising, like everything that is part of manufacturing a product, is a cost. Ultimately, the consumer pays for the cost of advertising. But the industry argues that advertising helps make more goods and services available to the consumer, and that the resulting competition keeps prices lower.*

*2.* Advertising causes people to buy products they do not need. *Says media scholar Michael Schudson,*

> *Most blame advertising for the sale of specific consumer goods, notably luxury goods (designer jeans), frivolous goods (pet rocks), dangerous goods (cigarettes), shoddy goods (some toys for children), expensive goods that do not differ at all from cheap goods (nongeneric over-the-counter drugs), marginally differentiated products that do not differ significantly from one another (laundry soaps), and wasteful goods (various unecological throw-away convenience goods).* [21]

> *The advertising industry contends that the ultimate test of any product is the marketplace, and that advertising may stimulate consumers to try a new product or a new brand, but consumers will not continue to buy an unsatisfying product.*

# Going for the Green

In this article, *The Wall Street Journal's* advertising reporter **Joann S. Lublin** says that "green" advertising campaigns for environmentally safe products are causing controversy.

TWO NEW reports on the controversial "green" labeling issue highlight the problems of devising and policing advertising claims about the environmental safety of various products.

A report from a task force of 10 state attorneys general and a separate report from ad agency J. Walter Thompson conclude that consumer confusion over environmental claims is mounting.

Because they don't understand what most of the terms mean, "people don't have a lot of faith in green labeling," says Lois Kaufman, president of Environmental Research Associates, Princeton, N.J., pollsters on environmental issues.

The attorneys general's task force . . . asks the federal government to draft national standards, an effort that has already begun. It urges, in the meantime, that businesses devise specific and substantive environmental claims backed by reliable evidence. The report wants companies to avoid vague phrases such as "environmentally friendly" and clarify whether a claim is for a package or a product. (It tells how one consumer tried to recycle the plastic wrappers — along with a trash bag full of dirty diapers — from a diaper package labeled "recyclable.")

Because of such confusion, the J. Walter Thompson report finds, corporate environmental messages aren't getting through. Most consumers would stop buying a product they know to be environmentally unsafe, according to the nationwide survey by the agency, a unit of WPP Group. But only 14% of the 1,000 Americans polled could recall environmental advertising for a particular company, while 56% said they knew about companies whose actions have hurt the environment.

"'Green' advertising isn't as effective as it could be," says Peter Kim, JWT's research director, because most businesses have yet to educate customers about the environmental benefits of their products. Instead, Mr. Kim adds, "advertisers are still struggling [to determine] what should be the right 'green' advertising message." Those that succeed, he believes, "will have a positive halo for the 1990s." . . .

The Wall Street Journal, *Nov. 8, 1990, p. B-8.*

The American Association of Advertising Agencies sponsored a campaign to combat the negative view of advertising.

*3.* Advertising reduces competition and thereby fosters monopolies. *Critics point to the rising cost of advertising, especially television, which limits which companies can afford to launch a new product or a new campaign. The industry argues that advertising is still a very expensive way to let people know about new products. "The cost of launching a nationwide advertising campaign may be formidable," writes Louis C. Kaufman, "but the cost of supporting larger, nationwide sales forces for mass-marketed goods would be greater still."[22]*

To answer these and other criticisms (see Impact/Perspective, Going for the Green), the American Association of Advertising Agencies (called the 4As) introduced — what else? — an advertising campaign to explain their point of view. The AAAA ads questioned the assumptions many people make about advertising (see above).

Does advertising work? According to media scholar Michael Schudson,

*Apologists are wrong that advertising is simply information that makes the market work more efficiently — but so too are the critics of advertising who believe in its overwhelming power to deceive and to deflect human minds to its ends. Evaluating its impact is more difficult than these simplicities of apology and critique will acknowledge.* [23]

# How Ad Agencies Work

ABOUT 6,000 advertising agencies are in business in the United States, but only 452 of them collect $1 million or more a year. Advertising agencies buy time and space for the companies they represent. For this, they are usually paid a commission (commonly 15 percent). Many agencies also produce television and radio commercials and print advertising for their clients.

Depending on the size of the agency, the company may be divided into as many as six departments: marketing research, media selection, creative activity, account management, administration, and public relations.

*Marketing research* examines the product's potential, where it will be sold, and who will buy the product. Agency researchers may survey the market themselves or contract with an outside market research company to evaluate potential buyers.

*Media selection* suggests the best combination of buys for a client — television, newspapers, magazines, billboards.

*Creative activity* thinks up the ads. The "creatives" write the copy for TV, radio, and print. They design the graphic art and often they produce the commercials. They also verify that the ad has run as many times as it was scheduled to run.

*Account management* is the liaison between the agency and the client. Account executives handle client complaints and suggestions and also manage the company team assigned to the account.

*Administration* pays the bills, including all the tabs for the account executives' lunches with clients.

Advertisers are always seeking new ways to catch consumers' attention. The San Francisco company CTA Lasers offers a new dimension with laser advertising, projecting an ad for American Airlines into the evening sky.

*Public relations* is an extra service that some agencies offer for companies that don't have a separate public relations office.

All of these departments work together on an ad campaign. An advertising campaign is a planned effort that is coordinated for a specific time period. A campaign could last anywhere from a month to a year, and the objective is a coordinated strategy to sell a product or a service. Typically, the company assigns the account executive a team of people from the different departments to handle the account. The account executive answers to the people who control the agency, usually a board of directors.

The members of the campaign team coordinate all types of advertising — print and broadcast — to make sure they share consistent content. After establishing a budget based on the client's needs, the campaign team creates a slogan, recommends a strategy for the best exposure for the client, approves the design of print and broadcast commercials, and then places the ads with the media outlets.

# The Advertising Industry Today

t HE ADVERTISING business and the media industries are interdependent — that is, what happens in the advertising business directly affects the media industries. And the advertising business is very dependent on the nation's economic health. If the national economy is expanding, the advertising business and the media industries prosper. If the nation falls into a recession, advertisers typically reduce their ad budgets, which eventually leads to a decline in advertising revenue for the agencies and also for the media industries where the agencies place their ads. During a recession, advertisers also may change their advertising strategies — choosing radio over television because it is much less expensive, for example.

The advertising industry today therefore must be very sensitive to economic trends. The success of an ad agency is best measured by the results an ad campaign brings. The agency must analyze the benefits of different types of advertising and recommend the most efficient combination for their clients.

## TV Commercials

Even though the cost seems exorbitant, sponsors continue to line up to appear on network television. "Advertisers must use television on whatever terms they can get it, for television is the most potent merchandising vehicle ever devised," writes TV producer Bob Shanks in his book *The Cool Fire: How to Make It in Television.* Shanks is talking about national advertisers who buy network time — companies whose products can be advertised to the entire country at once.

Minutes in every network prime-time hour are divided into 10-, 15-, and 30-second ads. Shanks describes how an advertiser today fits into the networks' prime-time plan:

*When the networks have chosen the program[s], contracted with suppliers to make them, and have announced their fall schedules (usually around April 15), the major agencies and clients are invited to presentations of those schedules and for screenings of the pilots. From these encounters they will decide about or recommend which shows they think they should buy into.*

Then the client faces a series of questions:

*Do I need that night or time of night or season? What precedes and follows the show? What will the other networks be playing against it? What is the station line-up? Live clearance? What has been the track record of the production team? The leads? Will the star do the commercials? The lead-ins? The sales convention? Not just how many people are likely to watch, but what audience composition in terms of my product — young, old, children, women, men, educated, disposable income? How short a commitment can I make? How much will it cost? Does the network really believe in it and will they promote and advertise it? Then, finally, more practically, and a lot more humanly — what choice do I have anyway?[24]*

If an advertiser wants to reach the broad national market, television is an expensive choice because the average price for a 30-second TV commercial is $120,000. The price tag can go as high as $1 million for a widely watched program such as the Super Bowl.

National advertising on programs like *The Cosby Show* is bought by national advertising agencies, which handle the country's biggest advertisers — Procter & Gamble and McDonald's, for example. These companies usually have in-house advertising and public relations departments, but most of the advertising strategy and production of commercials for these companies is handled by the agencies. National agencies buy advertising space based on a careful formula, calculated on a cost-per-thousand (CPM) basis — the cost of an ad per one thousand people reached.

Making a TV commercial for national broadcast is more expensive per minute than making a television program. The price to produce a TV commercial can run as much as $1 million a minute. That may be why, as one producer said, "the commercials are the best things on TV."[25]

TV commercials are expensive because each company wants its ads to look different from the rest. This often involves special effects and unusual sets. "One writer came up with the idea of putting a five-story box of detergent out on an open plain, to be worshiped by hundreds of people," writes advertising critic Jonathan Price. "They went to Yugoslavia to build the thing, and as soon as it was built, rain came. For three weeks. The box fell over. So they went to Israel. They built another box. Protesters showed up: The film crew was desecrating an ancient shrine."[26]

**9.2** ➤

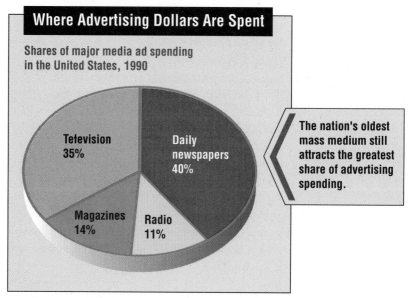

**Where Advertising Dollars Are Spent**

Shares of major media ad spending
in the United States, 1990

Television
35%

Daily
newspapers
40%

The nation's oldest
mass medium still
attracts the greatest
share of advertising
spending.

Magazines
14%

Radio
11%

SOURCE: Data from *The Veronis, Suhler & Associates Communications Industry Forecast*, June 1991.

Network television commercials certainly are the most visible type of advertising, but not everyone needs the reach of network television. The goal of well-placed advertising is to deliver the best results to the client for the lowest cost, and this may mean looking to other media.

## Other Media

Different types of media deliver different types of audiences. Network television delivers a large, diverse audience, at a high price. Agencies also buy less expensive time and space in local television, radio, newspapers, and magazines to target a specific audience by demographics: age, education, sex, and income (see Figure 9.2). Language also can be a targeting factor (see Impact/Profile, A New Ad Language: Spanish). A radio station with a rock format delivers a different group from an easy-listening station. *The New York Times* delivers a different reader from the *Honolulu Advertiser*. *Sports Illustrated* targets a different group from *The Ladies' Home Journal*.

The competition among different media for advertisers is heavy:

## 30 Million Viewers Have Discovered How To Watch Your 15-Second Commercial In Just 2½ Seconds

It's tough enough to try to sell somebody something in 15 seconds. It's impossible in 2½. No matter how much money and production value you pour into the spot.

Which leads to the ultimate question: Is there life after zapping?

Yes. In the pages of magazines and newspapers where there are no remote controls. Only close-up involvements.

Print offers a more than viable alternative to TV. Here your ads are welcomed as sources of news and information, not resented as sources of interruption and irritation.

Most important, your ads are *read*. With all of the implications that the act of reading suggests. When people read they think. And when they think, you have the opportunity to talk *to* them instead of at them. To present your sales story with literate copy that can both enlighten and excite. Words and pictures to be studied and reviewed at leisure.

So if you're concerned about the time compression in TV, rely on the time expansion in magazines and newspapers where time is measured in minutes rather than seconds.

Print works. Because readers don't zap your ads. They buy from them.

Print advertisers creatively argue the advantages of print over broadcast advertising.

• *The American Newspaper Publishers Association commissions a study that reveals that only one in five prime-time adult viewers could remember the last ad they had seen on television.*

• *Print advertisers claim that remote channel changers zap many TV ads, making them an unreliable way to deliver an audience.*

• Time *advertises that more airline customers read its magazine than read* Newsweek.

• Newsweek *advertises that it delivers more people for the money than* Time.

• Cosmopolitan *says that airline companies should advertise in its magazine because women who travel often don't watch daytime television.*

• *"Radio is the medium working women don't have to make time for," boasts the Radio Advertising Bureau (RAB). While working women spend 15 percent of their daily media time reading a newspaper, they spend half of their media time with radio, says the RAB.* [27]

Advertising agencies gather demographic information provided by Nielsen and Arbitron for broadcast and by the Audit Bureau of Circulations for print; the audience is converted into numbers. Based on these numbers, agencies advise advertisers about ways to reach buyers for their products.

# A New Ad Language: Spanish

This profile of Hispanic broadcaster Danny Villanueva offers insight into the history of Spanish broadcasting. Advertisers today are just beginning to understand the targeted marketing that Villanueva pioneered more than 25 years ago.

**d**ANNY VILLA-NUEVA'S father was a migrant minister, and Danny is very much his father's son. "I've always looked at my television station as my pulpit, my stage," Danny says. "I was brought up to believe that we have an obligation to do public service."

Villanueva, whose career spanned 25 years at Los Angeles Hispanic station KMEX-TV, says that to be successfully involved in Spanish-language television, he must be involved with the community. Spanish-language media *is* community media, he says.

For Villanueva, 54, that commitment has meant an exhausting career, usually filled with 18-hour days. He has served on more than 20 community and professional boards, including National Junior Achievement, the Greater Los Angeles Chamber of Commerce, the American Red Cross, and the National Conference of Christians and Jews. He was named Commissioner of Boxing for the 1984 Summer Olympics.

He also has been hospitalized four times for stomach problems, including ulcers. And in their 34 years of marriage, Danny and his wife Myrna have never take a vacation together.

KMEX-TV had been on the air for less than two years when Villanueva started working there in 1964 as a part-time sportscaster. As Villanueva worked his way up to station manager and then general manager, he was faced with pitching advertisers on an audience that was not documented by any ratings service.

The Hispanic audience became a "special buy," which meant that Villanueva found himself making client calls, trying to convince advertisers to support the station. "I remember pitching my little heart out at a huge company in Milwaukee and when it was over I asked, 'Are there any questions?' And one man looked at me and said, 'Why don't you people learn English?' I think he had another agenda in mind."

By 1987, Villanueva had been general manager at KMEX for 15 years. He was also an owner, director, and senior vice president of a group

Danny Villanueva

of ten Hispanic stations, including KMEX, called Spanish International Communications Corporation (SICC). KMEX formed the largest part of the group.

The Spanish audience had matured. Spanish-language TV offered viewers the same familiar mix of programs as English-language TV — comedy, entertainment, musicals, feature films, children's shows, public affairs, and news. Two special hits were the novelas (Spanish-language soap operas) and *Sabado Gigante*, a 3-hour Saturday night game show.

Then, in a move that surprised many industry observers, Hallmark and First Chicago Venture Capital bought SICC in 1987 for $300 million. "We started this company from absolute scratch," says Villanueva. "Ours was a license that nobody wanted and the company was sold for $300 million. We have now become the *In* medium.

"What used to be the anchor around our necks — that we were a Spanish-language UHF company — is now our redeeming glory. We are the ultimate narrowcasting medium." Villanueva's share of the sale was about $30 million. In June 1989, Villanueva left his job at KMEX to become an adviser on the Hallmark board.

Why have advertisers begun to look differently at the Hispanic audience? "It's dawning on them that we are a much younger community," says Villanueva. (L.A. is 30 percent Hispanic, but over 50 percent of the schoolchildren are Hispanic. Over 60 percent of the kindergartners are Hispanic.)

"Advertisers are beginning to see the massive numbers coming and they want to jump in on that market. In the end, we're asking advertisers to judge Spanish broadcasting using the same ruler they use for other markets — the delivery of homes and the existence and viability of the audience."

Today's Hispanic market is concentrated in what are called the Eight Power States — California, Arizona, New Mexico, Texas, Florida, New Jersey, New York, and Illinois. The challenge, says Villanueva, will be to expand beyond those states to the Denvers, the Austins, the Hartfords, the Bakersfields, and the Philadelphias — cities with measurable, but not massive, Hispanic populations.

"We did all the things that you have to do to build a company, and now Spanish is in style. One of the things that has sustained our Spanish culture over the centuries is respect for our elders. And the way we show this respect is that we try to do better. We should never underestimate or minimize the contributions of those who went before us."

# Local Advertising

Karen's Yogurt Shoppe, a small downtown business, does not need to advertise on *Cheers* or in *The New York Times*. Karen and other local businesses only need to reach their neighbors. Businesses larger than the yogurt shop, such as a car dealer or a furniture store, may buy local television or radio time, but most of the local advertising dollar goes to newspapers.

A local advertising agency can design a campaign, produce the ad, and place the ad just like the national agencies, but on a much smaller scale. And some small companies design and place their own ads directly with the local media.

To attract customers, local media often help companies design their ads. Newspapers, for example, will help a small advertiser prepare an ad using ready-made art. A radio or television station may include the services of an announcer or access to a studio in the price for a series of spots. Broadcast stations sometimes trade ads for services offered by the advertiser — dinner for two at the local restaurant in return for two spot ads, for example. Then the station gives the dinners away on one of its programs.

**Advertising Sales Representatives.** What if you manufacture sunglasses in Dubuque, Iowa, and you hire a local advertising agency to sell your product nationally? The agency tells you that they believe a good market for your product exists on the West Coast. How is the agency going to find out the most efficient way to sell your sunglasses in Los Angeles?

In this situation, many advertising agencies would contact a **rep firm** — a company of advertising sales representatives who sell advertising time and space in their market to companies outside the area. In this case, the agency in Dubuque would first decide who were the most likely customers for your sunglasses. If the agency decided that L.A.-area males age 18–24 are the best potential customers, the agency would budget a certain amount of money for advertising in the Los Angeles area and then call the ad reps there.

The rep firm, in return, takes a percentage (usually 15 percent) of the advertising dollars they place. Ad reps are, in effect, brokers for the media in their markets.

Each rep firm handles several clients. Some ad reps sell only broadcast advertising and some specialize in print ads, but many rep firms sell all types of media. In this case, each L.A. ad rep would enter the demographics ("demos") for your product into a computer. Based on ratings, readership, and the price for the ads, each rep would come up with a CPM (cost per thousand people reached) for your product. The rep then would recommend the most efficient buy — how best to reach the people most likely to want your sunglasses.

Each rep then presents an L.A. advertising plan for your product to the agency in Dubuque. Usually the buy is based on price — the medium with the lowest CPM gets the customer. But a rep who cannot match the lowest CPM might offer incentives for you to choose his or her plan: If you agree to provide 50 pairs of sunglasses, for example, the rep's radio station will give away the glasses as prizes during a local program, each time mentioning the name of your product. So even though the ad time you buy will cost a little more, you will also get promotional announcements every time the station gives away a pair of sunglasses. Other ad reps might offer different packages.

The agency in Dubuque then would decide which package is the most attractive and present that proposal to you. This entire process can take as little as 24 hours for a simple buy such as the one for your sunglasses account, or several weeks for a complicated campaign for a big advertiser.

**A Local Agency Goes National.** Local advertising agencies rarely venture beyond the regional market, but in 1985, a small agency in Nashville, Tennessee, had an idea. Why not take a very successful local ad campaign and use it in different parts of the country for different products? The idea worked because the central actor in the commercials, Jim Varney, portrayed someone audiences love to hate.

Varney plays Ernest P. Worrel (the P is for Power Tool), "a gangly redneck who looks as if he were born to lean against a gas pump." Ernest is nosy and overbearing. He always interrupts at the wrong time. And he's a hit. Consider this commercial:

> Ernest stands behind a Thanksgiving dinner table, sticks his nose into the camera lens and addresses his long-suffering neighbor, Vern. "You know, Vern," he says in his tobacco-cured baritone, "times like this when family and friends get together are so special. Like our relationship with our Northwest Ford dealer." Then, after a 10-second pitch, he says, "Shall I carve? What'll it be, Vern, light or dark?" He takes a chain saw from behind his back and, as the giblets fly, saws through the turkey, the plate and the table.[28]

Carden & Cherry, the agency that created the ads, originally used Ernest in a commercial for a local dairy. But then they discovered they could repeat the same gags for different advertisers in different markets. Ernest now has been seen by about half the people in the United States, but in different ads for different companies in different parts of the country.

*Your ol' Buddy, Ernest*

Carden & Cherry Advertising, of Nashville, Tennessee, capitalized on a memorable face by using Jim Varney in its ads to portray obnoxious character Ernest P. Worrel. The agency took a very successful local ad campaign and used it in different parts of the country to sell different products.

Each advertiser gets a minimum of six Ernest commercials, with different jokes in each commercial. In contrast to the elaborate, expensive commercials created by larger agencies, Carden & Cherry typically made 12 ads in one day (26 is the record) at Mr. Cherry's house, using a hand-held camera. By doing everything the wrong way (according to standard agency practices), Carden & Cherry succeeded.

## Advertising Regulation

Government protection for consumers dates back to the beginning of this century when Congress passed the Pure Food and Drug Act in 1906, mainly as a protection against patent medicine ads (see Edward Bok's campaign against patent medicine advertising, Chapter 3). The advertising industry itself has adopted advertising standards, and in some cases the media have established their own codes.

Government oversight is the main deterrent against deceptive advertising, however. This responsibility is shared by several government agencies.

*1.* The Federal Trade Commission (FTC), *established in 1914, can "stop business practices that restrict competition or that deceive or otherwise injure consumers."*[29] *If the FTC determines that an ad is deceptive, the commission can order the advertiser to stop the campaign.*

*The commission also can require corrective advertising to counteract the deception. In 1991, for example, a consumer group asked the FTC to launch an investigation of products that appear in movies, claiming that the product appearances are advertisements and that the film companies should be required to list the products in the screen credits.*

*2.* The Food and Drug Administration (FDA) *oversees claims that appear on food labels or packaging. If the FDA finds that a label is deceptive, the agency can require the advertiser to stop distributing products with that label. Orange juice that is labeled "fresh," for example, cannot be juice that has been frozen first.*

*3.* The Federal Communications Commission (FCC) *enforces rules that govern the broadcast media. The FCC's jurisdiction over the broadcast industry gives the commission indirect control over broadcast advertising. In the past, the FCC has ruled against demonstrations of products that were misleading and against commercials that the FCC decided were tasteless.*

Other government agencies, such as the Environmental Protection Agency and the Consumer Product Safety Agency, also can question the content of advertisements. Advertising agencies have formed the National Advertising Review Board (NARB) to hear complaints against advertisers. This effort at self-regulation parallels those of some of the media industries, such as the movie industry's ratings code and the recording industry's record labeling for lyrics.

# Facing the Future

The future of advertising will parallel changes in the media, in technology, and in demographics. As more U.S. products seek international markets, advertising must be designed to reach those markets. American agencies today collect nearly half of the *world's* revenue from advertising (see Figure 9.3 for the top ten agencies by worldwide income).

## The Top Ten U.S. Ad Agencies by Gross Income

Worldwide gross income,
1990 (millions)

| | Agency | Worldwide gross income, 1990 (millions) |
|---|---|---|
| 1 | Young & Rubicam | $1,001 |
| 2 | Saatchi & Saatchi Advertising Worldwide | $826 |
| 3 | Ogilvy & Mather Worldwide | $775 |
| 4 | McCann-Erickson Worldwide | $745 |
| 5 | BBDO Worldwide | $724 |
| 6 | Backer Spielvogel Bates Worldwide | $716 |
| 7 | J. Walter Thompson Co. | $691 |
| 8 | Lintas: Worldwide | $677 |
| 9 | DDB Needham Worldwide | $625 |
| 10 | Grey Advertising | $583 |

SOURCE: Data from *Advertising Age*, March 25, 1991.

International advertising campaigns are becoming more common for global products, such as Coca-Cola and McDonald's, and this has meant the creation of international advertising. Cable News Network (CNN) announced in 1991 that it would be selling advertising on CNN worldwide, so that any company in any nation with CNN's service could advertise its product to a worldwide audience. Overall, billings outside the United States are commanding an increasing share of U.S. agencies' business (Figure 9.4).

A second factor in the future of advertising is changing technology. As new media technologies create new outlets, the advertising community must adapt. Perhaps future advertising campaigns will reach your home computer screen. Or a tennis instructional video could include advertising for tennis products. And one company is using lasers to create advertising in the sky (see page 311).

A third factor in the future of advertising is shifting demographic patterns. As the ethnicity of the nation evolves, marketing programs must adapt to reach new audiences. Future television ads could include dialogue in both English and Spanish. Some national ad campaigns already include multilingual versions of the same ad, targeted for different audiences.

The challenges for the advertising business are as great as for the media industries. The advertising industry will do what it has always done to adapt —

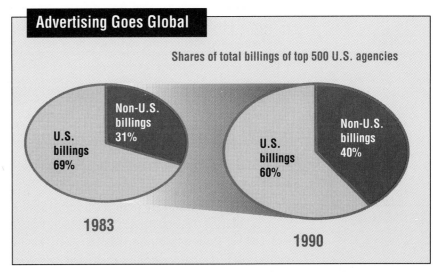

## Advertising Goes Global

Shares of total billings of top 500 U.S. agencies

U.S. billings 69%

Non-U.S. billings 31%

U.S. billings 60%

Non-U.S. billings 40%

1983

1990

SOURCE: Data from *Advertising Age*, March 29, 1989, and March 25, 1991.

follow the audience. The challenge for advertising in the 1990s will be to learn how to efficiently match the audience to the advertising messages the media deliver.

**IN FOCUS**

**Advertising**

• Advertising carries the messages that come to you from the sponsors who pay for the American media.

• As early as 1200 B.C., the Phoenicians painted messages on stones to advertise. In 600 B.C., ship captains sent criers around to announce that their ships were in port. In the 13th century A.D., the British began requiring trademarks to protect buyers.

• Newspapers were the first medium to use advertising, in 1704. Magazines, radio, and television followed.

• Daniel Boorstin says that advertising in America shares three characteristics: repetition, an advertising style, and ubiquity.

• Advertising can catch your attention, according to Jib Fowles, in 15 ways, including playing on your need to nurture, your need for attention, and your need to escape.

• Advertising provokes three main criticisms: advertising adds to the cost of products; advertising causes people to buy products they do not need; and advertising reduces competition and thereby fosters monopolies.

• Today's advertising agencies use sophisticated technology to track demographics to help deliver the audience the advertiser wants.

• The advertising business and the media industries are interdependent — what happens in the advertising business directly affects the media industries. And the advertising business is very dependent on the nation's economic health.

• The industry is divided into national and local advertising. Advertising sales representatives broker local accounts to out-of-town advertisers.

• The media compete with each other for the advertising dollar, and some media are better than others for certain products.

• Protection for consumers from misleading advertising comes from government regulation (Federal Trade Commission, Food and Drug Administration, and Federal Communications Commission, for example); from advertising industry self-regulatory groups (National Advertising Review Board, for example); and from codes established by the media industries.

• The future of advertising will parallel the development of international markets; the refinement and expansion of new media technologies; and changing demographics.

**10** *You may think that the cash rebate program offered by many of today's car manufacturers is a new idea, but*

*Henry Ford announced in 1914 that if he sold 300,000 Model Ts that year, each customer would receive a rebate. When the company reached its goal, Ford returned $50 to each buyer.[1] This was good business. It also was good public relations.*

*Like Henry Ford, public relations people today work to create favorable images —*

**Public Relations**

*for corporations, public officials, products, schools, hospitals, and associations.*

Scholars have defined three methods to encourage people to do what you want them to do: power, patronage, and persuasion. Power involves ruling by law, but it can also mean ruling by peer pressure — someone does something because their friends do. Patronage is a polite term for bribery — paying someone with favors or money to do what you want.

The third method — persuasion — is the approach of public relations. Like advertising, public relations is not a mass medium. Public relations is a media support industry. In the classic definition, public relations involves creating an understanding for, or goodwill toward, a company, a person, or a product.

# Origins and Growth of Public Relations

ONE OF the first political leaders to realize the importance of public relations was Augustus Caesar, who commissioned statues of himself in the first century to be erected throughout the Roman Empire to enhance his image.[2] Many political leaders have ordered heroic images of themselves printed on coins and stamps.

Today's public relations approach can be traced to the beginning of the 20th century. Journalists were an important reason for the eventual emergence of the public relations profession.

Before 1900, business had felt that it could work alongside the press, even ignore it. Many stories that appeared in the press promoted companies that bought advertising. Then the Industrial Revolution arrived, and some industrialists exploited workers and collected enormous profits. Ida Tarbell and Lincoln Steffens began to make business people uncomfortable, writing stories for magazines like *McClure's* about the not-so-admirable characteristics of some companies (see pages 90–92).

*No longer could the railroads butter up the press by giving free passes to reporters. No longer would the public buy whitewashed statements like that of coal industrialist George F. Baer, who in 1902 told labor to put their trust in "the Christian men whom God in His infinite wisdom has given control of the property interests of the country."[3]*

President Theodore Roosevelt fed public sentiment against the abuses of industry when he started his antitrust campaigns.

*With the growth of mass-circulation newspapers, Roosevelt's canny ability to dominate the front pages demonstrated a new-found power for those with causes to promote. He had a keen sense of news and knew how to stage a story so that it would get maximum attention. His skill forced those he fought to develop similar means. He fully exploited the news media as a new and powerful tool of presidential leadership, and he remade the laws and the presidency in the process.*[4]

The first publicity firm, called The Publicity Bureau, opened in Boston in 1900 to head off the growing public criticism of the railroad companies. The best-known early practitioner of public relations was Ivy Lee, who began his PR career by opening an office in New York with George F. Parker. Lee and Parker represented coal magnate George F. Baer when coal workers went on strike. A former newspaper reporter, Lee issued a "Declaration of Principles" that he mailed to city editors. This declaration became a manifesto for early public relations companies to follow.

Reacting to criticism that The Publicity Bureau had worked secretly to promote the railroads, Lee wrote:

*This [the firm of Lee & Parker] is not a secret press bureau. All our work is done in the open. We aim to supply news. . . . In brief, our plan is, frankly and openly, on behalf of business concerns and public institutions, to supply to the press and public of the United States prompt and accurate information concerning subjects which it is of value and interest to the public to know about.*[5]

Lee and Parker dissolved their firm in 1908 when Lee went to work as a publicity agent for the Pennsylvania Railroad. Eventually John D. Rockefeller hired Lee to counteract the negative publicity that began with Tarbell's investigation of Standard Oil (Lee worked for the Rockefellers until he died in 1934).

The idea of in-house corporate public relations grew as Chicago Edison Company and American Telephone & Telegraph began promotional programs. The University of Pennsylvania and the University of Wisconsin opened publicity bureaus in 1904, and the Washington, D.C., YMCA hired a full-time publicist to oversee fund-raising in 1905 — the first time a publicist was hired for this job.[6]

During World War I, the government set up the Committee on Public Information, organized by former newspaper reporter George Creel, blurring the line between propaganda and publicity. Creel recruited journalists, editors, artists, and teachers to raise money for Liberty Bonds and to promote the nation's participation in the war. One of the people who worked for Creel was Edward L. Bernays. Both Bernays and Ivy Lee have been called the father of public relations.

In what was the largest public relations drive of its time, the Office of War Information promoted the role of the United States in World War II.

In 1923, Bernays wrote the first book on public relations, *Crystallizing Public Opinion*, and taught the first course on the subject. Bernays was interested in mass psychology — how to influence the opinions of large groups of people. Procter & Gamble, General Motors, and the American Tobacco Company were among his clients. "Public relations," Bernays wrote in 1955, "is the attempt, by information, persuasion, and adjustment, to engineer public support for an activity, cause, movement, or institution."[7] In 1985, Bernays further defined public relations as "giving a client ethical advice, based on research of the public, that will win the social goals upon which the client depends for his livelihood."[8]

To sell the New Deal in the 1930s, Franklin D. Roosevelt used every tactic he knew. Comfortable with the press and the public alike, and advised by PR expert Louis McHenry Howe, FDR *projected an image of self-confidence and happiness — just what the American public wanted to believe in. He talked to them on the radio. He smiled for the cameras. He was mentioned in popular songs. He even allowed himself to be one of the main characters in a Rodgers and Hart musical comedy (played by George M. Cohan, America's favorite Yankee Doodle Dandy).[9]*

The requirements for someone to work in public relations in the 1930s were loose, and many people who said they worked in public relations were press agents who were not above tricks to get attention for their clients. Henry Rogers, co-founder of what was then the world's largest entertainment PR firm, Rogers & Cowan (based in Beverly Hills), admitted that in 1939 he created a "best-dressed" contest to promote little-known actress Rita Hayworth.

There had been no contest, but Rogers dubbed Hayworth the winner of this fictional event. *Look* magazine gave Hayworth a ten-page spread. "Press agents, and that's what we were, would dream up all sorts of phony stories," he said. "Journalists knew they were phony but printed them because they looked good in print."[10]

To gain support for the nation's entry into World War II, the federal government mounted the largest public relations drive in its history, which centered around the Office of War Information, led by former newscaster Elmer Davis. Public relations boomed with the postwar economy, and more women began to enter the field.

Doris E. Fleischman was among the first women in public relations when she joined her husband, Edward L. Bernays, in his PR firm. Fleischman was an equal partner with Bernays in their public relations business. An early advocate of public relations as a profession for women, Fleischman wrote in 1931 that "one finds women working side by side with men in forming the traditions and rules that will govern the profession of the future."[11]

Two other women who were public relations pioneers were Leone Baxter and Anne Williams Wheaton. Baxter formed Baxter and Whitaker in San Francisco with her husband, Clem Whitaker — the first public relations agency to specialize in political campaigns. And in 1957, President Dwight Eisenhower appointed Anne Williams Wheaton as his associate press secretary.[12]

# Development of Ethics Codes

During the 1950s, the question of ethics in public relations arose publicly when Byoir and Associates, hired by a railroad company to counteract the expansion of trucking, was charged with creating "front" organizations to

Doris Fleischman, a public relations pioneer, began her career in the 1920s.

speak out against the trucking industry. In court, Byoir's agency argued that they were exercising free speech. The U.S. Supreme Court in 1961 upheld Byoir's right to represent a client even if the presentation was dishonest, but this left the ethical issue of honesty unresolved.

The Public Relations Society of America established its first code of ethics in 1954 and expanded that code in 1959 with a Declaration of Principles.[13] That ethics code still exists today to guide the business of public relations (excerpts from the PRSA code are in Chapter 14). PR professionals continue to argue among themselves about the differences between the profession's beginnings as press agentry (which often meant fabricating stories) and the concept of ethically representing a client's business, as Edward L. Bernays described.

Public relations grew throughout the 1960s and 1970s with the encouragement of television, the federal government, and corporate America. In 1961, for example, the federal government had 1,164 people working as writer-editors and public affairs specialists. Today the total number of people working in federal government public information jobs is nearly 4,000,[14] making the federal government the nation's largest single employer of public information people. (Public information is the name given to the job of government public relations.)

# How Public Relations Works

PUBLIC RELATIONS is an industry of specialties. The most familiar public relations areas are financial public relations, product public relations, and crisis public relations, but there are many other specialty areas.

## Financial Public Relations

People in financial public relations provide information primarily to business reporters. "Business editors like a PR staff that can provide access to top management," wrote James K. Gentry in the *Washington Journalism Review*, "that knows its company well or can find needed information quickly, that demonstrates ethics and honesty and that knows and accepts the difference between news and fluff."

Gentry then listed comments gathered from editors about what makes a bad PR operation:

• *"Companies that think they can hide the truth from the public or believe it's none of the public's business."*

• *"I despise it when a PR person intercepts our calls to a news source but then isn't capable of answering our questions."*

• *"When they hire an outside PR firm to handle the job."*

• *"The 'no-comment' attitude. When they have little or no interest in going beyond the press release."*

• *"People who either get in the way of your doing your job, complain too much or are no help at all."*[15]

# Product Public Relations

Product PR uses public relations techniques to sell products and services. Many companies have learned that seeking publicity for a product often is less expensive than advertising the product. Public relations "is booming partly because of price," reports *The Wall Street Journal*. A PR budget of $500,000 is considered huge, while an ad budget that size is considered tiny.

*At its best, PR can work better than advertising. Coleco Industries Inc. kicked off its Cabbage Patch Kids in 1983 with press parties thrown in children's museums, to which editors and their children were invited — and at which all received dolls to "adopt." "Reporters who adopted dolls felt a part of the process," a Coleco spokeswoman says. They had "a personal interest in . . . continuing to publicize it."*[16]

The initial publicity for the Cabbage Patch dolls snowballed, as Cartier's used the dolls to display jewelry in its windows and First Lady Nancy Reagan gave dolls to two Korean children who were in the United States for surgery. Richard Weiner, who handled the publicity, charged Coleco $500,000.

On a smaller budget, the Wieden & Kennedy agency in Seattle contracted Bigger Than Life, Inc., which makes large inflatables, to manufacture a 2½-story pair of tennis shoes. (See Impact/Perspective, These Size 2½-Story Shoes Were Made for . . . Gawking!) The company attached the shoes to the Westin Copley Place hotel during the Boston Marathon and to the Westin Hotel in downtown Cincinnati during the March of Dimes walk-a-thon.

Pictures of the shoes appeared in *The New York Times, The Cincinnati Enquirer*, and in newspapers as far away as Japan. Wieden & Kennedy estimated that buying the same advertising would have cost $7 million.

# Crisis Public Relations

This aspect of public relations goes back as far as Edward Bernays responding to the charges against Standard Oil. The term *crisis public relations* has been used to describe the situation facing Johnson & Johnson after their product Tylenol was identified as the carrier of a poison that killed seven people in and near Chicago in 1982.

Johnson & Johnson and Burson-Marsteller, their PR agency, were credited with exceptional professionalism in handling the crisis. The Public Relations Society of America honored the companies for their performance. This is an example of responsible public relations in a crisis — when PR must counteract overwhelming negative information.

"The poisonings called for immediate action to protect the consumer," explained Johnson & Johnson's Lawrence G. Foster, who was vice president of public relations at the time, "and there wasn't the slightest hesitation about being completely open with the news media. For the same reasons, Johnson & Johnson decided to recall two batches of the product, and later to withdraw it nationally. During the crisis phase of the Tylenol tragedy, virtually every public relations decision was based on sound, socially responsible business principles, which is when public relations is most effective."[17]

Johnson & Johnson sampled public opinion about its activities with nightly telephone surveys. Pulling the product from the shelves cost $100 million, but as soon as Tylenol was out of the stores, the company was viewed as acting responsibly. The challenge then was to rebuild the product's 37 percent share of the market.

The 2,500-member Johnson & Johnson sales force visited retailers and people in the medical community to rebuild confidence in Tylenol. Then Burson-Marsteller organized a televised 30-city satellite press conference for 600 journalists to give local media an equal chance at a nationwide story, which ensured broad coverage.

After relaunch of the product, Tylenol immediately regained a 24 percent share of the market and later regained its position as the nation's top-selling brand.[18]

In 1987 the Chrysler Corporation faced a crisis of integrity when a federal grand jury delivered a 16-count indictment against the company, charging that Chrysler sold 60,000 cars and trucks as new when company managers already had driven the cars up to 400 miles with the odometers disconnected. At first Chrysler denied that "the company or any of its employees had done anything illegal or improper."

Within days, *The Wall Street Journal* consulted several public relations experts and asked for their advice. What should Chrysler do? Here are the suggestions they offered:

• *Admit the mistake. This will limit the damage because then the incident will be a one-day story.*

• *Admit the mistake and say you're sorry. Claim that the problem is not ethical, but technical.*

**Publicity is the cheapest form of advertising because it attracts media (and thus the public's) attention without the expense of purchasing advertising space. This article by Sheila McLaughlin of *The Cincinnati Enquirer* about giant sneakers is a good example of how the Rockport Shoe Company used publicity to its best advantage.**

SNEAKERS. TENNIS shoes. Call them what you will. But a pair of inflated white sports shoes, each spanning 2½ stories on the north wall of the Westin Hotel, is a publicity stunt that has downtown visitors doing a double-take.

Speculation abounded Sunday among those on Fountain Square.

"It could be from the Heart Mini–Marathon, or for the 2½-mile run this morning that ended up at the stadium," said Mike Krieg of Fairfield.

But given 30 seconds, he changed his mind. Krieg was sure those shoes were made for walking.

"If they were running shoes, they'd probably have a Nike swoosh on them."

Dave Hollingsworth of Cincinnati Carriage was as baffled as his customers. "Everybody's been asking me, but I don't have the answer. I tell them we're working on it."

"Isn't it some kind of promotion for Wrangler?" he yelled over his shoulder to a co-worker.

Clifton resident Rick Meadows tried to solve the mystery with an eyewitness account.

He said he and a friend were downtown about midafternoon Saturday when they saw two men on a scaffold secured above an inflated shoe. The other shoe was against the building, deflated.

"I left to buy some lottery tickets and when I came back they were inflating the other one. Those things are pretty wild though," Meadows said.

Even the Westin staff was stumped.

"I believe they're part of a promotion with the March of Dimes WalkAmerica," said Hugh Moore, assistant manager of the Westin's front office.

"All I know is that they cover 2½ floors of the hotel."

Executive committee member Michael Proulx of the March of Dimes confirmed Moore's guess.

The Rockport Shoe Co., which makes walking shoes and is one of the sponsors of WalkAmerica, agreed to let Cincinnati borrow the shoes for a week, said Laura Kennedy, director of public information for the March of Dimes.

Next Sunday, 4,500 walkers are expected to participate in a 30-kilometer walk-a-thon through Greater Cincinnati to raise money for research in birth defects. Fountain Square will serve as both starting point and finish line.

About 1,500 more will join in similar community events in the 15-county area served by the Greater Cincinnati chapter, Proulx said.

This giant pair of shoes, commissioned by the Wieden & Kennedy agency in Seattle, was created for $30,000 by Bigger Than Life, Inc., manufacturers of giant inflatables. Photographs of the shoes appeared in major newspapers across the country. *The Cincinnati Enquirer*, for example, ran a story (opposite) about the shoes when they appeared in Cincinnati to promote the March of Dimes WalkAmerica.

As an example of crisis public relations, Chrysler Chairman Lee Iacocca faced the press in 1987 to respond to a federal indictment against Chrysler.

• *Hide. Say no one is available to talk about it.*

• *Put Chrysler Chairman Lee Iacocca on television to admit his mistake, saying that he's "damn mad and that it won't happen again."*

• *Announce formally that you are halting the practice and that any cars driven extensively in the future will be sold as demonstrators.*

• *Attack the idea that the buyer has to be the first person behind the wheel for the car to be considered new. Say that the corporate executives were testing the product to make sure it worked right.*

• *Begin an ad campaign that says, "Nobody tests cars the way we test cars."*[19]

Which decision would you make? A week after the indictment, Lee Iacocca held a press conference to acknowledge "mistakes in judgment," saying Chrysler would extend the warranty on any vehicles it had used with disconnected odometers.

Iacocca said that disconnecting the odometers was "just dumb." But selling 40 cars as new that had been seriously damaged in accidents and then repaired, said Iacocca, "went beyond dumb and reached all the way out to stupid." Iacocca said Chrysler would replace the repaired cars with new cars. Chrysler was taking the action, said Iacocca, to repair the damage that had been done "in the court of public opinion." Iacocca's quick reaction diffused criticism of Chrysler's original mistake.

The Chrysler episode and the Tylenol crisis indicate how important specialization in crisis public relations can be within the public relations business. (To see how *not* to handle a crisis, see Impact/Perspective, Critics Fault Exxon for Handling of Alaskan Oil Spill.)

# PR Agencies Today

STIMATES OF the number of people in the country involved in public relations range from 100,000 to 134,000,[20] and more than 5,000 firms in the United States offer PR-related services. The largest public relations firms employ more than 1,000 people. Several major corporations have 100 to 400 public relations specialists, but most public relations firms have fewer than four employees.[21]

Public relations people often deal with advertising agencies as part of their job, and because PR and advertising are so interrelated, several large public relations firms have joined several large advertising agencies. J. Walter Thompson (advertising) acquired Hill & Knowlton (PR) for $28 million. Young & Rubicam (advertising) bought Burson-Marsteller and Marsteller Inc. (PR) for about $20 million.[22] In 1987, J. Walter Thompson Group was itself bought by a London firm, WPP Group PLC, for $566 million. These combined agencies can offer their clients both public relations and advertising help.

The difference between public relations and advertising at the nation's largest agencies can be difficult to discern. Advertising is an aspect of marketing that aims to sell products. People in advertising usually *aren't* involved in a company's policymaking. They implement the company's policies after company executives decide how to sell a product or a corporate image or an idea.

Public relations people, in comparison, usually *are* involved in policy. A PR person often contributes to decisions about how a company will deal with the public, the press, and its own employees.

**Public relations practitioners always point to the importance of knowing how to handle a crisis. In the case of the Exxon oil spill, detailed here by Allana Sullivan and Amanda Bennett of *The Wall Street Journal*, the company's treatment of the crisis became an example of what *not* to do.**

WHEN CRISIS strikes a big company, the chief executive officer is often one of the first to step forward to take responsibility publicly. . . .

Exxon Corp. [wasn't] so prompt.

In the week [after] a grounded Exxon supertanker sent a huge oil spill spreading over Alaskan waters [in March 1989], the company . . . dispatched its top shipping executives to the scene. It . . . sent in planes, cleanup crews and at least one attorney. It . . . stationed three public relations people there to field questions about the spill, the largest ever in U.S. waters.

But it wasn't until . . . a week after the spill that Exxon chairman and chief executive Lawrence Rawl emerged to comment publicly. He told the Reuter news service that the U.S. Coast Guard and Alaskan officials were to blame for the holdup in efforts to clean up the spill. "I don't want to point fingers, but the facts are, we're getting a bad rap on that delay," he said. . . . He also appeared on the MacNeil/Lehrer Newshour and apologized to the people of the U.S. and Alaska for the spill.

But Mr. Rawl's delay in responding drew criticism from analysts and consultants. "It doesn't help the public image for the CEO to sit back for so long," says Paul Shrivastava, associate professor of management at New York University's graduate school of business and director of its industrial-crisis center. Mr. Rawl, he adds, "is behaving very typically of CEOs who . . . hope [the problem] will go away."

. . . Analysts, academics

Fisherman John Thomas holds an oil-slicked sea bird recovered in the Prince William Sound, Alaska.

and consultants say the top officer's presence in an emergency can be an important symbol. "When the most senior person in the company comes forward, it's telling the whole world that we take this as a most serious concern," says Harry Nicolay, a crisis management consultant in Boston. . . .

In their own crises, other chief executives have maintained that no one else could better represent the company. Says Lawrence G. Foster, a Johnson & Johnson vice president: "Regardless of how many public relations people you have, the chairman is the single most responsible spokesman a company has."

In Exxon's case, Mr. Rawl's lack of visibility is just one striking note in a decidedly mixed crisis-management effort. On the one hand, the company has been blunt about its own responsibilities. . . . But others fault the company for its tardy and confused response. Cleanup crews were late on the scene, and early public relations efforts were sketchy and uninformed at Exxon's main U.S. offices.

Exxon's usual public relations office for its U.S. operations — one man and an answering machine in Houston — was swamped with calls. When others were brought in to field questions, they referred callers to public relations officials in Alaska, only to find that overloaded telephone lines couldn't handle the traffic. Even Exxon executives complained that they couldn't get the information they needed and were relying on news wires.

The president of Exxon Co. U.S.A., William Stevens, didn't fly to the site of the spill until President Bush decided to send three representatives to survey the situation. . . .

Part of Exxon's troubles apparently stemmed from its own decentralized structure. Because the accident occurred at a U.S. operation, the entire responsibility for organizing public relations fell to the one-man shop in Houston. Also, the decentralization left Mr. Rawl getting his information secondhand in the early stages. Before he was dispatched to Valdez, Mr. Stevens was being briefed by phone from Alaska — and in turn was briefing Mr. Rawl.

---

*"Critics Fault Chief Executive of Exxon on Handling of Recent Alaskan Oil Spill,"* The Wall Street Journal, *March 31, 1989, B-1.*

# Types of Clients

Public relations people work for several types of clients, including governments, business and industry, and nonprofit organizations.

**Government.** As noted previously, the federal government is the nation's largest employer of public information people. State and local governments also hire people to handle PR. Related to government are PR people who work for political candidates and for lobbying organizations. Media consultants also are involved in political PR. These people counsel candidates and officeholders about how they should present themselves to the public through the media.

**Education.** Universities, colleges, and school districts often hire public relations people to promote these educational institutions and to handle press attention to the consequences of decisions that educators make.

**Nonprofit Organizations.** This includes hospitals, churches, museums, and charities. Hospital PR is growing especially fast as different health care agencies compete with each other for customers.

**Industry.** AT&T's early appreciation of the public relations business was one type of industry PR. Many industries are government-regulated, so this often means that the industry PR person works with government agencies on government-related issues that affect the industry, such as utility rate increases or energy conservation programs.

**Business.** This is the best-known area of public relations. Large companies keep an in-house staff of public relations people, and these companies also often hire outside PR firms to help on special projects. Product publicity is one of the fastest-growing aspects of business-related public relations.

Within many large businesses are people who handle corporate PR, sometimes called financial PR. They prepare annual reports and gather financial data on the company for use by the press. They also may be assigned directly to the executives of a corporation to help establish policy about the corporation's public image. And many companies sponsor charity events to increase their visibility in the community.

In an example of corporate public relations, General Telephone Company of California (GTE) lent technical assistance, equipment, charitable contributions, volunteers, graphics, printing, and media assistance to the World

GTE garnered both public recognition and an award for its sponsorship of and participation in the World Games for the Deaf. GTE employees formed one of the teams in the "Tell-A-Bike Relay."

Games for the Deaf. GTE was the first major sponsor of the Games. Two thousand athletes from 45 nations competed in 144 events in 13 sports.

The "Tell-A-Bike Relay" consisted of two teams of eight experienced cyclists apiece, riding from Santa Barbara to Santa Monica. Instead of passing batons, each team passed a message. One team was a deaf team, the other a hearing team made up of GTE employee volunteers. The hearing team spoke the message; the deaf team signed it.

As a result of this and many other efforts, the California Public-Private Partnership Commission recognized GTE and the World Games for the Deaf with its award in the public initiatives category.

## Athletic Teams and Entertainment Organizations. A

professional sports team needs someone to travel with the team and handle the

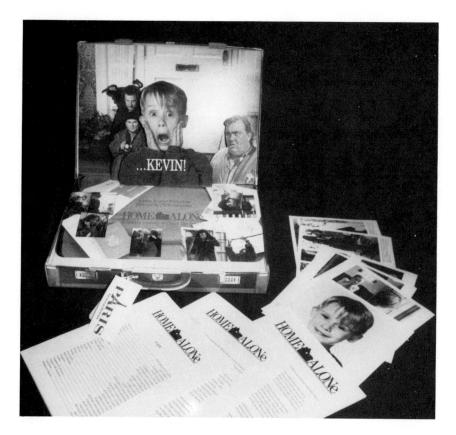

Public relations people try to create excitement for their entertainment clients. This unique press kit for *Home Alone* arrived in a cardboard suitcase, filled with photos and press releases to promote the movie.

press requests that inevitably come at each stop. Sports information people also are responsible for the coaches' and the owner's and the team's relationship with the fans. College and university sports departments often hire public relations people to handle inquiries from the public and from the press.

In 1939, Henry Rogers learned how to use press agentry to gather publicity for Rita Hayworth. Today, entertainment public relations agencies promote movies (see above), and they also handle TV personalities and well-known athletes who appear on the lecture circuit.

**International.** As the nation's consumer market broadens, more attention is being given to developing business in other countries. This means more opportunities in international PR. Hill & Knowlton and Burson-Marsteller, for example, are the two biggest U.S. public relations firms now operating in Japan.[23]

# The PR Job

What do public relations people do? Their responsibilities include the following.

**Writing.** News releases, newsletters, correspondence, reports, speeches, booklet texts, radio and TV copy, film scripts, trade paper and magazine articles, institutional advertisements, product information, and technical materials.

**Editing.** Special publications, employee newsletters, shareholder reports, and other communications for employees and for the public.

**Media Relations and Placement.** Contacting news media, magazines, Sunday supplements, freelance writers, and trade publications with the intent of getting them to publish or broadcast news and features about or originated by the organization. Responding to media requests for information or spokespersons.

**Special Events.** Arranging and managing press conferences, convention exhibits, open houses, anniversary celebrations, fund-raising events, special observances, contests, and award programs.

**Speaking.** Appearing before groups and arranging platforms for others before appropriate audiences by managing a speakers' bureau.

**Production.** Creating art, photography, and layout for brochures, booklets, reports, institutional advertisements, and periodicals; recording and editing audio- and videotapes; preparing audiovisual presentations.

**Research.** Gathering data to help an organization plan programs; monitoring the effectiveness of public relations programs. This is a fast-growing area of public relations that includes focus groups to test message concepts; research to target specific audiences; surveys of a company's reputation to use for improving the company's image; employee and public attitude surveys; and shareholder surveys to improve relations with investors.

**Programming and Counseling.** Establishing a program for effective public relations within the company.

**Training.** Working with executives and other people within the organization to prepare them to deal with the media.

**Management.** Overseeing the costs of running the public relations program; paying the bills.[24]

# Public Relations and the Media

Public relations work often means finding ways to attract the attention of the press. Says Seymour Topping, managing editor of *The New York Times*,

*PR people do influence the news, but really more in a functional manner rather than in terms of giving new editorial direction. We get hundreds of press releases every day in each of our departments. We screen them very carefully for legitimate news, and very often there are legitimate news stories. Quite a lot of our business stories originate from press releases. It's impossible for us to cover all of these organizations ourselves.*[25]

People in public relations provide **publicity**, which creates events and presents information so the press and the public will pay attention. Publicity and advertising differ: An advertising message is paid for; publicity is free. Advertising is a *controlled* use of media, because the message and where it will appear are governed by the person or company that places the ad. Publicity is considered an *uncontrolled* use of the media, because the public relations person provides information to the press but has no control over how the information will appear — the press writes the story. "We know how the media work," says David Resnicow of the PR firm Ruder Finn & Rotman, "and we make judgments on that, providing access to events as it becomes necessary."[26]

It is precisely because people in the media and people in PR know how each other work that they argue about the role of public relations in the news. (See Impact/Profile, Video News Releases.) In 1979, the *Columbia Journalism Review* studied the relationship between corporate public relations and *The Wall Street Journal* by examining the stories in the *Journal* on a specific day and comparing the stories to press releases issued by PR people.

Specific companies were mentioned in 111 articles. Nearly half the news stories in the *Journal* that day, *CJR* reported in its analysis, were based solely on press releases. In 32 of the stories that were based on press releases, reporters paraphrased the releases almost verbatim; in the 21 remaining cases, only a small amount of additional reporting had been done.

The *Journal*'s executive director, Frederick Taylor, responded to *CJR*'s analysis by saying, "Ninety percent of daily coverage is started by a company making an announcement for the record. We're relaying this information to our readers."[27]

In a specific example of what is called press release journalism, *New York Times* reporter Douglas C. McGill published a story in the March 6, 1987, *Times* about the discovery of the original model that Michelangelo used to create his famous statue of David. McGill attributed the story to Professor Frederick Hartt, who had made the discovery.

Hartt had signed a contract with Abbeville Press to write a book about the Michelangelo discovery, and the book's photographer was David Finn, the chief executive officer of the public relations agency Ruder Finn & Rotman. In March 1987, two public relations people from Ruder Finn & Rotman had called McGill at the *Times* and offered him the story.

McGill added considerable research to the story, but when the connection was discovered, McGill told *Manhattan inc.* magazine that he felt uncomfortable. "I wasn't especially happy that the story was handed to me by a public relations agent. But once I heard about it, I thought it was an important story for *Times* readers no matter who it came from. The whole thing made me uneasy. It showed a high degree of sophistication from Ruder Finn."[28]

Clever ways to attract attention are trademarks of today's successful public relations professional. According to Jeff and Marie Blyskal, who interviewed hundreds of PR people for their book *PR: How the Public Relations Industry Writes the News*:

*At the highest level of the profession, PR people are low-key, candid, creative, knowledgeable, warm, witty, charming, friendly, personable, self-confident. The best ones communicate as well as or better than some of the best journalists today; they are true communications technicians. We have found few hollow shells of human beings, bereft of moral conviction and marching in step with whatever "orders" their clients or employers bark out. Many were genuinely excited about their profession; some were swell-headed; only a few harkened back to their journalism days to assure us they were really "okay."*

*Then, too, we saw no cabals or international PR conspiracies to control the public's mind — though quietly controlling minds is, in fact, what PR people attempt to do on a case-by-case basis. PR people have chosen their profession, and most seem reasonably satisfied with being effective advocates for their clients. . . . Some will even admit that what they do is manipulation, but manipulation with a noble, higher goal in mind:*

# Video News Releases

Video news releases (VNRs) are a growing form of public relations. In this article, freelance writer **Robert Buchanan** describes VNR production and the spreading use of VNRs in the media as "free video."

**a**T 34, [Robin] Bossert is second in command at Armstrong Information Services, which is a sort of news agency, or rather, a *sponsored* news agency: It produces ready-to-roll television stories called "video news releases," or VNRs, on behalf of corporate clients and distributes them free of charge to news programs and talk shows. VNRs are the hot ticket in Hypeland these days. The better ones look and sound exactly like bona fide news features — and they're routinely broadcast as such — but they put the squeeze on unsuspecting viewers with subtle and sometimes not so subtle commercial messages. . . .

"This went out last October," Bossert says, slapping a cassette into his VCR. "Thirty-two stations picked it up, and the total audience was something like 2,800,000." He pushes the play button. "New Kind of Water Powers Marathon Runners," reads the screen. The opening shot is a standard view of the Verrazano Bridge on Marathon Sunday. Hordes stream toward Brooklyn. *The New York Marathon is the largest marathon, with over twenty thousand runners competing*, begins a newsy-sounding voice. *That means a lot of physical courage and a lot of plain sweat. One runner in a single marathon can lose between five and ten pounds due to water loss — and this can be a major source of dehydration.*

"We send the story out with the voice-over on one channel so they can knock it out and put in their anchorman," says Bossert. "We send it out with a script so he can just read off it if he wants to pretend he's the reporter."

*No one knows about the problems*, the announcer continues, *better than Fred Lebow, originator of the New York Marathon.* Cut to a bearded sprite in a nylon track suit, standing on the jogging path that circles the reservoir in Central Park. A superimposed caption identifies him as "Fred Lebow, New York Road Runners Club."

Bossert leans over again. "We never put titles [in]," he says. "The ones you see are just for the client. We just put instructions along with the script, because every station has its own typeface. . . . Plus every station has its Action News logo or whatever."

Lebow, meanwhile, is explaining the importance to the marathoner of maintaining a steady intake of water. To back him up, there's stock footage of racers passing a midcourse water station and grabbing cups from the outstretched arms of volunteers, all without breaking stride. Most runners seem to slosh a lot of water; the pavement glistens with spillage.

It's at this point that the announcer begins his windup. *The problem in every marathon is getting water to the runners in a* *way they can use. It's often a miracle if it ever gets to where it's needed most — the runner's mouth. Preformed Tetra-Brik cartons, with seven layers of paper, plastic and foil, help protect liquids. Its special brick shape and easy-open top makes getting water a snap and a runner's life easier.*

The concluding scenes of the clip are set back at the reservoir. A self-conscious group of runners shuffles up to the camera, sure-handedly gripping Tetra-Briks but somewhat tentatively sipping at the sharp, tiny straws that protrude from them. Interviewed, one of them says, "It works a lot better, because when you're running along and you have to pick up a cup, you spill a lot of water and this is much better." A paid actor? Bossert shakes his head. "Let me tell you, people love to be on camera, and they'll say anything." . . .

Outside the New York metropolitan area, this kind of "news" is more and more prevalent. Bossert says that Armstrong, which employs eight people and bills about $1 million a year, maintains "good relations" with perhaps two hundred stations between here and L.A., and enjoys an average success rate of 30 percent with each mass mailing of a VNR. Captains of the VNR industry — there are half a dozen hybrid "broadcast PR" agencies bigger than Armstrong in Manhattan — say they're simply riding a wave of demand for footage. . . .

In the case of the Tetra-Brik spot, Bossert says, several stations combined Armstrong footage with their own interviews of local athletes who were en route to New York for the marathon.

In general, though, Bossert contends, "they use the whole thing, because it's time-consuming to mess with the package, and they know this package is professional." But even if you see only five seconds of a VNR like Tetra-Brik's, if you but glimpse a runner's hand holding a squarish foil-and-paper carton perforated by a single straw, then you've got the message.

*From "Not Necessarily the News: Are Video Press Releases Turning TV Journalism into 'Promo at Eleven'?"* Manhattan inc. 4, no. 4 (April 1987): 45–49.

*defending or advancing the cause of their client. There are two sides to every story, goes the argument. They are, in a sense, the equivalent of attorneys in the court of public opinion.*[29]

# Facing the Future

Like the future of advertising, the future of public relations is closely tied to the future of the media industries. The basic structure of the business will not change, but public relations practitioners will find themselves facing the same challenges as people in the advertising business.

Growing international markets will mean that, in the future, many U.S. public relations firms will expand overseas. Global communications will mean that public relations agencies will work internationally on some projects, and that the agencies will have to adjust to the cultural differences that global exposure brings.

New technologies will mean new ways to deliver public relations messages, such as the video news release. Eventually, satellite technology may streamline all video, giving PR agencies the same access to distributing video to news organizations that the news organizations now possess themselves.

And, as in the advertising industry, shifting demographic patterns will mean growing potential markets for public relations services.

**IN FOCUS**

**Public Relations**

• Modern public relations emerged at the beginning of the 20th century as a way for business to respond to the muckrakers and to Theodore Roosevelt's antitrust campaign.

• The first publicity firm in the country, called The Publicity Bureau, opened in Boston in 1900.

• The best-known early practitioner of public relations was Ivy Lee, who wrote a "Declaration of Principles" to respond to the secret publicity activities of The Publicity Bureau.

• The Chicago Edison Company and American Telephone & Telegraph were the first companies to begin in-house promotional programs.

• The Committee on Public Information, headed by George Creel, promoted the war effort during World War I. The Office of War Information, headed by newscaster Elmer Davis, promoted the country's efforts during World War II.

• Edward L. Bernays wrote the first book on public relations, *Crystallizing Public Opinion*. Both Bernays and Ivy Lee have been called the father of public relations.

• Franklin Roosevelt, assisted by public relations expert Louis McHenry Howe, successfully used public relations to promote the New Deal.

• Among the pioneering women who joined the public relations business were Doris E. Fleischman, Leone Baxter, and Anne Williams Wheaton. Doris Fleischman and Edward Bernays were equal partners in the Bernays public relations firm. Doris Fleischman was an early advocate of public relations as a career for women.

• The Public Relations Society established the profession's first code of ethics in 1954.

• Public relations expanded quickly in the 1960s and 1970s to accommodate television, the federal government, and corporate America.

• Today it is estimated that between 100,000 and 134,000 people work in public relations nationwide. More than 5,000 firms offer PR-related services.

• Public relations people work in government, education, industry, business, for nonprofit agencies, athletic teams, entertainment companies, and in international public relations.

• Public relations people use persuasion and publicity to attract attention for their clients.

• The main difference between advertising and public relations is that advertising messages are controlled and public relations messages are uncontrolled.

• The trademark of today's public relations is a sophisticated approach to news. People who work in public relations have been called "attorneys in the court of public opinion."

• Public relations agencies face the same challenges as advertising agencies: expanding worldwide markets, the development of new technologies, and changing demographic patterns.

IV

Issues
and
Effects

**11**

*In 1822, James Madison observed about the media's role in a democracy that "a popular government, without popular information, or the means of acquiring it, is but a prologue to a farce or a tragedy; or perhaps both."[1]*

*One hundred years later, political columnist Walter Lippmann wrote, "The press is no substitute for institutions. It is like the beam of a searchlight that moves restlessly about, bringing one episode and then another out of darkness into vision."[2]*

**Ownership Issues and Press Performance Issues**

Because the media are this country's main source of information, it is important to examine who owns the media and how well journalists, working within that system of ownership, fulfill their responsibility of reporting on events. How well does today's system of media ownership in the United States allow the media to bring the important and necessary "popular information" to the people, as envisioned by Madison? How well do journalists shine that searchlight to bring "one episode and then another out of darkness into vision," as Lippmann described? That is what this chapter is about.

# Ownership Issues

IN SOME media industries, ownership is controlled by more companies today than in the 1950s. There are six major movie studios today, for example, compared to the Big Five and the Little Three of the 1940s; the number of companies that own broadcast stations has increased since the 1940s, and so has the number of magazine publishers. The number of companies that publish newspapers and the number of companies that produce records, however, have declined.

Overall, American media ownership has been contracting rather than expanding since its heyday in the 1960s. The emergence of some new media, such as cable, is inviting more people into the media business, but the trend is for fewer companies to own more media businesses and for fewer companies to own more aspects of the media business. Here is some media ownership information compiled from previous chapters, with some new facts added (see also Figure 11.1):

• *The top ten newspaper chains own one-fifth of the nation's dailies; group owners (companies that own more than one newspaper) hold three out of four newspapers published in America every day.*

• *Twenty corporations control more than 50 percent of annual magazine revenue.*

• *Nearly 40 percent of the nation's radio stations are network affiliates.*

• *More than half of the nation's TV stations are network affiliates.*

## Where Ten Media Giants Get Their Revenues

### 1989 revenues (millions of dollars)

| | Company | News-papers | Maga-zines | Radio and TV | Cable TV | Other | Total |
|---|---|---|---|---|---|---|---|
| 1 | Capital Cities/ABC | 491 | 376 | 3,585 | 315 | – | 4,767 |
| 2 | Time Warner | – | 1,855 | – | 2,720 | – | 4,575 |
| 3 | Gannett | 2,852 | – | 408 | – | 258 | 3,518 |
| 4 | General Electric | – | – | 3,392 | – | – | 3,392 |
| 5 | CBS | – | – | 2,960 | – | – | 2,960 |
| 6 | Advance Publications | 1,745 | 842 | – | 295 | – | 2,882 |
| 7 | Times Mirror | 2,066 | 306 | 103 | 333 | – | 2,808 |
| 8 | TCI | – | – | – | 2,353 | – | 2,353 |
| 9 | Knight-Ridder | 1,988 | – | – | – | 273 | 2,261 |
| 10 | News Corporation | 284 | 713 | 700 | – | 506 | 2,203 |

SOURCE: Data from *Advertising Age*, August 12, 1991.

• *Almost all of America's movies are distributed by one of the six large studios.*

• *The majority of recording company profits are collected from six major labels.*

• *America's top six book publishing companies account for 30 percent of total annual publishing revenue.*

• *The nation's top ten advertising agencies bill more than $50 billion dollars annually in worldwide business.* [3]

Media concentration involves four trends:

*1.* Concentration of ownership *within one industry, such as print and broadcast chain ownership and broadcast network affiliation.*

*2. The number of* cross-media ownerships — *companies that own more than one type of medium.*

*3. The role of* conglomerate ownership — *companies that own media properties and also are involved in businesses other than the media business.*

*4. The attempts of some companies to achieve* vertical integration — *companies that control several aspects of a single media industry, such as production and distribution (see Chapter 1 for more information about these categories).*

In 1961, *New Yorker* press critic A. J. Liebling warned about the danger of one-newspaper towns:

*As the number of cities in the United States with only a single newspaper ownership increases, news becomes increasingly nonessential to the newspaper. In the mind of the average publisher, it is a costly and uneconomic frill, like the free lunch that saloons used to furnish to induce customers to buy beer. . . . With the years, the quantity of news in newspapers is bound to diminish from its present low. The proprietor, as Chairman of the Board, will increasingly often say that he would* like *to spend 75 cents now and then on news coverage but that he must be fair to his shareholders.*[4]

Today less than 3 percent of American cities have competing newspapers. Liebling's fears could apply to all forms of ownership concentration. The issue of concentration centers on one question, what former newspaper editor Norman E. Isaacs calls "the internal war between public purpose and making money" and what the book publishing industry calls the war between "culture and commerce."

"For an author, the increased concentration means decreased access to the market and fewer outlets for publication," write economists Michael J. Robinson and Ray Olszewski, summarizing statements made by the Authors Guild about concentration in the publishing industry. "Its impact on the marketplace for ideas . . . is to introduce the risk of corporate pressure being placed on editors and on the production process, pressure that would not be a problem with the existence of independent companies. Mergers and acquisitions reduce the number of diverse and antagonistic sources."[5]

In the advertising business, some executives are even more candid. "It's big for big's sake," one advertising executive told *The Wall Street Journal*. "Advertising is really a personal service," said a second ad executive, "and the bigger it gets, the more impersonal it becomes."[6]

Today's media companies are profit-centered. They are owned by people who want to make money. As in all industries, there are people who want to make money quickly and people who take the long-term view about profits, but certainly none of them wants to lose money.

Traditionally making money has been a goal supported by the vast majority of Americans. But the way these companies make money is the debate. Does the legacy of First Amendment protection for news-gathering organizations mean that they have a special responsibility to provide the information people need in a democracy? Should entertainment-producing companies provide a diversity of cultural outlets for creativity? Will the adoption of corporate values benefit or harm the mass media industries?

# Why Media Properties Are Selling

The two biggest examples of turnover in ownership are the newspaper and broadcast industries. Several factors have affected the market for these properties.

*1. Newspaper and broadcast properties are attractive investments. Many report profits of 10 percent a year, which is about double the profit for a U.S. manufacturing company.*

*2. Newspapers and broadcast stations are scarce commodities. Because the number of newspapers has been declining and the number of broadcast stations is government-regulated, only so many properties are available. As with all limited commodities, this makes them attractive.*

*3. Many newspapers, especially, have gone through a cycle of family ownership. If the heirs to the founders of the business are not interested in joining the company, the only way for them to collect their inheritance is to sell the newspaper.*

*4. Newspapers and broadcast stations are easier to buy than to create. Because these businesses require huge investments in equipment, they are expensive to start up.*

*5. In broadcasting, the major factor that is encouraging ownership changes is deregulation. This has allowed people who have never been in the broadcast business before to enter this industry, using bank loans to pay for most of their investment. Deregulation is the main reason for the huge surge in changes of ownership in the 1980s (see Figure 11.2). But deregulation can have other effects, too (see Impact/Perspective, Broadcast Programmers Respond to Deregulation).*

Some of these new owners approach broadcast properties as they would any other business — hoping to invest the minimum amount necessary. They hope to hold onto the property until the market is favorable and then sell at a huge profit. In 1986, for example, a company named Kohlberg-Kravis sold KTLA-TV in Los Angeles to the Tribune Company (owner of TV stations in Atlanta, New Orleans, and Denver; the *Chicago Tribune*, the New York *Daily News*, five

11.2 ➤

## Broadcasting's Ownership Changes, 1938–1990

Number of radio and television stations sold in the United States, with average price per transaction

| Year | Number of transactions | | | | Average price per each FCC-approved transaction | |
| | Radio only | TV only | Radio/ TV | Total | Radio only | TV only |
| --- | --- | --- | --- | --- | --- | --- |
| 1938 | 20 | – | – | 20 | $46,039 | – |
| 1946 | 52 | – | – | 52 | $441,589 | – |
| 1956 | 316 | 21 | 24 | 361 | $103,049 | $849,066 |
| 1966 | 367 | 31 | 11 | 409 | $208,811 | $986,259 |
| 1976 | 413 | 32 | 1 | 446 | $437,442 | $3,389,364 |
| 1986 | 959 | 128 | 192 | 1,279 | $1,553,838 | $21,168,098 |
| 1988 | 845 | 70 | 106 | 1,021 | $2,179,443 | $25,796,493 |
| 1990 | 1,045 | 75 | 60 | 1,180 | $831,230 | $9,292,698 |

SOURCE: Data from "37 Years of Station Transactions," *Broadcasting Yearbook, 1991*, p. ix.

radio stations, 15 cable television systems, and the Chicago Cubs). The Tribune Company paid $510 million—twice the amount Kohlberg-Kravis paid for KTLA three years earlier.[7]

# Advantages of Concentration

Supporters of concentrated ownership say that a large company can bring advantages that a small company could never afford—training for the employees, higher wages, and better working conditions. John C. Quinn, executive vice president for news for Gannett, says:

*A publisher's instinct for good or evil is not determined by the number of newspapers he owns. A group can attract top professional talent, offering training under a variety of editors, advancement through a variety of opportunities. . . . It can invest in research and development and nuts-and-bolts experience necessary to translate the theories of new technology into the practical production of better newspapers.*

*Concentrated ownership can provide great resources; only independent, local judgment can use the resources to produce a responsible and responsive local newspaper. That measure cannot be inflated by competition nor can it be diluted by monopoly.*[8]

William A. Henry III of *Time* magazine, who won a Pulitzer Prize at the *Boston Globe*, points out that several of the newspapers that are considered the nation's best — *The New York Times,* the *Los Angeles Times*, and the *Washington Post* — are chain newspapers, although he acknowledges that these three are still dominated by family owners who hold the majority of stock.

The same arguments that are made against chain ownership can be made against independent ownership, he says.

*Most independent owners run papers in ways that comfort them, their friends and their general social class.*

*A great many reporters have gotten into trouble over the years by going after buddies or business associates of the owners. And a great many more have compromised themselves by writing puffy, uncritical pieces about cultural institutions, department stores, restaurants or socialites favored by the owner or his spouse.*[9]

# Disadvantages of Concentration

The major arguments of those who support concentration are that a corporation can offer financial support to a small newspaper or broadcast station and that responsible, autonomous local management is the key to successful group ownership. Yet several studies have proved that chain newspapers are more likely to support the favored candidates in elections, and that in presidential elections, 85 percent or more of the papers in a chain endorse the same candidate.[10]

This is an example of the consequences of corporate control that forms the major argument against group ownership — that concentration limits the diversity of opinion and the quality of culture available to the public and reduces what scholars call *message pluralism.*

In an article in *The New Republic* entitled "Invasion of the Gannettoids," former newspaper reporter Philip Weiss described what he says happens when corporate culture takes over American journalism:

*The problem with Gannett isn't simply its formula or its chairman, but the company's corporate culture. The product is the company — cheerful, superficial, self-promoting, suspicious of ideas, conformist, and implicitly authoritarian. But the Gannett story is more, too. For as many as 6 million daily readers, most of them in one-newspaper towns, Gannett serves as chief interpreter and informer about society — and does so unsustained by ideals of independence or thoroughness.* [11]

The loss of message pluralism in television angers critics the most, since broadcasting still is licensed to serve the public "interest, convenience, and necessity." Broadcasters argue that this requirement is out of date because it was adopted when broadcast outlets were scarce. Today, broadcasters say many channels of information are available to the public.

But Ben H. Bagdikian, Dean Emeritus, Graduate School of Journalism at

# Broadcast Programmers Respond to Deregulation

Stories like this one by **Bob Davis** are becoming more common as all broadcast stations look for ways to save money. At issue is whether broadcast stations, licensed by the government, can fulfill their public responsibilities if they drop news, public affairs, and children's programming.

t O SOME people in Whatcom County, Wash., no news is bad news. . . .
Federal broadcast deregulation gave KVOS, the county's only television station, the freedom to drop its sole half-hour local newscast. And shortly afterward, the CBS affiliate did just that, replacing the un-profitable show with periodic, minute-long "news capsules."

KVOS "cut off maybe 40 percent of Whatcom County (population 113,700) from

U.S. (television) news," says Tim Douglas, mayor of Bellingham, Wash. "It's a big loss." KVOS says money saved from cutting the news show saved the station.

For many years a debate has raged over whether the government should force radio and television stations to run programs that attract small audiences but nevertheless may serve some public good. About five years ago [in 1981], the Federal Communications Commission began eliminating programming guidelines and

government pressure to make broadcasters run news, public affairs and children's programming.

Now, in the fallout, both opponents and proponents of broadcast deregulation see proof for their positions. . . .

Still, neither denies that deregulation has led to the demise of many shows. The argument is whether that's good or bad.

For instance, one Boston TV station, WNEV, started producing several local information shows in late 1982 after

IMPACT/
PERSPECTIVE

University of California, Berkeley, describes how the loss of message pluralism can affect every aspect of communication:

*It has always been assumed that a newspaper article might be expanded to a magazine article which could become the basis for a hardcover book, which, in turn, could be a paperback, and then, perhaps a TV series and finally, a movie. At each step of change an author and other enterprises could compete for entry into this array of channels for reaching the public mind and pocketbook. But today several media giants own these arrays, not only closing off entry points for competition in different media, but influencing the choice of entry at the start.* [12]

the FCC awarded the station to a coalition of businessmen, academics and programming activists. But the shows flopped in the ratings. One magazine-style news-and-interview show, *Look*, fared so poorly that the station's management cut it to one hour a week from two hours in September 1983. And the station, under no regulatory pressure to run public-interest programs, dropped the shortened show six months later and replaced it with game shows. . . .

On the radio, news departments, long hurt by sagging advertising, have been cut back. In Peoria, Ill., Chuck Collins, news director of WXCL radio, says the lack of regulatory pressure freed managers from the obligation of running news shows. As a result of deregulation, he says, management slashed the news staff to three from seven, reduced the number of newscasts

and didn't replace the public affairs director after he died. Now, he says, WXCL often can't cover stories in person or do features. "We just have time for surface reporting," he says. . . .

Nowhere is the debate over deregulation more tenaciously fought than in children's programming. Action for Children's Television, a Cambridge, Mass., group, says deregulation is to blame for fewer educational children's shows. The group also claims there has been a flood of TV cartoons based on popular toys because the FCC no longer regulates the commercial content of kids' shows.

Chuck Sherman, president of WHOI-TV in Peoria, says there are fewer good children's shows because of dismal economics in educational children's programming. And clearly, unlike the old days of regulatory demands, he feels no

pressure to run children's shows. Deregulation has "broken down the old (television network) oligarchy," he says. "We're in a more competitive environment. Why should every station have to do children's programming every day? There's Nickelodeon (a cable channel of kids' shows) and PBS." His station carries *Quincy* reruns and game shows in the afternoon instead of kids' shows because he is trying to build an adult audience. "If I put on a kids' program, I'll lose my audience."

*"Broadcasters, Absent Regulation, Kill News Shows — but Is That Bad?"* The Wall Street Journal, *Oct. 16, 1986, p. 33.*

IMPACT/
PERSPECTIVE

# Press Performance Issues

**B**ECAUSE THE First Amendment to the U.S. Constitution prescribes freedom of the press, it is important to examine how well the press uses that freedom to report on events. To understand how well the press performs, you must first understand who journalists are and how they work. Then you can examine how the public feels about the way members of the press do their job.

## Today's Journalists

The latest study of just who journalists are comes from *The American Journalist: A Portrait of U.S. News People and Their Work*, published in 1986 to update a 1971 study that tried to determine journalists' characteristics. Authors David H. Weaver and G. Cleveland Wilhoit surveyed 1,001 American journalists about their jobs. According to Weaver and Wilhoit's 1986 study, today's "typical" U.S. journalist "is a white Protestant male who has a bachelor's degree, is married and has children, is middle-of-the-road politically, is thirty-two years old, and earns about $19,000 a year."[13]

Weaver and Wilhoit cautioned that this typical portrait is misleading because there are:

*substantial proportions of women, non-Protestant, single, politically left and right, young and old, and relatively rich and poor journalists working in this country for a variety of news media, including daily and weekly newspapers, radio and television stations, news magazines, and news services.*

In the following list, Weaver and Wilhoit compared their findings with the conclusions of the 1971 study.

1. The size of the journalistic workforce has increased *61 percent during the 1970s, with the great percentage of growth in radio and television.*

2. There appears to be a dramatic decline in the percentage (not necessarily the actual number) of journalists in the Northeast, and significant increases in the percentages working in the North Central and South.

3. The proportions of journalists working in different regions of the country more closely match the population percentages in those regions than in *1971*, *largely because of the growth of the number of broadcast journalists in the North Central and South.*

4. U.S. journalists in *1982–83 are younger and more often female than in 1971. Broadcast journalists are significantly younger than those working for the print media, and minority journalists are younger on the average than nonminorities.*

5. More journalists are leaving the field after age forty-five than in *1971, primarily because of low salaries.*

6. There has been a significant gain in the proportion of women journalists employed in U.S. media during the *1970s. Overall, the proportion of women journalists has increased from about one-fifth in 1971 to about one-third in 1982–83, and this proportion is likely to increase further, given the 60 percent enrollment of women in U.S. journalism schools.*

7. The largest increases in the percentages of women journalists have occurred in the broadcast media. The proportions of women employed as journalists in the various U.S. media are more consistent in *1982–83 than in 1971.*

8. There are proportionately fewer blacks, Hispanics, and Jews in U.S. journalism in *1982–83 than in 1971, although the actual numbers are up somewhat. This finding suggests that although efforts to recruit and retain women journalists in U.S. news media have been successful, such efforts with regard to minorities have not been effective.*

9. Politically, many more journalists place themselves in the middle of the scale than in *1971, and significantly fewer put themselves on the right. That suggests that U.S. journalists as a whole are becoming more centrist, not more leftist as some researchers have argued.*

10. We find much less difference overall in the political leanings of journalists working for prominent and nonprominent organizations than Johnstone found in *1971, although we do find managers in the nonprominent organizations to be the most conservative, and staffers in the prominent media to be the most inclined to say they are Democrats. We do not find the managers in the prominent organizations to be left of the staffers, as was found in 1971.* [14]

Of the journalists surveyed by Weaver and Wilhoit, 22.1 percent classified themselves as "a little to the left" or "pretty far to the left," 57.5 percent called themselves middle-of-the-road, and 17.9 percent called themselves "a little to the right" or "pretty far to the right." (2.5 percent didn't answer.)

It has not been shown in any comprehensive survey of news gathering that people with liberal or conservative values insert their personal ideology directly into their reporting and that the audience unquestioningly accepts one point

News values often are influenced by the way journalists cover important public events. Here, photojournalists surround professor Anita Hill, testifying in 1991 at the Clarence Thomas confirmation hearings.

of view. The belief in this one-to-one relationship can be traced to the **magic bullet theory**, which was disproved long ago (see page 378).

But the assumption that journalists' personal beliefs directly influence their professional performance is common. Although the reporting of some journalists and columnists can certainly be cited to support this idea, the majority of journalists, says media scholar Herbert J. Gans, view themselves as detached observers of events:

*Journalists, like everyone else, have values, [and] the two that matter most in the newsroom are getting the story and getting it better and faster than their prime competitors — both among their colleagues and at rival news media. Personal political beliefs are left at home, not only because journalists are trained to be objective and detached, but also because their credibility and their paychecks depend on their remaining detached. . . .*

*The beliefs that actually make it into the news are professional values that are intrinsic to national journalism and that journalists learn on the job. However, the professional values that particularly antagonize conservatives (and liberals when they are in power) are neither liberal nor conservative but reformist, reflecting journalism's long adherence to good-government Progressivism.* [15]

Some press critics, in fact, argue that journalists most often present establishment viewpoints and are unlikely to challenge prevailing political and social values.[16] In addition, the pressure to come up with instant analyses of news events may lead to conformity in reporting.

In mid-May 1989, for example, thousands of people gathered in Tiananmen Square to demonstrate against the Chinese government. Angered by the demonstrations, the government sent troops to clear the Square, and hundreds of people were killed and injured, most of them students. In his analysis of the way the press reported on the violence, press critic David Shaw argued that journalists misread and misreported events as a pro-democracy uprising that could not be stopped. Shaw called this "consensus journalism" — the tendency among many journalists covering the same event to report similar quick conclusions about the event, rather than to report conflicting interpretations (see Impact/Perspective, Consensus Journalism).

# News Values

News organizations often are criticized for presenting a consistently slanted view of the news. But as Weaver and Wilhoit observed, news values often are shaped by the way news organizations are structured and the routines they follow. The press in America, it is generally agreed, don't tell you what to think, but do tell you what and whom to think *about*. This is called **agenda-setting**.

There are two types of agenda-setting: the flow of information from one news organization to another and the agenda of information that flows from news organizations to their audiences.

In the first type of agenda-setting, the stories that appear in the nation's widely circulated print media provide ideas to the other media. The print media, for example, often identify certain stories as important by giving them attention, so that widely circulated print media can set the news agenda on some national issues. (See Impact/Perspective, Second-Hand News.)

To analyze the second type of agenda-setting — the picture of the world that journalists give to their audiences — is to examine the social and cultural values that journalists present to the public. The most significant recent study of news values was offered by Herbert J. Gans in his book *Deciding What's News*.

Gans identified eight enduring values that emerged in his study of different types of news stories over a long period of time: ethnocentrism, altruistic democracy, responsible capitalism, small-town pastoralism, individualism, moderatism, order, and leadership. These values, said Gans, often help define what is considered news.

# Consensus Journalism

According to press critic **David Shaw**, the press coverage of the dramatic events in China in May 1989 shows that consensus journalism can result when journalists fail to take the time for more complex, analytical reporting.

t IAN AN Men Square: More than a million Chinese demonstrated against their government [in May 1989], and the American media assured their readers and viewers that China would never be the same — that the democratic genie was permanently out of the totalitarian bottle. . . .

. . . Why? Why do the media sometimes arrive at an instantaneous consensus on issues, events, and individuals that would seem open to widely varying, even conflicting interpretations? How does this "conventional wisdom" develop?

Many of the more than 60 journalists and public opinion specialists the [Los Angeles] *Times* interviewed recently about the phenomenon attributed its growth to the tendency of reporters to talk to the same sources all the time. Others pointed to a "herd mentality" in the media — "the nation's herd of independent minds," in [*Time* magazine columnist Charles] Krauthammer's phrase. Still others cited conditions ranging from geographic myopia and ideological bias to manipulation by government officials, laziness, homogeneity, timidity, and insecurity in the press corps and the absence of such volatile, fundamentally divisive issues as Vietnam, Watergate, or the civil rights movement.

But most of those interviewed said the growing trend toward consensus journalism derived largely from the pervasiveness and impact of television, with its demands for speed, brevity, and conformity.

These demands affect print

reporters as well as television reporters; knowing that television will almost inevitably be first, newspaper and magazine journalists often try to provide the analysis that television may lack the air time to do. But in trying to rush this analysis into print to compete with the ever-increasing speed of television, many reporters and columnists reflexively reach for the simplest, safest, most obvious explanations.

Journalists required to write daily stories on developing events "don't think deeply enough and . . . don't take enough time. . . ; there's too much instant consensus . . ." says R. W. Apple, deputy Washington bureau chief for *The New York Times*.

The longstanding imperatives of daily journalism — the crush of events and the rush to meet deadlines — have been exacerbated in recent years by computers, satellites, and the other miracles of modern communications technology. The media *can* communicate faster, so the media *does* communicate faster — if not necessarily with greater perspicacity or originality. . . .

Technology notwithstanding, "reporters are only human," and many journalists invoked this phrase to explain

why they are often so quick to form a consensus — whether by discussing an issue or event with each other or by independently arriving at the same judgments. . . .

In China, the U.S. media thought the troops wouldn't attack the protesters, and even when they did, the media remained convinced that China had been forever changed by the protests, that freedom — not repression and executions — would follow.

Major upheavals have hit China at the end of each of the last four decades, though, and the current Chinese leaders — like their predecessors, terrified of anarchy in so vast a population — have remained authoritarian, determinedly faithful to their violent revolutionary roots.

So why did the massacre and repression surprise so many journalists?

"We all, to one degree or another, got sucked in by the prospect that these were the 1980s version . . . the Oriental version of the Concord Bridge," [NBC News Anchor Tom] Brokaw says. "I think that we were unsophisticated. . . . I suppose what I fault us all on in China is that we took a really typical Western attitude toward it and failed to see

it for its Chinese aspects, both culturally and politically."

Reporters on the scene in Beijing were "part of a euphoric environment," says Henry Muller, managing editor of *Time* magazine. "They were witnesses to something absolutely amazing" that coincided with what reporters from democracies would like to see happen. "They became so engrossed in what was going on that they lost their ability to be as purely analytical of the events as they should have been."

Daniel Schorr, senior news analyst for National Public Radio, says he, too, was "swept away" by what happened in Tian An Men Square, and he subsequently told his listeners that he shouldn't have called the event in China "irreversible" and would immediately "expunge the word 'irreversible' from my commentator's vocabulary."

*"Consensus Journalism: How Media in China Gave Stories the Same 'Spin,'"* Los Angeles Times, *Aug. 25, 1989, p. 1.*

These three magazine covers demonstrate the potential for consensus journalism, when major media organizations focus their attention on a single interpretation of the same story.

American news conveys the ideas of:

Ethnocentrism. *America is a nation to be valued above all others. "While the news contains many stories that are critical of domestic conditions, they are almost always treated as deviant cases, with the implication that American ideas, at least, remain viable," says Gans.*

Altruistic democracy. *Politics should be based on public service and the public interest. The news media expect all public officials to be scrupulously honest, efficient, and public-spirited.*

Responsible capitalism. *Open competition will create increased prosperity for everyone. Business people should not seek unreasonable profits, and they should not exploit workers or customers.*

Small-town pastoralism. *Small agricultural or market towns are favored over other settlements. Suburbs are usually overlooked as a place where news happens. Big cities are viewed as places with "urban" problems.*

Individualism. *A heroic individual is someone who struggles against difficulties and powerful forces. Self-made people are admired.*

Moderatism. *Moderation is valued, excesses and extremism are not.*

Order. *Importance is placed on political order. "The values in the news derive largely from reformers and reform movements, which are themselves elites. Still, the news is not simply a compliant supporter of elites, or the establishment, or the ruling class; rather, it views nation and society through its own set of values and with its own conception of the good social order."*

Leadership. *Attention is focused on leaders. The president is seen as the nation's primary leader and protector of the national order.* [17]

These values exist throughout American society and, indeed, come from historical assumptions based in our culture. As Gans suggests, this news ideology both supports and reflects elements of the social order.

# The Public and the Press

Two astute observers of the press who have been critical of its performance are James Reston and Norman Corwin. "The truth is that most American newspaper people are really more interested in dramatic spot news, the splashy story, than in anything else," said *New York Times* columnist James Reston. "They want to be in on the big blowout, no matter how silly, and would rather write about what happened than whether it made any sense."[18]

Broadcast producer and writer Norman Corwin said about local television news people:

*The average local newscast, almost everywhere in the country, is a kind of succotash served in dollops and seasoned by bantering between anchorpersons, sportspersons, weatherpersons and person-persons. And these people had better be good-looking, sparkling or cute — weathermen with party charm, anchorladies with good teeth and smart coiffures, sportscasters with macho charisma. It doesn't matter if they have a news background or not.* [19]

Reston and Corwin are members of the media who are critical of their own profession. The public's perception of how well members of the press perform their responsibility is equally important; only recently have the media begun to survey the public for their opinions about the news media.

Since 1986 Times Mirror has sponsored several ongoing studies of the public's feelings about the press conducted by the Gallup organization. For these surveys, Gallup has personally interviewed 1,000–3,021 people nationwide and then doubled back to ask the same respondents additional questions to clarify earlier findings. Among the findings of these surveys, which Times Mirror calls *The People & the Press*, are:

• *By a ratio of 4 to 1, the people who were surveyed said that the major news organizations* — The Wall Street Journal, *CBS News, ABC News, NBC News,* Newsweek, *and* Time — *are believable.*

• *79 percent of the people surveyed said that news organizations "care about how good a job they do"; 72 percent said the press is "highly professional."*

• *In 1989, a majority (54 percent) said reporters get the facts straight; 44 percent said the press was often inaccurate. The inaccuracy rating has increased 10 percent since 1985 (see Figure 11.3).*

# Second-Hand News

**In this article, Barbara Matusow describes one type of agenda-setting: the passing of information and ideas from one news organization to another.**

THE *Washington Post* runs a story about a reporter for the Voice of America being mobbed by adoring students in China. That night, Sam Donaldson interviews the reporter on ABC's *Nightline.*

The *Philadelphia Inquirer* profiles a woman who auditions animals for David Letterman's Stupid Pet Tricks. A few weeks later she shows up on Philadel-

phia station KYW-TV's *Evening Magazine.*

*USA Today* probes the problems of single people in a week-long series. The editors are deluged with telephone calls from radio program hosts who want to interview *USA Today's* experts on the air.

The *Wall Street Journal* features a story about a Miami lawyer who has a phenomenal record of beating drunk-driving charges for his clients.

Stories on CNN, NBC's *Today* show, ABC's *Good Morning America* and CBS's *60 Minutes* follow.

What's going on here? Do radio and TV originate any of the stories they air? The answer is yes when it comes to breaking news. For features, long-range trends, and investigative stories, however, broadcasters remain woefully dependent on the print press for leads and story ideas. "It's frightening to

- *In 1989, more than two-thirds of the people (68 percent) said that journalists tend to favor one side, compared to 53 percent who felt the press were biased in 1985 (see Figure 11.3).*

- *The press is "pretty independent," according to 33 percent of the people, but 62 percent said the press is "often influenced by the powerful," including the federal government, big business, advertisers, and special-interest groups.*

- *77 percent of the people interviewed in 1989 said that the press invades people's privacy. This was the most widely held criticism among the people surveyed.*

- *The people who have negative opinions about the press are those who consume the most news and are among the most vocal and powerful segments of American society.* [20]

think of how much we depend on newspapers," says Susan Mercandetti, a producer on *Nightline.* "If you haven't read the papers before you get to work, you haven't done your job."

"Let's say you come up with a really great story," says CBS *Nightwatch* Associate Producer Heidi Berenson. "So you tell the producer, 'Listen, I'm telling you, this is going to be big.' But unless you really push, I mean, go to the mat, no one is interested. Then, all of a sudden, the story appears in the papers and you say, 'Oh, my God.'"

Often, television news reporters take a story they see in the newspaper and advance it or develop additional information. Sometimes, assignment editors simply hand a reporter a clip and say, "Go do this." After *The Wall Street Journal* ran

a long piece last June on how cocaine trafficking had developed from a cottage industry into a relatively stable multinational business, the reporter, Thomas E. Ricks, got a call from a CBS correspondent. *The CBS Evening News* wanted to do the same story, the caller confided, and he asked Ricks for the names of his sources. . . .

Local news operations also pursue original stories more vigorously than they used to, but they are even more hampered than the networks by skimpy reporting staffs. KNBC, a reasonably ambitious station in Los Angeles that fields a staff of 19 reporters, can scarcely compete with the *Los Angeles Times*, which has 320 full-time and 20 part-time reporters covering southern California. One solution being adopted by a few stations around the country is "piggy-

backing." WAGA-TV in Atlanta has opened "bureaus" in two suburban newspapers and is planning to open a third shortly. The reporter stationed at the *Gwinnett Daily News* covers Atlanta's northern suburbs, reporting live from the newsroom with the newspaper's logo on prominent display. . . .

"The people who say TV has supplanted print as the biggest source of news are only half right," says Jeff Greenfield [ABC News]. "Maybe they get their news from radio and TV, but the agenda is still shaped to a large degree by print, especially *The New York Times*, the *Washington Post*, *The Wall Street Journal* and the news magazines."

*"Second-Hand News: How TV Feeds on Print,"* Washington Journalism Review 9, no. 2 (March 1987): 45–47.

IMPACT/
PERSPECTIVE

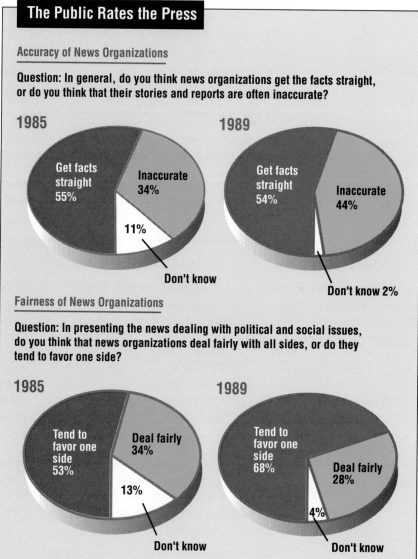

**The Public Rates the Press**

Accuracy of News Organizations

Question: In general, do you think news organizations get the facts straight, or do you think that their stories and reports are often inaccurate?

1985

Get facts straight 55%

Inaccurate 34%

11%

Don't know

1989

Get facts straight 54%

Inaccurate 44%

Don't know 2%

Fairness of News Organizations

Question: In presenting the news dealing with political and social issues, do you think that news organizations deal fairly with all sides, or do they tend to favor one side?

1985

Tend to favor one side 53%

Deal fairly 34%

13%

Don't know

1989

Tend to favor one side 68%

Deal fairly 28%

4%

Don't know

SOURCE: Data from *The People & the Press,* 1989.

These surveys are the most comprehensive of their kind undertaken to date. They show that members of the public seem to support the press as an institution, but with specific misgivings about the way journalists do their job. It is also important to note that the people who pay the most attention to the news are the most critical about how the press performs.

Furthermore, the public is not a cheering section roused to its feet to defend the First Amendment. In fact, only one in three people surveyed by Gallup was able to cite the First Amendment as the source of press freedoms in America.

After the first survey appeared, Times Mirror received nearly 8,000 letters from people commenting on the results. One person wrote: "No question: No free press, no democracy. They go together like pie and ice cream." But a second person wrote, "Does a free press strengthen democracy? Absolutely, but it must be a *responsible press*. It must be *honest*. It must have *integrity*. And it must be willing to admit its mistakes *as loudly* as it claims its triumphs."[21]

# Understanding Ownership and Press Performance

THE MEDIA system described by Walter Lippmann and James Madison at the beginning of this chapter delivers a diversity of messages and opinions to an alert and informed public that uses this information to make intelligent decisions.

Media ownership that becomes concentrated in a few corporations could limit the society's access to "popular information, or the means of acquiring it" that Madison foresaw as an essential part of democratic government. A press that does not fulfill its public duty as "the beam of a searchlight" that Lippmann described risks losing the freedom that the First Amendment prescribes.

To maintain the public's trust, the owners of media companies and members of the press must be willing to undergo constant scrutiny about whether they are meeting their responsibilities. A critical view of ownership issues and press performance issues is important because the American media were founded in the belief that the press will perform conscientiously and that the public will have access to a variety of ideas and opinions through diverse media outlets.

• Ownership issues center around: (1) concentration; (2) cross-media ownership; (3) conglomerate ownership; (4) vertical integration.

• Media properties are selling rapidly because they are attractive investments; they are scarce commodities; they are easier to buy than to launch; many newspapers have gone through a cycle of family ownership; broadcast deregulation has lifted many restrictions.

• The major arguments of people who support concentration are that a corporation can offer financial support and that responsible local management is the key to successful group ownership.

• The major argument against group ownership is that concentration limits the diversity of opinion and the quality of culture available to the public — the loss of message pluralism.

• *The American Journalist* study (1986) indicates that today's "typical" journalist is a Protestant white male, 32 years old, with a bachelor's degree, is married and has children, is middle-of-the-road politically, and earns about $19,000 a year. The study also found that today's journalists are younger and more often female than in 1971.

• The press in America doesn't tell you what to think. It does tell you what and whom to think about. This is called agenda-setting.

• There are two types of agenda-setting: the flow of information from one news organization to another (the broadcast media, for example, often develop stories that first appeared in the print media) and the flow of information from news organizations to their audiences.

• Consensus journalism, as described by press critic David Shaw, is the tendency of journalists covering the same event to report similar quick conclusions about the event, rather than to report conflicting interpretations.

• Herbert J. Gans in his book *Deciding What's News* identified eight enduring news values: ethnocentrism, altruistic democracy, responsible capitalism, small-town pastoralism, individualism, moderatism, order, and leadership.

• *The People & the Press* survey sponsored by the *Los Angeles Times* found that most people believe that news organizations care about how well they do their jobs; more than two-thirds of the people surveyed said journalists tend to favor one side; 62 percent felt that the press is influenced by special interests; 77 percent of the people felt the press invades people's privacy; people who say they consume the most news also are most critical of the press' performance.

**12**

*How do the media affect what we do? When* People's

Court *became a series on TV, small-claims filings in*

*some cities rose 50 percent.*[1] *On November 7, 1991, within minutes after basketball*

*star Earvin "Magic" Johnson announced on TV that he had tested positive for the*

*HIV virus, callers flooded the San Francisco AIDS Foundation hotline at more than*

*15 times the normal rate.*[2]

*These two examples of media effects are anecdotal evi-*

**Media Effects**

*dence—pieces of a very complex picture. Today scholars*

understand that the media have different effects on different types of people with differing results. Generalizations about the media's effects are easy to make but difficult to prove. "We do not fully understand at present what the media system is doing to individual behavior, much less to American culture," say William L. Rivers and Wilbur Schramm. "The media cannot simply be seen as stenciling images on a blank mind. That is too superficial a view of the communication process."[3]

# Assessing the Impact: Media Studies

THE CONCEPT that the media have different effects on different types of people is relatively new. Early media observers felt that an absolute one-to-one relationship existed between what people read, heard, and saw and what people did with that information. They also believed that the effects were the same for everyone.

The magic bullet theory, sometimes called the hypodermic needle theory, alleged that ideas from the media were in direct causal relationship to behavior. The theory held that the media could inject ideas into someone the way liquids are injected through a needle. This early distrust of the media still pervades many people's thinking today, although the theory has been disproved.

Media research, like other social science research, is based on a continuum of thought, with each new study advancing slightly the knowledge from the studies that have come before. This is what has happened to the magic bullet theory. Eventually, the beliefs that audiences absorbed media messages uncritically and that all audiences reacted the same to each message were proven untrue. Research disclosed that analyzing media effects is a very complex task.

Some media research existed before television use became widespread in the mid-1950s, but TV prompted scholars to take an even closer look at the media's effects. Two scholars made particularly provocative assertions about how the media influence people's lives. David M. Potter and Marshall McLuhan arrived at just the right moment—when the public and the scholarly community were anxiously trying to analyze media's effects on society.

In his book *People of Plenty*, published in 1954, Potter first articulated an important idea: that American society is a consumer society driven primarily by advertising. Potter, a historian, asserted that American advertising is rooted in American abundance.

*Advertising is not badly needed in an economy of scarcity, because total demand is usually equal to or in excess of total supply, and every producer can normally sell as much as he produces. . . . It is when potential supply outstrips demand—that is, when abundance prevails—that advertising begins to fulfill a really essential economic function.*

Potter then warned about the dangers of advertising. "Advertising has in its dynamics no motivation to seek the improvement of the individual or to impart qualities of social usefulness. . . . It has no social goals and no social responsibility for what it does with its influence."[4] Potter's perspective was important in shaping the critical view of modern advertising. *People of Plenty* is still in print today.

In the 1960s, Canadian Marshall McLuhan piqued the public's interest with his phrase "The medium is the message," which he later parodied in the title of his book *The Medium Is the Massage*. One of his conclusions was that the widespread use of television was a landmark in the history of the world, "retribalizing" society and creating a "global village" of people who use media to communicate.

McLuhan suggested that electronic media messages are inherently different from print messages—to watch information on TV is different from reading the same information in a newspaper. McLuhan never offered systematic proof for his ideas, and some people criticized him as a charlatan, but his concepts still are widely debated.

Scholars who analyze the media today look for patterns in media effects, predictable results and statistical evidence to document how the media affect us. Precisely because the media are ubiquitous, studies of their effects on American society are far from conclusive. In this chapter you will learn about some of the major studies that have examined the media's effects and some of the recent assertions about the role that the media play in our lives.

Media research today includes media effects research and media content analysis. Effects research tries to analyze how people use the information they receive from the media—whether political advertising changes people's voting behavior, for example (see the discussion of *The People's Choice*, pages 383–384). Content analysis examines what is presented by the media—how many children's programs portray violent behavior, for example (see George Gerbner, page 380). Sometimes these two types of analysis (effects research and content studies) are combined in an attempt to evaluate what effect certain content has on an audience.

# The Payne Fund Studies

The prestigious Payne Fund sponsored the first major study of media, conducted in 1929. It contained 12 separate reports on media effects. One of these studies concentrated on the effects of movies on children. In his interviews, researcher Herbert Blumer simply asked teenagers what they remembered about the movies they had seen as children.

Using this unsystematic approach, he reported that the teenagers had been greatly influenced by the movies because they *said* they had been greatly influenced. Blumer's conclusion and other conclusions of the Payne Fund studies about the media's direct one-to-one effect on people were accepted without question, mainly because these were the first major studies of media effects, and the results were widely reported. This became known as the magic bullet theory.

The Payne Fund studies also contributed ammunition for the Motion Picture Producers and Distributors Association Production Code, adopted in 1930, which regulated movie content (see Chapter 6).

# The Cantril Study

The Martians who landed in New Jersey on the Mercury Theater "War of the Worlds" broadcast of October 30, 1938 (see page 125) sparked the next major study of media effects, conducted by Hadley Cantril at Princeton University. The results of the Cantril study contradicted the findings of the Payne Fund studies and disputed the magic bullet theory.

The Cantril researchers wanted to find out why certain people believed the Mercury Theater broadcast and other people did not. After interviewing 135 people, Cantril concluded that high critical thinking ability was the key. Better-educated people were much more likely to decide that the broadcast was a fake. This might seem to be a self-evident finding today, but the importance of the Cantril study is that it differentiated among listeners: People with different personality characteristics interpreted the broadcast differently.

# The Lasswell Model

In 1948, Harold D. Lasswell designed a model to describe the process of communication that is still used today. Lasswell said this process can be analyzed by answering five questions:

*Who?*
*says what?*
*on which channel?*
*to whom?*
*with what effect?*

In other words, Lasswell said that the process of communication can be analyzed by determining who the sender is and what the sender says. Next, you must identify which channel — meaning method — of communication the sender used. Then you must examine the audience and define the effect on that audience. Because Lasswell described the communication process so succinctly, most of the communications research that followed has attempted to answer his five questions.

# Studies of Television

The 1950s were a time of adjustment to the addition of the new medium of television, which was seen first as a novelty and then as a necessity. Since 1960, four of the major studies of the effects of television have focused on children.

*Television in the Lives of Our Children*, published in 1961 by Wilbur Schramm, Jack Lyle, and Edwin Parker, was the first major study of the effects of television on children. Researchers interviewed 6,000 children and 1,500 parents, as well as teachers and school officials.

Schramm and his associates reported that children were exposed to television more than to any other mass medium. On an average, 5-year-old children watched television 2 hours every weekday. TV viewing time reached 3 hours by the time these children were 8 years old. In a finding that often was subsequently cited, Schramm said that from the ages of 3 to 16, children spent more time in front of the television set than they spent in school.

Children used television for fantasy, diversion, and instruction, Schramm said. Children who had troubled relationships with their parents and children who were classified as aggressive were more likely to turn to television for fantasy, but Schramm could find no serious problems related to television viewing. Schramm also found, in support of Cantril, that different children showed different effects.

*Television and Social Behavior*, a six-volume study of the effects of television, was funded by $1 million appropriated by Congress in 1969 after the violent decade of the 1960s. The U.S. Department of Health, Education and Welfare, which sponsored the study, appointed a distinguished panel of social scientists to undertake the research.

"OKAY, WE CAN WATCH A LIVE EXECUTION ON PUBLIC TV, A MERCY KILLING ON CHANNEL TWO, AN ABORTION ON CHANNEL SEVEN OR JUST KICK BACK AND SPEND THE EVENING PLAYING *NAZI DEATH CAMP NINTENDO!...*"

The study's major findings, published in 1971, concerned the effects of television violence on children. A content analysis of one week of prime-time programming, conducted by George Gerbner of the University of Pennsylvania, reported that eight out of ten prime-time shows contained violence. The conclusions of *Television and Social Behavior* failed to make a direct connection between TV programming and violent behavior, however. The report said only that there was a "tentative" indication that television viewing caused aggressive behavior. According to the study, this connection between TV violence and aggressive behavior affected only *some* children who were already classified as aggressive children and *only* in certain environments.

Even though the report avoided a direct statement about violent behavior in children as a result of television viewing, the U.S. Surgeon General called for immediate action against violence on television. The television industry dismissed the results as inconclusive.

Several subsequent studies since 1971 have suggested that television violence causes aggression among children. In their 1988 book *The Early Window: Effects of Television on Children and Youth*, psychologists Robert M. Liebert and

Joyce Sprafkin urged caution in drawing broad conclusions about the subject:

*Studies using various methods have supported the proposition that TV violence can induce aggressive and/or antisocial behavior in children. Whether the effect will hold only for the most susceptible individuals (e.g., boys from disadvantaged homes) or whether it will hold for a wider range of youngsters obviously depends in part upon the measure being used. . . . The occurrence of serious violent or criminal acts results from several forces at once. Researchers have said that TV violence is a cause of aggressiveness, not that it is the cause of aggressiveness. There is no one, single cause of any social behavior.* [5]

**Television Advertising to Children.** The effects of advertising on adults have been widely analyzed, but in 1979 the advertising of children's products became an object of serious government attention with the release of the 340-page report *Television Advertising to Children* by the Federal Trade Commission.

The report, based on a 2-year study, was designed to document the dangers of advertising sugar-based products to children, but imbedded in the report was some provocative information about children's advertising. Children are an especially vulnerable audience, said the FTC. The report concluded:

• *The average child sees 20,000 commercials a year, or about 3 hours of TV advertising a week.*

• *Many children regard advertising as just another form of programming and do not distinguish between programs and ads.*

• *Televised advertising for any product to children who do not understand the intent of the commercial is unfair and deceptive.*

The report called for a ban on advertising to very young children, a ban on sugared products in advertising directed to children under age 12, and a requirement for counter-ads with dental and nutritional information to balance any ads for sugared products. [6]

This report and subsequent research about children's advertising suggest that younger children pay more attention to television advertising than older children. But by sixth grade, children adopt what has been called a "global distrust" of advertising. [7]

**Television and Behavior.** *Television and Behavior: Ten Years of Scientific Progress and Implications for the Eighties*, published in 1982 by the National Institute of Mental Health, compiled information from 2,500 individual studies of television. According to the National Institute of Mental Health, three findings of these 2,500 studies, taken together, were that:

*1. A direct correlation exists between televised violence and aggressive behavior, yet there is no way to predict who will be affected and why.*

*2. Heavy television viewers are more fearful, less trusting, and more apprehensive than light viewers.*

*3. Children who watch what the report called "pro social" programs (programs that are socially constructive, such as* Sesame Street*) are more likely to act responsibly.*

Most of the latest studies of the media's role have continued to reinforce the concept that different people in different environments react to the media differently.

# The Media and National Politics

THE MEDIA have transformed politics in ways that could never have been imagined when President Franklin D. Roosevelt introduced what were called Fireside Chats in 1933. Roosevelt was the first president to use the media effectively to stimulate public support. The newest technology of FDR's era — radio — gave him immediate access to a national audience. Roosevelt's media skill became an essential element in promoting his economic programs. Today, politics and the media seem irreversibly dependent on each other, one of the legacies of Roosevelt's presidency.

## The Fireside Chats

In March 1933, just after he was inaugurated, FDR looked for a way to avoid a financial panic after he announced that he was closing the nation's banks. For a week the country cooled off while Congress scrambled for a solution. On the Sunday night eight days after his inauguration, Roosevelt used radio to calm the nation's anxiety before the banks began to reopen on Monday. FDR went down to the basement of the White House to give his first Fireside Chat.

There was a fireplace in the basement, but no fire was burning. The president could not find his script, so he borrowed a mimeographed copy from a reporter. In his first address to the nation as president, FDR gave a banking lesson to his audience of 60 million people: "I want to talk for a few minutes with the people of the United States about banking. . . . First of all, let me state the simple fact that when you deposit money in a bank, the bank does not put the money into a safe deposit vault. It invests your money in many different forms." When he finished, he turned to people in the room and asked, "Was I all right?"[8] America had its first media president, an elected leader talking directly to the people through the media.

Roosevelt's chats are cited as a legendary example of media politics, yet he gave only eight of them in his first term of office. His reputation for press access also was enhanced by his other meetings with the press — in 13 years in office he held more than 900 press conferences.

# The People's Choice

The first major study of the influence of media on politics was *The People's Choice*, undertaken precisely because FDR seemed to be such a good media politician. This comprehensive examination of voter behavior in the 1940 presidential election was quite systematic.

Researchers Paul Lazarsfeld, Bernard Berelson, and Hazel Gaudet followed 3,000 people in rural Erie County, Ohio, from May to November 1940 to determine what influenced the way these people voted for president. The researchers tracked how people's minds changed over the 6-month period and then attempted to determine why. (It is important to remember that this study was undertaken before television. Radio became the prevailing medium for political advertising in 1932, when the two parties spent more money for radio time than for any other item.[9])

What effect, the researchers wanted to know, did the media have on people's choosing one candidate over another? The results were provocative. Lazarsfeld and his colleagues found that only 8 percent of the voters in the study were actually *converted*. The majority of voters (53 percent) were *reinforced* in their beliefs by the media, and 14 percent were *activated* to vote. Mixed effects or no effects were shown by the remaining 25 percent of the people.

Lazarsfeld said that opinion leaders, who got their information from the media, shared this information with their friends. The study concluded that instead of changing people's beliefs, the media primarily activate people to vote and reinforce already-held opinions. *The People's Choice* also revealed that:

- *Family and friends had more effect on people's decisions than the media did.*

- *The media had different effects on different people, reinforcing Cantril's findings.*

- *A major source of information about candidates was other people.*

This finding that opinion leaders often provide and shape information for the general population was a bonus — the researchers hadn't set out specifically to learn this. This transmittal of information and ideas from mass media to opinion leaders to friends and acquaintances is called the **two-step flow** of communication.

# The Unseeing Eye

In 1976, a second study of the media and presidential elections, called *The Unseeing Eye: The Myth of Television Power in National Elections*, revealed findings that paralleled those of *The People's Choice*. With a grant from the National Science Foundation, Thomas E. Patterson and Robert D. McClure supervised interviews with 2,707 people from early September to just before Election Day in the November 1972 race between George McGovern and Richard Nixon. The study did not discuss political media events, but it did analyze television campaign news and political advertising. (The role of journalists and news reporting is discussed in Chapter 11.)

The researchers concluded that although 16 percent of the people they interviewed were influenced by political advertising, only 7 percent were manipulated by political ads. The researchers defined people who were influenced as those who decided to vote for a candidate based mostly on what they knew and only slightly on what the ads told them. The 7 percent of the people in the survey who were manipulated, according to Patterson and McClure, were people who cited political advertising as a major factor in their choices. Patterson and McClure concluded that political advertising on TV has little effect on most people.

*By projecting their political biases, . . . people see in candidates' commercials pretty much what they want to see. Ads sponsored by the candidate who shares their politics get a good response. They like what he has to say. And they like him. Ads sponsored by the opposing candidate are viewed negatively. They object to what he says. And they object to him.* [10]

It is important to remember, however, that in some elections a difference of a few percentage points can decide the outcome. This is why political advertising continues to play such an important campaign role, in an effort to reach the percentage of the population that remains vulnerable.

**Television and Politics.** So far no convincing systematic evidence has been presented to show that the media change the voting behavior of large groups of people. Yet since before John F. Kennedy debated Richard Nixon during the 1960 presidential campaign, a deeply felt view has persisted among many people that the media — television in particular — have changed elections and electoral politics.

Kennedy's debate with Nixon in 1960 was the first televised debate of presidential candidates in American history. Kennedy's appearance in the debates often is credited for his narrow victory in the election. In his book *Presidents and the Press*, media scholar Joseph C. Spear wrote:

*As the panel began asking questions, Nixon tended to go on the defensive, answering Kennedy point by point and ignoring his huge audience beyond the camera. Kennedy, by contrast, appeared rested, calm, informed, cocksure. Whatever the question, he aimed his answer at the millions of Americans viewing the program in their living rooms.*

*It was an unmitigated disaster for Nixon. In the second, third, and fourth debates, he managed to recover somewhat from his initial poor performance, but it was too late. Surveys showed that an overwhelming percentage of the television audience had judged Kennedy the victor.* [11]

One legacy of Kennedy's television victory is that today, national political campaigns depend almost entirely on TV to promote presidential candidates. Television is a very efficient way to reach large numbers of people quickly, but campaigning for television also distances the candidates from direct public contact (see Impact/Perspective, Campaigning for Television). Television advertising also is very expensive, and the cost of national campaigns in the last 20 years has skyrocketed (see Figure 12.1). According to University of Southern California political scientist Herbert Alexander, gubernatorial and senatorial candidates devote 40 to 60 percent of their campaign budgets to advertising.

Alexander is quick to point out that not all of this money goes to television. In congressional elections, according to Alexander, "fewer than half the candidates use TV. Many of them are in districts like Los Angeles, where the

The Nixon-Kennedy debates in 1960 triggered arguments over the effect of TV on politics. After reviewing one of his TV appearances, Kennedy said, "We wouldn't have had a prayer without that gadget."

media markets are much larger than the political jurisdictions."[12] Television advertising in these larger markets delivers a much bigger audience than the candidates need, so they will use direct mail or print advertising. But if you were running for Congress in Des Moines, Iowa, you might choose to use television because your entire district would be included in the local television station's coverage, says Alexander.

In presidential politics, the cost of radio and television advertising is rising quickly. During the 1980 presidential election, Republican media expenditures were $16.7 million; the Democrats spent $20.5 million. In the next presidential election, the Republicans spent $23.9 million and the Democrats $21.5 million. Total media expenditures by both parties grew nearly $8.2 million in four years.[13]

Congressional candidates in 1986 spent an estimated $450 million, which was $121 million more than in 1984. Then California Senator Pete Wilson (now governor) set a record for campaign expenditure in the 1989 U.S. Senate race: $14.7 million.[14]

## The Rising Cost of Running for President

Costs of the U.S. presidential/vice presidential election campaigns, 1972-1988 (millions of dollars)

| | 1972 | | 1976 | | 1980 | | 1984 | | 1988 | |
|---|---|---|---|---|---|---|---|---|---|---|
| | Nixon | McGovern | Ford | Carter | Reagan | Carter | Reagan | Mondale | Bush | Dukakis |
| Media cost | $ 8.2 | $ 7.2 | $11.6 | $ 9.7 | $16.7 | $20.5 | $23.9 | $21.5 | $31.5 | $23.5 |
| Total campaign cost | $61.4 | $21.2 | $23.1 | $23.4 | $31.7 | $29.2 | $47.3 | $45.0 | $54.4 | $54.4 |
| Percentage of cost for media | 13.4% | 34.0% | 50.2% | 41.5% | 52.6% | 70.2% | 50.5% | 47.8% | 58.0% | 43.0% |

## 12.1

SOURCE: Data from Christopher H. Sterling and Timothy R. Haight, *The Mass Media: Aspen Institute Guide to Communication Industry Trends*, New York/London: Praeger Publishers, 1977, p. 219; Herbert E. Alexander, *Financing the 1980 Election*, Lexington, Mass.: D.C. Heath, 1983; Herbert E. Alexander and Brian A. Haggerty, *Financing the 1984 Election*, Lexington, Mass.: D. C. Heath, 1987; and Herbert E. Alexander and Monica Bauer, *Financing the 1988 Election*, Boulder, Colo.: Westview Press, 1991.

Historian James David Barber describes the public's role in politics:

*Particularly since television has brought national politics within arm's length of nearly every American, the great majority probably have at least some experience of the quadrennial passing parade. But millions vote their old memories and habits and interests, interpreting new perceptions that strike their senses to coincide with their prejudices and impulses.*

*At the other end of the participation spectrum are those compulsive readers of* The New York Times *who delve into every twitch and turn of the contest. Floating in between are large numbers of Americans who pick up on the election's major events and personalities, following with mild but open interest the dominant developments. Insofar as the campaign makes a difference, it is this great central chunk of The People who swing the choice. They respond to what they see and hear. They are interested but not obsessed. They edit out the minor blips of change and wait for the campaign to gather force around a critical concern. They reach their conclusions on the basis of a widely shared common experience. It is through that middling throng of the population that the pulse of politics beats most powerfully, synchronizing to its insistent rhythm the varied vibrations of discrete events.* [15]

The rising cost of running for public office can exclude people without the means to raise huge sums of money. If "The People who swing the choice," described by Barber, cannot easily participate in the political process, eventually they may choose not to participate at all, eroding the number of people who run for office, vote in elections, and work in political campaigns.

Today, the media are essential to American politics, changing the behavior of politicians as well as the electorate, raising important questions about governance and the conduct of elections.

# Campaign-ing for Television

In this article, *New York Times* political reporter **R. W. Apple, Jr.**, covering the 1988 election campaign, describes the role that television plays in a modern political race.

i SUPPOSE it's terrific stuff for the consultants and pollsters, this new style of campaigning they've invented, but I don't think the candidates enjoy it much, and it sure isn't much fun for the likes of me. I'll never grouse again about standing outside a Pittsburgh plant gate at 7 A.M. on a cold October morning, listening to what the workers tell the candidates, or watching yet another Republican rally with yet another balloon drop. At least you got a chance to talk to some real voters at events like that; now the only way you come into contact with voters is in the columns of a computer printout. It's more illuminating, I suppose, to learn that 43 percent of white urban women with high-school educations and incomes of less than $25,000 a year are going to vote Democratic this time because they think the economy is going to hell, but it isn't as satisfying, somehow, as listening to the slightly disconnected lucubrations of Helen Hovercraft of Marshalltown, Iowa, who used to tell you about the grocery bills and what she'd read and seen about the two candidates and what her father

# Some Ideas for Future Research

ECAUSE MEDIA research is a continuing process, new ideas will emerge in the next decade from today's ideas and studies. A sampling of some provocative recent ideas and studies that could extend the current boundaries of media research follows.

used to say about politicians and their promises.

The cardinal aphorism of the year came from Bob Shrum, the Democratic consultant. . . . Shrum said that a campaign rally this year consisted of three people around a television set. He was talking about California, where he helped to make his quip true, but it was more or less true everywhere. The business of getting elected to the Senate has become so obscenely expensive that most candidates have to spend most of their time raising money for commercials. In South Dakota this year, they spent $8.50 per head of population, which would amount to $150 million in a state the size of New York, and they didn't raise it from the farmers and the tractor dealers. They raised it from the PACs [political action committees] in Wash-

ington and New York and California, either on the phone or in person, then gave it to filmmakers in Washington and New York and California to turn into 30-second spots attacking their opponents for having psoriasis. . . .

In Florida, I spent most of a day in my hotel room, watching TV, on the theory that at least once I should see the commercials interspersed with soap operas and ball games, the way most people do. It was a good idea, but half the time, the commercials and the programs looked identical. Bob Graham and Paula Hawkins were so busy trying to portray themselves as implacable foes of drugs that what you got was politics as *Miami Vice*. Except that candidates don't dress nearly as well as actors, and you only have to watch *Miami Vice* once.

In Georgia, I thought I had discovered a variation from the pattern when I found out that Wyche Fowler was spending a lot of time driving around the rural parts of the state in his old car, talking one-on-one, or at least one-on-three, to the good old boys who were said to consider him too much of a city slicker. But then a leading campaign consultant told me that the real reason for the jaunts was that they made such great film for the commercials.

After a while, I came to see the point of the Texas street philosopher quoted by my colleague Phil Gailey, who said the voters were being forced to choose between the evil of two lessers. . . .

*"Glued to the Tube from Buffalo to Boise,"* Washington Journalism Review 9, *no. 1 (January 1987): 18.*

# Spiral of Silence

Elisabeth Noelle-Neumann has asserted that because journalists in all media tend to concentrate on the same major news stories, the audience is assailed on many sides by similar information. Together, the media present the consensus; journalists reflect the prevailing climate of opinion. As this consensus spreads, people with divergent views, says Noelle-Neumann, may be less likely to voice disagreement with the prevailing point of view. Thus, because of a "**spiral of silence**," the media gain more influence because opponents of the consensus tend to remain silent. The implication for future research will be to ask whether the media neutralizes dissent and creates a pattern of social and cultural conformity.

# Children's Viewing Habits

Many studies about children and television, such as the National Institute of Mental Health report, have concentrated on the effects of portrayals of violence. But in 1981, a California study suggested a link between television viewing and poor school performance.

The California Assessment Program (CAP), which tests academic achievement, included a new question on the achievement test: "On a typical weekday, about how many hours do you watch TV?" The students then were given a choice ranging from zero to 6 or more hours.

An analysis of the answers from more than 10,000 sixth graders to that question was matched with the children's scores on the achievement test. The results suggested a consistent relationship between viewing time and achievement. Students who said they watched a lot of television scored lower in reading, writing, and mathematics than students who didn't watch any television. The average scores for students who said they viewed 6 or more hours of television a day were 6 to 8 points lower than for children who said they watched less than a half-hour of television a day.

Because the study didn't include information about the IQ scores or income levels of these students, the results cannot be considered conclusive. The study simply may show that children who watch a lot of television aren't studying. But the results are particularly interesting because of the number of children who were included in the survey. [16]

When I Was Short

Further research could examine whether children are poor students *because* they watch a lot of television or whether children who watch a lot of television are poor students for other reasons.

# Stereotyping

Journalists often use shorthand labels to characterize ethnic and other groups. In his 1922 book *Public Opinion*, political journalist Walter Lippmann first identified the tendency of journalists to generalize about other people based on fixed ideas.

*When we speak of the mind of a group of people, of the French mind, the militarist mind, the bolshevik mind, we are liable to serious confusion unless we agree to separate the instinctive equipment from the stereotypes, the patterns, the formulae which play so decisive a part in building up the mental world to which the native character is adapted and responds. . . . Failure to make this distinction accounts for oceans of loose talk about collective minds, national souls, and race psychology.* [17]

The portrayal of women and ethnic groups by the media has been a subject of significant contemporary debate since the civil rights movement in the late 1960s. Two new ways to think about stereotyping have been suggested by Tania Modleski and Earle Barcus.

**Women.** Critics of the stereotyping of women point to today's media and their inaccurate portrayals. But in her book *Loving with a Vengeance: Mass-Produced Fantasies for Women*, Tania Modleski says the portrayal in popular fiction of women in submissive roles began nearly 250 years ago with the British novel *Pamela*, published in England in 1740 and first published in America by Benjamin Franklin in 1744.

Modleski's historical content analysis of gothic novels, Harlequin Romances, and soap operas reveals:

> *In Harlequin Romances, the need of women to find meaning and pleasure in activities that are not wholly male-centered such as work or artistic creation is generally scoffed at. Soap operas also undercut, though in subtler fashion, the idea that a woman might obtain satisfaction from these activities. . . . Indeed, patriarchal myths and institutions are, on the manifest level, wholeheartedly embraced, although the anxieties and tensions they give rise to may be said to provoke the need for the texts in the first place.*[18]

The implication in Modleski's research is that women who read romance novels will believe they should act like the women in the novels they read.

**Ethnic Groups.** Media research on the portrayal of ethnic groups usually has concentrated on content analysis of how ethnic people are depicted when they appear. But researcher Earle Barcus says that members of ethnic groups often are noticeable by their absence in the media, rather than their presence.

Barcus analyzed 38 hours of children's TV programs shown in Boston in a study he conducted for Action for Children's Television. He reported that of the 1,145 characters who appeared in the programs, only 42 were African-American, and 47 belonged to other minority groups: 3.7 percent of the characters were African-American, 3.1 percent were Hispanic, and 0.8 percent were Asian.

Barcus' findings demonstrate that children's television programs historically have been very slow to reflect their audience's ethnic variety.

# *No Sense of Place*

In his book *No Sense of Place*, published in 1985, Joshua Meyrowitz provided new insight into television's possible effects on society. In the past, says Meyrowitz,

Calvin and Hobbes

*parents did not know what their children knew, and children did not know what their parents knew they knew. Similarly, a person of one sex could never be certain of what a member of the other sex knew. . . . Television undermines such behavioral distinctions because it encompasses children and adults, men and women, and all other social groups in a single informational sphere or environment. Not only does it provide similar information to everyone but, even more significant, it provides it publicly and often simultaneously.* [19]

This sharing of information, says Meyrowitz, means that subjects that were rarely discussed between men and women, for instance, and between children and adults, have become part of the public dialogue.

A second result of television viewing is the blurring of the distinction between childhood and adulthood, says Meyrowitz. When print dominated the society as a medium, children's access to adult information was limited. The only way to learn about "adult" concepts was to read about them, so typically a child was not exposed to adult ideas or problems, and taboo topics remained hidden from children.

In a video world, however, any topic that can be portrayed in pictures on television challenges the boundaries that print places around information. This, says Meyrowitz, causes an early loss of the naiveté of childhood.

*Television removes barriers that once divided people of different ages and reading abilities into different social situations. The widespread use of television is equivalent to a broad social decision to allow young children to be present at wars and funerals, courtships and seductions, criminal plots and cocktail parties. . . . Television thrusts children into a complex adult world, and it provides the impetus for children to ask the meanings of actions and words they would not yet have heard or read about without television.*[20]

Meyrowitz concedes that movies offered similar information to children before television, but he says the pervasiveness of television today makes its effects more widespread. Television is blurring social distinctions — between children and adults, and between men and women.

# Understanding Media Effects

**S**CHOLARS ONCE thought that media effects were easy to measure, as a direct relationship between media messages and media effects. But contemporary scholars now know that media effects are difficult to document. Complicating the current study of media effects is the increase in the variety and number of available media sources.

Communications scholar Neil Postman (see Impact/Perspective, Looking at Television) poses some of the questions that should be asked about media effects:

- *"What are the main psychic effects of each [media] form?"*

- *"What is the main relation between information and reason?"*

- *"What redefinitions of important cultural meanings do new sources, speeds, contexts and forms of information require?"*

- *"How do different forms of information persuade?"*

- *"Is a newspaper's 'public' different from television's 'public'?"*

- *"How do different information forms dictate the type of content that is expressed?"*[21]

These questions should be discussed, says Postman, because "no medium is excessively dangerous if its users understand what its dangers are. . . . This is an instance in which the asking of the questions is sufficient. To ask is to break the spell."[22]

# Looking at Television

In this excerpt from his book *Amusing Ourselves to Death*, communications professor **Neil Postman** maintains that television has transformed our culture from a society based on words to a society based on images.

THE SINGLE most important fact about television is that people *watch* it, which is why it is called "television." And what they watch, and like to watch, are moving pictures — millions of them, of short duration and dynamic variety. It is in the nature of the medium that it must suppress the content of ideas in order to accommodate the requirements of visual interest; that is to say, to accommodate the values of show business.

Film, records and radio (now that it is an adjunct of the music industry) are, of course, equally devoted to entertaining the culture, and their effects in altering the style of American discourse are not insignificant. But television is different because it encompasses all forms of discourse. No one goes to a movie to find out about government policy or the latest scientific advances. No one buys a record to find out the baseball scores or the weather or the latest murder. No one turns on radio anymore for soap operas or a presidential address (if a television set is at hand). But everyone goes to television for all these things and more, which is why television resonates so powerfully throughout the culture. Television is our culture's principal mode of knowing about itself. Therefore — and this is the critical point — how television stages the world becomes the model for how the world is properly to be staged. It is not merely that on the television screen entertainment is the metaphor for all discourse. It is that off the screen the same metaphor prevails. As typography once dictated the style of conducting politics, religion, business, education, law and other important social matters, television now takes command. In courtrooms, classrooms, operating rooms, board rooms, churches and even airplanes, Americans no longer talk to each other, they entertain each other. They do not exchange ideas; they exchange images. They do not argue with propositions; they argue with good looks, celebrities and commercials. For the message of television as metaphor is not only that all the world is a stage but that the stage is located in Las Vegas, Nevada.

Amusing Ourselves to Death *(New York: Viking Penguin, 1985), pp. 92–93.*

• Media scholars look for patterns in the effects of media, rather than anecdotal evidence.

• David Potter, in *People of Plenty*, described the United States as a consumer society driven by advertising.

• Canadian scholar Marshall McLuhan introduced the term *global village* to describe the way the media bring people together through shared experience.

• The magic bullet theory, developed in the 1929 Payne Fund studies, asserted that media content had a direct causal relationship to behavior.

• Hadley Cantril challenged the magic bullet theory. Cantril found that better-educated people listening to "War of the Worlds" were more likely to detect that the broadcast was fiction. Today scholars believe that the media have different effects on different people.

• In 1948, political scientist Harold D. Lasswell described the process of communication as: Who? says what? on which channel? to whom? with what effect?

• In 1961, Wilbur Schramm and his associates revealed that children used TV for fantasy, diversion, and instruction. Aggressive children were more likely to turn to TV for fantasy, said Schramm, but he could find no serious problems related to TV viewing.

• The 1971 report to Congress, *Television and Social Behavior*, made a faint causal connection between TV violence and children's violent behavior, but the report said that only some children were affected, and these children already had been classified as aggressive.

• Several subsequent studies have suggested that TV violence causes aggression among children. Researchers caution, however, that TV violence is not *the* cause of aggressiveness, but only *a* cause of aggressiveness.

• The Federal Trade Commission report, *Television Advertising to Children*, said that children see 20,000 commercials a year and that younger children are much more likely to pay attention to TV advertising than older ones.

• The summary study by the National Institute of Mental Health in 1982 asserted that a direct connection exists between televised violence and aggressive behavior, but there is no way to predict who will be affected and why.

• Media politics began in 1933 with President Franklin Roosevelt's Fireside Chats. John F. Kennedy broadened the tradition when he and Richard Nixon appeared in the nation's first televised debate of presidential candidates in 1960.

• The first major study of politics and the media, *The People's Choice*, concluded that only 8 percent of the voters in the study were actually converted by media coverage of the 1940 campaign.

• The 1976 study *The Unseeing Eye* revealed that only 7 percent of the people in the study were manipulated by TV ads. The researchers concluded that political advertising has little effect on most people.

• The rising cost of national political campaigns is directly connected to the expense of television advertising. Television is a very efficient way to reach large numbers of people quickly, but campaigning for television also distances the candidates from direct public contact.

• Communications scholar Neil Postman says that television has changed the United States from a society based on words to a society based on images.

• Some promising areas for future media research are: how audiences are influenced by the consensus view presented by the media; how the media stereotype women and ethnic groups; the connection, if any, between students' academic performance and the time students spend watching television; and the way a video world blurs social distinctions among people.

**13**

*According to the precedent-setting* New York Times *v.*

*Sullivan case, which helped define press freedom, the*

*media's role is to encourage "uninhibited, robust and wide open debate." Arguments*

*among the public, the government, and the media about the best way for the media to*

*maintain this public trusteeship form the core of challenges and rebuttals to legal and*

*regulatory limits on the media. Writes* New York Times *columnist Tom Wicker,*

*"Even though absolute press freedom may sometimes have*

*to accommodate itself to other high constitutional*

**Legal and Regulatory Issues**

values, the repeal or modification of the First Amendment seems unlikely. . . . If the true freedom of the press is to decide for itself what to publish and when to publish it, the true responsibility of the press must be to assert and defend that freedom."[1]

The media are businesses operating to make a profit, but these businesses enjoy a special trust under the U.S. Constitution. The legal and regulatory issues faced by the media are attempts by the government to balance this special trust with (1) the interests of individuals and (2) the interests of government.

# Freedom of the Press

ALL LEGAL interpretations of the press' responsibilities attempt to determine exactly what the framers of the U.S. Constitution meant when they included the First Amendment in the Bill of Rights in 1791. The First Amendment established the concept that the press should operate freely:

*Congress shall make no law respecting an establishment of religion, or prohibiting the free exercise thereof; or* **abridging the freedom of speech, or of the press;** *or the right of the people peaceably to assemble, and to petition the Government for a redress of grievances.*

In his book, *Emergence of a Free Press*, Leonard W. Levy explained:

*By freedom of the press the Framers meant a right to engage in rasping, corrosive, and offensive discussions on all topics of public interest. . . . The press had become the tribune of the people by sitting in judgment on the conduct of public officials. A free press meant the press as the Fourth Estate, [as] . . . an informal or extraconstitutional fourth branch that functioned as part of the intricate system of checks and balances that exposed public mismanagement and kept power fragmented, manageable, and accountable.*[2]

A discussion of the restrictions and laws governing the press today can be divided into six categories: (1) federal government restrictions; (2) prior restraint; (3) censorship; (4) libel; (5) privacy; and (6) the right of access.

# Government Attempts to Restrict Press Freedom

a T LEAST four times in U.S. history before 1964, the federal government felt threatened enough by press freedom to attempt to restrict that freedom. These four notable attempts to restrict the way the media operate were: the Alien and Sedition Laws of 1798, the Espionage Act of 1918, the Smith Act of 1940, and the Cold War congressional investigations of Communists in the late 1940s and early 1950s. All four of these challenges were attempts by the government to control free speech.

## The Alien and Sedition Laws of 1798

Under the provisions of the Alien and Sedition Laws of 1798, 15 people were indicted, 11 people were tried, and ten were found guilty. The Alien and Sedition Laws, as discussed in Chapter 2, set a fine of up to $2,000 and a sentence of up to two years in jail for anyone who was found guilty of speaking, writing, or publishing "false, scandalous and malicious writing or writings" against the government, Congress, or the president. The laws expired in 1801, and when he became president in that year, Thomas Jefferson pardoned everyone who had been found guilty under the laws.[3]

## The Espionage Act of 1918

Although Henry Raymond challenged censorship of Civil War reporting (see page 51), journalists and the general population during that war accepted the idea of government control of information. But during World War I, Congress passed the Espionage Act of 1918. Not all Americans supported U.S. entry into the war, and to stop criticism, the Espionage Act made it a crime to say or write anything that could be viewed as helping the enemy. Under the act,

Senator Joseph McCarthy explains his theory of communism during the Army-McCarthy hearings. Army counsel Joseph N. Welch, whose colleague had been declared subversive by McCarthy, is seated at the table.

877 people were convicted. Many, but not all, of them were pardoned when the war ended.[4]

The most notable person cited under the Espionage Act of 1918 was Socialist party presidential candidate Eugene V. Debs, who was sentenced to two concurrent ten-year terms for giving a public speech against the war. At his trial Debs said, "I have been accused of obstructing the war. I admit it. Gentlemen, I abhor war. I would oppose the war if I stood alone."[5] Debs was released from prison by a presidential order in 1921.

# The Smith Act of 1940

During World War II, Congress passed the Smith Act of 1940, which placed some restrictions on free speech. Only a few people were cited under it, but the press was required to submit stories for government censorship. President Roosevelt created an Office of Censorship, which worked out a voluntary "Code of Wartime Practices" with the press. It spelled out what information the press would not report about the war, such as troop and ship movements. The military retained power to censor all overseas war reporting.[6] The Office of Censorship also issued guidelines for news broadcasts and commentaries, called the *Code of Wartime Practices for American Broadcasters* (see page 404). The government exercised special influence over broadcasters because it licensed broadcast outlets.

# HUAC and the Permanent Subcommittee on Investigations

The fourth major move challenging the First Amendment protection of free speech came in the late 1940s and early 1950s, culminating with the actions of the House Committee on Un-American Activities against the Hollywood Ten (see page 215) and the Army-McCarthy hearings before the Permanent Subcommitee on Investigations presided over by Senator Joseph R. McCarthy.

These congressional committees set a tone of aggressive Communist-hunting. (See Impact/Profile, Dalton Trumbo of the Hollywood Ten, Chapter 6.) When television broadcasts of McCarthy's investigation of Communist influence in the army and other reports eventually exposed his excesses, McCarthy's colleagues censured him by a vote of 67 to 22, but while they were being held, the hearings established a restrictive atmosphere that challenged free expression.

# Prior Restraint

PRIOR RESTRAINT means censoring information before the information appears or is published. The framers of the Constitution clearly opposed prior restraint by law. However, in 1931 the U.S. Supreme Court established the circumstances under which prior restraint could be justified.

# Excerpts from the 1943 *Code of Wartime Practices for American Broadcasters*

## News Broadcasts and Commentaries

It is requested that news in any of the following classifications be kept off the air unless made available for broadcast by appropriate authority or specifically cleared by the Office of Censorship.

(a) Weather — Weather forecasts other than those officially released by the Weather Bureau.

(b) Armed forces — Types and movements of United States Army, Navy, and Marine Corps units, within or without continental United States.

## Programs

(a) Request programs — No telephoned or telegraphed requests for musical selections should be accepted. No requests for musical selections made by word-of-mouth at the origin of broadcast, whether studio or remote, should be honored.

(b) Quiz programs — Any program which permits the public accessibility to an open microphone is dangerous and should be carefully supervised. Because of the nature of quiz programs, in which the public is not only permitted access to the microphone but encouraged to speak into it, the danger of usurpation by the enemy is enhanced.

(c) Forums and interviews — During forums in which the general public is permitted extemporaneous comment, panel discussions in which more than two persons participate, and interviews by authorized employees of the broadcasting company, broadcasters should devise methods guaranteeing against the release of any information which might aid the enemy . . .

(d) Special-events reporting (ad lib) — Reporters and commentators should guard against use of descriptive material which might be employed by the enemy in plotting an area for attack . . .

## Foreign Language Broadcasts

(a) Personnel — The Office of Censorship, by direction of the president, is charged with the responsibility of removing from the air all those engaged in foreign language broadcasting who, in the judgment of appointed authorities in the Office of Censorship, endanger the war effort of the United Nations by their connections, direct or indirect, with the medium.

(b) Scripts — Station managements are requested to require all persons who broadcast in a foreign language to submit to the management in advance of broadcast complete scripts or transcriptions of such material.

(c) Censors and monitors — In order that these functions can be performed in a manner consistent with the demands of security, station managers are reminded that their staffs should include capable linguists as censors and monitors whose duty it will be to review all scripts in advance of broadcast and check them during broadcast against deviation . . .

Broadcasters should ask themselves, "Is this information of value to the enemy?" If the answer is "Yes," they should not use it. If doubtful, they should measure the material against the Code . . .

The Office of Censorship
Byron Price, Director
December 1, 1943.

U.S. Government Office of Censorship, *Code of Wartime Practices for American Broadcasters*. Washington, D.C.: Government Printing Office, 1943, pp. 1–8.

# Near v. Minnesota

J. M. Near published the weekly *Saturday Press*, which printed the names of people who were violating the nation's Prohibition laws. Minnesota authorities obtained a court order forbidding publication of *Saturday Press*, but the U.S. Supreme Court overturned the state's action. In *Near* v. *Minnesota* in 1931, the Court condemned prior restraint but acknowledged that the government could limit information about troop movements during war and could control obscenity. The Court also said that "the security of community life may be protected against incitements to acts of violence and the overthrow of orderly government."[7]

*Saturday Press* had not violated any of these prohibitions, so the court order was lifted. But future attempts to stop publication were based on the *Near* v. *Minnesota* decision, making it a landmark case.

In two important cases since *Near*, courts were asked to bar publication of information to protect national security. In two other situations the federal government took action to prevent journalists from reporting on the government's activities.

# The Pentagon Papers

In June 1971, *The New York Times* published the first installment of what has become known as the Pentagon Papers, excerpts from what was properly titled *History of U.S. Decision-Making Process on Vietnam Policy*. The Pentagon Papers detailed decisions that were made about the Vietnam War during the Kennedy and Johnson administrations. The documents were labeled top secret, but they were given to the *Times* by one of the report's authors, Daniel Ellsberg, an aide to the National Security Council. Ellsberg said he believed that the papers had been improperly classified and that the public should have the information.

After the first three installments were published in the *Times*, Justice Department attorneys received a restraining order against the *Times*, which stopped publication for two weeks while the *Times* appealed the case. While the case was being decided, the *Washington Post* began publishing the papers, and the *Post* was stopped, but only until the *Times* case was decided by the U.S. Supreme Court.

In *New York Times Co.* v. *United States*, the Court found that the government had failed to prove that prior restraint was necessary. The *Times* and the *Post*

Daniel Ellsberg, author of the Pentagon Papers, and his wife Barbara after a court hearing in Los Angeles.

then printed the papers, but publication had been delayed for two weeks. It was the first time in the nation's history that the federal government had stopped a newspaper from publishing. Legal fees cost the *Post* and the *Times* more than $270,000.[8]

## *The Progressive Case*

The second instance of prior restraint happened in 1979 when editors of *The Progressive* magazine announced that they planned to publish an article by Howard Morland about how to make a hydrogen bomb. The author said the article was based on information from public documents and from interviews with government employees. The Department of Justice brought suit in Wisconsin, where the magazine was published, and received a restraining order to stop the information from being printed (*United States* v. *The Progressive*). *The Progressive* did not publish the article as planned.

In 1971, a federal court temporarily stopped *The New York Times* from publishing the last two installments of the Pentagon Papers, even though the first three installments had already appeared, as shown here.

Before the case could reach the Supreme Court, a Wisconsin newspaper published a letter from a man named Charles Hansen that contained much the same information as the Morland article. Hansen sent eight copies of the letter to other newspapers, and the *Chicago Tribune* published it, saying that none of the information was proprietary.[9] Six months after the original restraining order, *The Progressive* published the article.

## Grenada

In an incident that never reached the courts but was a type of prior restraint, the Reagan administration in 1983 kept reporters away from the island of Grenada, where the administration had launched a military offensive. This caused a press blackout beginning at 11 P.M. October 24, 1983.

The administration didn't officially bar the press from covering the invasion, but the Pentagon refused to transport the press and then turned back

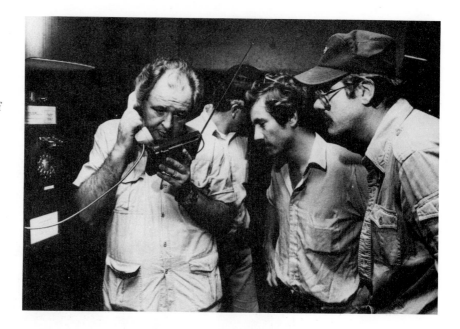

A member of the international press corps files a story from Bridgetown, Barbados, while listening to a short-wave radio for news of the 1983 invasion of Grenada, about 100 miles away.

press yachts and airplanes that attempted to enter the war zone. About a dozen print journalists and photographers were able to get in, but no television crews.

More than 400 journalists from 170 news organizations around the world who couldn't get to Grenada were left on Barbados, waiting for the news to get to them. Charles Lachman of the *New York Post* flew to Barbados, then to St. Vincent. Then he and some other reporters paid $6,000 to charter a boat to Grenada. It was five days after the invasion when they arrived and discovered that one of the casualties of the military's action had been a hospital.[10]

## News Blackouts and Press Pools

The gulf war posed the toughest battleground yet for the rights of reporters versus the rights of the military to restrict access.

On Saturday, February 23, 1991, about three weeks into the gulf war, the Defense Department announced the first total news blackout in U.S. military history. For 24 hours, defense leaders were told to issue no statements about the actions of U.S. troops. Military officials said that instantaneous transmission of information from the battlefield meant that live TV pictures could be picked up by Iraq. Press organizations protested the ban, but the military argued that modern communications technology necessitated the blackout.

Pentagon rules for war coverage, reached in cooperation with journalists, imposed stricter limits on reporting in the Persian Gulf than in any other U.S. war. The rules required that reporters travel in small "pools," escorted by public affairs officers. Every story produced by the pool was then subject to military censorship. The pools had been created in response to reporters' complaints about news blackouts during the Grenada incident. And an unprecedented number of journalists from around the world — 1,300 in Saudi Arabia alone — posed a formidable challenge for military press officers.

In a commentary protesting the restrictions, *The New Yorker* magazine said, "The rules, it is clear, enable the Pentagon to promote coverage of subjects and events that it wishes publicized and to prevent reporting that might cast it, or the war, in a bad light."[11] Yet, by an overwhelming majority, the public approved of the press restrictions. In a *Los Angeles Times* poll of nearly 2,000 people two weeks after the fighting started, 79 percent of the people polled approved of the Pentagon's restrictions and 57 percent favored even further limits.[12]

When the war ended, many members of the U.S. press in the Middle East complained bitterly about their lack of access, but the military, and the public, seemed satisfied with the new rules for wartime coverage. (See Impact/Perspective, TV and the Gulf War.)

# TV and the Gulf War

In this article, written in the middle of the gulf war, *Los Angeles Times* TV writer **Rick Du Brow** contends that the public was satisfied with the war pictures presented by the press because the pictures made very tasteful television.

**i**T'S NO wonder that polls show Americans strongly support military restrictions of the media in the Gulf War.

Patriotism and national security are prime factors. But there's also this:

Television is the public's primary source of news images, including local TV, where comical weather reporters and sportscasters, lightweight anchors and ratings sweeps series — such as a recent one on aphrodisiacs — hardly inspire confidence.

Given this trivialization of the news, isn't it logical that TV viewers would gravitate to well-versed, authoritative military spokesmen who clearly have prepared for media combat in this first instant satellite war?

This can be dangerous, of course — Big Brother. And polls also show that the public thinks the press, overall, is doing a good job.

But the increasing entertainment values in news — from local TV to reality spin-offs such as the tabloid shows "Hard Copy" and "A Current Affair," not to mention their supermarket kin — are coming home to roost.

The excesses of such aberrations as airhead happy-talk news simply are not going to add to believability. Upbeat war features, sure. But credibility, no.

One is reminded of the film "Network" when a character tells a TV executive: "War, murder, death are all the same to you as bottles of beer."

But public confidence in TV seemed sky-high at the start of the war when CNN's Bernard

Shaw, Peter Arnett and John Holliman became America's sweethearts as they broadcast historic reports on the outbreak of hostilities from a Baghdad hotel room.

The fact that restrictions then became the big media story is a pity because, as the war threatened to get uglier on TV with ground action, it became clear that attempts to withhold the ugliness from home viewers were part and parcel of policy.

Is this right?

Maybe, if you're running the show and have government interests as first priority. But should the networks engage in complicity, which is what they are doing in agreeing that viewers should not see the extreme horrors of war?

Walter Porges, vice president of news practices for ABC, says that "the executive producers of each broadcast" decide on the content and generally "put on only what they'd like to see in their living rooms."

David Miller, director of foreign news for NBC, adds: "We have our standards of taste. We don't want to offend the viewer. We're not grotesque. We maintain prudent standards."

This is all in keeping with standard network practice. But it may strike some as unique that TV would want to present the most distasteful act of all — war — in a relatively tasteful manner so that it is acceptable in people's living rooms.

Ed Turner, CNN vice president of news-gathering, says: "You've got to have a proper amount of video that reflects an honest record of what occurred. You can't be dishonest. You have got to show that people get killed and that it isn't innocent."

And in a CBS interview before he was reported missing, correspondent Bob Simon said: "There is a rule now that we cannot show a soldier who is in severe agony or shock. We hope we don't have to film that." But, he added, it "will be part of the war."

Viewers, however, apparently are satisfied with the war on TV as it's being presented.

At another time, in another war, the saying was, "Loose lips sink ships." Now, everybody has loose lips, and what they say is transmitted around the world instantly. And the public is behind the new TV-war restrictions.

Perhaps, however, only so long as we win easily.

But thus far, the government has shown plenty of moxie in finding persuasive spokesmen — such as its man in Riyadh, Saudi Arabia, Marine Brig. Gen. Richard I. Neal, a homey fellow bound to engender public confidence.

Nonetheless, the hard images of war pop up on TV in unlikely places. On Tuesday night, in a CNN feature about "warriors of yesterday," a World War II veteran recalled turning to his friend during combat and "suddenly, half his head disappeared."

TV commentator Linda Ellerbee, discussing the subtle interaction of TV and politics, once said: "We are all raised to believe that the camera doesn't lie, when in fact nothing lies so easily as the camera. Every time you point a camera at something, you're pointing it away from something."

The truth, of course, is neutral. But not in a war. Especially a popular one.

Los Angeles Times, *Feb. 21, 1991*, *A-8, p. 18.*

# I read banned books.
## AMERICAN SOCIETY OF JOURNALISTS & AUTHORS

The American Society of Journalists and Authors, the nation's largest organization of freelance writers, sponsored the "I Read Banned Books" campaign to combat censorship.

The fact that the government could successfully stop the press is significant. When should the government be able to prevent information from reaching the public? The Supreme Court has not yet specifically answered this question, and the press and publishers remain vulnerable to government restrictions.

# Censorship

DIFFERENT MEDIA industries historically have reacted differently to threats of censorship, which usually concern matters of morality, especially obscenity. In America, censorship is almost always an issue after the fact. Once the material is printed or displayed, it can be judged obscene and therefore censored. The motion picture and recording industries have accepted some form of self-regulation to avoid government intervention. The electronic media are governed by laws in the federal criminal code against broadcast obscenity, and the federal Cable Act of 1984 bars obscenity on cable TV.

Print media have been the most vigorous defenders of the right to publish. The print media, of course, were the earliest media to be threatened with censorship, beginning with the philosopher Plato, who suggested in 387 B.C. that Homer's *Odyssey* be expurgated for immature readers.

Publisher H. L. Mencken sells a copy of *The American Mercury* magazine on the streets of Boston in April 1926.

## Local Efforts

More than 2,000 years after Homer's *Odyssey* was threatened with censorship, Boston officials banned the sale of the April 1926 issue of H. L. Mencken's magazine *The American Mercury*. The local Watch and Ward Society had denounced a fictional story in the magazine as "salacious." The title character of the story, "Hatrack," was a prostitute whose clientele included members of various religious congregations who visited her after church.

In Boston, surrounded by his supporters, Mencken sold a copy of the magazine at a prearranged time to a member of the Watch and Ward. The chief of the Boston Vice Squad arrested Mencken and marched him to jail, where he spent the night before going to court the next morning.

"Mencken passed an uneasy night," says Mencken's biographer Carl Bode, "knowing that he could be found guilty and perhaps even be imprisoned. . . .

Returning to court he listened to Judge Parmenter's brief analysis of the merits of the case and then to his decision: 'I find that no offense has been committed and therefore dismiss the complaint.'" Mencken spent $20,000 defending the *Mercury* but, according to Bode, "the net gain for both the *Mercury* and Mencken was great. The *Mercury* became the salient American magazine and Mencken the international symbol of freedom of speech."[13]

Mencken was defending his magazine against local censorship, and until 1957, censorship in America remained a local issue because the U.S. Supreme Court had not considered a censorship case. Today censorship still is primarily a local issue, but two landmark Supreme Court cases — *Roth* v. *United States* and *Miller* v. *California* — established the major criteria for local censorship.

### Roth v. United States.
Two cases were involved in this 1957 decision. Samuel Roth was found guilty in New York of sending obscenity through the mail, and David S. Alberts was found guilty of selling obscene books in Beverly Hills. The case carries Roth's name because his name appeared first.

The Supreme Court upheld the guilty verdict and established several precedents:

• *Obscenity is not protected by the First Amendment;*

• *Obscenity is material "utterly without redeeming social importance";*

• *Sex and obscenity are not synonymous. Obscene material is material that appeals to "prurient [obsessively sexual] interest";*

• *A test of obscenity is "whether to the average person, applying contemporary community standards, the dominant theme of the material taken as a whole appeals to prurient interest."*[14] *(This last description of obscenity has become known as the* **Roth test**.)

### Miller v. California.
In the late 1960s, a California court found Marvin Miller guilty of sending obscene unsolicited advertising material through the mail. The case reached the U.S. Supreme Court in 1973. The decision described just which materials a state could censor and set a three-part test for obscenity.

States could censor material that met this three-part local test for obscenity, according to the Supreme Court. The local court should determine:

*1. Whether "the average person, applying contemporary community standards," would find that the work, taken as a whole, appeals to the prurient interest.*

*2. Whether the work depicts or describes, in a patently offensive way, sexual conduct specifically defined by the applicable state law.*

*3. Whether the work, taken as a whole, lacks serious literary, artistic, political, or scientific value — often called the* **LAPS test**.[15]

The combination of the Roth and Miller cases therefore established a standard for obscenity, leaving the decision on specific cases to local courts. The result for the nation has been widely differing standards in different parts of the country because local juries decide what is offensive in their communities. Books that are available to readers in some states are unavailable in other states.

**School Boards as Censors.** Many censorship cases begin at school and other local government boards, where parents' groups protest books, magazines, and films that are available to students. For example:

• *A school board in New York removed 11 books from school libraries, including the novels* Slaughterhouse-Five *by Kurt Vonnegut, Jr., and* Black Boy *by Richard Wright, plus a work of popular anthropology,* The Naked Ape *by Desmond Morris.*

• *A school district in California required students to have parental permission to read* Ms. *magazine in the school library.*

• *A school board in Minnesota banned four books, including* Are You There, God? It's Me, Margaret *by Judy Blume, a writer well known for her young adult books.*

• *The state of Alabama ordered 45 textbooks pulled from the shelves after a federal judge said the books promoted "secular humanism."*[16]

One-third of all censorship incidents involve attempts to censor library books and school curricula.[17] These types of cases usually are reversed on appeal, but while the specific issues are being decided, the books, magazines, and films are unavailable. And censorship efforts are increasing. (See Impact/ Perspective, Library Card Keeps Kids in Their Place.)

# National Efforts

**The Meese Commission on Pornography.** Censorship activities were encouraged from the federal level by the issuance in July 1986 of the Final Report of the Attorney General's Commission on Pornography, called the Meese Commission (named for Attorney General Edwin Meese). The 1986 report totally reversed the conclusion of the 1970 Commission on Obscenity and Pornography, which had found that no convincing evidence existed to show that pornography causes harm.

The 1986 commission concluded that pornography does cause harm, and that even when sexually explicit material doesn't portray violence, it may be harmful to society and the family. The 1986 commission urged Congress to require convicted pornographers to give up the profits from producing and distributing offensive material, but the commission's arguments were not convincing, and no substantial legislation resulted.

# Library Card Keeps Kids in Their Place

In this article, Associated Press reporter **Sarah Nordgren** describes a typical example of recent censorship by a local government board. A library's trustees voted to confine children under 14 to the children's room of the library — away from magazines such as *Time* and science fiction novels such as Ray Bradbury's *Fahrenheit 451*.

OAK LAWN, Ill. — See Dick and Jane run — as long as it's not from the children's room to the rest of the Oak Lawn Memorial Library, where trustees have adopted a "PG-13" library-card policy.

Beginning in September [1990], parents of children under age 14 . . . have the option of a library card that . . . restricts their young to the children's room of the library. Period.

Time magazine — in the periodical area — would be off limits. Ray Bradbury's book, "Fahrenheit 451" — in adult fiction — would be out of reach. So would "Who's Who" — upstairs in the library's reference section.

Trustees say in an age in which children are bombarded with violent and illicit images, the card will give parents the option of confining their children to appropriate reading material.

Parents who aren't interested in the special card may still get cards for their children that will give them free rein of the library.

"I think the issue here is parental rights," said Dave Gallagher, a seven-year trustee of the library who voted in favor of the plan at the board's June meeting.

"As far as I'm concerned, the whole policy puts it into the

**The Hazelwood Case.** In 1988, the U.S. Supreme Court for the first time gave public school officials considerable freedom to limit what appears in student publications. The case, *Hazelwood* v. *Kuhlmeier*, became known as the Hazelwood Case because the issues originated at Hazelwood High School in Hazelwood, Missouri.

The high school paper, funded mostly from the school budget, was published as part of a journalism class. The principal at Hazelwood regularly reviewed the school paper before it was published, but in this case he deleted two articles that the staff had written.

hands of the parent and takes it away from the library, a government body," said Gallagher. "The parent has a choice — and that's the key word here, choice."

Under the plan, kids wishing to leave the library's L-shaped children's area would be required to show a staff member their card. If they have the special juvenile card, they will not be allowed to leave the room.

The proposal, which passed, 3 to 1, with three members absent, has met with the approval of some parents.

"I wouldn't get the cards for my kids, but I wouldn't criticize the board for issuing them," Grace Kreten said recently as she browsed through the children's section with her children, 10-year-old Kelly and 6-year-old Peter.

"If you're on top of things as a parent, then the library doesn't have to be," Kreten said.

Twelve-year-old Jason Pollard, a fan of sports books, shrugged when asked about the new policy, saying "I don't care what they do."

Others questioned the wisdom of the policy.

"The library should be a place where everything is available," said Donna Kordas, who regularly brings her four children, ages 2 to 15, to the only library in this suburb south of Chicago.

Oak Lawn librarians refused to discuss the new policy.

Oak Lawn is not unique in instituting such a card — nearby Arlington Heights has a similar system already in place. Officials of the American Library Assn. said they feared the cards were a bad precedent.

"If just one parent signs that card that denies a child free access in the library, we've been set back," said association president Richard Dougherty. "Kids who read succeed. Anything that puts barriers in front of that is not good."

The association does not keep statistics on how many of the nation's 103,000 libraries have such systems, although the trend has been away from them, said Judith Krug, director of the association's Office for Intellectual Freedom.

"But every once in a while, like in Oak Lawn, the trend is reversed," she said.

Some child and adolescent psychiatrists also questioned the proposal.

"The more children read, the better off they are," said Dr. Aaron Esman, an adolescent psychiatrist who teaches at Cornell University Medical College in New York. "It almost doesn't matter what it is. For libraries to discourage children from reading is inappropriate developmentally and culturally disastrous."

Los Angeles Times, *July 15, 1990,* *p. A-8.*

IMPACT/
PERSPECTIVE

One of the deleted articles covered the issue of student pregnancy and included interviews with three students who had become pregnant while attending school, using pseudonyms instead of the students' names. The principal said he felt that the anonymity of the students was not sufficiently protected, and that the girls' discussion of their use or nonuse of birth control was inappropriate for a school publication. By a vote of 5–3, the U.S. Supreme Court agreed.

"Even though the legal rights of children have gained broader recognition in recent years, it remains that children are not adults and that they have no explicit or implied right to behave with the full freedom granted to adults," wrote Jonathan Yardley, a *Washington Post* columnist. "Freedom entails the responsibility to exercise it with mature judgment, and this neither young children nor adolescents possess."

The same newspaper, however, carried an editorial that opposed the decision. "Even teenagers," the *Post* editorial said, "should be allowed to publish criticism, raise uncomfortable questions and spur debate on subjects such as pregnancy, AIDS and drug abuse that are too often a very real aspect of high school culture today."

The decision is significant because it may change the way local officials monitor school publications. At Hazelwood, however, the principal's action drew the attention of the *St. Louis Post-Dispatch*, which published the censored articles, bringing them a much wider audience than the students at Hazelwood High.

# Libel Law

"AMERICANS HAVE increasingly begun to seek the refuge and vindication of litigation," writes legal scholar Rodney A. Smolla in his book *Suing the Press*. "Words published by the media no longer roll over us without penetrating; instead, they sink in through the skin and work inner damage, and a consensus appears to be emerging that this psychic damage is serious and must be paid for."[18]

Four cases show how prominent the media are as targets of litigation:

• *In 1983, actress Carol Burnett sued the* National Enquirer *for $10 million for implying in an article that she was drinking too much and acting rude in a Washington, D.C., restaurant.*

• *In late 1984, General William C. Westmoreland filed a $120 million suit against CBS, charging that he was defamed in a 1982 CBS documentary,* The Uncounted Enemy: A Vietnam Deception.

• *At the same time that jurors were hearing the Westmoreland case, former Israeli Defense Minister Ariel Sharon sought $50 million in a libel suit against* Time *magazine, claiming that* Time *wrongly characterized his role in a 1982 massacre of Palestinian refugees.*

• *In 1989 entertainer Wayne Newton was awarded $6 million in damages after he sued NBC-TV for a story that linked him to organized-crime figures. NBC appealed the case.*

These four cases involve the law of **libel**, which is only one recognized restraint on press freedom in the United States. (A libelous statement is one that unjustifiably exposes someone to ridicule or contempt.) All of these cases indicate the media's legal vulnerability.

How can the country accommodate both the First Amendment concept of a free press and the right of the nation's citizens to keep their reputations from being unnecessarily damaged?

L. B. Sullivan (second from right), whose case formed the basis for the *New York Times* v. *Sullivan* libel decision, with his attorneys after winning in the Montgomery County (Alabama) court. The U.S. Supreme Court later overturned the lower court's decision.

# The Sullivan Case

Modern interpretation of the free speech protections of the First Amendment began in 1964 with the landmark *New York Times* v. *Sullivan* case. With this case, the U.S. Supreme Court began a process that continues today to define how the press should operate in a free society. Many of today's arguments about the free press' role in a libel case derive from this decision.

The Sullivan case began in early 1960 in Alabama, where civil rights leader Dr. Martin Luther King, Jr., was arrested for perjury on his income tax form (a charge of which he was eventually acquitted). The Committee to Defend Martin Luther King bought a full-page ad in the March 29, 1960, *New York Times*, which included statements about harassment of King by public officials and the police. The ad included a plea for money to support civil rights causes. Several notable people were listed in the ad as supporters, including singer Harry Belafonte, actor Sidney Poitier, and former First Lady Eleanor Roosevelt.

L. B. Sullivan, who supervised the police and fire departments as commissioner of public affairs in Montgomery, Alabama, demanded a retraction from the *Times*, even though he had not been named in the ad. The *Times* refused, and Sullivan sued the *Times* for libel in Montgomery County, where 35 copies of the March 29, 1960, *Times* had been distributed for sale.[19]

The trial in Montgomery County lasted three days, beginning on November 1, 1960. The jury found the *Times* guilty and awarded Sullivan $500,000. Eventually the case reached the U.S. Supreme Court. In deciding the suit, the Court said that although the *Times* might have been negligent because it did not spot some misstatements of fact that appeared in the ad, the *Times* did not deliberately lie — it did not act with what the court called *actual malice*. To prove libel, a *public official* must show that the defendant published information with *knowledge of its falsity* or out of *reckless disregard* for whether it was true or false, the court concluded.[20] The Sullivan decision thus became the standard for subsequent libel suits: Public officials in a libel case must prove actual malice.

### *Gertz* v. *Robert Welch.*

Three important cases further defined the Sullivan decision. A 1974 decision in *Gertz* v. *Robert Welch* established the concept that the expression of opinions is a necessary part of public debate, and so opinions — an editorial or a restaurant review, for example — cannot be considered libelous. The Gertz case also expanded the definition of public *official* to public *figure*. Today people involved in libel suits are separated into *public figures* and *private figures*.

The criterion that divides people into public and private figures is very important. People who are defined as private citizens by a court must show only that the libelous information was false and that the journalist or news organization acted negligently in presenting the information. *Public figures must show* not only that the libelous information was false but that the information was published with *actual malice* — that the journalist or the news organization knew the information was untrue or that the journalist or news organization deliberately overlooked facts that would have proved that the published information was untrue.

### *Herbert* v. *Lando.*

A 1979 decision in *Herbert* v. *Lando* established the concept that because a public figure suing for libel must prove actual malice, the public figure can use the discovery process (the process by which potential witnesses are questioned under oath before the trial to help define the issues to be resolved at the trial) to determine a reporter's state of mind in preparing the story. Because of this decision, reporters today are sometimes asked in a libel suit to identify their sources and to give up notes and tapes of the interviews they conducted to write their stories.

***Masson v. New Yorker Magazine.*** In 1991, the U.S. Supreme Court reinstated a $10 million libel suit brought against *The New Yorker Magazine* by psychoanalyst Jeffrey M. Masson. Masson charged that author Janet Malcolm libeled him in two articles in *The New Yorker* and in a book when she deliberately misquoted him. Malcolm contended that the quotations she used were tape recorded or were written in her notes.

Malcolm wrote, for example, that Mr. Masson said, "I was like an intellectual gigolo." However, this exact phrase was not in the tape recorded transcript of her interview. Masson contends that he never used the phrase.

The case offers the potential for arguments about just what quotation marks in a story mean — whether quoted material must be verbatim, for example; or whether a journalist can change grammar and syntax, or edit rambling sentences, to give the sense of what the speaker said. The Masson case is the most recent example of the Court's continuing interest in defining the limits of libel.

# Charges and Defenses for Libel

Today's libel law involves four elements. To prove libel, someone must show that:

*1. The statement was communicated to a third party;*

*2. People who read or saw the statement would be able to identify the person, even if that person was not actually named;*

*3. The statement injured someone's reputation or income or caused mental anguish;*

*4. The journalist or the print or broadcast organization is at fault.*

Members of the press and press organizations that are faced with a libel suit can use three defenses: truth, privilege, and fair comment.

**Truth.** The first and best defense against libel, of course, is that the information is true. True information, although sometimes damaging, cannot be considered libelous. Publishing true information, however, can still be an invasion of privacy, as explained later in this chapter. Furthermore, truth is a successful defense only if truth is proved to the satisfaction of a judge or jury.

**Privilege.** The press is free to report what is discussed during legislative and court proceedings, even though the information presented in the proceedings by witnesses and others may be untrue or damaging. This is called *qualified privilege.*

**Fair Comment.** The courts also have carefully protected the press' freedom to present opinions. Because opinions cannot be proved true or false, the press is free to comment on public issues and to laud a play or pan a movie, for example.

# Today's Libel Laws and the Media

The four cases listed at the beginning of this section all involved public figures. The jury in the Carol Burnett case originally awarded her $1.6 million, but the amount was reduced to $150,000 on appeal. The Westmoreland case was settled before it went to the jury. CBS issued a statement acknowledging that Westmoreland had acted faithfully in performing his duties, but the combined legal costs for both parties were more than $18 million.[21]

In the Sharon case, the jury found that *Time* had defamed Sharon and reported false information but that the magazine did not act with actual malice, so no judgment was levied against *Time.* Sharon's legal costs were $1 million. The jury that awarded Wayne Newton $19.2 million in 1986 said that NBC knew the broadcasts were false and that the network and the defendants intended to injure Newton. When NBC appealed the case, the court sided with NBC.

In several of these cases, members of the press were faulted for their reporting methods, even when the news organizations were not found guilty. Although *Time* magazine was exonerated in the Sharon case, for example, the jury issued a statement that said that "certain *Time* employees, particularly correspondent David Halevy, acted negligently and carelessly in reporting and verifying the information which ultimately found its way into the published paragraph of interest in this case."[22] These cases show that the press must always be diligent. (See Impact/Perspective, How to Get Sued for Libel.)

Most successful libel judgments eventually are reversed or reduced when they are appealed. According to a study of all the libel suits brought in the United States from 1974 through 1984, only about 10 percent of the cases were won; another 15 percent of them were settled, usually without the payment of any money. And although 20 judgments of $1 million or more were awarded between 1980 and 1984, none of these had been upheld on appeal. However, in 1988 a $3.05 million award in the case of *Brown and Williamson* v. *CBS* was upheld, an amount four times larger than any other upheld award.[23]

The major cost of a libel suit for the media is not the actual settlement but the defense lawyers' fees. Large media organizations carry libel insurance, but a small newspaper, magazine, book publisher, or broadcast station may not be able to afford the insurance or the legal fees. The average libel case today costs about $150,000 in legal fees alone.[24] These costs sometimes cause the press to be self-censoring.

"Since the Supreme Court ruled in favor of *The New York Times* in *New York Times* v. *Sullivan* in 1964, no country in the world has offered more legal protection for those wishing to speak out frankly and fearlessly," writes eminent libel lawyer Floyd Abrams. "Yet today, American libel law manages to achieve the worst of two worlds: It does little to protect reputation. It does much to deter speech."[25]

Abrams has proposed three major changes in American libel law:

# How to Get Sued for Libel

In this article, media attorney **Bruce Sanford** outlines when the press is the most vulnerable to libel suits: reporting on sensitive subjects, covering people who are most likely to sue, and being careless.

## The Five Most Dangerous Areas

Alarm bells are supposed to go off in an editor's head whenever a story contains a statement that could injure someone's reputation. Words that, if false, have the potential to be libelous change with time and place. In the 1950s, falsely branding someone a "Commie" was certainly libelous. To do so today still might be libelous, but not as certainly as inaccurately terming someone a "roommate to an AIDS victim."

Wrongly identifying someone in Greenwich Village as a CIA agent might endanger his life and limb, not to mention his reputation, but doing the same thing in Columbus, Georgia, might get him the key to the city.

Currently, the five most dangerous areas for prompting libel suits seem to be any words or expressions touching on:

• Child abuse

• Lying

• Corruption of public officials

• Affiliation with organized crime

• Law enforcement bungling

## The Five Most Litigious Types of People

• Prosecutors

• Generals

• Police

• School officials

• Lawyers

1. *Publishers and broadcasters should be encouraged to print corrections quickly. When the media do offer timely corrections, no suit would be allowed.*

2. *Damages should be limited to amounts actually lost by those who sue. Abrams suggests the actual amount of lost wages should be awarded, and that the limit on emotional injury be $100,000.*

3. *The court should be able to require that the losing side pay the legal fees for the winning side.*[26]

"The libel explosion does chill the courage of the press," says legal scholar Rodney A. Smolla, "and in that chill all of us suffer, for it threatens to make the press slavishly safe, pouring out a centrist, spiceless paste of consensus thought. All of us lose if we permit the trivialization of free speech."[27]

**IMPACT/ PERSPECTIVE**

# Privacy Law

t HE PUBLIC seems to feel that invasion of privacy is one of the media's worst faults. As noted in Chapter 11, three out of four people interviewed in the Times Mirror survey said that news organizations invade people's privacy. However, libel suits are much more common in the United States than suits about invasion of privacy. Because there is no Supreme Court decision covering privacy like *New York Times* v. *Sullivan* covers libel, each of the states has its own privacy protections for citizens and its own restrictions on how reporters can get the news and what can be published.

Privacy is an ethical as well as legal issue (see Chapter 14 for a discussion of the ethics of privacy). Generally, the law says that the media can be guilty of invasion of privacy in four ways:

1. *By intruding on a person's physical or mental solitude.*

2. *By publishing or disclosing embarrassing personal facts.*

3. *By giving someone publicity that places the person in a false light.*

4. *By using someone's name or likeness for commercial benefit.*

If they are successful, people who initiate privacy cases can be awarded monetary damages to compensate them for the wrongdoing. However, most privacy cases do not succeed.

## Physical or Mental Solitude

The courts in most states have recognized that a person has a right not to be pursued by the news media unnecessarily. A reporter can photograph or question someone on a public street or at a public event, but a person's home and office are private. For this reason, many photographers request that someone who is photographed in a private situation sign a release form, designating how the photograph can be used.

One particularly notable case establishing this right of privacy is *Galella* v. *Onassis*. Jacqueline Onassis, widow of former President John F. Kennedy, charged that Ron Galella, a freelance photographer, was pursuing her unnecessarily. He had used a telephoto lens to photograph her on private property and he had pursued her children at private schools. Galella was ordered to stay 25 feet away from her and 30 feet away from her children.

## Embarrassing Personal Facts

The personal facts the media use to report a story should be newsworthy, according to the courts. If a public official is caught traveling with her boyfriend on taxpayers' money while her husband stays at home, information about the boyfriend is essential to the story. If the public official is reported to have contracted AIDS from her contact with the boyfriend, the information probably is not relevant to the story and could be covered under this provision of privacy law.

In reality, however, public officials enjoy very little legal protection from reporting about their private lives. Information available from public records, such as court proceedings, is not considered private. If the public official's husband testifies in court about his wife's disease, this information could be reported.

## False Light

A writer who portrays someone in a fictional version of actual events should be especially conscious of **false-light** litigation. People who believe that what a writer or photographer *implies* about them is incorrect (even if the portrayal is flattering) can bring a false-light suit.

The best-known false-light suit is the first, *Time Inc.* v. *Hill*. In 1955, *Life* magazine published a story about a Broadway play, *The Desperate Hours*, that portrayed a hostage-taking. The author of the play said he based it on several real-life incidents. One of these involved the Hill family, a husband and wife and their five children who had been taken hostage in their Philadelphia home by three escaped convicts. The Hills told police that the convicts had treated them courteously, but the Hills were frightened by the events and eventually moved to Connecticut.

When *Life* decided to do the story about the play, the cast went to the Hills' old home, where *Life* photographed the actors in scenes from the play — one son being roughed up by the convicts and a daughter biting a convict's hand. None of these incidents had happened to the Hills, but *Life* published the photographs along with a review of the play.

The Hills sued Time Inc., which owned Life magazine, for false-light invasion of privacy and won $75,000, which eventually was reduced to $30,000. When the case went to the U.S. Supreme Court, the Court refused to uphold the decision, saying that the Hills must prove actual malice.[28] The Hills dropped the case, but *the establishment of actual malice* as a requirement in false-light cases *was important*.

In 1974, in *Cantrell* v. *Forest City Publishing Co.*, the U.S. Supreme Court held that a reporter for the Cleveland *Plain Dealer* had wrongly portrayed the widow of an Ohio man who was killed when a bridge collapsed. The story talked about the woman as if the reporter had interviewed her, although he had only interviewed her children. She was awarded $60,000 in her false-light suit, and the Supreme Court upheld the verdict. "Eight justices held that a properly instructed jury had come to the correct conclusion in finding actual malice," writes legal scholar Ralph L. Holsinger. "There was enough evidence within the story to prove that the reporter's word portrait of Mrs. Cantrell was false. The story indicated that he had seen her and perhaps had talked with her. He had done neither."[29]

Only a few false-light cases have been successful, but the lesson for the press is that truthful portrayal of people and events avoids the problem altogether.

# Right of Publicity

This facet of privacy law is especially important in the advertising and public relations industries. A portable toilet seems a strange fixture to use to establish a point of law, but a case brought by *Tonight Show* host Johnny Carson demonstrates how the right of publicity protects someone's name from being used to make money without that person's permission.

In *Carson* v. *Here's Johnny Portable Toilets*, Carson charged in 1983 that a Michigan manufacturer of portable toilets misappropriated Carson's name to sell the toilets. The manufacturer named his new line "Here's Johnny Portable

Toilets," and advertised them with the phrase "The World's Foremost Commodian." Carson said he did not want to be associated with the product and that he would be. Since he began hosting *The Tonight Show* in 1957, he said, he had been introduced by the phrase "Here's Johnny." The court agreed that "Here's Johnny" violated Carson's right of publicity.

This right can cover a person's picture on a poster or name in an advertisement. In some cases, this right is covered even after the person dies, so that the members of the immediate family of a well-known entertainer, for example, are the only people who can authorize the use of the entertainer's name or likeness.

# Fair Trial and Right of Access

t HE ANSWERS to two other questions that bear on press freedoms and individual rights remain discretionary for the courts: When does media coverage influence a jury so much that a defendant's right to a fair trial is jeopardized? And how much access should the media be granted during a trial?

## Fair Trial

The best-known decision affecting prejudicial press coverage of criminal cases is *Sheppard* v. *Maxwell*. In 1954, Dr. Samuel Sheppard of Cleveland was sentenced to life imprisonment for murdering his wife. His conviction followed reams of newspaper stories, many of which proclaimed his guilt before the jury had decided the case. The jurors, who went home each evening, were told by the judge not to read newspapers or pay attention to broadcast reports, but no one monitored what the jurors did.

Twelve years later, lawyer F. Lee Bailey took Sheppard's trial to the U.S. Supreme Court, where the conviction was overturned on the premise that Sheppard had been a victim of a biased jury. In writing the decision, Justice Tom C. Clark prescribed several remedies. He said that the reporters should have been limited to certain areas in the courtroom, that the news media should not have been allowed to interview the witnesses, and that the court should have forbidden statements outside of the courtroom.

## Courtroom Access

The outcome of the Sheppard case led to many courtroom experiments with restrictions on the press. The most widespread practices were restraining (gag) orders and closed proceedings. With a gag order, the judge limited what the press could report. Closed proceedings excluded the press from the courtroom. But since 1980, several court cases have overturned most of these limitations so that today the press is rarely excluded from courtroom proceedings, and the exclusion lasts only as long as it takes the news organization to appeal to a higher court for access.

Cameras in the courtroom is a sticky issue between judges, who want to avoid the disruption that cameras present, and broadcast newspeople, who want to photograph what is going on. In selected cases, however, cameras have been allowed to record complete trials. In 1984, for example, Cable News Network broadcast the entire trial of six men who were charged with raping a woman in New Bedford, Massachusetts. Cameras in the courtroom is a state-by-state decision. Some states allow cameras during civil but not criminal trials. Other states ban them altogether. The courts and the press are not yet completely comfortable partners.

# Government Regulation

LL OF the American media are expected to abide by the country's laws. Regulation of the media comes from government agencies that oversee aspects of the media business. The print industry is not specifically regulated by any government agency. The largest single area of regulation comes from the Federal Communications Commission, which oversees broadcasting. Other regulating agencies, such as the Federal Trade Commission, scrutinize specific areas that relate to the media, such as advertising.

Today's Federal Communications Commission: (left to right) Andrew Barrett, James Quello, Chairman Alfred C. Sikes, Sherrie Marshall, Erwin Duggan.

# Broadcast Regulation

The concept behind broadcast regulation since 1927 has been that the airwaves belong to the public and that broadcasters are trustees operating in the public interest. The history of U.S. broadcast regulation can be traced to government's early attempt to organize the airwaves (see Radio Act of 1912 and Radio Act of 1927, Chapter 4). The Federal Communications Commission, based in Washington, D.C., now has five commissioners, who are appointed by the president and approved by the Senate. Each commissioner serves a five-year term, and the chairperson is appointed by the president.

FCC regulation today touches almost every aspect of station operations. Most importantly, U.S. broadcast stations must be licensed by the FCC to operate. Because the print media are unregulated by any government agency, the government exercises more direct control over the broadcast media than over the print media.

Like the print media, broadcasters must follow court rulings on issues such as libel, obscenity, and the right of privacy. But broadcast stations also must follow the regulations that the FCC establishes regarding campaign advertising, for example, and obscenity. The FCC also governs how often stations can be sold and who can own broadcast properties (see Ownership Issues, Chapter 11).

The five major regulatory issues that affect broadcast coverage of public issues and broadcast programming are: must-carry requirements for cable; broadcast content restrictions; the equal opportunities (often called equal time or equal access) requirement; the fairness doctrine; and syndicated exclusivity.

**Must-Carry Requirements for Cable.** In 1986, the FCC reached an agreement between cable and commercial broadcasters about what must be carried on cable systems. The broadcasters had argued that cable should be required to carry all TV stations within each cable jurisdiction. Cable operators felt that the commercial broadcast stations were crowding their channels; they wanted the discretion to decide who should be on which channel.

The FCC essentially agreed with the cable operators. This puts commercial broadcasters in the position of negotiating with the cable company about what will be carried on the cable and which channel the station will be allocated. This has economic implications for broadcasters because the cable audience is included in describing a station's total audience to advertisers. If a cable operator decides not to carry a broadcast station, the broadcast station loses part of its audience.

**Broadcast Content Restrictions.** The FCC in the past had been very careful not to regulate broadcast content, but in April 1987, it announced new fines for "indecent" programming. Under the new rules, the agency could impose fines of up to $2,000 a broadcast.

Most stations maintain their own program standards, and before the announcement the FCC had limited its censorship actions to "the seven dirty words" made famous by comedian George Carlin. Under the new ruling, the FCC said it would take action against shows that contain explicit descriptions of sexual or excretory activities — even if the shows don't contain those famous dirty words. FCC regulations ban indecent programming between the hours of 6 A.M. and 10 P.M., when children are most likely to be listening.

In 1989, in the first major action by Alfred Sikes, the FCC's new chairman under President Bush, the FCC initiated action against three stations accused of airing sexually explicit talk shows. Then in 1990, the FCC announced a 24-hour-a-day ban on "indecent" radio and television programs and fined several radio stations, including the station that broadcast talk show host Howard Stern.

Broadcasters challenged the FCC in court, and in 1991, a federal court ruled that the 24-hour ban was unconstitutional, but the 6 A.M. to 10 P.M. restrictions still apply.

**Equal Time.** The equal time section of the Communications Act says that a broadcast station that makes advertising time available to one candidate for public office in a primary or general election must make the same amount of time and about the same audience available to all candidates for that office. The audience at 1 A.M., for example, is much smaller than at 8 P.M., so each candidate for the same office must be offered access to an equivalent audience.

This requirement covers non-news programming only, which in effect means paid political advertising. If a station gives free non-news time to one candidate, all candidates for that office must be offered the same amount of time. Once a candidate buys time for a political ad, the station cannot censor that ad in any way and the candidate can only be charged the lowest rate that the station charges commercial advertisers. All candidates must be charged the same rate.

**The Fairness Doctrine.** This doctrine is easily confused with the equal time provision. But the equal time provision covers only candidates for public office; the fairness doctrine covers issues. Broadcasters who air opinions on controversial topics were required by the FCC to give opponents a reasonable opportunity to respond.

In 1984, in an atmosphere of deregulation, the FCC began an attempt to eliminate the fairness doctrine, saying that it was unconstitutional because it unfairly prescribed what broadcasters could put on the air.

In 1987, a U.S. appeals court determined that the fairness doctrine was a *regulation* enforced by the Federal Communications Commission, but it was *not a law*. This gave the FCC the authority to eliminate the doctrine, which the FCC did in August 1987. Several members of Congress subsequently introduced legislation to make the fairness doctrine a law, free from FCC interpretation. Such a law passed Congress in 1987, but President Reagan vetoed it, so currently there is no fairness doctrine for broadcasters.

**Syndicated Exclusivity.** In 1988, the FCC approved rules that reduce how often an audience can see reruns of shows like *Star Trek* in the same market. Beginning in 1989, TV broadcast stations negotiated contracts that allowed them exclusive rights for syndicated programming. Broadcasters call this **syndex** for short.

This means that if a broadcaster pays for the exclusive rights to run a syndicated program like *Star Trek* in a specific broadcast market, the cable operator in that market will have to black out the shows or run other programs.

The FCC had dropped a rule similar to syndex in 1980, and since then cable operators had been able to carry the signals from out-of-town "superstations" such as WTBS in Atlanta and WGN in Chicago, even when those stations transmitted programs that had been bought by local broadcasters. The syndex decision was one possible sign of sympathy for *re-regulation* of broadcasting under the Bush administration.

# Broadcast Deregulation and Re-Regulation

Because members of the FCC are appointed by the president, the FCC's actions can swing widely from one administration to the next. In the 1980s, during the Reagan administration, the FCC strongly favored a philosophy of **deregulation**, which meant that several regulations on broadcasting were lifted. This deregulation followed the Reagan philosophy of a free marketplace for business.

During the 1980s, FCC actions included changes in the regulations that affect:

• Children's programs. *The FCC changed the rules requiring that television stations provide "informative" children's programming, and rejected restrictions on advertising to children. Children's cartoons can be based on toys (such as* Smurfs) *that are then marketed to children.*

• Public service. *The FCC loosened guidelines requiring nonentertainment programming and coverage of community issues. TV stations once were required to devote 5 percent of their air time to news, public affairs, and informational programming.*

• Community assessment. *The FCC dropped requirements that station executives conduct regular formal interviews with community leaders to assess local needs and interests (called ascertainment).*

• Commercials. *The FCC eliminated the requirements about how long commercials can be and how many commercials can be broadcast, which allows more commercials per hour.*

• Station ownership. *The FCC raised the limit on group ownership of TV stations and AM and FM radio stations from seven to 12 each. The only restriction is that one company can have no more than 25 percent of the national audience.*

• Station transfer. *The FCC allowed stations to be sold as soon as they were purchased, rather than a minimum of every three years.*

The FCC under President Bush has slowly moved the commission to a policy of *re-regulation*. The first act of the current FCC, under Chairman Alfred Sikes, was to try to ban indecent programming from radio (see page 432). Although this action failed, the FCC has successfully reinstated price controls for cable television, limiting how much cable operators can charge for their services, and — in a reversal of the Reagan-era FCC — the Sikes FCC has set limits on children's advertising.

Critics complain that the limits are rather modest (ads are limited to 10½ minutes per hour on weekend children's programs and 12 minutes during the week), but the FCC is sending a signal to broadcasters that stricter oversight is likely in the 1990s.

# Advertising and Public Relations Law and Regulation

Advertising and public relations are governed by legal constraints and by regulation.

**Legal Issues.** *New York Times* v. *Sullivan* (see page 420) was a crucial case for advertisers as well as for journalists. Since that decision, two other important court cases have defined the advertising and public relations businesses — the Central Hudson case for advertising (which is defined as "commercial speech" under the law) and the Texas Gulf Sulphur case for public relations.

*Central Hudson case.* In 1980, in *Central Hudson Gas & Electric Corp.* v. *Public Service Commission*, the U.S. Supreme Court issued the most definitive opinion yet on commercial speech. During the energy crisis atmosphere of the 1970s, the New York Public Utilities Commission had banned all advertising by public utilities that promoted the use of electricity. Central Hudson Gas & Electric wanted the ban lifted, and so the company sued the commission. The commission said the ban promoted energy conservation; the Supreme Court disagreed, and the decision in the case formed the basis for commercial speech protection today. "If the commercial speech does not mislead, and it concerns lawful activity," explains legal scholar Ralph Holsinger, "the government's power to regulate it is limited. . . . The state cannot impose regulations that only indirectly advance its interests. Nor can it regulate commercial speech that poses no danger to a state interest."[30]

The decision prescribed standards that commercial speech must meet to be protected by the First Amendment. The main provisions of the standards are that (1) the advertisement must be for a lawful product and (2) the advertisement must not be misleading. This has become known as the *Hudson test.*

To be protected, then, an advertisement must promote a legal product and must not lie. This would seem to have settled the issue, but controversy continues. Should alcohol advertising be banned? What about advertisements for condoms or birth control pills? Courts in different states have disagreed on these questions, and no Supreme Court decision on these specific issues exists, leaving many complex questions undecided. The Hudson test remains the primary criteria for determining what is protected commercial speech.

*The Texas Gulf Sulphur case.* The most important civil suit involving the issue of public relations occurred in the 1960s in *Securities and Exchange Commission* v. *Texas Gulf Sulphur Company.* The Texas Gulf Sulphur (TGS) Company discovered ore deposits in Canada in late 1963 but did not announce the discovery publicly. TGS quietly purchased hundreds of acres surrounding the ore deposits. Although TGS officers began to accumulate more shares of the stock, the company issued a press release that said that the rumors about a discovery were "unreliable."

When TGS announced that it had made a "major strike," the company was taken to court by the Securities and Exchange Commission. The U.S. court of appeals ruled that TGS officers had violated the disclosure laws of the Securities and Exchange Commission. The court also ruled that TGS had issued "a false and misleading press release." Company officers and their friends were punished for withholding the information.

*The case proved conclusively that a company's failure to make known material information (information likely to be considered important by reasonable investors in determining whether to buy, sell, or hold securities) may be in violation of the antifraud provision of the Securities and Exchange Acts. The TGS case remains today as a landmark in the history of public relations law.* [31]

The decision in the Texas Gulf Sulphur case means that public relations people can be held legally responsible for information that is not disclosed about their companies. This case, although nearly 30 years old, says that public relations people at publicly held corporations (businesses with stockholders) are responsible, not only to their companies, but also to the public.

**Regulatory Issues.** The main regulatory agency for advertising and public relations issues is the Federal Trade Commission (FTC), although other agencies such as the Securities and Exchange Commission and the Food and Drug Administration sometimes intervene to question advertising practices.

In 1914, the Federal Trade Commission assumed the power to oversee deceptive interstate advertising practices under the Federal Trade Commission Act. Today, the FTC's policy covering deceptive advertising says: "The

Commission will find an act or practice deceptive if there is a misrepresentation, omission or other practice that misleads the consumer acting reasonably in the circumstances, to the consumer's detriment."[32] The FTC can fine an advertiser who doesn't comply with an FTC order.

The Federal Trade Commission's five members serve seven-year terms. They are appointed by the president and confirmed by the Senate, and no more than three of the members can be from one political party. The commission acts when it receives a complaint that the staff feels is worth investigation. The staff can request a *letter of compliance* from the advertiser, with the advertiser promising to change the alleged deception without admitting guilt.

Next, the advertiser can argue the case before an administrative law judge, who can write a consent agreement to outline what the advertiser must do to comply with the law. A cease-and-desist order can be issued against the advertiser, although this is rare.

Finally, because the FTC's members are presidential appointees, the commission's actions often reflect the political climate under which they operate. In the 1970s the FTC became a very active consumer advocacy agency. This was challenged in the 1980s, when presidential policy favored easing regulations on business practices.

Under President Bush in the 1990s, the FTC has begun to move aggressively to cite companies for wrongdoing. For example, the FTC has charged a toymaker with misrepresenting the performance of its toys. In another instance, the author of a book on how to obtain government grants was cited by the FTC for misleading consumers after he appeared in an advertisement for his book.

*The Wall Street Journal* reports:

> *Regulations governing advertising haven't changed. . . . But lawyers say the ad industry relaxed during the Reagan administration, when the industry was largely left alone to regulate itself. Under the Bush administration, things have changed. FTC Chairwoman Janet Steiger has made it clear that [advertising] agencies — in certain circumstances — will be held responsible for their part in allegedly deceptive advertising.*[33]

In summary, legal and regulatory issues governing advertising and public relations, then, are stitched with the same conflicting values that govern all aspects of media law and regulation. The courts, the FCC, the FTC, and other government agencies that monitor the media industries are the major arbiters of ongoing constitutional clashes that attempt to balance the business needs of the media industries, the constitutional guarantee of freedom of speech, and the government's role as a public interest representative.

• Until 1964, the First Amendment faced four notable government challenges: the Alien and Sedition Laws of 1798, the Espionage Act of 1918, the Smith Act of 1940, and the Cold War congressional investigations of Communists in the late 1940s and early 1950s.

• Prior restraint has rarely been invoked by American courts. The two most recent cases involved the publication of the Pentagon Papers by *The New York Times* and the publication of directions to build a hydrogen bomb in *The Progressive* magazine. In both cases, the information eventually was printed, but the intervention of the government delayed publication.

• Attempts by the Reagan administration to limit reporters' access to Grenada in October 1983 were a subtle form of prior restraint.

• Pentagon rules for 1991 war coverage, reached in cooperation with journalists, imposed stricter restrictions on reporting in the Persian Gulf than in any other U.S. war.

• *Roth* v. *United States* established the Roth test for obscenity: "whether to the average person, applying contemporary community standards, the dominant theme of the material taken as a whole appeals to prurient interest."

• *Miller* v. *California* established a three-part local test for obscenity: whether "the average person, applying contemporary community standards," would find that the work, taken as a whole, appeals to the prurient interest; whether the work depicts or describes, in a patently offensive way, sexual conduct specifically defined by the applicable state law; and whether the work, taken as a whole, lacks serious literary, artistic, political, or scientific value — often called the LAPS test.

• The 1986 Final Report of the Attorney General's Commission on Pornography totally contradicted the findings of a similar study done in 1970. The 1986 report called for a nationwide crackdown on obscenity, linking sex crimes and other antisocial behavior to hard-core pornography. The commission's arguments were not convincing and no substantial legislation resulted.

• In the 1988 Hazelwood case, the U.S. Supreme Court for the first time gave public school officials considerable freedom to limit what appears in student publications.

• In 1964, the *New York Times* v. *Sullivan* case set a libel precedent, establishing the concept that to be successful in a libel suit, a public official must prove actual malice.

• *Gertz* v. *Robert Welch* established the concept that the expression of opinions is a necessary part of public debate. Because of the *Herbert* v. *Lando* decision, reporters today can be asked in a libel suit to identify their sources and to surrender their notes. The *Masson* v. *New Yorker Magazine* decision defined the journalist's responsibility for direct quotations.

• To prove libel, a person must show that the statement was communicated to a third party; that people who read or saw the statement would be able to identify the person, even if that person was not actually named; that the statement injured the person's reputation or income or caused mental anguish; and that the journalist or the print or broadcast organization is at fault.

• The press can use three defenses against a libel suit: truth, privilege, and fair comment.

• Invasion-of-privacy lawsuits are much less common than libel suits. There is no U.S. Supreme Court decision governing invasion of privacy, so each state has its own interpretation of this issue.

• Generally, the media can be guilty of invading someone's privacy by intruding on a person's physical or mental solitude, publishing or disclosing embarrassing personal facts, giving someone publicity that places the person in a false light, using someone's name or likeness for commercial benefit.

• *Sheppard* v. *Maxwell* established the legal precedent for limiting press access to courtrooms and juries.

• Unlike print, the broadcast media are regulated by a federal agency, the Federal Communications Commission. The five regulations that affect broadcast coverage of public issues and broadcast programming are: the must-carry requirement for cable; broadcast content restrictions; the fairness doctrine; the equal time requirement; and syndicated exclusivity. The fairness doctrine was eliminated by the FCC in 1987; Congress passed legislation to make the fairness doctrine a law, but President Reagan vetoed it, so currently there is no fairness doctrine for broadcasters.

• A major regulatory issue affecting entertainment programming is syndicated exclusivity (syndex), which gives broadcasters exclusive rights to run a syndicated program in a specific market.

• The FCC under President Bush has slowly moved to a policy of re-regulation, reversing the deregulation policy of President Reagan.

• The Hudson test for advertising means that, to be protected by the First Amendment, an advertisement must promote a legal product and must not lie.

• The Texas Gulf Sulphur case established the concept that a publicly held company is responsible for any information it withholds from the public.

• The main government agency regulating advertising is the Federal Trade Commission that, in the 1990s, is expected to adopt a more stringent policy of monitoring advertisers than in the 1980s.

**14** *"Most of us would rather publish a story than not,"*

*explained journalist Anthony Brandt in an* Esquire

*magazine article about ethics. "We're in the business of reporting, after all; most of us*

*believe the public should know what's going on, has a right to know, has, indeed a*

*responsibility to know, and that this right, this responsibility, transcends the right*

*to privacy, excuses our own pushiness, our arrogance, and therefore ought to protect us*

*from lawsuits even when we are wrong.*

**Ethical Practices**

*"But most reporters also know there are times when*

publishing can harm or ruin people's lives. Members of the press sometimes print gossip as truth, disregard the impact they have on people's lives, and are ready to believe the worst about people because the worst sells. . . . We in the media have much to answer for."[1]

Discussions about how journalists answer for what they do center on *ethics*. The word derives from the Greek word *ethos*, meaning the traditions or guiding spirit that govern a culture. Part of America's culture is the unique First Amendment protection given to the press, so any discussion of ethics and the American media acknowledges the cultural belief that the privilege accorded to the press by the First Amendment carries with it special obligations. Among these obligations are professional ethics.

Journalists as a group are no more likely to exploit their positions than people in other professions, but when journalists make the wrong ethical choices, the consequences can be very damaging. "It may well be that if journalism loses touch with ethical values, it will then cease to be of use to society, and cease to have any real reason for being," writes media ethics scholar John Hulteng. "But that, for the sake of all of us, must never be allowed to happen."[2]

Journalists sometimes make poor ethical judgments because they work quickly and their actions can be haphazard; because the lust to be first with a story can override the desire to be right; because they sometimes don't know enough to question the truthfulness of what they're told; because they can win attention and professional success quickly by ignoring ethical standards; and because journalists sometimes are insensitive to the consequences of their stories for the people they cover. Consider these actual situations:

*1.* Creating composite characters. *A journalist for a prestigious magazine admitted that he sometimes embroidered the events he wrote about or created composite characters in his articles without telling his readers. Was the journalist presenting fiction as fact, or was he simply using journalistic license?*

*2.* Insider friendships. *A nationally syndicated political columnist coached a presidential candidate before a televised debate and then praised the candidate's performance on a nationwide TV program. Did the columnist get too close to a news source, or did he simply help a friend?*

*3.* Reporting personal information. *A reporter verified that a well-known public figure was dying of AIDS, although the news figure would not admit his illness. The reporter printed the information. Did the reporter infringe on the person's privacy, or did the readers deserve to know about the extent of this growing health hazard?*

*4.* Portraying sensational events. *A public official committed suicide by calling a press conference and then shooting himself in the head. A television station showed the complete tape of the event on its evening news. Did the station exploit a morbid story for its shock value, or will the public understand this type of tragedy better by witnessing the event?*

# Defining Ethical Dilemmas

THICAL DILEMMAS faced by the media can be described using four categories: truthfulness, fairness, privacy, and responsibility. Falsehood is the issue for the journalist who embroidered characters in example 1. Bias is the question for the columnist who coached the presidential candidate in example 2. Invasion of privacy is the debate facing the reporter who published the AIDS information in example 3. And the television station that broadcast the tape of the public official's suicide in example 4 could be criticized for acting irresponsibly.

Some ethical debates are easier to resolve than others. These four incidents and several other examples are described here to demonstrate how vulnerable the media can be to ethical lapses.

## Truthfulness

Truthfulness in reporting means more than accuracy and telling the truth to get a story. Truthfulness also means not misrepresenting the people or the situations in the story to readers or viewers. Another aspect of truthfulness is the responsibility of government officials to not use the media for their own ends — called **disinformation**.

**Misrepresentation.** The journalist described in example 1 was *New Yorker* magazine writer Alistair Reid, who acknowledged in 1984 that in more than 20 years as a writer for *The New Yorker*, he had modified facts five separate times. In a "Letter from Barcelona," Reid had described some Spaniards sitting in "a small, flyblown bar" jeering at a televised speech by Spanish chief of state

Francisco Franco. In fact, Reid said he watched the speech at the home of a onetime bartender, and two of the main characters were composites. This was particularly surprising because *The New Yorker* prides itself on its fact-checking department. Reid said that he created the fictional environment and characters to protect his sources from retribution by the government.

A more celebrated case of a journalist embroidering the facts is Janet Cooke, who was a reporter for the *Washington Post* in 1980 when she wrote "Jimmy's World," a story about an 8-year-old heroin addict. After she was awarded the Pulitzer Prize for the story in April 1981, reporters began to check up on her background, and the *Post* learned that she had lied on her résumé. The editors then questioned her for several hours about the story. She was allowed to resign.

"'Jimmy's World' was in essence a fabrication," she wrote in her resignation letter. "I never encountered or interviewed an 8-year-old heroin addict. The September 19, 1980, article in *The Washington Post* was a serious misrepresentation which I deeply regret. I apologize to my newspaper, my profession, the Pulitzer board and all seekers of the truth."[3]

A month later, columnist Michael Daly of the New York *Daily News* resigned, admitting that he had invented a British soldier in a story about Ireland. He said he had re-created the adventures of "Christopher Spell" from a description given to him by another soldier, who had witnessed the events. "The question of reconstruction and using a pseudonym — I've done it a lot," said Daly. "No one has ever said anything."[4]

Misrepresenting people by creating composite characters, as in these three cases, causes readers to question the facts in all stories: Which are actual people and which are composites? Is the story fiction or fact? (Another type of potential misrepresentation — made possible by technology — is discussed in the Impact/Perspective, Alterations of Photos Raise Host of Legal, Ethical Issues.)

**Disinformation.** In October 1986, the press learned that in August 1986 the Reagan administration had launched a disinformation campaign to scare Libyan leader Moammar Qadhafi. Selected U.S. government sources had planted stories with reporters that U.S. forces were preparing to strike Libya. The first report of the bogus preparations appeared in the August 25, 1986, *Wall Street Journal*.

On the basis of this story and a statement by White House spokesman Larry Speakes that the article was "authoritative," other newspapers, including the *Washington Post*, carried the story. This brings up the ethical question of the government's responsibility not to use the press for its own ends. State Department spokesman and former television reporter Bernard Kalb resigned when he learned about the disinformation campaign, saying "Faith in the word of America is the pulsebeat of our democracy."

In 1988, the Drug Enforcement Administration (DEA) admitted it had used police nationwide to stage phony drug seizures and attract press attention to help DEA agents gain the confidence of drug kingpins. Law enforcement officials defended the practice as a way to outsmart criminals; the press responded that scams like these raise ethical questions similar to the planted Qadhafi story. How is the public to differentiate between true stories and those that are planted by the government?

# Fairness

Fairness implies impartiality — that the journalist has nothing personal to gain from a report, that there are no hidden benefits to the reporter or to the source from the story being presented. Criticism of the press for unfairness results from debates over close ties that sometimes develop between reporters and the people they write about — called *insider friendships*; reporters who accept personal or financial benefits from sources, sponsors, or advertisers — callect *conflicts of interest*; and reporters who pay their sources for stories — called *checkbook journalism*.

**Insider Friendships.** The columnist in example 2 was ABC News commentator George Will; the candidate was Ronald Reagan. In 1980, Will coached candidate Reagan before he faced President Jimmy Carter for a televised debate. On the ABC program *Nightline*, after the debate, Will compared Reagan's performance to that of a "thoroughbred." In 1983, when Will's actions were reported, Will admitted that he would not do the same thing again.

In 1987, *The Wall Street Journal* reported that in December 1986, ABC's Barbara Walters had carried a private message from arms merchant Manucher Ghorbanifar to President Reagan after she conducted an exclusive interview with Ghorbanifar for an ABC story. Ghorbanifar was a central figure in the arrangements during 1985 and 1986 between the White House and the Iranian government to send arms to Iran in exchange for American hostages. Walters did not report on ABC that she had delivered a message to the president.

"After the interviews, Mr. Ghorbanifar asked to speak with Ms. Walters again and asked that she send his views to the president," stated network spokesman Tom Goodman. "Believing that her information could be of assistance to the remaining hostages (held in Lebanon), and before informing her

# Alterations of Photos Raise Host of Legal, Ethical Issues

Today's technology makes it possible to drastically change photographs. The ethical issues this presents for photographers, editors, and publishers are discussed by reporter **Clare Ansberry** in this article from *The Wall Street Journal.*

SEEING IS believing, they say. Sure.

See the eye-catching picture on the jacket of the best-selling book, "A Day in the Life of America"? See the cowboy riding under the moon? Well, in the original photograph, the cowboy hadn't been riding right under the moon, but editors used computers to alter the composition.

Or consider the dreamy advertisement for Peachtree Doors Inc., which shows a girl staring out her window into the star-studded night. Actually, the picture was assembled from three different photos, including an indoor studio picture.

While a picture may be worth a thousand words, the stories they tell are increasingly fibs. According to the Rochester Institute of Technology, one of 10 color reproductions has been altered — meaning something has been added, deleted or moved. That percentage promises to grow with the proliferation of equipment to take and store pictures electronically.

## Visual Sleights of Hand . . . Some 500 companies already own computer equipment that can quickly alter a photo's colors or move its elements around or combine several shots. In five years, that number is expected to triple as the systems become less expensive.

Visual sleights of hand — say, airbrushing wrinkles from shirts and faces — have long been common in advertising and photography. But the new technology is raising a host of fresh ethical and legal issues — and making a growing number of photographers and others ill at ease.

"Who knows what is real anymore?" sighs Len Kaltman, director of marketing for Comstock, a firm that catalogs and sells thousands of photos in New York.

Mr. Kaltman's question has bearing in the area of copyright laws. For example, how much can you change a copyrighted picture — altering or adding colors — without ruining the integrity of the picture? And when you create a new photo out of several different shots, who owns the copyright? . . .

Policing copyright violations is a nightmare when an art director has the ability to pick a sun from one photograph and a bird from another to create one picture electronically. "It would be such a pain to look for pieces of your picture everywhere," says Nancy Madlin, senior editor for Photo District News, a monthly publication for commercial artists. . . .

Altering a photograph [also] raises ethical issues. When National Geographic's editors several years ago moved two of

This cover provoked controversy about the ethics of altering photographs.

the pyramids of Giza closer together so they would fit on the magazine's cover, "people said, 'My God, they can't move pyramids,'" recalls Richard Clarkson, a contract photographer for Sports Illustrated who was formerly associated with National Geographic. Thomas Kennedy, National Geographic's director of photography, says, "There was so much negative fallout that we'd be extremely reluctant to do that again."

Patti Richards, spokeswoman for Collins Publishers Inc., which published "A Day in the Life of America," says

editors altered that book's jacket shot for "marketing reasons." The cowboy scene, although dramatic, was horizontal and all of its elements wouldn't fit on a book jacket; so editors had to fudge electronically to avoid cropping one of the key elements.

"The cover sells the book. You want people to stop and notice," Ms. Richards says, adding that pictures inside aren't altered. "I wouldn't say any of us feel particularly great about doing it, but it seems to be a technology that others use."

At Newsweek, it's taboo to retouch news photos but permitted for feature or fashion pictures, says picture editor Karen Mullarkey. For example, a recent story about the movie "Rain Man" featured a picture of Dustin Hoffman and Tom Cruise standing side by side — although the two actors had been photographed separately. Says Ms. Mullarkey: "That's different from news. If you start doing that with news, you undermine your reputation."

**'Judgment Calls'** One cover of Time Inc.'s short-lived Picture Week magazine showed Nancy Reagan and Raisa Gorbachev sitting side by side under the headline "Nancy meets Raisa," even though they had never met. The two shots were

merged electronically to avoid an obvious line down the middle. "We tried to blend them together so it wouldn't be so harsh," says Richard B. Stolley, Time Inc.'s editorial director. "But you could tell by the backgrounds that the two women weren't sitting together in the same room."

Mr. Stolley adds: "You have to be very careful you don't distort the veracity of the picture. By retouching a photo in a variety of subtle ways, you can make something really more dramatic than it is or should be."

That's what worries Mr. [Roger] Ressmeyer, the freelance photographer. He would be concerned, for instance, if a magazine or a newspaper made a sunset behind President Bush brilliant when it had actually been a duller orange. "If an image is manipulated, I think the reader should know that," he says. "Photographs are supposed to be the truth."

The Wall Street Journal, *January 26, 1989, p. B-1.*

management, Ms. Walters did that and also gave her information to the appropriate editors" at the network.[5]

*New York Times* reporter Judith Miller, who covered the Middle East for three years, criticized Walters for becoming a participant in a story she covered. "We're in the business of publishing what we know. . . . We don't deliver messages," said Miller.[6]

Part of the job of being a reporter is learning to be friendly with many different types of people. In both the Walters and Will examples, the reporters became part of the stories they were supposed to be covering. How can the public trust a reporter who becomes more than an outside observer of events and instead takes part in the story? Insider friendships can remove a reporter's necessary detachment.

**Conflicts of Interest.** Reporters with conflicts of interest are divided between at least two loyalties, and the ethical question is: How will the stories the reporters write and the integrity of the organizations for which they work be affected?

In 1984, *The Wall Street Journal* fired stock tip columnist R. Foster Winans for allegedly leaking stories in advance to a group of friends who paid Winans for his help and then used the information to make profitable stock market investments. An investigation by the Securities and Exchange Commission had prompted the *Journal* to question Winans.

In 1985, Winans was found guilty of 59 counts of fraud and conspiracy. "What made the conduct here a fraud was that Winans knew he was not supposed to leak the timing or contents of his articles or trade on that knowledge," wrote Judge Charles E. Stewart in his decision on the case. "Here, the fraudulent taking and misuse of confidential information stolen from *The Wall Street Journal* placed immediately in jeopardy probably its most valuable asset — its reputation for fairness and integrity."[7] Winans was sentenced to 18 months in jail, $5,000 in fines, 5 years' probation, and 400 hours of community service.

A different type of conflict of interest happens when reporters accept free meals and passes to entertainment events (freebies) and free trips (junkets). In a 1986 survey of 34 newspapers, nearly half said they accepted free tickets to athletic events, and nearly two-thirds accepted free tickets to artistic events.[8]

In 1986, Walt Disney World invited journalists from all over the world to attend its 15th anniversary celebration in Orlando, Florida, and more than 10,000 journalists and their guests accepted the invitation. Most of the press guests let Disney pay for the hotel, transportation, and meals. *Variety* called the event "one of the biggest junkets in showbiz history," at an estimated cost to Disney, the airlines, hotels, and tourism agencies of $8 million. In an editorial about the junket, *The New York Times* said: "Accepting junkets and boondoggles does not necessarily mean that a reporter is being bought — but it inescapably creates the appearance of being bought."[9]

**Checkbook Journalism.** In 1975, CBS paid $100,000 to H. R. Haldeman, a top aide to ex-President Nixon during the Watergate scandal, for two interview programs. In 1984, NBC paid a woman named Helen Hage a finder's fee to get the network an interview with Libya's Colonel Qadhafi. CBS News Executive Vice President Howard Stringer criticized the payment, saying, "We don't think you should pay for a terrorist."[10]

When Pulitzer Prize-winning journalist Teresa Carpenter decided to write a book about a Tufts University Medical School professor who murdered a Boston prostitute, she says other writers were offering money to all the main people involved in the case. According to Carpenter, even the owner of a local massage parlor, who was a minor figure in the case, left a message on Carpenter's phone machine that said, "Without compensation there will be no information."[11]

After New York's "Son of Sam" serial killer David Berkowitz signed a lucrative film and book deal, the state passed a law to prohibit criminals from profiting from such contracts. But on December 10, 1991, the U.S. Supreme Court overturned the law as an infringement on free speech.

Besides the ethical questions about whether journalists and criminals should profit from crime, there are other hazards in any kind of checkbook journalism. One danger is that a paid interviewee will sensationalize the information to bring a higher price, so the interviewee's veracity cannot always be trusted. The second hazard is that such interviews often become the exclusive property of the highest bidder, shutting out smaller news organizations and independent journalists from the information. A third possibility is that the person who is paid by the news organization to comment could possibly carry a hidden agenda, such as in an incident involving ABC News and former U.S. Secretary of State Henry Kissinger.

In 1989, ABC News paid Kissinger to appear on ABC to analyze how the United States should respond to the events in Tiananmen Square. The student demonstrations in China threatened U.S. business ties there. Neither ABC nor Kissinger revealed during Kissinger's commentary that Kissinger's company had extensive investments in China at the time.

Can an influential person who is being paid for his analysis comment dispassionately about events when those events could affect his business? What responsibility did ABC have to tell its audience about Kissinger's ties to China?

# Privacy

Reporting on AIDS and on rape are the most visible examples of a complex ethical dilemma: How does the press balance the goal of truthfulness and fact-finding with the need for personal privacy? Is the private grief such a report may cause worth the public good that can result from publishing the information?

**Reporting on AIDS.** Because the majority of people who die from AIDS are homosexual, announcing that a person's illness is AIDS can reflect on the person's private sexual behavior. One argument in favor of the press reporting the nature of the illness in these cases is that covering up the information means that the public won't understand the widespread extent of the public health problem that AIDS represents.

"Covering up the truth, by doctors or journalists, stigmatizes other sufferers — the less widely the disease is acknowledged, the less easily they can be accepted. And it shields communities and industries from understanding the full, devastating effect of AIDS," argued *Newsweek* in a story called "AIDS and the Right to Know."[12] The counterargument is that a person's illness and death is strictly a private matter and that publishing the information will harm the person's reputation.

The case of the public figure with AIDS in example 3 describes two recent situations. In 1986, New York lawyer Roy Cohn died of AIDS without acknowledging before his death that he suffered from the disease. Entertainer Liberace also withheld information about his illness before he died in 1987.

Roy Cohn became a public figure in the 1950s during the McCarthy hearings (see page 215), as counsel for the Senate committee investigating Communist activity in the 1950s. As a lawyer in the 1980s, he defended many organized-crime figures, and he lived a high-profile existence in New York City. A week before Cohn died, columnists Jack Anderson and Dale Van Atta published a story saying that Cohn was being treated with azidothymidine (AZT), used exclusively for AIDS patients.

Journalist William Safire criticized Anderson and Van Atta in *The New York Times*, saying "Doctors with some sense of ethics and journalists with some regard for a core of human privacy are shamed by [this] investigative excess."[13] After Cohn's death, *Harper's* magazine published copies of the hospital records on which Van Atta had based his column.

Liberace's illness was first revealed in the *Las Vegas Sun* about two weeks before he died. *Sun* publisher Brian Greenspun appeared on ABC's *Nightline* to defend publishing the information before the entertainer's death. Because

only the *Sun* had access to the documentation, other members of the media who wrote about Liberace's illness attributed the information to the *Sun*. After Liberace died, the Riverside County coroner confirmed that Liberace suffered from a disease caused by AIDS.

A third example of a story about someone dying of AIDS represents one journalist's answer to the debate. *Honolulu Star-Bulletin* Managing Editor Bill Cox announced in a column published September 1, 1986, that he was going on disability leave because he had AIDS. "As a journalist," he wrote, "I have spent my career trying to shed light in dark corners. AIDS is surely one of our darkest corners. It can use some light."[14]

**Reporting on Rape.** Privacy also is an important issue in reporting on rape cases. Common newsroom practice forbids the naming of rape victims in stories. In 1989, editor Geneva Overholser of *The Des Moines Register* startled the press community when she wrote an editorial arguing that newspapers contribute to the public's misunderstanding of the crime by withholding, not only the woman's name, but an explicit description of what happened.

In 1990, the *Register* published a five-part series about the rape of Nancy Ziegenmeyer, with Ziegenmeyer's full cooperation. Ziegenmeyer had contacted the *Register* after Overholser's column appeared, volunteering to tell her

# The Des Moines Register

On the witness stand, Nancy Ziegenmeyer identifies her assailant.

## IT COULDN'T HAPPEN TO ME: ONE WOMAN'S STORY

On Sunday, Feb. 25, 1990, The Des Moines Register published the first of five consecutive parts of an emotional, gripping and powerful story. It is the story of a rape: the rape of Nancy Ziegenmeyer, a 29-year-old woman from a small Iowa town.

It is an unusual story for a newspaper to publish. Some of those unusual circumstances — the victim's decision to be identified and to share her feelings throughout her 14-month ordeal; the graphic description of the rape; the infusion of race as an issue in the reporting of this rape — prompted Geneva Overholser, editor of The Register, to write a column that appeared on the same day as the first installment.

Her column appeared that day on the front page of The Register's opinion section. It appears in this reprint on Page 16.

The *Des Moines Register* series about the rape of Nancy Ziegenmeyer focused attention on the ethics of publishing the names of rape victims with their consent.

story. The Ziegenmeyer series has provoked wide-ranging debate among editors about this aspect of privacy.

Is there more benefit to society by printing the victim's name, with the victim's permission, than by withholding it? Should the press explicitly describe sexual crimes, or is that merely sensationalism, preying on the public's salacious curiosity?

The Cohn, Liberace, and Ziegenmeyer cases demonstrate how complex privacy issues in today's society have become. When is it in the public interest to divulge personal information about individuals? Who should decide?

# Responsibility

The events that journalists choose to report and the way they use the information they gather reflect on the profession's sense of public responsibility. Most reporters realize that often they change the character of an event by covering that event. The mere presence of the media magnifies the importance of what happens.

The media can be exploited by people in trouble or by people who covet the notoriety that media coverage brings. And the media can exploit an event for its shock value to try to attract an audience. The following two specific examples demonstrate how differently individual media organizations and individual members of the media interpret their responsibility to the public.

**A TV Suicide.** Many television stations refuse to show any of the events connected with a suicide. Even the sound of a gunshot from inside a house may be edited out of broadcast news footage.

The event described in example 4 happened in January 1987. The media faced an unusual ethical dilemma when Pennsylvania State Treasurer R. Budd Dwyer, who was under investigation for fraud, called a news conference, presented a brief statement, then pulled a .357 Magnum from inside a cloth bag and shot himself in the mouth in front of two dozen reporters, photographers, and camera operators. Videotape and photos of the complete sequence of events leading up to the suicide and the suicide itself were available for the media to use in presenting the story. A wire service photo, for example, showed Dwyer at the exact moment he pulled the trigger. Dwyer's suicide became a media event.

Dwyer's death would not have attracted attention outside of Pennsylvania except for the public way he chose to die. In a throwback to the 1928 New

The on-camera suicide of former Pennsylvania State Treasurer R. Budd Dwyer in 1987 sparked an ethical debate over what the public should see.

York *Daily News* front-page execution photograph of Ruth Snyder (see page 57), some newspapers—including one edition of the *Los Angeles Times*—printed a photograph of the morbid moment. Some Pennsylvania television stations, including WHTM in Harrisburg, rebroadcast the entire event. ABC, CBS, NBC, and CNN refused to broadcast the suicide, although they showed Dwyer at the press conference before he killed himself.[15]

Many newsworthy events concern people who are under stress, and several ethical questions linger from the media's portrayal of the Dwyer suicide: Is the recording of an event justification for showing it? How can the media prevent being used by people who want to attract attention? Should limits be set on the media's role in satisfying the public's curiosity about morbid events? Should some private agonies remain private? (For a reporter's-eye view of these questions, see Impact/Perspective, Reporters and the Tragedies They Cover.)

**A Live TV Drug Raid.** In December 1986, the Tribune Entertainment Company presented a special program called *American Vice: The Doping of a Nation*, featuring former ABC reporter Geraldo Rivera. Tribune broadcast the program to 163 stations throughout the country. Rivera accompanied law enforcement officials in Florida, Texas, and California to show on-camera drug raids. He provided the live commentary as the drug teams made their arrests, and he also acted as executive producer.

The live format provided immediacy, but it also brought some ethical risks. Among the people arrested were Terry Rouse (in Channelview, Texas) and Manuel Chavez (in San Jose, California). Charges against both people were subsequently dropped when it was determined that they were visiting the people who were arrested and had no connection to the drug activity.

*Los Angeles Times* media columnist Howard Rosenberg wrote:

*This was live TV at its most revolting, with cops kicking down doors and bagging alleged pushers in front of TV cameras that beamed coast-to-coast pictures of suspects*

# Reporters and the Tragedies They Cover

**In this excerpt from a column by *New York Times* reporter Anna Quindlen, she describes the pain of being a journalist as she enters and leaves people's lives like a "hit-and-run driver."**

FOR MOST of my adult life, I have been an emotional hit-and-run driver, that is, a reporter. I made people like me, trust me, open their hearts and their minds to me and cry and bleed onto the pages of my neat little notebooks, and then I went back to a safe place and I made a story out of it. I am good at what I do, and so often the people who read those stories cried, too. When they were done they turned the page and when I was done I went on to another person, another story, went from the cop's wife whose husband had never come home to the impoverished 80-year-old Holocaust survivor to the family with the missing child. I stepped in and out of their lives as easily as I did a pair of shoes in the morning, and when I was done I wrote my piece and I went home, to the husband who had not been killed, the bank account that was full, the child safe in his high chair. Sometimes I carried within me, for a day or a week or sometimes even longer, the resonances of their pain. But they were left with the pain itself.

*"Hers,"* The New York Times, *April 10, 1986, p. 16.*

*along with apparently innocent bystanders. In the confusion, it was hard telling who was who, and the ultimate disposition of these cases will never be known. A woman was led away under the white glare of TV lights. Was she charged? Was she guilty? No time to worry about smearing the innocent. "This is real life," Rivera said.* [16]

The Tribune Company's defense of the program was that it merely portrayed events as they occurred. "That's what the newspapers are doing," said Tribune spokesman Jack Devlin. "We were merely reporting the news as it happened." [17]

Are members of the media, as Devlin contends, merely conduits for information? Or do they have a responsibility to protect the interests of the people they cover — in this case, the innocent as well as the guilty? And how did Rivera's presence during the drug raids change the event from a private to a public arrest? Does the Tribune Company have any responsibility to the people involved to report who actually faced charges and who was released? How is live TV coverage different from newspaper coverage of the same event?

# Philosophical Principles

SCHOLARS CAN only prescribe guidelines for moral decisions, because each situation presents its own special dilemmas. First it is important to understand the basic principles that underlie these philosophical discussions.

In their book *Media Ethics*, Clifford G. Christians, Kim B. Rotzoll, and Mark Fackler identify five major philosophical principles underlying today's ethical decisions: Aristotle's golden mean, Kant's categorical imperative, Mill's principle of utility, Rawls' veil of ignorance, and the Judeo-Christian view of persons as ends in themselves.

• Aristotle's golden mean. *"Moral virtue is appropriate location between two extremes."* This is a philosophy of moderation and compromise, often called the golden mean. *The journalistic concept of fairness reflects this idea.*

• Kant's categorical imperative. *"Act on that maxim which you will to become a universal law."* Eighteenth-century philosopher Immanuel Kant developed this idea, an extension of Aristotle's golden mean. Kant's test — that you make decisions based on principles that you want to be universally applied — is called the categorical imperative. *This means you would act by asking yourself the question, "What if everyone acted this way?"*

• Mill's principle of utility. *"Seek the greatest happiness for the greatest number." In the 19th century, John Stuart Mill taught that the best decision is one with the biggest overall benefit for the most human beings.*

• Rawls' veil of ignorance. *"Justice emerges when negotiating without social differentiations." John Rawls' 20th-century theory supports an egalitarian society that asks everyone to work from a sense of liberty and basic respect for everyone, regardless of social position.*

• Judeo-Christian view of persons as ends in themselves. *"Love your neighbor as yourself." Under this longstanding ethic of religious heritage, people should care for one another — friends as well as enemies — equally and without favor. Trust in people and they will trust in you.* [18]

In American society, none of these five philosophies operates independently. Ethical choices in many journalistic situations are not exquisitely simple. What is predictable about journalistic ethics is their unpredictability. Therefore, journalists generally adopt a philosophy of "situational" ethics — because each circumstance is different, individual journalists must decide what is best in each situation.

Should the press adopt Rawls' idea of social equality and cover each person equally, or should public officials receive more scrutiny than others because they maintain a public trust? Is it a loving act in the Judeo-Christian tradition to allow bereaved parents the private sorrow of their child's death by drowning, or is the journalist contributing to society's greater good by warning others about the dangers of leaving a child unattended? Questions like these leave the press in a continually bubbling cauldron of ethical quandaries.

# How the Media Define Ethics

ETHICAL DILEMMAS might seem easier to solve with a rule book nearby, and several professional media organizations have tried to codify ethical judgments to ensure the outcomes in difficult situations. Codes of ethics can be very general ("Truth is our ultimate goal" — Society of Professional Journalists, Sigma Delta Chi); some are very specific ("We will no longer

*"This might not be ethical. Is that a problem for anybody?"*

accept any complimentary tickets, dinners, junkets, gifts or favors of any kind" — *The San Bernardino* [Calif.] *Sun*); some are very personal ("I will try to tell people what they ought to know and avoid telling them what they want to hear, except when the two coincide, which isn't often" — CBS commentator Andy Rooney). [19]

Some ethical decisions carry legal consequences — for example, when a journalist reports embarrassing facts and invades someone's privacy (see Chapter 13). First Amendment protections shield the media from government enforcement of specific codes of conduct, except when ethical mistakes are also judged by the courts to be legal mistakes.

In most cases, however, a reporter or a news organization that makes an ethical mistake will not face a lawsuit. The consequences of bad ethical judgments usually involve damage to the newsmakers who are involved and to the individual journalist, damage to the reputation of the news organization where the journalist works, and damage to the profession in general.

Professional codes of ethics set a leadership tone for a profession, an organization, or an individual. Several groups have attempted to write rules governing how the media should operate. Television stations that belonged to the National Association of Broadcasters, for example, once subscribed to a code of conduct developed by the NAB. This code covered not only news reporting but also entertainment programming.

One provision of the NAB code said "Violence, physical or psychological, may only be projected in responsibly handled contexts, not used exploitatively. Programs involving violence should present the consequences of it to its victims and perpetrators." Members displayed the NAB Seal of Approval before broadcasts to exhibit their compliance with the code.

In 1976, a decision by a U.S. federal judge in Los Angeles abolished the broadcast codes, claiming that the provisions violated the First Amendment. Today codes of ethics for both print and broadcast are voluntary, with no absolute penalties for people who violate the rules. These codes are meant as guidelines. Many media organizations, such as CBS News, maintain their own detailed standards and hire people to oversee ethical conduct. Other organizations use guidelines from professional groups as a basis to develop their own philosophies. Advertising and public relations organizations also have issued ethical codes.

# Codes of Ethics

Three widely used codes of ethics are the guidelines adopted by the Society of Professional Journalists, the Radio-Television News Directors Association, and the Public Relations Society of America.

### The Society of Professional Journalists Code of Ethics.

The Sigma Delta Chi code lists 18 specific canons for journalists (such as "Nothing of value should be accepted"). The following list quotes directly from the code's major points:

• *The public's right to know of events of public importance and interest is the overriding mission of the mass media. The purpose of distributing news and enlightened opinion is to serve the general welfare. Journalists who use their professional status as representatives of the public for selfish or other unworthy motives violate a high trust.*

• *Freedom of the press is to be guarded as an inalienable right of people in a free society. It carries with it the freedom and the responsibility to discuss, question, and challenge actions and utterances of our government and of our public and private institutions. Journalists uphold the right to speak unpopular opinions and the privilege to agree with the majority.*

• *Journalists must be free of obligation to any interest other than the public's right to know the truth.*

• *Good faith with the public is the foundation of all worthy journalism.*

• *Journalists at all times will show respect for the dignity, privacy, rights, and well-being of people encountered in the course of gathering and presenting the news.*

• *Journalists should actively censure and try to prevent violations of these standards, and they should encourage their observance by all newspeople. Adherence to this code of ethics is intended to preserve the bond of mutual trust and respect between American journalists and the American people.*[20]

## Radio-Television News Directors Association Code of Broadcast News Ethics.
The RTNDA offers a seven-point program for broadcasters:

1. *Strive to present the source or nature of broadcast news material in a way that is balanced, accurate and fair.*

   A. *They will evaluate information solely on its merits as news, rejecting sensationalism or misleading emphasis in any form.*

   B. *They will guard against using audio or video material in a way that deceives the audience.*

   C. *They will not mislead the public by presenting as spontaneous news any material which is staged or rehearsed.*

   D. *They will identify people by race, creed, nationality or prior status only when it is relevant.*

   E. *They will clearly label opinion and commentary.*

   F. *They will promptly acknowledge and correct errors.*

2. *Strive to conduct themselves in a manner that protects them from conflicts of interest, real or perceived. They will decline gifts or favors which would influence or appear to influence their judgments.*

3. *Respect the dignity, privacy and well-being of people with whom they deal.*

4. *Recognize the need to protect confidential sources. They will promise confidentiality only with the intention of keeping that promise.*

5. *Respect everyone's right to a fair trial.*

6. *Broadcast the private transmissions of other broadcasters only with permission.*

7. *Actively encourage observance of this Code by all journalists, whether members of the Radio-Television News Directors Association or not.*[21]

**The Public Relations Society of America.** The Code of Professional Standards, first adopted in 1950 by the Public Relations Society of America, has been revised several times since then. Here are some excerpts:

• *A member shall deal fairly with clients or employers, past, present, or potential, with fellow practitioners, and with the general public.*

• *A member shall adhere to truth and accuracy and to generally accepted standards of good taste.*

• *A member shall not intentionally communicate false or misleading information, and is obligated to use care to avoid communication of false or misleading information.*

• *A member shall be prepared to identify publicly the name of the client or employer on whose behalf any public communication is made.*

• *A member shall not guarantee the achievement of specified results beyond the member's direct control.*[22]

# Three Responses to Criticism

Prescriptive codes of ethics are helpful in describing what journalists should do, and informal guidelines can supplement professional codes (see Impact/ Perspective, Ethics Clinic). Moreover, most journalists use good judgment. But what happens when they don't? People with serious complaints against broadcasters sometimes appeal to the Federal Communications Commission (see Broadcast Regulation, Chapter 13), but what about complaints that must be handled more quickly? The press has offered three solutions: press councils, readers' representatives, and correction boxes.

**Press Councils.** *Press councils* originated in Great Britain. They are composed of people who formerly worked or currently work in the news business, as well as some laypeople. The council reviews complaints from the public, and when the members determine a mistake has been made, the council reports its findings to the offending news organization.

**Bob Steele**, who directs the ethics program at the Poynter Institute for Media Studies, offers a ten-step approach to ethical decisionmaking in this article from *The Quill*, published by the Society of Professional Journalists.

d OING ETHICS is more than simply applying common sense to a moral dilemma.

At the common sense level we are analyzing questions by weighing various values and applying some level of critical thinking. There is nothing wrong with that approach. It is just not enough. Moral reasoning compels us to include ethical principles in the process of making decisions on ethical matters.

This approach to ethical decisionmaking places a premium on the *process* with less emphasis on the results. It does not ignore *what* people decide and do. Rather it stresses the *how* and *why* elements of decisionmaking.

This process approach to doing ethics relates closely to what Professor Ed Lambeth of the University of Missouri calls "craftsmanship" in ethical reasoning. It is a wonderful term, reflecting the development of one's skill at making sound ethical decisions.

It may therefore be logical to assume that good ethical decisionmaking can be a product of careful reflection *and* consistent application.

One approach to increasing the quality of ethical decisionmaking is using a model for processing dilemmas. Asking good questions is an essential part of making good decisions. *Making good decisions,* not getting the right answer, is the key.

The 10 questions we've developed at the Poynter Institute for Media Studies are:

# 1. What happened and is happening?

You need as much specificity as possible on the facts in the case. Clarify confusing or conflicting information. Add missing pieces of the puzzle.

# 2. What are my journalistic goals?

Don't lose sight of your responsibility to provide important and meaningful information [to] the public; the ethic of social responsibility, stewardship and independence.

# 3. What are my ethical concerns?

Balance your journalistic goals with truth-telling, promise-keeping and minimizing harm. Consider fairness and justice in relationships and for individual rights.

# 4. Do I need more points of view?

Do you include different perspectives? Do you have a diversity of "voices" in terms of gender, age, race, etc.?

# 5. Who are the stakeholders?

Have you considered the impact on all those affected by your decisions and actions? Stakeholders include the public, your news organization, special-interest groups and you, yourself.

# 6. What are the consequences of my action?

Weigh the good and bad results, for individuals and groups, for long- and short-term consequences.

# 7. What if the roles were reversed?

Put yourself in the stakeholders' shoes, including the readers/listeners/viewers.

# 8. Am I doing what is right?

Would your actions conflict with your personal ethics? Can you justify the exceptions, or are you rationalizing?

# 9. What are my alternatives?

A sound ethical decision is often found on the continuum between extremes. Brainstorm to maximize good consequences and minimize bad ones.

# 10. Can I justify my decision and actions?

Can you look yourself in the eye? Can you face your family and friends with an open explanation?

*Doing* ethics means that you develop and practice these decision-making skills on a regular basis. Consider a news department retreat, half-day workshops, brown-bag lunches, or impromptu small-group sessions to tackle a case study by applying moral reasoning in a systematic fashion.

*Doing* ethics takes commitment. Working hard at making good ethical decisions will go a long way toward making right decisions.

---

The Quill 79, *no. 2 (March 1991): 36.*

In 1973, the Twentieth Century Fund established a National News Council in the United States, which eventually was funded through contributions from various news organizations. The council was composed of 18 members from the press and the public. The council was disbanded in 1984, largely because some major news organizations stopped giving money to support the idea, but also because several news managers opposed the council, arguing that the profession should police itself.

In its 11 years of existence, the council received thousands of complaints. Most of them were dismissed as too trivial or too local, but of the 242 complaints that completed the review process, the council faulted the press in 82 cases.[23] Even when the press was judged to have been wrong, however, the council had no enforcement power. The results were published in professional publications, but the public at large rarely heard about the council's activities.

Media ethics scholar John Hulteng writes:

*It would seem that — as with the [ethical] codes — the great impact of the press councils is likely to be on the responsible editors, publishers and broadcasters who for the most part were already attempting to behave ethically. . . . An additional value of the councils may be the mutual understanding that grows out of the exchange across the council table between the members of the public and the managers of the media. These values should not be dismissed as insignificant, of course. But neither should too much be expected of them.[24]*

**Readers' Representatives.** The *readers' representative* (also called an ombudsman) is a go-between at a newspaper who responds to complaints from the public and regularly publishes answers to criticism in the newspaper. About two dozen newspapers throughout the country, including the *Washington Post, The Kansas City Star*, and the Louisville *Courier-Journal*, have tried the idea, but most newspapers still funnel complaints directly to the editor.

**Correction Box.** The *correction box* is a device that often is handled by a readers' representative but also has been adopted by many papers without a readers' representative. The box is published in the same place, usually a prominent one, in the newspaper every day. As a permanent feature of the newspaper, the correction box leads readers to notice when the newspaper retracts or modifies a statement. It is used to counter criticism that corrections sometimes receive less attention from readers than the original stories.

Readers' representatives and correction boxes are used by many papers to help handle criticism of the newspapers and to avert possible legal problems that some stories foster. But these solutions address only a small percentage of issues. In newsrooms every day, reporters face the same ethical decisions that all people face in their daily lives — whether to be honest, how to be fair, how to be sensitive, and how to be responsible.

The difference is that, unlike personal ethical dilemmas that other people can debate privately, reporters and editors publish and broadcast the results of their ethical judgments and those judgments become public knowledge — in newspapers, magazines, books, and on radio and television. So potentially, the media's ethical decisions can broadly affect society.

# The Importance of Professional Ethics

A profession that accepts ethical behavior as a standard helps to guarantee a future for that profession. The major commodity the press in America has to offer is information, and when the presentation of that information is weakened by untruth, bias, intrusiveness, or irresponsibility, the press gains few advocates and acquires more enemies. Writes John Hulteng:

*The primary objective of the press and those who work with it is to bring readers, listeners, and viewers as honest, accurate, and complete an account of the day's events as possible. . . . The need to be informed is so great that the Constitution provides the press with a First Amendment standing that is unique among business enterprises. But as with most grants of power, there is an accompanying responsibility, not constitutionally mandated but nonetheless well understood: that the power of the press must be used responsibly and compassionately.* [25]

**IN FOCUS**

**Ethical Practices**

• The word *ethics* derives from the Greek word *ethos*, which means the traditions or guiding spirit that govern a culture.

• Journalists' ethical dilemmas can be discussed using four categories: truthfulness; fairness; privacy; and responsibility.

• Truthfulness means more than telling the truth to get a story. Truthfulness also means not misrepresenting the people or the situations in the story to readers or viewers. In addition, truthfulness means that government agencies should not knowingly provide disinformation to the press.

• Fairness implies impartiality. Criticism of the press for unfairness results from insider friendships, conflicts of interest, and checkbook journalism.

• Two important recent press invasion of privacy issues are the publication of the names of AIDS victims and the publication of the names of rape victims.

• Responsibility means that reporters and editors must be very careful about the way they use the information they gather. Events that are broadcast live, such as the suicide of Pennsylvania State Treasurer R. Budd Dwyer and the drug raids broadcast by Geraldo Rivera, offer especially perilous ethical situations.

• Five philosophical principles underlying the practical application of ethical decisions are: Aristotle's golden mean; Immanuel Kant's categorical imperative; John Stuart Mill's principle of utility; John Rawls' veil of ignorance; and the Judeo-Christian view of persons as ends in themselves.

• Several media professions have adopted ethical codes to guide their conduct. Three of these codes are the guidelines adopted by the Society of Professional Journalists, Sigma Delta Chi; the Radio-Television News Directors Association; and the Public Relations Society of America.

• The U.S. press' three responses to press criticism have been to create press councils, to employ readers' representatives, and to create correction boxes. The National Press Council, created in 1973, was disbanded in 1984. These solutions address only a small percentage of the issues.

**15**

*Students often assume that media in most countries*

*throughout the world operate like the U.S. media. But*

*media industries in different countries are as varied as the countries they serve. Can*

*you match the following media situations with the countries where:*

*1. A Saturday afternoon television program regularly shows topless women frol-*

*icking in a hot springs bath;   2. A top rock star abandoned his very successful*

*career to become the lone public critic of his country's*

*government repression;*

**Global Media**

*3. A government limits each FM radio station to playing popular hits only 50 percent of the time;*

*4. Journalists were not allowed to report on incidents of unrest and were required, by government decree, to leave the location as soon as trouble erupted;*

*5. A magazine announced that it would distribute free copies of its next issue from a central point in the city, and a free-for-all erupted when thousands of people jammed the area to grab a copy;*

*6. Soap operas appear on television six nights a week, and actors regularly pitch sponsored products — as many as 17 per show — within the program's storylines.* [1]

The explicit TV programs appear in Japan, where nudity and discussions of discrete bodily functions in programming and advertising are common. The rock star is named Hou (pronounced Ho) Dejian, and in 1990, one year after demonstrations against the government in China's Tiananmen Square, Hou became a full-time dissident. The Canadian Radio-Television and Telecommunications Commission enforces the 50 percent pop music limitation for Canadian radio.

The banning of journalists occurred in South Africa under state of emergency regulations, first instituted in 1985 and renewed every year thereafter until 1990, when the regulations were eased by South African President F. W. de Klerk. The West German magazine *Stern* announced the free distribution of copies in East Berlin in March 1990, just a few days before the German vote on unification of East and West Germany. And sponsored products regularly appear in Brazilian soap operas (*telenovelas*), where the actors and the Brazilian networks are paid for the ads.

These examples help demonstrate the complexity of defining today's international media marketplace, which clearly is a marketplace in rapid transition. To discuss global media, this chapter is divided into three sections: (1) world media systems; (2) news and information flow; and (3) the new global media marketplace.

# World Media Systems

iT HAS been more than three decades since scholars began using the four theories of the press described in Chapter 1 to define the world's press systems (the Soviet theory, the authoritarian theory, the libertarian theory, and the social responsibility theory). At today's transitional period in global history, even the recent addition of the developmental theory of the press still leaves many press systems beyond convenient categorization.

The print media form the basis for press development in North America, Australia, Western Europe, and Eastern Europe, where two-thirds of the world's newspapers are published.[2] Many developing countries matured after electronic media were introduced in the 1920s, and newsprint in these countries often is scarce or government-controlled, making radio their dominant communications medium. Radio receivers are inexpensive, and many people can share one radio.

Television, which relies on expensive equipment, is in widespread use in prosperous nations and in urban areas of developing countries, yet most countries still have only one television service, usually run by the government.[3] In most developing countries, all broadcasting — television and radio — is owned and controlled by the government.

What follows is a description of today's press systems by region: Western Europe and Canada; Eastern Europe; the Middle East and North Africa; Africa; Asia and the Pacific; and Latin America and the Caribbean.

## Western Europe and Canada

Western European and Canadian media prosper under guarantees of freedom of expression similar to the First Amendment, but each nation has modified the idea to reflect differing values. For example, in Great Britain the media are prohibited from reporting on a trial until the trial is finished. France and Greece, unlike the United States, give more libel protection to public figures than to private citizens.

Scandinavian journalists enjoy the widest press freedoms of all of Western Europe, including almost unlimited access to public documents. Of the Western nations, Canada is the most recent country to issue an official decree supporting the philosophy of press freedom. In 1982, Canada adopted the Canadian Charter of Rights and Freedoms. Before 1982, Canada did not have its own constitution, and instead operated under the 1867 British North America Act, sharing the British free press philosophy.[4]

Johannes Gutenberg's invention of movable type rooted the print media in Western Europe. Today, Western European and Canadian media companies produce many fine newspapers. *The Globe and Mail* of Toronto, *The Times* of London, *Frankfurter Allgemeine* of Germany, *Le Monde* of France, and Milan's *Corriere della Sera* enjoy healthy circulations. Whereas Canadian journalists seem to have adopted the U.S. value of fairness as a journalistic ethic, Western European newspapers tend to be much more partisan than the U.S. or Canadian press, and newspapers (and journalists) are expected to reflect strong points of view.

As in the United States, however, the print media in Western Europe are losing audience to broadcast and cable. Government originally controlled most of Western Europe's broadcast stations. A board of 12 governors, appointed by the queen, supervises the British Broadcasting Corporation (BBC), for example. To finance the government-run broadcast media, countries tax the sale of radios and TVs or charge users an annual fee. Broadcasting in Western Europe is slowly evolving to private ownership and commercial sponsorship.

Western Europeans watch less than half as much television as people in the United States — an average of 3 hours a day per household in Europe, compared to 7 hours a day per household in the United States. One reason for the difference in viewing time may be that most Western European TV stations don't go on the air until late afternoon. In the majority of countries, commercials are shown back-to-back at the beginning or the end of a program.[5]

Europe gets much of its programming from the United States. Of 125,000 hours of TV broadcast in Western Europe each year, only 20,000 hours are produced in Europe. Most of the programming comes from the United States, with a few shows imported from Australia and Japan.[6] U.S. imports are attractive because programs such as *L.A. Law*, which is very popular in Western Europe, are cheaper to buy than to produce.

The European Community (EC) plans to create a single, unified European market by the end of 1992; the policy adopted by the EC establishes "Television Without Frontiers" to promote an open marketplace for television programs among countries in the EC and between EC countries and the United States.

Some members of the EC (especially France) have proposed quotas to limit imported TV programs, charging that U.S. imports are an example of "cultural

For *The Wall Street Journal*, global publishing means targeting the same wealthy audience in Europe and Asia as in the United States. (Note the average income figures for the *Journal's* readership, as stated in the ad.)

# Think globally. Act locally.

It's become almost a cliché to say that business is now global. But that makes it no less true or significant. The Wall Street Journal has made a strong commitment to covering the whole world of business. The Wall Street Journal Europe and The Asian Wall Street Journal are proof of that commitment.

Our international editions are reported, written, and edited for their respective audiences. They're not simply satellite-fed versions of our American newspaper. In fact, over 71% of Wall Street Journal Europe subscribers are European, and 66% of Asian Wall Street Journal subscribers are Asian.

One strength both publications share with the U.S. Journal is the quality of their readership. For The Wall Street Journal Europe: 72% hold top management positions; average household income is US$229,500. For The Asian Wall Street Journal: 71% hold top management positions; average household income is US$183,500.

If you're looking to reach the world's most affluent, influential decision-makers where they live and work, you need The Wall Street Journal around the world.

For more information, call David Manchee (212) 808-6691, Peter Harper (415) 986-6886, or your local Journal sales representative.

## THE WALL STREET JOURNAL.
### THE WORLD'S BUSINESS DAILY. IT WORKS.

imperialism." Countries who favor quotas fear that the importation of U.S. programs imposes a concentration of U.S. values on their viewers. The United States opposes such quotas, of course, because Western European commercial broadcasting offers a seemingly insatiable market for recycled U.S. programs.

# Eastern Europe

The democratization of Eastern Europe is transforming the media in these countries at an unprecedented pace because the media under communism were so closely tied to the government. Some examples:

• *In the six months after the Berlin Wall opened in 1990, circulation of East Germany's national newspapers* Neues Deutschland *and* Junge Welt *dropped 55 percent as the East German population, hungry for news from the West, embraced the flashy West German mass circulation daily* Bild. [7]

• *In Poland, Eastern Europe's first private television station, Echo, went on the air in February 1990, with a total cash investment of $15,000. The station broadcast programs from the windowless janitor's room of a student dormitory.* [8]

• *One week after the 1991 failed coup in the Soviet Union, President Mikhail Gorbachev fired the directors of the Soviet news agency Tass, who had supported the coup.* [9] *Then, on December 25, 1991, Gorbachev resigned. Within 24 hours, President Boris N. Yeltsin of Russia announced that the government would maintain control of the nation's broadcast media.*

Everette E. Dennis, executive director of the Gannett Center for Media Studies, and Jon Vanden Heuvel described the Eastern European challenges in a report issued after a Gannett-sponsored 1990 fact-finding trip:

*Mass communication in the several countries of the region was reinventing itself. While grassroots newspapers and magazines struggled for survival, new press laws were being debated and enacted; elements of a market economy were coming into view; the media system itself and its role in the state and society were being redefined, as was the very nature of journalism and the job description of the journalist, who was no longer a propagandist for the state.* [10]

Eastern Europe in transition is defining a new balance between the desire for free expression and the indigenous remnants of a system of government control.

In many of these countries, the media played a central role in upsetting the established power structure. Often one of the first targets of the revolutionary movements was the nation's broadcast facilities.

For example, in Romania in 1989, opposition leaders of the National Salvation Committee and sympathetic employees barricaded themselves in a Bucharest TV station, rallying the audience to action. "Romania was governed from a hectic studio littered with empty bottles, cracked coffee mugs and half-eaten sandwiches, and run by people who had not slept in days," The Associated Press reported.[11]

Television in the Eastern bloc countries developed under Communist direction because the Communist governments were in power before TV use was widespread. Radio broadcasting also was tightly controlled, although foreign broadcasts directed across Eastern European borders, such as Voice of America and Radio Free Europe, usually evaded jamming attempts by Radio Moscow.

In addition, print media were strictly controlled under communism, with high-ranking party officials forming the core of media management. Because paper supplies are limited, newspapers rarely exceed 12 pages. *Pravda*, the Soviet Union's oldest newspaper, was founded in 1912 by revolutionary leader Vladimir Lenin, who said that a newspaper should be a "collective propagandist," a "collective agitator," and a "collective organizer."[12] The Eastern European nations developed their press policies following the Soviet model.

In the late 1980s, President Mikhail Gorbachev relaxed media controls as part of his policy of *glasnost*. (See Impact/Perspective, St. Petersburg Tunes in to MTV.) In 1988, the first paid commercials (for Pepsi-Cola, Sony, and Visa credit cards) appeared on Soviet TV, and in 1989, the Soviet daily newspaper *Izvestia* published its first Western ads (including a full-page ad for perfume and wines from the French firm Pechiney and a quarter-page ad for Dresdner, a German bank).

In 1990, the Supreme Soviet outlawed media censorship and gave every citizen the right to publish a newspaper.[13] Within five months, more than 100 newspapers began publication. Then, showing how quickly government positions can change, in early 1991 Gorbachev asked the Supreme Soviet to suspend these press freedoms, but they refused.[14] Less than a year later, the Soviet Union had been replaced by the Commonwealth of Independent States. Press policy under the newly-formed commonwealth remains uncertain.

As the Eastern European governments change and realign themselves, the adjustments facing Eastern European media are unprecedented. According to Dennis and Vanden Heuvel:

*Once the revolution came, among the first acts of new government was to take (they would say liberate) electronic media and open up the print press. Permitting free and eventually*

# St. Petersburg Tunes in to MTV

**In this article from the *Los Angeles Times*, Elizabeth Shogren chronicles the first day that MTV appeared in the Soviet Union — March 8, 1991. When Shogren wrote this article, St. Petersburg was called Leningrad.***

MOSCOW — STARTING today, Leningrad cable television viewers can tune in around-the-clock to the same music videos that millions of people are watching simultaneously in 25 other countries.

MTV has made it as the first foreign television channel to contract to broadcast to the Soviet Union.

"It's a real breakthrough," William Roedy, managing director and chief executive officer of MTV Europe, said on Thursday. "One of MTV's mottoes is, 'breaking down barriers,' and this is one more wall that has come down and that will be impossible to build up again."

MTV will be broadcast 24 hours a day over Leningrad Cable Television, which is now received by 140,000 households,

---

*The city was renamed in September 1991 after the failed coup in the Soviet Union. St. Petersburg was the city's original name before the Russian Revolution.*

or about half a million viewers, Roedy said.

"MTV is one of the few programs that can cross international cultural and language barriers — music is the international language," Roedy said in a telephone interview from Leningrad. "We're being compared to Czar Peter the Great for opening [for Russia] a window on the world."

The programing will be paid for by Lenceltel, a joint venture of the Leningrad City Council and Rutter-Dunn Communications Inc. of Columbus, Ohio.

"Like lots of other Soviet broadcasters, we used to pirate MTV programs," Boris P. Belyayev, deputy general director of Leningrad Cable Television, said. "Now we have legal right to the programs.". . .

In its three years, MTV Europe has spread to 21 million households in 25 countries, Roedy said.

Although the main language of MTV Europe is English, the program's staff comes from 14

countries, so the show has a more international flavor than the American version. It also shows videos from a wider assortment of European artists than the American counterpart.

Initially, there will be no translation provided for MTV in Leningrad, but some translation may be added in the future, according to Yuri A. Gerasimov, deputy director of Lenceltel.

MTV already enjoys wide popularity among Soviet teenagers and young adults, who will be targeted as the main audience for the new 24-hour cable channel, Gerasimov added.

"But this is not just a musical event but also a political event," Gerasimov said. "For decades, rock was restricted here. Now Leningraders can tune into rock videos 24 hours a day. It's a big success of *perestroika* and democratization."

---

Los Angeles Times, *March 8, 1991*, p. F-24.

*independent media was a vital beginning for democracy in several countries and a clear break with the past. The freeing up of the media system, speedily in some countries and incrementally in others, was the lifting of an ideological veil without saying just what would replace it.* [15]

# Middle East and North Africa

Press history in the Middle East and North Africa begins with the newspaper *Al-Iraq*, first published in 1817, although the first daily newspaper didn't begin until 1873. With one exception, development of the printed press throughout this region follows the same pattern as in most developing countries: More newspapers and magazines are published in regions with high literacy rates than in regions with low literacy rates. The exception is Egypt, where less than half the people are literate, yet Cairo is the Arab world's publishing center. [16] *Al Ahram* and *Al Akhbar* are Egypt's leading dailies.

The Middle Eastern press is tightly controlled by government restrictions, through ownership and licensing, and it is not uncommon for opposition newspapers to disappear and for journalists to be jailed or leave the country following political upheaval.

*Following the revolution in Iran, all opposition and some moderate newspapers were closed, and according to the National Union of Iranian Journalists (now an illegal organization), more than 75 percent of all journalists left the country, were jailed, or no longer work in journalism.* [17]

The Palestinian press, for example, is subject to censorship by the Israeli government, and all Palestinian newspapers and magazines must receive Israeli government permission to be published. [18]

The foreign-language press is especially strong in the Middle East because of the large number of immigrants in the area. And foreign radio is very popular. Radio and television are almost completely controlled by the governments within each country, and television broadcasts only a few hours each night. So radio signals beamed from Europe have become the region's alternative affordable source of news.

*Because of tight censorship, newspapers and television stations in the Arab world frequently reflect the biases or outright propaganda of their governments. But radio broadcasts from outside the region travel easily across borders and long distances, and many Arabs regard those stations as the most reliable sources of unbiased news.* [19]

The BBC (based in London) and Radio Monte Carlo (based in Paris) are the main across-the-border program sources.

Also, because of careful government control of television programming, another alternative medium has emerged — the VCR.

*Saudi Arabia and some of the Gulf countries have the highest VCR penetration levels in the world, in spite of the high cost of the equipment. And since only Egypt, Turkey, Lebanon, and Israel have copyright laws, pirated films from Europe, the United States, India, and Egypt circulate widely in most countries. . . . The widespread availability of content that cannot be viewed on television or at the cinema (Saudi Arabia even forbids the construction of cinemas) has reduced the popularity of broadcast programming.*[20]

In the Middle East, as in other developing regions, the government-owned media are perceived as instruments of each country's social and political programs. The rapid spread of technological developments such as the VCR, however, demonstrates new challenges to the insulated Middle Eastern media cocoon.

# Africa

Most of the new nations of Africa were born after 1960, a remarkable year in U.S. media history that witnessed the Kennedy-Nixon debates and the maturing of U.S. television as a news medium. African history is a record of colonialism, primarily by the British, French, Dutch, and Portuguese, and the early print media were created to serve the colonists, not the native population.

The first English-language newspaper in sub-Saharan Africa, the *Capetown Gazette and African Advertiser*, appeared in 1800; a year later, the first black newspaper, the *Royal Gazette and Sierra Leone Advertiser*, appeared in Sierra Leone.

French settlement in Africa is reflected in the pages of *Fraternité-Matin*, the only major daily in French Africa. A Portuguese settler founded *Noticias*, published in Mozambique. In Kenya, three tabloid newspapers enjoy wide circulations with relative independence: the English-language *Daily Nation* and *The Standard* and the Swahili daily *Taifa Leo*.

Media scholar L. John Martin describes the African media landscape:

*Africans have never had an information press. Theirs has always been an opinion press. Advocacy journalism comes naturally to them. To the extent that they feel a need for hard news, that need is satisfied by the minimal coverage of the mass media, especially*

Newspaper vendors offer a variety of choices on a street in Lagos, Nigeria.

*of radio. Soft news — human interest news or what [media scholar Wilbur] Schramm has called immediate-reward news — is equally well transmitted through the folk media, such as the "bush telegraph" or drum; the "grapevine," or word-of-mouth and gossip; town criers and drummers; traditional dances, plays; and song.*[21]

Martin points out that African culture is very diverse, with an estimated 800 to 2,000 language dialects, making it impossible to create a mass circulation newspaper that can appeal to a wide readership. The widest circulating publication is a magazine called *Drum*, published in South Africa but also distributed in West Africa and East Africa.

Today, most newspapers in South Africa, for example, are owned and edited by whites, who publish newspapers in English and in Afrikaans, a language that evolved from South Africa's 17th century Dutch settlers. South Africa's first Afrikaans newspaper, *Di Patriot*, began publishing in 1875.

South Africa's highest circulation newspaper is the *Star*, which belongs to the Argus Group, South Africa's largest newspaper publisher with holdings in several other African states.

From 1985 to 1990, the South African government demonstrated its distaste for dissident speech when it instituted strict limits on domestic and international news coverage in the region. Because of violent demonstrations supporting the opposition African National Congress, President P. W. Botha declared a state of emergency in the country in 1985. In 1988, the government suspended the *New Nation* and four other alternative publications.[22] These suspensions and the regulations that prevented journalists from covering unrest show the power of government to limit reporting on dissent.

Broadcasting and African independence emerged at about the same time; the result is that today, radio is a much more important medium in Africa than print or television. Because literacy rates are lower in Africa than in many other regions of the world, radio is very accessible because it is the cheapest way for people to follow the news.

Some governments charge license fees for radio sets, which are supposed to be registered, but many radios go unregistered. Most stations accept advertising, but the majority of funding for radio comes from government subsidies.[23]

Less than 2 percent of the African public owns a TV set.[24] Television in the region is concentrated in the urban areas, and TV broadcasts last only a few hours each evening. Says L. John Martin, "TV remains a medium of wealthy countries."[25]

# Asia and the Pacific

The development of media in this region centers primarily in four countries: Japan's prosperous mix of public and private ownership; Australia's media barons with their entrepreneurial fervor; India's phenomenal media growth; and the People's Republic of China, with its sustained government-controlled media monopoly.

**Japan.** Japan boasts more newspaper readers than any other nation in the world. Japan's three national daily newspapers are based in Tokyo — *Asahi Shimbun*, *Yomiuri Shimbun*, and *Mainichi Shimbun*. These three papers, each of them more than 100 years old, account for almost half of the nation's newspaper circulation.

Broadcast media in Japan developed as a public corporation called the Japanese Broadcasting Corporation (NHK). During World War II, NHK became a propaganda arm of the government, but after the Japanese surrender, the United States established the direction for Japanese broadcasting. Japan created a licensing board similar to the Federal Communications Commission,

On November 25, 1991, Japan became the first country to begin broadcasting high-definition television (HDTV) programs. Here, people stop on a street in Tokyo to watch a broadcast. An HDTV set costs more than $30,000.

but an operating board similar to Great Britain's BBC. Japan also decided to allow private broadcast ownership.

As a result of this, Japan today has a mixed system of privately owned and publicly held broadcast media. NHK continues to prosper and, says broadcast scholar Sydney W. Head:

*NHK enjoys more autonomy than any other major public broadcasting corporation. In a rather literal sense, the general public "owns" it by virtue of paying receiver fees. The government cannot veto any program or demand that any program be aired. It leaves the*

*NHK free to set the level of license fees and to do its own fee collecting (which may be why it rates as the richest of the world's fee-supported broadcasting organizations).*[26]

Private ownership is an important element in the Japanese media, and many broadcasting operations are owned by newspaper publishers. NHK owns many more radio properties than private broadcasters; NHK shares television ownership about equally with private investors.[27]

**Australia.** In Australia, acquisitions by media magnates skyrocketed in the 1980s, and today Australian-turned-American citizen Rupert Murdoch controls an astounding 60 percent of Australia's newspaper circulation, which includes the *Daily Telegraph Mirror* in Sydney and *The Herald-Sun* in Melbourne.

Murdoch, although somewhat burdened with debt because of his binge of acquisitions in the 1980s (see Impact/Profiles, Four Moguls of the Media, Chapter 1), emerged in the 1990s as Australia's uncontested print media baron after the other major Australian media family, the Fairfaxes, fell into bankruptcy in December 1990.

Broadcasting in Australia is dominated by Australian Broadcasting Corporation (ABC), modeled after the BBC. Three nationwide commercial networks operate in the country, but all three were suffering financial difficulties as the 1990s began, a legacy "of the heydays of the 1980s, when aspiring buyers, backed by eager bank lenders, paid heady prices for broadcast and print assets," reported *The Wall Street Journal*.[28]

**India.** Entrepreneurship also is an important element in the print media of India, which gained independence from Britain in 1947. Forty years following independence, in 1987, Indian print media had multiplied 1,000 times — from 200 publications in 1947 to nearly 25,000 publications in 1987.[29]

Broadcasting in India follows its British colonial beginnings, with radio operating under the name All India Radio (AIR) and TV as Doordarshan ("distance view"). Doordarshan uses satellite service to reach remote locations, bringing network TV to four out of five people. As in most developing countries, the network regularly broadcasts programs aimed at improving public life, about subjects such as family planning, health, and hygiene.

**People's Republic of China.** Social responsibility is a very important element of media development in the People's Republic of China, where a media monopoly gives government the power to influence change. At the center of Chinese media are the two party information sources, the newspaper *People's Daily* and Xinhua, the Chinese news agency. These two sources set the tone for the print media throughout China, where self-censorship maintains the government's direction.

Broadcasting in China, as in India, offers important potential for social change in a vast land of rural villages. China's three-tier system for radio includes a central national station; 100 regional, provincial, and municipal networks; and grassroots stations that send local announcements and bulletins by wire to loudspeakers in outdoor markets and other public gathering places.[30]

A television set is a prized possession in China, where the Chinese have bought some U.S. programs and accepted some U.S. commercials, but generally produce the programming themselves. The 1989 demonstrations in Tiananmen Square cooled official enthusiasm for relationships with the West, and Chinese media today sometimes use information and entertainment programming from the West to show the dangers of Western influence, proving the power and the reach of a government media monopoly.

# Latin America and the Caribbean

In Latin America, where hectic political change is the norm, media have been as volatile as the region. Media are part of the same power structure that controls politics, business, and industry; family dynasties often characterize Latin American media ownership.

Romulo O'Farrill, Jr., chairman of the board of Televisa in Mexico, owns more than 150 TV stations and eight newspapers. Mario Vásquez Raña owns more than 50 Mexican newspapers. His name became familiar in the United States in 1986 when he bought a controlling interest in United Press International, but he sold his interest a year later.

In Santiago, Chile, the Edwards family has owned *El Mercurio* since 1880; the El Mercurio newspapers now total at least 14. *O Estado de São Paulo* in Brazil, owned by the Mesquita family, has represented editorial independence in the region for more than 50 years, and often is mentioned as one of the country's best newspapers. Argentina's *La Prensa* refuses government subsidies and has survived great conflicts with people like former dictator Juan Peron, who shut down the newspaper from 1951 to 1955.[31]

Home delivery for newspapers and magazines is uncommon in Latin America; the centers of print media merchandising are street-corner kiosks, where vendors offer a variety of publications. *Manchete*, published in Brazil, is one of the most widely circulated national magazines, similar in size and content to *Life* magazine.[32]

Broadcasting operates in a mix of government and private control, with government often owning a few key stations and regulating stations that are privately owned. But the pattern is varied.

Cuba's broadcast media are totally controlled by the government, for example. In Costa Rica and Ecuador, almost all of the broadcast media are privately owned. In Brazil, private owners hold most of the radio stations and television networks, including TV Globo Network, which claims to be the world's fourth largest network (after the United States' three TV networks).[33]

As in many other developing regions, Latin American media often are targets for political and terrorist threats, and a journalist's life can be very hazardous.

*Threats to journalists come not only from governments but from terrorist groups, drug lords, and quasigovernment hit squads as well. Numerous news organizations have been bombed, ransacked, and destroyed by opponents. Dozens of Latin American journalists have been murdered for their beliefs or for writing articles that contain those beliefs.*[34]

Journalists face danger in this region because the media represent potential opposition to the political power of a country's leadership. Perhaps more than in any other part of the world, the Latin American media are woven into the fiber of the region's revolutionary history.

# News and Information Flow

COUNTRIES IN Latin America and in many other developing nations have criticized what they believe is a Western bias to the flow of information throughout the world. These countries charge that this imposes cultural imperialism (see pages 470–471), centered in Western ideology.

The reason for this criticism is that, in fact, most of the major international news services are based in the West. The Associated Press, United Press International, Reuters (Great Britain), Agence France-Presse (France), Deutsche Presse-Agentur (Germany), and Agencia Efe (Spain) supply news to the print and broadcast media. Visnews, based in Great Britain, and the U.S.-based Cable News Network (CNN) and World International Network (WIN) offer international video services. Rupert Murdoch's Sky Television merged with British Satellite Broadcasting in 1990 to become British Sky Broadcasting, delivering programs by satellite.

Despite Western dominance of global news organizations, many regions of the world support information services within their own countries and even within their regions. Middle East News Agency (MENA), based in Egypt, serves all of the countries of the Middle East while News Agency of Nigeria (NAN) limits services to Nigeria, for example.

Within the last 15 years, news services outside the Western orbit have been created — Asian-Pacific News Network in Japan; Caribbean News Agency (CANA); Pan-African News Agency (PANA); Non-Aligned News Agency (NANA), linking the nonaligned nations with the national news agencies, based in Yugoslavia; and Inter Press Service (IPS), based in Rome but created as an "information bridge" between Europe and Latin America.[35] In 1991, Japan Broadcasting Corporation announced plans to launch a world-wide news network, but cancelled its plans before the year's end, citing the projected start-up cost of more than $1 billion.

# New World Information and Communications Order

Even with the creation of these added sources of information, Western news services dominate. Critics of the present system of news and information flow have labeled this issue the New World Information and Communications Order (NWICO), saying that the current system is **ethnocentric**, which means promoting the superiority of one ethnic group (in this case the Western world) over another.

*Developing world media and newly independent governments have been highly critical of this situation, arguing that coverage from the major services contains ethnocentric occidental values that affect its content and presentation. Coverage from these media most often include political, economic, Judeo-Christian religious, and other social values that are not universal. . . . In addition, developing world media and governments have argued that Western ethnocentrism creates an unequal flow of information by providing a large stream of information about events in the developed world but only a very small flow from the developing world.[36]*

According to communications scholar Robert G. Picard, the New World Information and Communications Order proposes that in the future:

*. . . each nation must become self-reliant in communications capabilities so that it is not dependent on other nations and thus cannot be held subservient. The NWICO also adheres to the ideal that in developing domestic communications capabilities, each nation has the right to determine what the communications system within its boundaries will be, what should be communicated, and to what end.* [37]

Beginning in the 1970s, several international communications and journalism organizations have convened to address this issue, including UNESCO (United Nations Educational, Scientific, and Cultural Organization), the International Telecommunications Union (ITU), and the Movement of Non-Aligned Countries (MNAC).

# UNESCO's 1978 Declaration

The United Nations organization UNESCO adopted a declaration in 1978 supporting the principles of self-reliant communications and self-determination for countries as they establish their own communications policies. Critics of the statement, especially journalists, felt that some aspects of the declaration supported government control of the flow of information out of a country, because some news services are official government mouthpieces.

# The MacBride Report

Four years later, UNESCO, which had appointed a 16-member commission headed by Irish statesman Sean MacBride, received their recommendations at the general conference of UNESCO in Belgrade, Yugoslavia. These recommendations became known as the MacBride Report. The report listed 82 ways to help achieve the New World Information and Communications Order, but after the report was issued neither critics of the current status of communications nor those who opposed the report's recommendations were satisfied:

*The West objected to the report's skepticism about a free market in communication, including its opposition to advertising, for example; many NWICO supporters objected to its downplaying of government controls (for example, its advocacy of self-imposed rather than government codes of ethics for journalists).* [38]

The Belgrade conference passed a general resolution supporting NWICO, but in 1983, citing opposition to some of the principles outlined in the MacBride Report, the Reagan administration withdrew its $50 million in financial support for UNESCO, seriously crippling the organization because the United States had been its largest contributor.

UNESCO has since turned to other issues. The NWICO still remains a theoretical idea that scholars of global media continue to debate because of its implications for the international media community.

# The New Global Media Marketplace

ODAY'S MEDIA marketplace is increasingly global. Ted Turner and Rupert Murdoch (see Impact/Profiles, Chapter 1) are just two examples of media moguls who are moving into the global media marketplace. U.S. media companies are looking for markets overseas at the same time that overseas media companies are purchasing pieces of media industries in the United States and other countries. (See Impact/Perspective, Global Satellite Radio Network in the Year 2000?) MTV, as discussed earler in this chapter, is available 24 hours a day in St. Petersburg. Here are some more:

- *WPP Group, the world's largest advertising agency, is based in London. WPP Groups owns U.S. agencies J. Walter Thompson and Ogilvy & Mather. With 22,000 employees and 635 offices, WPP collected nearly $3 billion in worldwide advertising revenue in 1990.* [39]

- *Dow Jones & Co., publishers of* The Wall Street Journal, *also publish* The Wall Street Journal Europe *and* The Asian Wall Street Journal *(see page 471).*

- *The Japanese company Sony, with worldwide distribution of electronic equipment, owns Columbia Pictures and CBS Records. In 1990 Japan's Matsushita, which manufactures broadcast equipment, bought the U.S. film company MCA/Universal.*

# Global Satellite Radio Network in the Year 2000?

In this article from *The Wall Street Journal*, **Bob Davis** describes a proposal that would beam radio around the world. The U.S. Information Agency and two entrepreneurs have approached the FCC for approval of the $1 billion project.

t HE U.S. is quietly pursuing a plan to create a global radio network that would be run jointly by the government and private industry.

The network would use a $1 billion satellite system that would begin broadcasts of music, information and advertising around the year 2000. It would require a new generation of radios that can receive satellite broadcasts.

The proposal generally envisions private ownership of satellites and radio stations in the U.S. market and government ownership of satellites in foreign markets, according to people who heard a briefing on the plan.

The proposal is backed principally by the Commerce Department, the U.S. Informa-

tion Agency and the National Aeronautics and Space Administration. But already the plan is running into opposition from U.S. broadcasters, who fear that the proposed system would gobble up scarce broadcast frequencies and increase competition among radio stations. It also may kick up a storm within the Bush administration, where senior officials have fiercely opposed government direction of new commercial technologies.

Even so, the system has two big advantages. It would offer broadcasters and advertisers a way to reach a national and international market. And it would offer listeners crystalline sound quality by using digital technology to transmit signals.

The Commerce Department's Office of Space Commerce . . . invited a group of government and industry officials to a breakfast [on June 29, 1990] for their second, closed-door discussion of satellite radio. Two satellite entrepreneurs — Martin Rothblatt, president of a consulting group . . . called Marcor Inc., and Gary Noreen, president of Radio Satellite Corp., Pasadena, Calif. — are scheduled to address the group.

"Let's get started first in the U.S.," says Mr. Noreen, who proposes a system that would broadcast 10 stations nationally in 1993. "Then we can turn our system into a world-wide system." . . . At the first Commerce Department meeting, on April 17, [1990], H. Don Messer, USIA's satellite broadcast program manager, sketched his agency's plans for the system. According to a memo passed around at the meeting, the system would include as many as 100 radio stations that could broadcast anywhere in the world with a sound quality comparable to compact disks. Mr. Messer's memo called the plan "a fundamentally different, new radio broadcasting service from satellites."

For global reach, the USIA envisions four satellites in orbit, at a total cost of $700 million. A one-satellite system, costing $200 million, could cover the Americas, Europe and Africa, the memo said. The USIA is pushing the plan to increase its reach geographically, to cut its costs by sharing the satellite system with commercial broadcasters and to improve its quality, said participants in the Commerce Department meetings. The Voice of America, for instance, broadcasts on scratchy, short-wave frequencies and wants to augment its service with a better-resolution system. . . .

The proposal faces formidable political and technical obstacles. Most importantly, current radios can't receive satellite signals, so the agencies must persuade manufacturers to develop a new generation of receivers. It also will require the Federal Communications Commission to allocate a huge number of unused or currently used broadcast frequencies, which U.S. broadcasters will surely oppose. The National Association of Broadcasters, for instance, [has] tried to head off the satellite system by proposing a digital transmission system using conventional, land-based radio towers.

The two satellite entrepreneurs so far have made proposals to the FCC that closely mirror aspects of the federal proposal, but that would provide service by 1994. The systems would be privately owned. . . .

The two entrepreneurs already are taking potshots at each other. Mr. Noreen calls the Satellite CD proposal "silly" and grandiose. Mr. Rothblatt counters that Mr. Noreen's idea is too limited. "It's geared to truckers — people who like radio and a pager rolled into one," he says.

For its part, the FCC has asked for comment on the Satellite CD proposal. "It's getting a lot of discussion in and out of the agency," says Ray Laforge, an FCC engineer.

The Wall Street Journal, *June 26, 1990, p. B-1.*

## The Worldwide Market for U.S.-Made Movies

**Top markets for U.S. theatrical films, 1989**

(Rentals* to distributors, in millions of dollars)

| | |
|---|---|
| **U.S.** | **$1,780** |
| **Japan** | **202** |
| **Canada** | **153** |
| **France** | **128** |
| **W. Germany** | **118** |
| **U.K./Ireland** | **115** |
| **Spain** | **95** |
| **Italy** | **85** |
| **Australia** | **74** |
| **Sweden** | **39** |
| **Rest of world** | **340** |

Foreign rentals 43%

U.S. rentals 57%

**U.S. movies earn nearly half their theatrical rentals outside of the United States.**

* Rentals are the share of box-office revenues paid to distributors.

SOURCE: Data from Standard & Poor's *Industry Surveys*, March 14, 1991.

• *In 1990, Great Britain's Maxwell Communication bought two Hungarian newspapers and Bulgarian television channel BTV2. The same year, Germany's Axel Springer bought 20 Hungarian newspapers, and Italy's Silvio Berlusconi signed agreements in Czechoslovakia, Poland, and Hungary to provide programming for local TV stations in return for advertising time for Western advertisers.* [40]

All of these companies are positioning themselves to manage the emerging global media marketplace. This media marketplace includes news and information services, programming, films, and recordings as well as products and the advertising to sell those products. Foreign movie rentals, for example, account for an increasing share of U.S. moviemakers' box office income (Figure 15.1).

Fueling the move to global marketing is the decision by the European countries to eliminate all trade barriers among countries by the end of 1992 (see page 470). Advertisers spent more than $1 billion in 1990 to advertise

**15.2 ➤**

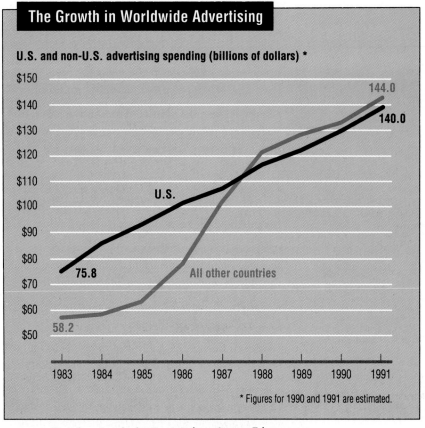

**The Growth in Worldwide Advertising**

U.S. and non-U.S. advertising spending (billions of dollars) *

[Figure: Line graph showing U.S. and "All other countries" advertising spending from 1983 to 1991. U.S. line rises from 75.8 in 1983 to 140.0 in 1991. "All other countries" line rises from 58.2 in 1983 to 144.0 in 1991.]

\* Figures for 1990 and 1991 are estimated.

SOURCE: Data from Standard & Poor's *Industry Surveys*, Feb. 7, 1991.

products across European national boundaries (called pan-European advertising).[41] A further sign of the times is the shrinking proportion of worldwide advertising expenditures accounted for by the United States, which has long been the world's advertising colossus. In recent years, non-U.S. advertising spending has finally overtaken the amount spent in the United States (Figure 15.2).

As more and more national media boundaries open up throughout the world, global advertising campaigns become essential. Today, news, information, and entertainment can move instantly from their home countries to become part of the global media dialogue. In the 1990s, the media industries and advertising are entering a media marketplace without boundaries, a global marketplace that is truly "transnational."

• The four theories of the press, plus the developmental theory, still leave many press systems beyond categorization.

• The print media form the basis for press development in North America, Australia, Western Europe, and Eastern Europe.

• Radio is often the dominant medium in developing countries; television is in widespread use in prosperous nations and in urban areas of developing countries, yet most countries still have only one TV service, usually run by the government.

• Western European and Canadian media today prosper under guarantees of freedom of expression similar to the First Amendment, although each nation has modified the idea to reflect differing values.

• Scandinavian journalists enjoy the widest press freedoms of all of Western Europe, including almost unlimited access to public documents; Canada is the most recent country to issue an official decree supporting press freedom.

• Western European newspapers tend to be much more partisan than either U.S. or Canadian newspapers.

• Western Europeans watch less than half as much TV as people in the United States; most TV stations in Europe don't go on the air until late afternoon.

• Most of Western European programming comes from the United States. U.S. programs are attractive to European broadcasters because buying U.S. programs is cheaper than producing their own.

• Some members of the European Community have proposed quotas on the importation of U.S. programs.

• Eastern Europe in transition is defining a new balance between the desire for free expression and the remnants of government control.

• In many Eastern European countries, the media played a central role in upsetting the established power structure.

• Television in these Eastern bloc countries developed under Communist direction because the Communist governments were in power before TV use was widespread; radio broadcasting also was tightly controlled.

• The Eastern European nations developed their press policies following the Soviet model.

• In the Middle East and North Africa, more newspapers and magazines are published in regions with high literacy rates than in regions with low literacy rates; the one exception is Cairo, Egypt, which is the Arab world's publishing center.

• The Middle Eastern press is tightly controlled by government restrictions, through ownership and licensing.

• Radio Monte Carlo and the BBC offer alternative radio programming across Middle Eastern borders. VCRs also are very popular.

• In the Middle East, as in other developing regions, the media are perceived as instruments of each country's social and political programs.

• African culture is very diverse, making it impossible to create a mass circulation newspaper that can appeal to a wide readership.

• Suspension of five publications in South Africa during the state of emergency during 1985–1990 demonstrates the power of government to limit reporting on dissent.

• Radio is a much more important medium in Africa than print because it is an inexpensive way for people to follow the news.

• The three major Japanese national dailies account for almost half of the nation's newspaper circulation.

• Japan today has a mixed system of privately owned and publicly held broadcast media.

• Entrepreneurs, including Rupert Murdoch, control large segments of Australia's media; Broadcasting in Australia is dominated by Australian Broadcasting Corporation (ABC).

• Since India's independence in 1947, the number of publications has increased 1,000 times; broadcasting in India follows its British colonial beginnings.

• Chinese media operate under a government monopoly, supported by a belief in the media's social responsibility.

• Media in Latin America are part of the power structure, and media often are owned by family dynasties.

• Journalists in Latin America face danger because the media represent a challenge to political power.

• The New World Information and Communications Order (NWICO), supported by UNESCO, advocated parity for the media in all countries.

• U.S. media companies are looking for markets overseas at the same time that overseas media companies are purchasing pieces of media industries in the United States and other countries.

# V

# Appendices

*This appendix is designed to familiarize you with some of the publications that will help you find background and current information about the media. Also included is a list of associations that can provide information about specific media businesses.*

*The study of media covers many areas of scholarship besides journalism and mass communication. Historians, psychologists, economists, political scientists, and sociologists, for example, often contribute ideas to media studies. This appendix therefore includes a variety of*

**Media Resources**

information sources from academic and industry publications as well as from popular periodicals.

# General Information

*The Wall Street Journal* is the best daily source of information about the business of the media. Although you won't find articles specifically about the media every day, you will find regular reports on earnings, acquisitions, and leaders in the media industries. *The Wall Street Journal Index* will help you find the articles you need.

The *Los Angeles Times'* daily section *Calendar* follows the media business very closely, especially television and movies, because the majority of these companies are based in Los Angeles. The *Los Angeles Times Index* lists stories in the *Times*.

*The New York Times* and the *Washington Post* also carry media information and both are indexed.

*Advertising Age* publishes special issues throughout the year focusing on newspapers, magazines, and broadcasting.

*Columbia Journalism Review* and *Washington Journalism Review* regularly critique developments in the print and broadcast industries. *Columbia Journalism Review* is published by New York's Columbia University Graduate School of Journalism. The University of Maryland College of Journalism publishes *Washington Journalism Review*.

*Communication Abstracts, Communication Research, Journal of Communication,* and *Journalism Quarterly* offer scholarly articles and article summaries about media issues. Journals that cover specific media topics include *Journalism History, Journal of Advertising Research, Newspaper Research Journal,* and *Public Relations Review*.

*U.S. Industrial Outlook,* published each year by the U.S. Department of Commerce, projects the expected annual earnings of American businesses, including the mass media industries.

*Advertising Age* publishes regular estimates of actual advertising receipts as each year progresses. McCann-Erickson in New York publishes annual projections of advertising revenue in a publication called *Insider's Report*. Included are ongoing tables on total advertising revenue for each year as well as a breakdown of national and local advertising.

Since 1973, Paine Webber in New York has sponsored an Annual Conference on the Outlook for the Media. Conference speakers include experts on newspapers, broadcasting, cable, advertising, magazine and book publishing, as well as media investment specialists. The results are published in an annual report, *Outlook for the Media*, issued each June.

*Broadcasting Yearbook* is an annual compilation of material about the broadcast industry. Also listed are syndicators, brokers, advertising agencies, and associations.

*Editor & Publisher Yearbook*, published annually, lists all U.S., and many foreign, newspapers. The yearbook also publishes newspaper statistics — the number of daily and weekly newspapers publishing in the U.S., for example.

*The Encyclopedia of American Journalism* by Donald Paneth (New York: Facts on File, 1983) is a very useful alphabetical guide to events and people in the history of journalism.

*Ulrich's International Periodicals Directory* lists magazines alphabetically and by subject.

*Standard Directory of Advertisers* lists advertisers by the types of products they sell — all the advertisers who handle automobile manufacturers, for example. *Standard Directory of Advertising Agencies* shows advertising agencies alphabetically, along with the accounts they manage.

# History and Background

*The Journalist's Bookshelf* by Roland E. Wolseley and Isabel Wolseley (Indianapolis: R. J. Berg, 1986) is a comprehensive listing of resources about American print journalism.

The classic history of American magazines is Frank Luther Mott's *History of American Magazines* (New York: D. Appleton, 1930).

An overview of radio and television history is provided by Christopher H. Sterling and John M. Kittross in *Stay Tuned: A Concise History of American Broadcasting*, 2nd ed. (Belmont, Calif.: Wadsworth, 1990). The classic television history is Eric Barnouw's *Tube of Plenty* (New York: Oxford University Press, 1975).

*A History of Films* by John L. Fell (New York: Holt, Rinehart & Winston, 1979) and *Movie-Made America* by Robert Sklar (New York: Random House, 1975) provide a good introduction to the history of movies.

Sterling and Kittross' *Stay Tuned* (listed earlier) provides some information about the recording industry. *This Business of Music* by Sidney Shemel and M. William Krasilovsky (New York: Billboard Publications, 1985) explains the way the recording industry works.

John P. Dessauer's *Book Publishing: What It Is, What It Does* (New York: R. R. Bowker, 1974) succinctly explains the book publishing business. A historical perspective and overview is available in *Books: The Culture & Commerce of Publishing* by Lewis A. Coser et al. (New York: Basic Books, 1982).

Three histories of American advertising are *The Making of Modern Advertising* by Daniel Pope (New York: Basic Books, 1983), *The Mirror Makers: A History of Twentieth Century American Advertising* by Stephen Fox (New York: Morrow, 1984), and *Advertising the American Dream* by Roland Marchand (Berkeley: University of California Press, 1985).

In 1923, Edward L. Bernays wrote the first book specifically about public relations, *The Engineering of Consent* (Norman: University of Oklahoma Press, reprinted in 1955). For an understanding of today's public relations business, you can read *This is PR: The Realities of Public Relations* by Doug Newsom, Alan Scott, and Judy VanSlyke Turk (Belmont, Calif.: Wadsworth, 1989).

For information about historical events and people in the media who often are omitted from other histories, you can refer to *Up From the Footnote: A History of Women Journalists* by Marion Marzolf (New York: Hastings House, 1977), *Great Women of the Press* by Madelon Golden Schilpp and Sharon M. Murphy (Carbondale: Southern Illinois University Press, 1983), and *The Dissident Press: Alternative Journalism in American History* by Lauren Kessler (Beverly Hills, Calif.: Sage, 1984).

# Indexes

The best place to begin specific mass media research is with an index. Indexes provide quick, comprehensive access to listings of articles about the mass media industries. Pick a subject heading about your topic (if you need help defining the heading to use, see the subject heading list beginning on page 504). Then check the most likely index from the following print index list that catalogs information about your topic. You may have to check two or more indexes to locate all the citations you need.

## Print Indexes

*Access: The Supplementary Index to Periodicals*

*Arts and Humanities Citation Index*

*Business Index*

*Business Periodicals Index*

*Communication Abstracts*

*Film Literature Index*

*Graphic Arts Literature Abstracts*

*Humanities Index*

*Index to Legal Periodicals*

*Journalism Monographs*

*Library Literature*

*Popular Periodicals Index*

*Reader's Guide*

*Trade and Industry Index*

*Ulrich's Periodicals Index*

**Electronic Databases.** In addition to print indexes, several electronic databases offer access to information about the media. Three things to remember about using electronic databases for research, however, are that:

*1. Most libraries charge fees for database searching based on the computer time required. To avoid unnecessary costs, define your subject as specifically as possible. A general request, such as "terrorism," for example, will give you too much unnecessary information. You should work with a database specialist (usually at your library) before making a request.*

*2. Many of the listings are duplicates. A reprinted article may appear in several different publications under different titles.*

*3. Electronic databases are good for current information only. Most electronic databases contain information only within the preceding five to ten years. If you want historical information, return to printed resources.*

DIALOG and BRS Information Technologies provide several electronic databases that are useful for mass media research. Among the electronic databases that are available from these two sources are:

• *AP News — national and international business news from the Associated Press.*

• *Biography Master Index — infomation on where prominent individuals are cited in various biographical sources.*

• *Dissertation Abstracts Online — access to citations on doctoral dissertations accepted at North American universities since 1861.*

• *Facts on File — news summaries of worldwide politics, government, business, and economics.*

• *Legal Resource Index — indexing of hundreds of major law journals and reviews.*

• *Magazine Index — articles, reviews, and features from general interest U.S. magazines.*

• *National Newspaper Index — carries indexes to* The Wall Street Journal, The New York Times, The Christian Science Monitor, *the* Los Angeles Times, *and the* Washington Post.

• *Newsearch — a daily index to 2,000 news stories and features from the National Newspaper Index and from popular magazines, trade and industry journals, legal periodicals, and press releases from PR Newswire.*

• *PR Newswire — complete text of news releases prepared by a variety of companies, public relations agencies, and city, state, federal and foreign governments.*

• *Sociological Abstracts — provides current research in political science, media, and sociology, including book chapters, journal articles, association papers, and conference reports.*

• *Ulrich's International Periodicals Directory and Irregular Serials and Annuals — a database version of the printed* Ulrich's International Periodicals Directory, *with information from 100,000 U.S. and foreign periodical publishers.*

• *UPI News — worldwide news and current events stories from the United Press International wire.*

Some libraries have access to other on-line services which include databases, such as VuText and Data-Times, with access to stories in many regional newspapers, such as the *Miami Herald* and the *Philadelphia Inquirer*, within 24 hours after the stories appear. These services also track AP and UPI news service stories and articles from the nation's majo᠂ newspapers.

**Other Indexes.** Three other indexes which are not on-line database indexes but are helpful are:

• *InfoTrac — disc retrieval system*

• *Magazine Index — available on microfilm*

• *Newspaper Index — available on miocrofilm*

These are not as current as electronic databases; they are usually about four months behind current issues. However, they are helpful shortcuts if you don't need timely data.

# Periodicals

Many magazines publish information about the mass media industries and support industries. The following is an alphabetical listing of the major magazines in each subject area. If a periodical is indexed, the name of the index appears in parentheses.

## ADVERTISING

*Advertising Age* (Business Periodicals Index)

*Adweek/Adweek: National Marketing Edition* (Business Periodicals Index)

*Inside Print*, formerly *Magazine Age*, publishes marketing ideas for advertisers and agencies

*Journal of Advertising* (Business Periodicals Index)

*Journal of Advertising Research* (Business Periodicals Index)

## BROADCASTING

*Broadcasting* (Business Periodicals Index)

*Cable Today*

*Cablevision*

*Electronic Media* (Ulrich's Periodicals Index)

*Emmy*, published by the Academy of Television Arts and Sciences (Access: The Supplementary Index to Periodicals)

*Federal Communications Law Journal* (Index to Legal Periodicals)

*Journal of Broadcasting and Electronic Media*, published by Broadcast Education Association (Communication Abstracts)

*RTNDA Communicator*, published by the Radio-Television News Directors Association

*TV Guide* (Access: The Supplementary Index to Periodicals)

*Television/Radio Age* (Business Periodicals Index)

*Video Week* (Ulrich's Periodicals Index)

## MAGAZINE AND BOOK PUBLISHING

*AB Bookman's Weekly*, collector books (Library Literature)

*Book Research Quarterly*, published by Rutgers University

*Bookwoman*, published by the Women's National Book Association

*COSMEP Newsletter*, published by the Committee of Small Magazine Editors and Publishers

*Folio*, the magazine for magazine management (Trade and Industry Index)

*Publishers Weekly*, the journal of the book industry (Business Periodicals Index)

## MOVIES

*American Film* (Arts and Humanities Citation Index)

*Film Comment*, published by the Film Society of Lincoln Center (Arts and Humanities Citation Index)

*Hollywood Reporter*

*Variety* (Business Index)

*Video Times*, covers video for home viewing

## NEWSPAPERS

*Editor & Publisher: The Fourth Estate* (Business Periodicals Index)

*Journalism Monographs*, published by the Association for Education in Journalism and Mass Communication (Communication Abstracts)

*Newspaper Financial Executive Journal*, published by International Newspaper Financial Executives (Encyclopedia of Business Information Sources)

*Newspaper Research Journal*, published by the Association for Education in Journalism and Mass Communication (Communication Abstracts)

*Presstime*, published by the American Newspaper Publishers Association (Graphic Arts Literature Abstracts)

*Quill*, published by the Society of Professional Journalists, Sigma Delta Chi (Humanities Index)

## PUBLIC RELATIONS

*Public Relations Journal* (Business Periodicals Index)

*Public Relations Quarterly* (Business Periodicals Index)

*Public Relations Review* (Communication Abstracts)

## RECORDINGS

*Billboard* (Business Periodicals Index)

*Cash Box* (Encyclopedia of Business Information Sources)

*Down Beat* (Reader's Guide)

*Music Index*, a separate index that covers articles on the music industry

*Music Journal* (Encyclopedia of Business Information Sources)

*Rolling Stone* (Popular Periodicals Index)

*Up Beat* (Encyclopedia of Business Information Sources)

## GLOBAL MEDIA

### Advertising

*International Journal of Advertising*, England (Ulrich's Periodicals Index)

*Affiliated Advertising Agencies International*, Colorado (Ulrich's Periodicals Index)

### Broadcasting

*A M P S Black Radio and Television Diary*, South Africa (Ulrich's Periodicals Index)

*World Radio T.V. (Complete Guide to International Broadcasting)*, New York (Ulrich's Periodicals Index)

### Movies

*Young Cinema and Theatre/Jeune Cinema et Theatre*, cultural magazine of the International Union of Students, Czechoslovakia

### Newspapers

*International Media Guide*, Newspapers Worldwide, Connecticut

### Periodicals

*International Media Guide*, Consumer Magazines Worldwide, Connecticut

### Public Relations

*International Public Relations Review*, England (Ulrich's Periodicals Index)

### Recordings

*Musical America International Directory of the Performing Arts*, ABC Leisure Magazines, Inc., New York

### Other

*Media International*, England (Ulrich's Periodicals Index)

*O P M A Overseas Media Guide* (Overseas Press and Media Association), England (Ulrich's Periodicals Index)

### MEDIA-RELATED TOPICS

*Censorship News*, published by the National Coalition Against Censorship

*Communication Research* (Communication Abstracts)

*Communications and the Law* (Index to Legal Periodicals)

*Entertainment Law Reporter*, covers motion pictures, radio, TV, and music (Index to Legal Periodicals)

*News Media and the Law*, published by Reporters Committee for Freedom of the Press (Index to Legal Periodicals)

*Nieman Reports*, published by the Nieman Foundation for Journalism at Harvard

# Finding Subject Headings for Mass Media Information

Because mass media information is often scattered throughout different types of references in the library, what follows is an alphabetical list of subject headings as they appear in the Library of Congress Subject Headings.

*Academy Awards (motion pictures)*

*Advertising, Magazine*

*Advertising, Newspaper*

*Advertising agencies*

*Advertising and public relations (often public relations is not listed separately)*

*Advertising, political*

*Audio-equipment industry*

# Finding Media Organizations

These organizations compile statistics and useful information about specific industries for their members and for the public. (To find out an association's current address and telephone number, check the *Encyclopedia of Associations*, available in printed form and as an on-line database.) The public information office and/or the office of research usually handles these requests.

*American Advertising Federation*

*American Association of Advertising Agencies*

*American Black Bookwriters Association*

*American Booksellers Association*

*American Library Association*

*American Newspaper Publishers Association (each state also has its own state association)*

*American Society of Newspaper Editors*

*Asian American Journalists Association*

*Associated Press Managing Editors Association*

*Association of American Publishers*

*Association for Education in Journalism and Mass Communication*

*Association of Independent Television Stations, Inc.*

*Association of National Advertisers*

*Audit Bureau of Circulations*

*Black American Cinema Society*

*Black Women in Publishing*

*Broadcast Education Association*

*Cabletelevision Advertising Bureau*

*International Association of Business Communicators*

*Investigative Reporters and Editors*

*Magazine Publishers Association*

*Motion Picture Association of America*

*National Association of Black Journalists*

*National Association of Broadcasters (each state also has its own state association)*

*National Association of Hispanic Journalists*

*National Black Public Relations Society*

*National Cable Television Association*

*Public Relations Society of America*

*Radio Advertising Bureau*

*Radio-Television News Directors Association*

*Recording Industry Association*

*Task Force on Minorities in the Newspaper Business*

*Television Bureau of Advertising*

*Women in Communications*

*Women in Film*

*World Institute of Black Communications/CEBA Awards*

*This appendix of 29 tables gives you, by subject, the*

*latest media statistics available. Tables B.1 through*

*B.24 track the media industries. Tables B.25, B.26, and B.27 cover advertising.*

*Tables B.28 and B.29 follow audience behavior.*

Media
Statistics

# Newspapers

## B.1 Number of Newspapers in United States, 1900–1990

| YEAR | DAILY NEWSPAPERS | WEEKLY NEWSPAPERS |
|------|------------------|-------------------|
| 1900 | 2,154 | 15,813 |
| 1918 | 2,166 | 14,724 |
| 1928 | 1,939 | 11,387 |
| 1938 | 1,936 | 10,728 |
| 1948 | 1,781 | 9,625 |
| 1958 | 1,751 | 9,006 |
| 1968 | 1,752 | 8,855 |
| 1978 | 1,783 | 7,980 |
| 1990 | 1,611 | 7,476* |

*1991 figures.
SOURCES: Data from Christopher H. Sterling and Timothy R. Haight, *The Mass Media: Aspen Institute Guide to Communication Industry Trends*, New York/London: Praeger, 1977, pp. 19–20; *Ayer Directory of Publications*, Philadelphia: Ayer Press, 1979, p. vii; American Newspaper Publishers Association, *'91 Facts about Newspapers*, Washington, D.C., April 1991, pp. 2, 18.

## B.2 U.S. Cities with Daily Newspapers, 1923–1991

| YEAR | TOTAL CITIES WITH NEWSPAPERS | CITIES HAVING ONLY ONE PAPER | CITIES HAVING TWO OR MORE PAPERS UNDER SEPARATE OWNERSHIP | |
|------|------------------------------|------------------------------|--------|-----------|
| | | | CITIES | % OF TOTAL |
| 1923 | 1,297 | 795 | 502 | 38.7% |
| 1933 | 1,426 | 1,183 | 243 | 17.0 |
| 1943 | 1,416 | 1,279 | 137 | 9.7 |
| 1948 | 1,392 | 1,283 | 109 | 7.8 |
| 1953 | 1,455 | 1,364 | 91 | 6.3 |
| 1958 | 1,447 | 1,377 | 70 | 4.8 |
| 1963 | 1,476 | 1,425 | 51 | 3.5 |
| 1968 | 1,493 | 1,450 | 43 | 2.9 |
| 1973 | 1,519 | 1,482 | 37 | 2.4 |
| 1986 | 1,525 | 1,478 | 47 | 3.1 |
| 1988 | 1,516 | 1,473 | 43 | 2.8 |
| 1991 | 1,511 | 1,435 | 37 | 2.4 |

SOURCES: Data from Christopher H. Sterling and Timothy R. Haight, *The Mass Media: Aspen Institute Guide to Communication Industry Trends*, New York/London: Praeger, 1977; American Newspaper Publishers Association, Washington, D.C., Joseph Lorfano, personal communication, December 13, 1991.

**B.3  Number, Percentage, and Circulation Share of Chain-Owned Daily Newspapers in United States, 1900–1990**

| YEAR | NUMBER OF CHAINS | NUMBER OF CHAIN-OWNED DAILIES | TOTAL NUMBER OF DAILIES | PERCENTAGE OF CHAIN-OWNED DAILIES | PERCENTAGE OF TOTAL DAILY CIRCULATION OF CHAIN-OWNED DAILIES | MEAN NUMBER OF DAILIES PER CHAIN |
|------|------|------|------|------|------|------|
| 1900 | 8   | 27    | —     | —    | 10.0% | 3.4 |
| 1910 | 13  | 62    | —     | —    | —     | 4.7 |
| 1923 | 31  | 153   | 2,036 | 7.8% | —     | 4.9 |
| 1930 | 55  | 311   | 1,942 | 16.0 | 43.4  | 5.6 |
| 1940 | 60  | 319   | 1,878 | 17.0 | —     | 5.3 |
| 1953 | 95  | 485   | 1,785 | 27.0 | 45.3  | 5.1 |
| 1960 | 109 | 552   | 1,763 | 31.3 | 46.1  | 5.1 |
| 1971 | 157 | 879   | 1,749 | 50.3 | 63.0  | 5.6 |
| 1986 | 146 | 1,217 | 1,657 | 73.0 | 80.0  | 8.3 |
| 1990 | 135 | 1,228 | 1,611 | 75.0 | 81.0  | 9.1 |

SOURCES: Data from Christopher H. Sterling and Timothy R. Haight, *The Mass Media: Aspen Institute Guide to Communication Industry Trends*, New York/London: Praeger, 1977, p. P-3; American Newspaper Publishers Association, *'91 Facts about Newspapers*, Washington, D.C., April 1991, p. 23, Newspaper Newsletter, Morton Research, January 31, 1991.

## B.4 Index of Daily Newspaper Readership in United States, by Age Group

| AGE GROUP | INDEX OF NEWSPAPER READERSHIP* |
|-----------|-------------------------------|
| 18–24 | 89.1 |
| 25–34 | 90.6 |
| 35–44 | 103.9 |
| 45–54 | 107.8 |
| 55–64 | 109.4 |
| 65 + | 103.1 |

*(100.0 = Adult Average)

SOURCE: Data from *The Veronis, Suhler & Associates Communications Industry Forecast*, June 1991, p. 146.

# Magazines

## B.5 Number of Periodicals in United States, 1936–1990

| YEAR | TOTAL NUMBER OF PERIODICALS |
|------|----------------------------|
| 1936 | 6,021 |
| 1946 | 5,985 |
| 1956 | 7,907 |
| 1966 | 9,102 |
| 1976 | 9,872 |
| 1986 | 11,328 |
| 1990 | 12,178 |

SOURCES: Data from Christopher H. Sterling and Timothy R. Haight, *The Mass Media: Aspen Institute Guide to Communication Industry Trends*, New York/London: Praeger, 1977, p. 27; Donald P. Boyden and John Krol, eds., *Gale Directory of Publications and Broadcast Media, 1990*, Vol. 3, Detroit, Gale Research Inc., 1989.

## B.6 Consumer Magazine Circulation in United States, 1961–1990

| YEAR | CIRCULATION (MILLIONS) |
|------|------------------------|
| 1961 | 192 |
| 1966 | 220 |
| 1971 | 243 |
| 1976 | 253 |
| 1981 | 289 |
| 1986 | 328 |
| 1990 | 367 |

SOURCE: Data from Magazine Publishers Association, *MPA Circulation of All A.B.C. Magazines, General and Farm*, May 1991.

## B.7 Magazine Circulation by Circulation Size in United States

| CIRCULATION SIZE | NUMBER OF MAGAZINES | PERCENT | TOTAL CIRCULATION (MILLIONS) | PERCENT |
|---|---|---|---|---|
| 10,000,000 + | 5 | 0.9 | 86 | 23.7% |
| 5,000,000–9,999,999 | 5 | 0.9 | 28 | 7.7 |
| 2,000,000–4,999,999 | 20 | 3.6 | 62 | 17.1 |
| 1,000,000–1,999,999 | 48 | 8.7 | 67 | 18.5 |
| 500,000–999,999 | 81 | 14.6 | 58 | 15.9 |
| 150,000–499,999 | 165 | 29.8 | 47 | 12.9 |
| Under 150,000 | 230 | 41.5 | 16 | 4.4 |

SOURCE: Data from Magazine Publishers Association, *MPA Circulation of All A.B.C. Magazines, General and Farm*, April 1990.

## B.8 Index of Magazine Exposure

| AGE GROUP | INDEX* |
|---|---|
| 18–24 | 121 |
| 25–34 | 115 |
| 35–44 | 122 |
| 45–54 | 108 |
| 55–64 | 80 |
| 65+ | 41 |

*100 = U.S. Average

SOURCE: Data from *Veronis, Suhler & Associates Communications Industry Forecast*, June 1991, p. 191.

# Radio

## B.9 Number of Radio Stations in United States, 1921–1991

| YEAR | AM TOTAL | FM | | FM TOTAL | TOTAL RADIO STATIONS |
| --- | --- | --- | --- | --- | --- |
| | | COMMERCIAL | EDUCATIONAL | | |
| 1921 | 5 | — | — | — | 5 |
| 1926 | 528 | — | — | — | 528 |
| 1936 | 616 | — | — | — | 616 |
| 1946 | 948 | 48 | 9 | 57 | 1,005 |
| 1956 | 2,824 | 540 | 123 | 663 | 3,487 |
| 1966 | 4,065 | 1,446 | 268 | 1,714 | 5,779 |
| 1976 | 4,463 | 2,767 | 804 | 3,571 | 8,034 |
| 1986 | 4,856 | 3,936 | 1,254 | 5,190 | 10,046 |
| 1991 | 4,986 | 4,402 | 1,442 | 5,844 | 10,830 |

SOURCES: Data from Christopher H. Sterling and Timothy R. Haight, *The Mass Media: Aspen Institute Guide to Communication Industry Trends*, New York/London: Praeger, 1977, pp. 43–44; *Broadcasting/Cablecasting Yearbook 1987*, p. A-2; *Broadcasting*, April 22, 1991, p. 69.

# Television

## B.10 Number of VHF and UHF Commercial and Educational Public Television Stations in United States, 1941–1990

| | VHF | | | UHF | | | TOTAL | | |
|---|---|---|---|---|---|---|---|---|---|
| | COMMERCIAL | EDUCATIONAL | TOTAL | COMMERCIAL | EDUCATIONAL | TOTAL | COMMERCIAL | EDUCATIONAL | TOTAL NUMBER OF STATIONS |
| 1941 | 2 | — | 2 | — | — | — | 2 | — | 2 |
| 1946 | 6 | — | 6 | — | — | — | 6 | — | 6 |
| 1956 | 344 | 13 | 357 | 97 | 5 | 102 | 441 | 18 | 459 |
| 1966 | 486 | 65 | 551 | 99 | 49 | 148 | 585 | 114 | 699 |
| 1976 | 513 | 97 | 610 | 197 | 155 | 352 | 710 | 252 | 962 |
| 1986 | 547 | 111 | 658 | 435 | 192 | 627 | 982 | 303 | 1,285 |
| 1990 | 552 | 125 | 677 | 563 | 229 | 792 | 1,115 | 354 | 1,469 |

SOURCES: Data from Christopher H. Sterling and Timothy R. Haight, *The Mass Media: Aspen Institute Guide to Communication Industry Trends*, New York/London: Praeger, 1977, p. 49; *Broadcasting/Cablecasting Yearbook 1987*, p. A-2; *Broadcasting*, Dec. 31, 1990, p. 77.

## B.11 Network Affiliate Television Stations in United States, 1947–1990

| | NBC AFFILIATES | | CBS AFFILIATES | | ABC AFFILIATES | | FOX AFFILIATES | | TOTAL STATIONS | TOTAL NETWORK STATIONS | |
|---|---|---|---|---|---|---|---|---|---|---|---|
| | NUMBER | PERCENT | NUMBER | PERCENT | NUMBER | PERCENT | NUMBER | PERCENT | | NUMBER | PERCENT |
| 1947 | 2 | 16.7% | 1 | 8.3% | 1 | 8.3% | — | — | 12 | 4 | 33% |
| 1957 | 205 | 43.5 | 180 | 38.2 | 60 | 12.7 | — | — | 471 | 445 | 94 |
| 1967 | 205 | 33.6 | 191 | 31.3 | 141 | 23.1 | — | — | 610 | 537 | 88 |
| 1977 | 212 | 29.1 | 210 | 28.8 | 190 | 26.1 | — | — | 728 | 612 | 84 |
| 1987* | 207 | 15.7 | 203 | 15.4 | 234 | 17.8 | 98 | 7.4 | 1,317 | 742 | 56 |
| 1990 | 205 | 14.0 | 359 | 24.4 | 223 | 15.2 | 134 | 9.1 | 1,469 | 921 | 63 |

*The 1987 total includes more than 300 recently licensed low-power TV stations, which accounts for part of the large drop in the percentage of affiliates.

SOURCES: Christopher H. Sterling and Timothy R. Haight, *The Mass Media: Aspen Institute Guide to Communication Industry Trends*, New York/London: Praeger, 1977, p. 53; *Broadcasting/Cablecasting Yearbook 1987*, Los Angeles: Times Mirror, 1987, pp. f-41, 48, 49, 55, 56; *FCC News*, no. 4478, Washington D.C.: Federal Communications Commission, July 31, 1987; *Broadcasting Yearbook 1991*, pp. F-32–39.

## B.12 Number of Radio and Television Stations Sold in United States, with Average Price per Transaction, 1938–1990

| YEAR | NUMBER OF TRANSACTIONS | | | | AVERAGE PRICE PER EACH FCC-APPROVED TRANSACTION | |
| | RADIO ONLY | TV ONLY | RADIO/ TV | TOTAL | RADIO ONLY | TV ONLY |
| --- | --- | --- | --- | --- | --- | --- |
| 1938 | 20 | — | — | 20 | $ 46,039 | — |
| 1946 | 52 | — | — | 52 | 441,589 | — |
| 1956 | 316 | 21 | 24 | 361 | 103,049 | $ 849,066 |
| 1966 | 367 | 31 | 11 | 409 | 208,811 | 986,259 |
| 1976 | 413 | 32 | 1 | 446 | 437,442 | 3,389,364 |
| 1986 | 959 | 128 | 192 | 1,279 | 1,553,838 | 21,168,098 |
| 1990 | 1,045 | 75 | 60 | 1,180 | 831,230 | 9,292,698 |

SOURCES: Data from Christopher H. Sterling and Timothy R. Haight, *The Mass Media: Aspen Institute Guide to Communication Industry Trends*, New York/London: Praeger, 1977, p. 92; "37 Years of Station Transactions," *Broadcasting Yearbook 1991*, p. ix.

## B.13 Top Ten TV Markets in United States, 1990

| MARKET | NUMBER OF TELEVISION HOMES | PERCENT OF TOTAL | NUMBER OF TV STATIONS |
| --- | --- | --- | --- |
| 1. New York | 7,043,900 | 7.68 | 21 |
| 2. Los Angeles | 4,939,400 | 5.38 | 25 |
| 3. Chicago | 3,124,800 | 3.41 | 17 |
| 4. Philadelphia | 2,704,400 | 2.95 | 21 |
| 5. San Francisco | 2,200,700 | 2.40 | 22 |
| 6. Boston | 2,105,800 | 2.29 | 20 |
| 7. Detroit | 1,923,580 | 2.10 | 10 |
| 8. Dallas-Ft. Worth | 1,728,900 | 1.88 | 18 |
| 9. Washington, D.C. | 1,701,700 | 1.85 | 14 |
| 10. Houston | 1,453,200 | 1.58 | 15 |

SOURCE: Data from Standard & Poor's *Industry Surveys*, Feb. 7, 1991, p. M-26.

# Cable

## B.14 Top Ten Cable System Operators, 1990

| SYSTEM OPERATOR | BASIC SUBSCRIBERS (THOUSANDS) |
|---|---|
| 1. TCI | 9,475 |
| 2. ATC | 4,700 |
| 3. UA Entertainment | 2,743 |
| 4. Continental | 2,674 |
| 5. Warner | 1,868 |
| 6. Comcast | 1,619 |
| 7. Cox | 1,616 |
| 8. Jones Intercable | 1,596 |
| 9. Cablevision Sys. | 1,583 |
| 10. Storer | 1,574 |

SOURCE: Data from Standard & Poor's *Industry Surveys*, June 6, 1991.

## B.15 Leading Cable Channels and Numbers of Subscribers

| BASIC SERVICE | | PAY SERVICE | |
|---|---|---|---|
| ESPN | 57.2 million | HBO | 17.3 million |
| CNN | 56.7 million | Showtime | 7.4 million |
| WTBS | 55.5 million | Cinemax | 6.4 million |
| USA | 54.1 million | Disney Channel | 5.7 million |
| Discovery Channel | 53.2 million | Bravo | 5.0 million |
| Nickelodeon | 53.2 million | The Movie Channel | 2.8 million |

SOURCE: Data from Standard & Poor's *Industry Surveys*, March 14, 1991.

## B.16  Cable Advertising Spending (Millions)

| YEAR | NATIONAL | LOCAL | TOTAL |
|------|----------|-------|-------|
| 1985 | $  594 | $130 | $  724 |
| 1986 | 676 | 179 | 855 |
| 1987 | 760 | 203 | 963 |
| 1988 | 942 | 254 | 1,196 |
| 1989 | 1,197 | 330 | 1,527 |
| 1990 | 1,375 | 415 | 1,790 |

SOURCE: Data from *The Veronis, Suhler & Associates Communications Industry Forecast*, June 1991, p. 94.

# Movies

## B.17  Number of Feature Films Released by the Major Distribution Companies in United States, 1930–1955

| YEAR | COLUMBIA | MGM | RKO | 20TH CENTURY | WARNER BROS. | UNITED ARTISTS | PARAMOUNT | UNIVERSAL | TOTAL |
|------|----------|-----|-----|--------------|--------------|----------------|-----------|-----------|-------|
| 1930–31 | 27 | 43 | 32 | 48 | 69 | 13 | 58 | 22 | 312 |
| 1935–36 | 36 | 43 | 43 | 52 | 58 | 17 | 50 | 27 | 326 |
| 1940 | 51 | 48 | 53 | 49 | 45 | 20 | 48 | 49 | 363 |
| 1945 | 38 | 31 | 33 | 27 | 19 | 17 | 23 | 46 | 234 |
| 1950 | 59 | 38 | 32 | 32 | 28 | 18 | 23 | 33 | 263 |
| 1955 | 38 | 23 | 13 | 29 | 23 | 35 | 20 | 34 | 215 |

SOURCE: Data from Christopher H. Sterling and Timothy R. Haight, *The Mass Media: Aspen Institute Guide to Communication Industry Trends*, New York/London: Praeger, 1977, p. 31.

**B.18  Number of Feature Films Released by the Major Distribution Companies in United States, 1960–1990**

| YEAR | COLUMBIA | MGM | 20TH CENTURY-FOX | WARNER BROS. | UNITED ARTISTS | PARAMOUNT | UNIVERSAL | BUENA VISTA | TRI-STAR | ORION | CANNON | TOTAL |
|---|---|---|---|---|---|---|---|---|---|---|---|---|
| 1960 | 35 | 18 | 49 | 17 | 23 | 22 | 20 | — | — | — | — | 184 |
| 1965 | 29 | 28 | 26 | 15 | 19 | 24 | 26 | — | — | — | — | 167 |
| 1970 | 28 | 21 | 14 | 15 | 40 | 16 | 17 | — | — | — | — | 151 |
| 1975 | 15 | * | 19 | 19 | 21 | 11 | 10 | — | — | — | — | 95 |
| 1986 | 17 | ** | 21 | 21 | 15 | 19 | 16 | 12 | 18 | 14 | 18 | 171 |
| 1990 | 14 | ** | 17 | 23 | 12 | 15 | 17 | 15 | 13 | 14 | — | 140 |

*Unavailable.

**Merged with United Artists.

SOURCES: Data from Christopher H. Sterling and Timothy R. Haight, *The Mass Media: Aspen Institute Guide to Communication Industry Trends*, New York/London: Praeger, 1977, p. 31; *Variety*, Jan. 7, 1987 and Dec. 24, 1990.

## B.19  Domestic and Foreign Films Released, 1917–1990

| YEAR | U.S. PRODUCED | IMPORTED | TOTAL |
|------|---------------|----------|-------|
| 1917 | 687 | — | 687 |
| 1926 | 740 | — | 740 |
| 1936 | 522 | 213 | 735 |
| 1946 | 378 | 89 | 467 |
| 1956 | 272 | 207 | 479 |
| 1966 | 156 | 295 | 451 |
| 1976 | 353 | 222 | 575 |
| 1986 | 409 | 218 | 627 |
| 1990 | 417 | 113 | 530 |

SOURCES: Data from Motion Picture Association of America; "Filming U.S. and Abroad 1976–86," *Variety*, Nov. 12, 1986; *Variety*, Jan. 7, 1987; *Variety*, Dec. 24, 1990. (These statistics do not include reissues.)

## B.20  Number of Motion Picture Theaters in United States, 1926–1990

| YEAR | FOUR-WALL THEATERS | | OUTDOOR THEATERS | TOTAL |
|------|--------|--------|------------------|-------|
|      | SILENT | SOUND | | |
| 1926 | 19,489 | — | — | 19,489 |
| 1936 | — | 15,858 | — | 15,858 |
| 1946 | — | 18,719 | 300 | 19,019 |
| 1956 | — | 14,509 | 4,494 | 19,003 |
| 1966 | — | 10,150 | 4,200 | 14,350 |
| 1976 | — | 12,197 | 3,635 | 15,832 |
| 1986 | — | 19,947 | 2,818 | 22,765 |
| 1990 | — | 22,774 | 915 | 23,689 |

SOURCES: Data from Christopher H. Sterling and Timothy R. Haight, *The Mass Media: Aspen Institute Guide to Communication Industry Trends*, New York/London: Praeger, 1977, p. 35; Motion Picture Association of America; *U.S. Economic Review*.

## B.21 Largest Movie Theater Chains in North America, 1990

| CHAINS | SCREEN TOTAL |
|---|---|
| 1. United Artists | 2,699 |
| 2. Cineplex Odeon | 1,940 |
| 3. American Multi-Cinema | 1,649 |
| 4. General Cinema | 1,444 |
| 5. Loews | 837 |
| 6. Carmike | 813 |
| 7. Cinemark | 645 |
| 8. National Amusements | 625 |
| 9. Hoyts | 610 |
| 10. Act III | 486 |

SOURCE: Data from *Variety*, Jan. 31, 1990, p. 20.


## B.22 U.S. Box Office Statistics, 1985–1990

| YEAR | NUMBER OF ADMISSIONS (MILLIONS) | AVERAGE TICKET PRICE | BOX OFFICE RECEIPTS (MILLIONS) |
|---|---|---|---|
| 1985 | 1,056 | $3.55 | $3,749 |
| 1986 | 1,017 | 3.71 | 3,778 |
| 1987 | 1,088 | 3.91 | 4,253 |
| 1988 | 1,085 | 4.11 | 4,458 |
| 1989 | 1,132 | 4.45 | 5,033 |
| 1990 | 1,058 | 4.75 | 5,022 |

SOURCE: Data from *The Veronis, Suhler & Associates Communications Industry Forecast*, June 1991, p. 108.

# Recordings

## B.23 Recording Industry Sales Profile, 1980–1989

| YEAR | UNITS (MILLIONS) | VALUE OF SHIPMENTS (MILLIONS) | PERCENT OF $ VALUE, BY FORMAT | | | | |
| | | | CASSETTES | CDS | LPS/EPS | SINGLES | 8-TRACK |
|---|---|---|---|---|---|---|---|
| *1989 | 800.7 | $6,464.1 | 51.7 | 40.0 | 3.4 | 4.8 | NIL |
| 1988 | 761.9 | $6,254.8 | 54.1 | 33.4 | 8.5 | 4.0 | NIL |
| 1987 | 706.8 | $5,567.5 | 53.2 | 28.6 | 14.2 | 3.9 | 0.1 |
| 1986 | 618.3 | $4,651.1 | 53.7 | 20.0 | 21.1 | 4.9 | 0.2 |
| 1985 | 653.0 | $4,387.8 | 55.0 | 8.9 | 29.2 | 6.4 | 0.6 |
| 1984 | 679.8 | $4,370.4 | 54.5 | 2.4 | 34.4 | 6.8 | 0.8 |
| 1983 | 578.0 | $3,814.3 | 47.5 | NM | 44.3 | 7.1 | 0.7 |
| 1982 | 577.7 | $3,641.6 | 38.0 | NM | 52.9 | 7.8 | 1.3 |
| 1981 | 635.4 | $3,969.9 | 26.8 | NM | 59.0 | 6.5 | 7.8 |
| 1980 | 683.7 | $3,862.4 | 20.1 | NM | 59.3 | 7.0 | 13.6 |

Sales represent manufacturers' shipments, net of returns; dollar values based on suggested retail prices, which often exceed actual prices.

NM — Not meaningful.

*Latest available.

SOURCE: Data from Standard & Poor's *Industry Surveys*, March 14, 1991, p. L-42.

# Books

## B.24  U.S. Book Title Output, 1900–1990

| YEAR | NEW BOOKS | NEW EDITIONS | TOTAL |
|------|-----------|--------------|-------|
| 1900 | 4,490 | 1,866 | 6,356 |
| 1906 | 6,724 | 415 | 7,139 |
| 1916 | 9,160 | 1,285 | 10,445 |
| 1926 | 6,832 | 1,527 | 8,359 |
| 1936 | 8,584 | 1,852 | 10,436 |
| 1946 | 6,170 | 1,565 | 7,735 |
| 1956 | 10,007 | 2,531 | 12,538 |
| 1966 | 21,819 | 8,231 | 30,050 |
| 1976 | 26,983 | 8,158 | 35,141 |
| 1986 | 33,556 | 5,605 | 39,161 |
| 1990* | 30,907 | 4,610 | 35,517 |

*Preliminary figures.

SOURCES: Data from Christopher H. Sterling and Timothy R. Haight, *The Mass Media: Aspen Institute Guide to Communication Industry Trends*, New York/London: Praeger, 1977, pp. 8–9; *Publishers Weekly*, March 13, 1987, and March 8, 1991.

## B.25  U.S. Advertising Expenditures, 1936–1990

| ADVERTISING MEDIUM | ESTIMATED EXPENDITURES (MILLIONS OF DOLLARS) | | | | | | |
|---|---|---|---|---|---|---|---|
| | 1936 | 1946 | 1956 | 1966 | 1976 | 1986 | 1990* |
| **NEWSPAPERS** | | | | | | | |
| National | 166 | 238 | 754 | 887 | 1,342 | 3,376 | 3,925 |
| Local | 676 | 917 | 2,469 | 3,978 | 8,276 | 23,614 | 28,935 |
| Total | 842 | 1,155 | 3,223 | 4,865 | 9,618 | 26,990 | 32,860 |
| **MAGAZINES** | | | | | | | |
| Weeklies | 67 | 202 | 440 | 658 | 748 | 2,327 | 2,845 |
| Women's | 57 | 127 | 166 | 280 | 457 | 1,376 | 1,730 |
| Monthlies | 30 | 76 | 152 | 316 | 584 | 1,614 | 2,310 |
| Total | 154 | 405 | 758 | 1,254 | 1,789 | 5,317 | 6,885 |
| **FARM PUBLICATIONS** | 12 | 36 | 73 | 70 | 86 | 192 | 215 |
| **TELEVISION** | | | | | | | |
| Network | — | — | 643 | 1,393 | 2,857 | 8,570 | 9,565 |
| Spot | — | — | 329 | 988 | 2,154 | 6,570 | 7,905 |
| Cable (national) | — | — | — | — | — | 752 | 1,375 |
| Local | — | — | 253 | 442 | 1,710 | 6,514 | 7,875 |
| Cable (local) | — | — | — | — | — | 179 | 415 |
| Total | — | — | 1,225 | 2,823 | 6,721 | 22,585 | 27,135 |
| **RADIO** | | | | | | | |
| Network | 75 | 200 | 60 | 63 | 105 | 423 | 495 |
| Spot | 23 | 98 | 161 | 308 | 518 | 1,348 | 1,655 |
| Local | 24 | 157 | 346 | 639 | 1,707 | 5,178 | 6,615 |
| Total | 122 | 455 | 567 | 1,010 | 2,330 | 6,949 | 8,765 |
| **DIRECT MAIL** | 319 | 334 | 1,419 | 2,461 | 4,786 | 17,145 | 23,590 |
| **BUSINESS PAPERS** | 61 | 211 | 496 | 712 | 1,035 | 2,382 | 2,875 |
| **OUTDOOR** | | | | | | | |
| National | 28 | 60 | 136 | 118 | 252 | 600 | 680 |
| Local | 10 | 26 | 65 | 60 | 131 | 385 | 475 |
| Total | 38 | 86 | 201 | 178 | 383 | 985 | 1,155 |
| **MISCELLANEOUS** | | | | | | | |
| National | 192 | 368 | 1,111 | 1,896 | 3,431 | 10,175 | 15,500 |
| Local | 190 | 290 | 837 | 1,361 | 3,121 | 9,420 | 5,280 |
| Total | 382 | 658 | 1,948 | 3,257 | 6,552 | 19,595 | 20,780 |
| **TOTAL** | | | | | | | |
| National | 1,030 | 1,950 | 5,940 | 10,150 | 18,355 | 56,850 | 74,665 |
| Local | 900 | 1,390 | 3,970 | 6,480 | 14,945 | 45,290 | 49,595 |
| **GRAND TOTAL** | $1,930 | $3,340 | $9,910 | $16,630 | $33,300 | $102,140 | $124,260 |

*Estimated.     SOURCES: Data from Robert J. Coen, *Estimated Annual Advertising Expenditures: 1936–1976*; McCann-Erickson, Inc.; *Advertising Age*, May 18, 1987, p. 82; Standard & Poor's *Industry Surveys*, Feb. 7, 1991.

## B.26 Top Ten U.S. Advertising Agencies
## by Worldwide Billings, 1990

| AGENCY | BILLINGS (MILLIONS OF DOLLARS) |
|---|---|
| 1. Young & Rubicam | $7,519.3 |
| 2. Saatchi & Saatchi Advertising | 5,709.4 |
| 3. Ogilvy and Mather Worldwide | 5,374.8 |
| 4. BBDO Worldwide | 5,221.7 |
| 5. McCann-Erickson Worldwide | 4,993.7 |
| 6. Backer Spielvogel Bates Worldwide | 4,899.1 |
| 7. J. Walter Thompson Co. | 4,852.3 |
| 8. DDB Needham Worldwide | 4,591.5 |
| 9. Lintas: Worldwide | 4,510.4 |
| 10. D'Arcy Masius Benton & Bowles | 4,406.7 |

SOURCE: Data from *Advertising Age*, March 25, 1991.

## B.27 Media Spending by Top Ten National Advertisers

| ADVERTISER | 1990 AD SPENDING (MILLIONS OF DOLLARS) |
|---|---|
| 1. Procter & Gamble Co. | $2,284.5 |
| 2. Phillip Morris Co. | 2,210.2 |
| 3. Sears, Roebuck & Co. | 1,507.1 |
| 4. General Motors Corp. | 1,502.8 |
| 5. Grand Metropolitan | 882.6 |
| 6. PepsiCo Inc. | 849.1 |
| 7. AT & T Co. | 796.5 |
| 8. McDonald's Corp. | 764.1 |
| 9. Kmart Corp. | 693.2 |
| 10. Time Warner | 676.9 |

SOURCE: Data from *Advertising Age*, Sept. 25, 1991, p. 1.

## B.28 Average Daily Per-Household Hours of Radio and Television Use in United States, 1931–1990

| YEAR | RADIO | TELEVISION | TOTAL HOURS |
|------|-------|------------|-------------|
| 1931 | 4:04 | — | 4:04 |
| 1935 | 4:48 | — | 4:48 |
| 1943 | 4:23 | — | 4:23 |
| 1946 | 4:13 | — | 4:13 |
| 1950 | 4:06 | 4:35 | 8:41 |
| 1955 | 2:12 | 4:51 | 7:03 |
| 1960 | 1:53 | 5:06 | 6:59 |
| 1965 | 2:27 | 5:29 | 7:56 |
| 1971 | 2:52 | 5:56 | 8:48 |
| 1975 | 3:16 | 6:07 | 9:23 |
| 1986 | 2:57 | 7:10 | 10:07 |
| 1990 | 2:59 | 7:02 | 10:01 |

SOURCE: Data from Christopher H. Sterling and Timothy R. Haight, *The Mass Media: Aspen Institute Guide to Communication Industry Trends*, New York/London: Praeger, 1977, p. 366; Radio Advertising Bureau; *Nielsen Report on Television 1990*.

## B.29 Time Spent Using Media, 1990

| MEDIUM | HOURS PER PERSON |
|--------|------------------|
| Television | 1,470 |
| Radio | 1,135 |
| Recorded Music | 235 |
| Newspapers | 175 |
| Consumer Magazines | 90 |
| Consumer Books | 95* |
| Home Video** | 50 |
| Movies | 12 |
| Total | 3,262 |

*1988 figures.
**Playback of prerecorded tapes only. Data is per household.
SOURCE: Data from *The Veronis, Suhler & Associates Communications Industry Forecast*, June 1991, p. 13.

# End Notes

**Chapter 1**

1. *Facts about Newspapers '90*, American Newspaper Publishers Association, p. 22; *Radio Facts for Advertisers 1990*, Radio Advertising Bureau, pp. 3–11; *The Magazine Handbook 1990–91*, Magazine Publishers Association, p. 100; *Nielsen Report on Television 1990*, A.C. Nielsen Co., p. 6; *Incidence of Motion Picture Attendance Among the Adult and Teenage Public July 1990*, Motion Picture Association of America; Barry Monush, *1991 International Television and Video Almanac* (New York: Quigley Publishing Company, Inc.), p. 18A; Recording Industry Association of America, Inc.; *Publishers Weekly* 235, no. 4 (Jan. 27, 1989):445; "Public Libraries in Fifty States and the District of Columbia, 1989" (Washington, D.C.: U.S. Department of Education, April 1991), p. 82; American Library Association.

2. *Industry Surveys*, Feb. 7, 1991, M-16. This is a projected estimate, based on *McCann-Erickson's Insider's Report*, December 1990. This does not include money spent for outdoor advertising and direct mail.

3. Melvin L. DeFleur and Everette E. Dennis, *Understanding Mass Communication*, 2nd ed. (Boston: Houghton Mifflin, 1986), p. 5. This is an abbreviated and modified version of DeFleur and Dennis' definition.

4. Joanne Lipman, "Mort Zuckerman Seeks to Influence Opinion, Not Just Own Land," *The Wall Street Journal*, Sept. 27, 1986, p. 1.

5. Ibid.

6. John Voland, "Turner Defends Move to Colorize Films," *Los Angeles Times*, Oct. 23, 1986, p. C-1.

7. Melinda Beck, Vincent Coppola, and Jonathan Alter, "The Movers and Shakers," *Newsweek*, April 1, 1986, pp. 54–55.

8. Edwin Diamond, "The Tisch Touch," *New York*, May 26, 1986, p. 33.

9. *Advertising Age* 62, no. 6 (Feb. 4, 1991):34; *Advertising Age* 62, no. 11 (March 11, 1991):36; *Industry Surveys*, Feb. 7, 1991, M-27.

10. These figures are from *U.S. Industrial Outlook 1991; Employment and Earnings*, U.S. Department of Labor, Bureau of Labor Statistics, January 1991, p. 95; *Variety*

340, no. 3 (July 25, 1991):51; *1990 Broadcast Equal Employment Opportunity Trend Report*, Federal Communications Commission.

11. Anthony Smith, *Goodbye Gutenberg* (New York: Oxford University Press, 1980), p. 6.

12. Plato, *Collected Works* (Princeton, N.J.: Phaedrus, 1961), pp. 520–21.

13. Smith, p. 5.

14. Ibid., p. 8.

15. Fred S. Siebert, Theodore Peterson, and Wilbur Schramm, *Four Theories of the Press* (Urbana: University of Illinois Press, 1963), p. 135.

**Chapter 2**  1. Richard Saul Wurman, *Information Anxiety* (New York: Doubleday, 1989), p. 33.

2. James Melvin Lee, *History of American Journalism*, 2nd ed. (New York: Garden City Publishing, 1923), p. 21.

3. Ibid., p. 22.

4. Livingston Rutherford, *John Peter Zenger* (Gloucester, Mass.: Peter Smith, 1963 [reprint of the first edition]), pp. 121–23.

5. Marion Marzolf, *Up from the Footnote* (New York: Hastings House, 1977), p. 2.

6. Ibid., pp. 1–11.

7. Edwin Emery and Michael Emery, *The Press and America*, 6th ed. (Englewood Cliffs, N.J.: Prentice-Hall, 1988), p.36.

8. Lee, p. 83.

9. Emery and Emery, p. 65.

10. Ibid., p. 81.

11. Anthony Smith, *Goodbye Gutenberg* (New York: Oxford University Press, 1980), pp. 13–14.

12. Lauren Kessler, *The Dissident Press* (Beverly Hills: Sage, 1984), p. 21.

13. Ibid.

14. Madelon Golden Schilpp and Sharon M. Murphy, *Great Women of the Press* (Carbondale: Southern Illinois University Press, 1983), p. 125.

15. Ida B. Wells, *The Crusade for Justice: The Autobiography of Ida B. Wells*, ed. Alfreda M. Duster (Chicago: University of Chicago Press, 1970), p. 42.

16. Emery and Emery, p. 137.

17. W. A. Swanberg, *Citizen Hearst* (New York: Bantam Books, 1971), p. 68.

18. Emery and Emery, p. 241.

19. Ibid., p. 575.

20. Phillip Knightley, *The First Casualty* (New York: Harcourt Brace Jovanovich, 1975), p. 276.

21. Donald Paneth, *Encyclopedia of American Journalism* (New York: Facts on File, 1983), p. 165.

22. Emery and Emery, p. 409.

23. Abe Peck, *Uncovering the Sixties: The Life and Times of the Underground Press* (New York: Pantheon Books, 1985), p. xiv.

24. Emery and Emery, p. 35.

25. James N. Dertouzos and Timothy H. Quinn, "Bargaining Responses to the Technology Revolution: The Case of the Newspaper Industry," *Labor Management Cooperation Brief*, U.S. Department of Labor, September 1985, p. 7.

26. Smith, p. 52.

27. Patrick Reilly, "Curley's Marching Orders," *Advertising Age* 60, no. 13 (March 27, 1989):64.

28. Smith, p. 48.

29. Patrick M. Reilly, "Newspapers are Paging Young Readers," *The Wall Street Journal*, May 6, 1991, p. B-1.

30. Ibid.

31. Ibid.

**Chapter 3**

1. Shirley Biagi, *NewsTalk I* (Belmont, Calif.; Wadsworth, 1987), p. 110.

2. Craig Endicott, "Top 300 Push Total Revenues Over $16 Billion," *Advertising Age* 61, no. 25 ( June 10, 1990):S6–S22.

3. Ruth Finley, *The Lady of Godey's, Sarah Josepha Hale* (New York: Arno Press, 1974 [1931 reprint]), p. 266.

4. Madelon Golden Schilpp and Sharon M. Murphy, *Great Women of the Press* (Carbondale: Southern Illinois University Press, 1983), p. 44.

5. Frank Luther Mott, *History of American Magazines* (New York: D. Appleton, 1930), p. I-584.

6. Donald Paneth, *Encyclopedia of American Journalism* (New York: Facts on File, 1983), p. 113.

7. Ibid., p. 208.

8. Ibid., p. 61.

9. Ibid., p. 63.

10. Ibid., p. 94.

11. Ibid., p. 319.

12. Ibid., p. 190.

13. James Playsted Wood, *Magazines in the United States*, 3rd ed. (New York: Ronald Press, 1971), pp. 33–34.

14. Ida Tarbell, *All in the Day's Work* (New York: MacMillan, 1939), pp. 235–39.

15. Edwin Diamond, "The Talk of 'The New Yorker,'" *New York* 18, no. 12 (March 25, 1985):14.

16. David Halberstam, *The Powers That Be* (New York: Knopf, 1979), p. 46.

17. W. A. Swanberg, *Luce and His Empire* (New York: Scribner's, 1972), p. 57.

18. Tamar Jacoby, "New Generation of Women's Publications," *The New York Times*, March 3, 1986, p. B-8.

19. Deidre Carmody, "A Guide to New Magazines Shows Widespread Vitality," *The New York Times*, Feb. 25, 1991, p. C-1.

20. Ibid.

21. Magazine Publishers Association, "Magazine Economics," *Magazine Magazine* 1, no. 1 (Fall 1985):23.

22. Eric Gelman and Sid Atkins, "Coping with the Ad Crunch," *Newsweek*, July 21, 1986, pp. 28–29.

23. James B. Kobak, "1984: A Billion-Dollar Year for Acquisitions," *Folio:* 14, no. 4 (April 1985):82–95.

24. Karlene Lukovitz, "The Next 10 Years: 24 Predictions for the Future," *Folio:* 11, no. 9 (September 1982):103.

**Chapter 4**

1. A. M. Sperber, *Murrow: His Life and Times* (New York: Freundlich, 1986), p. 168.

2. Radio Advertising Bureau, *Radio Facts for Advertisers 1990* (New York: Radio Advertising Bureau), pp. 3–11.

3. Irving Settel, *A Pictorial History of Radio* (New York: Citadel Press, 1960), p. 17.

4. Christopher H. Sterling and John M. Kittross, *Stay Tuned: A Concise History of American Broadcasting* (Belmont, Calif.: Wadsworth, 1978), p. 13.

5. Erik Barnouw, *Tube of Plenty* (New York: Oxford University Press, 1978), p. 9.

6. Ibid., p. 11.

7. Ibid., p. 13.

8. Ibid., p. 15.

9. Settel, p. 32.

10. Barnouw, p. 21.

11. Ibid., p. 20.

12. Ibid., pp. 30–31.

13. Ibid., p. 30.

14. Settel, p. 39.

15. Barnouw, p. 34.

16. Ibid., p. 36.

17. Ibid., p. 39.

18. Ibid., p. 43.

19. Ibid.

20. John R. Bittner, *Broadcast Law and Regulation* (Englewood Cliffs, N.J.: Prentice-Hall, 1982), p. 20.

21. Ibid., p. 57.

22. Settel, pp. 50–51.

23. Ibid., pp. 51–52.

24. Ibid., p. 52.

25. Laurence Bergreen, *Look Now, Pay Later: The Rise of Network Broadcasting* (New York: New American Library, 1980), pp. 77–78.

26. Edwin C. Hill, "Radio's New Destiny," *Radio Stars*, June 1933, p. 7.

27. Barnouw, p. 53.

28. Ibid., p. 55.

29. Bergreen, p. 62.

30. Ibid., pp. 62, 71.

31. Barnouw, p. 145.

32. Peter Fornatale and Joshua E. Mills, *Radio in the Television Age* (New York: Overlook Press, 1980), p. 7.

33. Ibid., p. 11.

34. Barnouw, p. 145.

35. Fornatale and Mills, p. 25.

36. Ibid., p. 20.

37. David R. MacFarland, *The Development of the Top 40 Radio Format* (New York: Arno Press, 1979), p. 46.

38. Ibid., p. 44.

39. Ibid.

40. Ibid., p. 53.

41. Broadcasting Publications, *Broadcasting/Cablecasting Yearbook 1990* (Washington, D.C.: Broadcasting Publications, 1990), p. A-3.

42. "Summary of Broadcasting and Cable," *Broadcasting* 120, no. 16 (April 22, 1991):69.

43. Standard & Poor's *Industry Surveys* 159, no. 5, Sec. 1 (February 7, 1991):M23.

44. Geraldine Fabrikant, "Hot Market for Radio Stations," *The New York Times*, July 25, 1986, p. D-1.

45. Fornatale and Mills, p. 64.

46. Eric Zorn, "Radio Lives!" reprinted from *Esquire* in *Readings in Mass Communication*, 6th ed., eds. Michael Emery and Ted Curtis Smythe (Dubuque, Iowa: Wm. C. Brown, 1986), pp. 340–41.

47. Ibid., p. 339.

**Chapter 5**  1. Jeff Greenfield, *Television: The First Fifty Years* (New York: Abrams, 1977), p. 11.

2. Ibid., pp. 52–53.

3. Erik Barnouw, *Tube of Plenty* (New York: Oxford University Press, 1975), p. 17.

4. Ibid., p. 5.

5. Ibid., p. 78.

6. Ibid., p. 90.

7. Les Brown, *Television: The Business Behind the Box* (New York: Harcourt Brace Jovanovich, 1971), p. 43.

8. Ibid.

9. Christopher H. Sterling and John M. Kittross, *Stay Tuned: A Concise History of American Broadcasting*, 2nd ed. (Belmont, Calif.: Wadsworth, 1990), p. 298.

10. Shirley Biagi, *NewsTalk II* (Belmont Calif.: Wadsworth, 1987), p. 140.

11. Ibid.

12. Greenfield, pp. 66–68.

13. A. M. Sperber, *Murrow: His Life and Times* (New York: Freundlich, 1986), p. 354.

14. Sterling and Kittross, p. 348.

15. Barnouw, p. 191.

16. Newton Minow, *Equal Time: The Private Broadcaster and the Public Interest* (New York: Atheneum, 1964), p. 51.

17. Ibid., p. 53.

18. Barnouw, p. 432.

19. Ibid., p. 317.

20. Ibid., p. 336.

21. Ibid., p. 339.

22. Greenfield, p. 234.

23. Ibid., p. 236.

24. Sterling and Kittross, p. 414.

25. Elizabeth Jensen, "Was the Cosby Show Worth It?" *Adweek* 39, no. 4 (Jan. 23, 1989):14–17.

26. Edwin Diamond, "The Big Chill: The Harsh New World of the Networks," *New York* 19, no. 31 (Aug. 11, 1986):25.

27. Peter Revzin, Peter Waldman, and Peter Gumbel, "Ted Turner's CNN Gains Global Influence and 'Diplomatic' Role," *Los Angeles Times*, Feb. 1, 1990, p. A-1.

28. "Year in Review: Sports," *Electronic Media* 10, no. 2 (Jan. 7, 1991):54.

29. Thomas Whiteside, "Cable-I," *The New Yorker* 61, no. 13 (May 20, 1985):78.

30. Ibid., p. 82.

31. Julie Amparano Lopez and Mary Lu Carnevale, "Fiber Optics Promises a Revolution of Sorts, If the Sharks Don't Bite," *The Wall Street Journal*, July 10, 1990, p. A-1.

32. Ibid.

**Chapter 6**
1. Jason E. Squire, ed., *The Movie Business Book* (New York: Simon & Schuster, 1983), p. 3.

2. Ibid., p. 2.

3. Robert Sklar, *Movie-Made America* (New York: Random House, 1975), p. 6.

4. Ibid., p. 9.

5. Tino Balio, *The American Film Industry* (Madison: University of Wisconsin Press, 1976), p. 27.

6. Sklar, p. 16.

7. Ibid., p. 36.

8. Ibid., p. 40.

9. Ibid., p. 37.

10. Balio, p. 75.

11. Jack C. Ellis, *A History of American Film*, 2nd ed. (Englewood Cliffs, N.J.: Prentice-Hall, 1985), p. 43.

12. George P. Johnson Film Collection, Special Collections, University of California, Los Angeles.

13. Ellis, p. 52.

14. Balio, p. 112.

15. Ibid., p. 114.

16. *Moving Picture World*, Feb. 1, 1919, p. 619.

17. G. S. Watkins, ed., *The Motion Picture Industry* (Philadelphia: American Academy of Political and Social Science, 1947), p. 140.

18. Motion Picture Association of America, *Motion Picture Production Code*, 1954, p. 2.

19. Ibid., pp. 2–5.

20. Balio, p. 209.

21. Ibid., p. 213.

22. Leonard Mosley, *Disney's World* (New York: Stein and Day, 1985), p. 164.

23. Dalton Trumbo, *Additional Dialogue: Letters of Dalton Trumbo: 1942–1962* (New York: M. Evans, 1970), p. 301.

24. Ibid., p. 102.

25. Balio, p. 372.

26. Ibid., p. 315.

27. "Stereophonic Sounds," from *Silk Stockings*, 1955.

28. Sklar, p. 389.

29. Motion Picture Association, "U.S. Economic Review," 1990, p. 5.

30. *The Veronis, Suhler & Associates Communication Industry Forecast,* June 1991, p. 108.

31. Squire, p. 345.

32. Ibid., pp. 155–56.

33. "The World Is Hollywood's Oyster," *Business Week* 3195, (Jan. 14, 1991):97.

34. Michael Cieply and Peter W. Barnes, "Movie and TV Mergers Point to Concentration of Power to Entertain," *The Wall Street Journal*, Aug. 21, 1986, p. 1.

35. Squire, p. 155.

36. Ibid., p. 150.

37. Ibid., pp. 296–97.

38. Ibid., p. 298.

39. Ibid., p. 399.

40. *Business Week*.

41. Cieply and Barnes.

42. Ibid.

43. Squire, p. 37.

**Chapter 7**

1. R. Serge Denisoff, *Solid Gold* (New Brunswick, N.J.: Transaction Books, 1975), p. 1.

2. James R. Smart, *A Wonderful Invention: A Brief History of the Phonograph from Tinfoil to the LP* (Washington: Library of Congress, 1977), p. 6.

3. Robert Metz, *CBS: Reflections in a Bloodshot Eye* (Chicago: Playboy Press, 1975), pp. 147–48.

4. Ibid., p. 151.

5. Ibid., p. 153.

6. James D. Harless, *Mass Communication: An Introductory Survey* (Dubuque, Iowa: Wm. C. Brown, 1985), p. 201.

7. David Pauly, "A Compact Sonic Boom," *Newsweek*, Dec. 6, 1985, p. 47; *U.S. Industrial Outlook 1991*, pp. 32–33.

8. Donald Alsop, "RCA Plugs Records the Way Other Firms Sell Corn Flakes," *The Wall Street Journal*, April 11, 1985, p. 33.

9. Ibid.

10. Jeffrey Zaslow, "New Rock Economics Make It Harder to Sing Your Way to Wealth," *The Wall Street Journal*, May 21, 1985, p. 1.

11. Stephen Holden, "Chart Fever: Watching the Hit Parades," *The New York Times*, June 21, 1987, p. H-24.

12. Zaslow.

13. Christopher H. Sterling and John M. Kittross, *Stay Tuned: A Concise History of American Broadcasting* (Belmont, Calif.: Wadsworth, 1978), p. 193.

14. Ronald P. Lovell and Philip C. Geraci, *The Modern Mass Media Machine* (Dubuque, Iowa: Kandall/Hunt, 1987), p. 346.

15. Stephen Kreider Yoder, "Digital Tape Is Inevitable; So Why the Delay?" *The Wall Street Journal*, Aug. 12, 1986, p. 29.

16. Harless, p. 214.

17. Robert Lindsey, "Payola's Return to Records Reported," *The New York Times*, March 6, 1985, p. A-14.

18. Michael Cieply, "A Few Promoters Dominate Record Business," *The Wall Street Journal*, April 18, 1986, p. 6.

19. Louis P. Sheinfeld, "Ratings: The Big Chill," *Film Comment* 22, no. 3 (May–June 1986):10.

20. Robert Epstein, "Now It's the Recording Industry's Turn to Face the Music," *Los Angeles Times*, Nov. 22, 1990, p. F-1.

21. John Rockwell, "Compact Disks Are Here to Conquer," *The New York Times*, Feb. 9, 1986, p. H-1.

22. Smart.

23. Metz, p. 146.

**Chapter 8**
1. E. B. White, *Letters of E. B. White, ed. Dorothy Lobrano Guth (New York: Harper & Row, 1976), p. 571.*

2. U.S. Department of Commerce, *U.S. Industrial Outlook 1987* (Washington: U.S. Government Printing Office), p. 27–12.

3. Lewis A Coser, Charles Kadushin, and Walter W. Powell, *Books: The Culture & Commerce of Publishing* (New York: Basic Books, 1982), p. 7.

4. Ibid.

5. James D. Hart, *The Popular Book* (Berkeley: University of California Press, 1950), p. 9.

6. Ibid., p. 57.

7. Ibid., p. 58.

8. Ibid.

9. Ibid., p. 138.

10. Ibid., p. 151.

11. Ibid., p. 185.

12. John P. Dessauer, *Book Publishing: What It Is, What It Does* (New York: R. R. Bowker, 1974), pp. 3–4.

13. Hart, p. 274.

14. Kenneth C. Davis, *Two-Bit Culture: The Paperbacking of America* (Boston: Houghton Mifflin, 1984), p. xii.

15. Ibid., p. 15.

16. Harvey Swados, "Paper Books: What Do They Promise?" *The Nation*, Aug. 11–18, 1951.

17. Davis, p. 266.

18. Ibid., p. 153.

19. Ibid., p. 266.

20. Ibid., p. 316.

21. Ibid., p. 266.

22. U.S. Department of Commerce, pp. 27–29.

23. Dessauer, p. 8.

24. Coser, Kadushin, and Powell, p. 7.

25. Ibid.

26. Ibid., p. 14.

27. Ibid., p. 43.

28. Laura Landro, "Publishers' Thirst for Blockbusters Sparks Big Advances and Big Risks," *The Wall Street Journal*, Feb. 3, 1986, p. 21.

29. Alex S. Jones, "For Waldenbooks, Reading Is More than a Pastime," *The New York Times*, reprinted in *The Sacramento Bee*, April 30, 1984, p. C-3.

30. U.S. Department of Commerce, pp. 27–29.

31. Coser, Kadushin, and Powell, p. 35.


**Chapter 9**
1. Daniel J. Boorstin, "The Rhetoric of Democracy," in *American Mass Media: Industries and Issues*, 3rd ed., eds. Robert Atwan, Barry Orton, and William Vesterman (New York: Random House, 1986), p. 37.

2. Ibid.

3. Robert Atwan, "Newspapers and the Foundations of Modern Advertising," in *The Commercial Connection*, ed. John W. Wright (New York: Doubleday, 1979), p. 16.

4. Edgar R. Jones, *Those Were the Good Old Days* (New York: Simon & Schuster, 1979), p. 35.

5. Ibid., p. 44.

6. Atwan.

7. Stephen Fox, *The Mirror Makers: A History of American Advertising and Its Creators* (New York: Morrow, 1984), p. 15.

8. Ibid., p. 32.

9. Ibid., p. 155.

10. Ibid., p. 210.

11. Ibid., p. 212.

12. Ibid.

13. Ibid., p. 213.

14. Erik Barnouw, *The Tube of Plenty* (New York: Oxford University Press, 1975), p. 187.

15. Boorstin.

16. Ibid.

17. Ibid.

18. Ibid.

19. Jib Fowles, "Advertising's Fifteen Basic Appeals," in *American Mass Media: Industries and Issues*, p. 43.

20. Ibid., pp. 46–52.

21. Michael Schudson, *Advertising: The Uneasy Persuasion* (New York: Basic Books, 1984), p. 13.

22. Louis C. Kaufman, *Essentials of Advertising*, 2nd ed. (New York: Harcourt Brace Jovanovich, 1987), p. 510.

23. Schudson, p. 13.

24. Bob Shanks, "Advertising Agencies and Sponsors," in *American Mass Media: Industries and Issues*, p. 59.

25. Jonathan Price, "Now a Few Words About Commercials . . ." in *American Mass Media: Industries and Issues*, p. 63.

26. Ibid., p. 60.

27. Radio Advertising Bureau, *Radio Facts for Advertisers 1989–1990* (New York: Radio Advertising Bureau), p. 28.

28. Timothy K. Smith, "Abominable Ernest of TV Commercials Noses Out Everyone," *The Wall Street Journal*, Nov. 20, 1985, p. 1.

29. Kaufman, p. 514.

**Chapter 10**

1. Fraser P. Seitel, *The Practice of Public Relations*, 2nd ed. (Columbus, Ohio: Charles E. Merrill, 1984), p. 40.

2. Theodore Lustig, "Great Caesar's Ghost," *Public Relations Journal*, March 1986, pp. 17–19.

3. Doug Newsom and Alan Scott, *This Is PR: The Realities of Public Relations*, 3rd ed. (Belmont, Calif.: Wadsworth, 1986), p. 40.

4. Scott M. Cutlip, Allen H. Center, and Glen M. Broom, *Effective Public Relations*, 6th ed. (Englewood Cliffs, N.J.: Prentice-Hall, 1985), p. 36.

5. Quoted in Sherman Morse, "An Awakening on Wall Street," *American Magazine* 62 (September 1906):460.

6. Cutlip, Center, and Broom, p. 39.

7. Edward L. Bernays, *The Engineering of Consent* (Norman: University of Oklahoma Press, 1955), pp. 3–4.

8. Craig Randall, "The Father of Public Relations: Edward Bernays, 93, Is Still Saucy," *United* 30, no. 11 (November 1985):50.

9. Newsom and Scott, p. 47.

10. "Interview: Henry Rogers," *PSA* 21, no. 10 (October 1986):70.

11. Doris E. Fleischman, "Public Relations — A New Field for Women," *Independent Woman*, February 1931, p. 58, as quoted in Susan Henry, "In Her Own Name?: Public Relations Pioneer Doris Fleischman Bernays," a paper presented to the Committee on the Status of Women Research Session, Association for Education in Journalism and Mass Communication, Portland, Oregon, July 1988.

12. Doug Newsom and Alan Scott in *This Is PR* are especially diligent about chronicling women's contributions to public relations. This specific information appears on p. 49.

13. Newsom and Scott, p. 50.

14. *Occupations of Federal White and Blue Collar Workers*, U.S. Office of Personnel Management, 1989.

15. James K. Gentry, "The Best and Worst Corporate PR," *Washington Journalism Review* 8, no. 7 (July 1986):38–40.

16. Joanne Lipman, "As Network TV Fades, Many Advertisers Try Age-Old Promotions," *The Wall Street Journal*, Aug. 26, 1986, p. 1.

17. Lawrence G. Foster, "The Role of Public Relations in the Tylenol Crisis," *Public Relations Journal*, March 1983, p. 13.

18. Jeff Blyskal and Marie Blyskal, "Making the Best of Bad News," *Washington Journalism Review* 7, no. 12 (December 1985):52.

19. "Dear Chrysler: Outsiders' Advice on Handling the Odometer Charge," *The Wall Street Journal*, June 26, 1987, p. 21.

20. The higher number comes from Robert Kendall, "Public Relations Employment: Huge Growth Projected," *Public Relations Review* 10, no. 3 (Fall 1984):13. *U.S. Industrial Outlook 1991*, pp. 52–55.

21. *County Business Patterns 1988*, U.S. Bureau of the Census, December 1990.

22. Newsom and Scott, p. 69.

23. "Japanese Said Lagging in PR," *Los Angeles Times*, reprinted in *The Sacramento Bee*, Dec. 8, 1986, p. C-3.

24. Summarized from a list of work assignments listed in Cutlip, Center, and Broom, p. 64.

25. Jeff Blyskal and Marie Blyskal, *PR: How the Public Relations Industry Writes the News* (New York: Morrow, 1985), p. 46.

26. Craig Bromberg, "Goliath Pitch Behind Times' 'David Story,'" *Manhattan, inc.* 4, no. 4 (April 1987):18.

27. Joanne Angela Ambrosio, "It's in the Journal, But This Is Reporting?" *Columbia Journalism Review* 18, no. 6 (March/April 1980):35.

28. Bromberg.

29. Blyskal and Blyskal, *PR*, p. 82.

**Chapter 11**

1. James Madison, letter to W. T. Barry, Aug. 4, 1822, in *Letters and Other Writings of James Madison, Fourth President of the United States, Vol. 3, 1816–1818* (Philadelphia: J. B. Lippincott, 1854), p. 276.

2. Walter Lippmann, *Public Opinion* (New York: Free Press, 1965), p. 229.

3. Additional information that has not appeared in preceding chapters is from Ben H. Bagdikian, *The Media Monopoly* (Boston: Beacon Press, 1983); American Newspaper Publishers Association; Laura Landro, "Book Industry Faces More Consolidation," *The Wall Street Journal*, March 13, 1987, p. 7; *Broadcasting Yearbook 1991* (Washington: Broadcasting Publications, 1991), p. A-3; *Advertising Age*, March 25, 1991, p. S-6; and *Standard & Poor's Industry Surveys*, Leisuretime Basic Analysis, March 14, 1991, Sec. 3, p. 43.

4. A. J. Liebling, *The Press* (New York: Ballantine, 1961), pp. 4–5.

5. Michael J. Robinson and Ray Olszewski, "Books in the Marketplace of Ideas," *Journal of Communication* 30, no. 2 (Spring 1980):82.

6. Joanne Lipman, "Ad Agencies Feverishly Ride a Merger Wave," *The Wall Street Journal*, March 9, 1986, p. 6.

7. Karen Rothmyer, "Hot Properties: The Media-Buying Spree Explained," *Columbia Journalism Review* 24, no. 4 (November/December 1986):40.

8. Benjamin M. Compaine, *Who Owns the Media?* (White Plains, N.Y.: Knowledge Industry Publications, 1979), p. 26.

9. William A. Henry III, "Learning to Love the Chains," *Washington Journalism Review* 8, no. 9 (September 1986):16.

10. Compaine, p. 26.

11. Philip Weiss, "Invasion of the Gannettoids," *The New Republic*, Feb. 2, 1987, p. 18.

12. Ben H. Bagdikian, "Conglomeration, Concentration, and the Media," *Journal of Communication* 30, no. 2 (Spring 1980):60.

13. David H. Weaver and G. Cleveland Wilhoit, *The American Journalist: A Portrait of U.S. News People and Their Work* (Bloomington: Indiana University Press, 1986), p. 12.

14. Ibid., pp. 38–39.

15. Herbert J. Gans, "Are U.S. Journalists Dangerously Liberal?" *Columbia Journalism Review* 24, no. 4 (November/December 1985):32–33.

16. See William A. Dorman, "Peripheral Vision: U.S. Journalism and the Third World," *World Policy Journal*, Summer 1986, pp. 419–46.

17. Herbert J. Gans, "The Messages Behind the News," in *Readings in Mass Communication*, 6th ed., eds. Michael Emery and Ted Curtis Smythe (Dubuque, Iowa: Wm. C. Brown, 1986), pp. 161–69.

18. James Reston, *The Artillery of the Press* (New York: Harper & Row, 1966), p. 49.

19. Norman Corwin, *Trivializing America: The Triumph of Mediocrity* (Secaucus, N.J.: Lyle Stuart, 1986), p. 33.

20. Times Mirror, *The People & the Press* (Los Angeles: Times Mirror, 1986), p. 30; Times Mirror, *The People & the Press* (Los Angeles: Times Mirror, 1989), pp. 25–26.

21. Times Mirror, *We're Interested in What You Think* (Los Angeles: Times Mirror, 1987), p. 8.

**Chapter 12**

1. Jeffrey Zaslow, "Clear Verdict: The People's Court Spurs Surge in Small-Claims Cases," *The Wall Street Journal*, March 6, 1987, p. 31.

2. Deb Kollars, "Callers Flood AIDS Hotlines; Johnson Cheered on 'Arsenio,'" *The Sacramento Bee*, November 9, 1991, p. A22.

3. Willaim L. Rivers and Wilbur Schramm, "The Impact of Mass Communications," in *American Mass Media: Industries and Issues*, 3rd ed., eds. Robert Atwan, Barry Orton, and William Vesterman (New York: Random House, 1986), pp. 11–12.

4. David M. Potter, *People of Plenty* (Chicago: University of Chicago Press, 1954), p. 167.

5. Robert M. Liebert and Joyce Sprafkin, *The Early Window*, 3rd ed. (New York: Pergamon Press, 1988), p. 161.

6. "Synopsis of FTC Staff Report on Television Advertising to Children," in *The Commercial Connection*, ed. John W. Wright (New York: Dell, 1979), pp. 340–42.

7. Scott Ward, cited in George Comstock et al., *Television and Human Behavior* (New York: Columbia University Press, 1978), p. 199.

8. James David Barber, *The Pulse of Politics: Electing Presidents in the Media Age* (New York: Norton, 1986), p. 150.

9. Ibid., p. 246.

10. Thomas E. Patterson and Robert D. McClure, *The Unseeing Eye: The Myth of Television Power in National Elections* (New York: Putnam, 1976), p. 113.

11. Joseph C. Spear, *Presidents and the Press* (Cambridge, Mass.: M.I.T. Press, 1984), p. 52.

12. Personal telephone conversation with Herbert Alexander, April 8, 1987.

13. Herbert E. Alexander, *Financing the 1980 Election* (Lexington, Mass.: D.C. Heath, 1983); Herbert E. Alexander and Brian A. Haggerty, *Financing the 1984 Election* (Lexington, Mass.: D.C. Heath, 1987).

14. Personal telephone conversation with Herbert E. Alexander, Sept. 14, 1989.

15. Barber, p. 6.

16. Mark Fetler, "Television Viewing and School Achievement." *Mass Communication Review Yearbook*, vol. 5 (Beverly Hills: Sage, 1985), pp. 447–61.

17. Walter Lippmann, *Public Opinion* (New York: Free Press, 1965), p. 61.

18. Tania Modleski, *Loving with a Vengeance: Mass-Produced Fantasies for Women* (New York: Methuen, 1982), p. 113.

19. Joshua Meyrowitz, *No Sense of Place* (New York: Oxford University Press, 1985), p. 92.

20. Ibid., p. 242.

21. Neil Postman, *Amusing Ourselves to Death* (New York: Viking Penguin, 1985), pp. 160–61.

22. Ibid.

**Chapter 13**

1. Tom Wicker, *On Press* (New York: Viking, 1978), p. 260.

2. Leonard W. Levy, *Emergence of a Free Press* (New York: Oxford University Press, 1985), pp. 272–73.

3. Ralph L. Holsinger, *Media Law* (New York: Random House, 1987), p. 14.

4. Ibid., p. 61.

5. Rodney A. Smolla, *Suing the Press* (New York: Oxford University Press, 1986), p. 46.

6. Peter Braestrup, *Battle Lines: Report of the Twentieth Century Fund Task Force on the Military and the Media* (New York: Priority Press, 1985), p. 29.

7. Holsinger, p. 35.

8. Sanford J. Ungar, *The Papers & The Papers: An Account of the Legal and Political Battle over the Pentagon Papers* (New York: Dutton, 1975), pp. 306–307.

9. Holsinger, pp. 48–49.

10. Jeff Blyskal and Marie Blyskal, *PR: How the Public Relations Industry Writes the News* (New York: Morrow, 1985), p. 15.

11. "Notes and Comment," *The New Yorker* LXVI, no. 51 (Feb. 4, 1991): 21.

12. Thomas B. Rosenstiel, "The Media Take a Pounding," *Los Angeles Times*, Feb. 20, 1991, p. A1.

13. Carl Bode, *Mencken* (Carbondale: Southern Illinois University Press, 1969), pp. 272–76.

14. Holsinger, pp. 332–33.

15. Ibid., pp. 340–41.

16. National Coalition against Censorship, *Books on Trial: A Survey of Recent Cases* (New York: National Coalition against Censorship, 1985), pp. 6–20.

17. Madalynne Reuter and Marianne Yen, "Censorship Rose 35 Percent over Previous Year, Study Finds," *Publishers Weekly*, Oct. 24, 1986, p. 13.

18. Smolla, p. 18.

19. Smolla, pp. 29–30.

20. Ibid., p. 50.

21. Holsinger, p. 161.

22. Peter McGrath and Nancy Stadtman, "What the Jury — and Time Magazine — Said," *Newsweek*, Feb. 4, 1985, p. 58.

23. "Media and Libel: Rising Losses," *Folio:* 17, no. 7 (July 1988): 24–25.

24. Ibid., p. 89.

25. Ibid., p. 34.

26. Ibid., p. 92.

27. Smolla, p. 257.

28. Holsinger, pp. 191–92.

29. Ibid., p. 192.

30. Ralph L. Holsinger, *Media Law*, 2nd ed. (New York: McGraw-Hill, 1991), p. 502.

31. Fraser P. Seitel, *The Practice of Public Relations*, 2nd ed. (Columbus, Ohio: Charles E. Merrill, 1984), p. 428.

32. Holsinger, p. 416.

33. Thomas R. King, "Agencies Give Legal Matters New Emphasis," *The Wall Street Journal*, Dec. 31, 1990, pp. 9–10.

**Chapter 14**

1. Anthony Brandt, "Truth and Consequences," *Esquire* 102, no. 4 (October 1984):27.

2. John Hulteng, *The Messenger's Motives: Ethical Problems of the News Media* (Englewood Cliffs, N.J.: Prentice-Hall, 1985), p. 221.

3. Tom Goldstein, *The News at Any Cost* (New York: Simon & Schuster, 1985), p. 217.

4. Ibid., p. 218.

5. "ABC: Walters Wrong to Be Iran Messenger," *The Sacramento Bee*, March 17, 1987, p. 1.

6. Ibid.

7. "Federal Judge Finds Winans, Two Others Guilty," *The Wall Street Journal*, June 25, 1985, p. 2.

8. M. L. Stein, "Survey on Freebies," *Editor & Publisher*, May 31, 1986, p. 11.

9. Alan Prendergast, "Mickey Mouse Journalism," *Washington Journalism Review* 9, no. 1 (January/February 1987):32.

10. Jane Mayer, "And You Thought the Big Drama Involving Qadhafi Was in London," *The Wall Street Journal*, May 1, 1984, p. 37.

11. Richard M. Levine, "Murder, They Write," *The New York Times Magazine*, Nov. 16, 1986, p. 132.

12. Jonathan Alter with Peter McKillop, "AIDS and the Right to Know," *Newsweek*, Aug. 18, 1986, p. 46.

13. Dale Van Atta, "Faint Light, Dark Print," *Harper's* 273, no. 1,638 (November 1986):57.

14. Ibid.

15. Howard Rosenberg, "Shot Heard 'Round the News Rooms," *Los Angeles Times*, Jan. 26, 1987, p. VI-1; and Mike Dunne, "Suicide Film Footage Has Media Edgy," *The Sacramento Bee*, Jan. 23, 1987, p. A-24.

16. Howard Rosenberg, "Is There No Control over Rivera's Kind of Journalism?" *Los Angeles Times*, reprinted in *The Sacramento Bee*, Dec. 6, 1986, p. A-24.

17. David Crook, "'Doping of a Nation' Roundly Criticized for Tarring of Reputations," *Los Angeles Times*, reprinted in *The Sacramento Bee*, Dec. 15, 1986, p. B-8.

18. Clifford G. Christians, Kim B. Rotzoll, and Mark Fackler, *Media Ethics*, 2nd ed. (New York: Longman, 1987), pp. 9–17.

19. Andy Rooney, "The Jounalist's Code of Ethics," in *Pieces of My Mind* (New York: Atheneum, 1984), pp. 59–60.

20. *The Quill* 61, no. 12 (December 1973):27.

21. Radio-Television News Directors Association, Code of Broadcast News Ethics, January 1988.

22. Public Relations Society of America, "Code of Professional Standards for the Practice of Public Relations," rev. 1983, p. 1.

23. Hulteng, p. 214.

24. Ibid., pp. 215–16.

25. John Hulteng, "Get It While It's Hot," *feed/back* 12, nos. 1 and 2 (Fall 1985/ Winter 1986):16.

**Chapter 15**

1. Damon Darlin, "Japanese Ads Take Earthiness to Levels Out of This World," *The Wall Street Journal*, Aug. 30, 1988, p. 1; Adi Ignatius, "Solo Act: In Beijing, Chinese Rock Star Is the Last Protester," *The Wall Street Journal*, May 31, 1990;

"Radio Station Penalized for Airing Too Many Hits," *The Wall Street Journal*, Aug. 29, 1988, p. A-16; Gordon S. Jackson, "The South African Press and the State of Emergency: An Assessment," a paper presented at the Association for Education in Journalism and Mass Communication, Minneapolis, August 1990; Tyler Marshall, "East Germans Dazzled by Western Press," *Los Angeles Times*, July 31, 1990, p. H-8; Julia Michaels, "Use of In-Program Ads Plays Big Role in Success of Brazilian TV Network," *The Wall Street Journal*, Jan. 4, 1989, p. B-5.

2. Lowndes F. Stephens, "The World's Media Systems: An Overview," *Global Journalism: Survey of International Communication*, 2nd ed. (New York: Longman, 1991), p. 62.

3. Ibid., p. 68.

4. Manny Paraschos, "Europe," *Global Journalism: Survey of International Communication*, 2nd ed. (New York: Longman, 1991), pp. 93–128.

5. Ibid., p. 96.

6. Philip Revzin and Mark M. Nelson, "European TV Industry Goes Hollywood," *The Wall Street Journal*, Oct. 3, 1989, p. A-18.

7. Marshall.

8. Blaine Harden, "'Maniacs' on TV Wake Up Poland," *Washington Post*, March 11, 1990, p. A-20.

9. Associated Press, "Media Chiefs Fired; Allegedly Backed Coup," *The Sacramento Bee*, Aug. 27, 1991, p. A-11.

10. Everette E. Dennis and Jon Vanden Heuvel, *Emerging Voices: East European Media in Transition* (New York: Gannett Center for Media Studies, October 1990), p. 2.

11. Mort Rosenblum, "TV Takes the Center Stage in Romanian Revolution," *The Sacramento Bee*, Dec. 17, 1989, p. A-11.

12. Paraschos, p. 124.

13. The Associated Press, "Ads for Comrades: Soviets Run U.S. Commercials," *The Sacramento Bee*, May 18, 1988, p. E-1; Mark J. Porubcansky, "Soviet Paper Finally Prints Capitalist Ads," *The Sacramento Bee*, Jan. 4, 1989, p. C-4; *Baltimore Sun*, "Censorship Outlawed in U.S.S.R.," *The Sacramento Bee*, June 13, 1990, p. A-8.

14. Laurie Hays and Andrea Rutherford, "Gorbachev Bids to Crack Down on Soviet Press," *The Wall Street Journal*, Jan. 17, 1991, p. A-8.

15. Dennis and Vanden Heuvel.

16. Christine Ogan, "Middle East and North Africa," *Global Journalism: Survey of International Communication*, 2nd ed. (New York: Longman, 1991), p. 130.

17. Ibid., p. 135.

18. Ibid.

19. Charles P. Wallace, "Radio: Town Crier of the Arab World," *Los Angeles Times*, Jan. 7, 1988, p. 1.

20. Ogan, pp. 139–40.

21. L. John Martin, "Africa," *Global Journalism: Survey of International Communication*, 2nd ed. (New York: Longman, 1991), p. 161.

22. Jackson, pp. 10–11.

23. L. John Martin.

24. Ibid., p. 190.

25. Ibid.

26. Sydney W. Head, *World Broadcasting Systems* (Belmont, Calif.: Wadsworth, 1985), p. 89.

27. Ibid., p. 90.

28. S. Karene Witcher, "Fairfax Group to be Placed in Receivership," *The Wall Street Journal*, Dec. 11, 1990, p. A-4.

29. Anne Cooper Chen and Anju Grover Chaudhary, "Asia and the Pacific," *Global Journalism: Survey of International Communication*, 2nd ed. (New York: Longman, 1991), p. 214.

30. Ibid., p. 240.

31. Michael B. Salwen, Bruce Garrison, and Robert T. Buckman, "Latin America and the Caribbean," *Global Journalism: Survey of International Communication*, 2nd ed. (New York: Longman, 1991), pp. 274–85.

32. Ibid.

33. Head, p. 27.

34. Salwen, Garrison, and Buckman, p. 305.

35. Ibid., p. 302.

36. Robert G. Picard, "Global Communications Controversies," *Global Journalism: Survey of International Communication*, 2nd ed. (New York: Longman, 1991), p. 74.

37. Ibid., p. 82.

38. Head, p. 381.

39. R. Craig Endicott, "WPP Biggest Ad Group; Burnett Top U.S. 'Brand'," *Advertising Age* 62, no. 16 (March 25, 1991):S-51.

40. Elizabeth Shogren, "Leningrad Tunes in to Its MTV Today," *Los Angeles Times*, March 8, 1991, p. F-24; Susan Greenberg, "Media Barons Garner Footholds in Eastern Europe," *The Sacramento Bee*, May 30, 1990, p. E-3.

41. Julie Skur Hill, "A Brave New World of Brands," *Advertising Age*, 62, no. 36 (Sept. 2, 1991):25.

# Glossary

**accreditation**  certification by the government of members of the press to cover government.

**affiliates**  broadcast stations that use broadcast network programming but are owned by companies other than the broadcast networks.

**agenda-setting**  the belief that members of the press do not tell people what to think but do tell people what and whom to think about.

**alternative press**  newspapers that become outlets for the voices of social protest; also called the dissident press.

**ancillary rights market**  the marketing of a movie beyond its theater audience, including television and videocassette sales.

**blanket licensing**  gaining authorization to use recorded music for broadcast by paying a fee.

**blind booking**  the practice of renting out films to exhibitors without showing the films to the exhibitors first.

**block booking**  the practice of scheduling a large number of movies for a theater, combining a few good movies with many second-rate features.

**channel**  in mass communication, the medium that delivers the message.

**concentration of ownership**  the trend among the media industries to cluster together in groups.

**consumer magazines**  all magazines sold by subscription or at newsstands, supermarkets, and bookstores.

**cooperative newsgathering**  first used by the New York Associated Press, with member newspapers sharing the expenses of acquiring news and returning any profits to the members.

**CPM** in advertising, cost-per-thousand, which is the cost of an ad per one thousand people reached.

**demand programming** request radio that is controlled completely by the listener.

**deregulation** in broadcasting, the elimination by the Federal Communications Commission in the 1980s of many of the government restrictions on broadcast programming and ownership.

**digital audio broadcast (DAB)** uses computer codes to send music and information, which eliminates the static and hiss of current broadcast signals.

**digital audiotape (DAT)** uses computer codes to produce recordings.

**disinformation** the planting by government sources of inaccurate information.

**dissident press** see *alternative press*.

**ethnocentric** the belief that certain cultural and social values, especially American values, are the only correct ones.

**false light** the charge that what a writer implied in a story about someone was incorrect.

**Federal Communications Commission (FCC)** the government agency that regulates broadcasting and cable.

**freelancers** journalists who write for more than one publication and are paid separately for each article they write.

**high definition television (HDTV)** provides a picture with a clearer resolution than on current television sets.

**jazz journalism** in a newspaper, the combination of large pictures and headlines to emphasize sex and violence.

**LAPS test** the local standard for obscenity established in *Miller* v. *California*: whether a work, taken as a whole, lacks serious Literary, Artistic, Political, or Scientific value.

**libel** a statement that damages a person's character or reputation by exposing that person to public ridicule.

**magic bullet theory** a belief that ideas from the media create a direct causal relationship to behavior.

**mass communication** communication from one person or group of persons through a transmitting device (a medium) to a large audience or market.

**mass media industries** used in *Media/Impact* to describe the seven types of media businesses: newspapers, magazines, radio, television, movies, recordings, and books.

**media** plural for medium.

**medium**   in mass communication, the transmitting device by which a message is carried.

**muckrakers**   turn-of-the-century magazine journalists who wrote articles to expose big business and corrupt government.

**narrowcasting**   in broadcasting, identifying a specific audience segment and specifically programming for that segment.

**news services**   originally called wire services, formed to provide information to print and broadcast news operations from locations throughout the world.

**O & O's**   broadcast stations that are Owned and Operated by a broadcast network.

**pass-along readership**   people who read a magazine by sharing the magazine with its original owner.

**payola**   a contraction of the words "payment" and "Victrola" (an early record player), used to describe the payment of a fee to a disc jockey in exchange for playing a recording on the air.

**penny paper**   first popularized by Benjamin Day of the *New York Sun* in 1833, the policy of dropping the price of a newspaper to a penny and supporting the production cost through advertising.

**photojournalism**   the use of photographs and text to tell a better story than either could tell alone.

**prime time**   in broadcasting, used to describe the hours between 7 p.m. and 11 p.m., when more people watch television than during any other period.

**prior restraint**   the power of government to stop information from being published or broadcast.

**publicity**   uncontrolled use of media by a public relations firm to create events and present information to capture press and public attention.

**rating**   the percentage of audience for a program compared to the total number of households with television sets.

**rep firm**   a company of advertising sales representatives who sell advertising time and space in their market to companies outside their geographic area.

**Roth test**   the local standard used to determine obscenity, established by the U.S. Supreme Court in *Roth* v. *United States*: whether to the average person, applying contemporary community standards, the dominant theme of the material taken as a whole appeals to prurient interest.

**selective perception**   the concept that different people perceive different messages differently.

**share**   an abbreviation for share-of-audience, which compares the audience for one show with the audience for another. Share means the percentage of the audience with TV sets on that is watching each program.

**situation comedy**   a program that establishes a fixed set of characters in either a home or work situation.

**small presses**   book publishers with fewer than 10 employees.

**spiral of silence**   the theory that people are unlikely to voice disagreement with the prevailing climate of opinion embraced by the media.

**subsidiary rights**   the rights to market a book for other uses — to make a movie, for example, or to print a character from the book on T-shirts.

**sweeps**   the most concentrated ratings period for local television stations, conducted in February, May, and November.

**syndex**   an abbreviation for "syndicated exclusivity," a negotiated contract by a broadcaster that gives the station the exclusive right to broadcast a syndicated program in a specific market.

**syndicates**   agencies and news organizations that sell articles for publication to appear in many different outlets simultaneously.

**syndicators**   services that sell programming to broadcast stations and cable.

**time-shifting**   the practice of people with a VCR who tape a program as it runs to watch later.

**two-step flow**   the transmittal of information and ideas from mass media to opinion leaders and then to their friends and acquaintances.

**vertical integration**   the process by which one company controls several related aspects of the media business simultaneously.

**yellow journalism**   highly emotional, often exaggerated or inaccurate reporting that emphasizes crime, sex, and violence.

# Index

on television, 165, 181
world market for U.S., 488
Movietone News, 158
MTV, 474, 485
Muckrakers, magazines, 90–92
Mullarkey, Karen, 447
Muller, Henry, 367
Murdoch, Rupert
control of Australian media by, 479, 484
magazine purchases by, 107
newspaper purchases by, 76
profile of, 12–14
Murray, Jim, 79
Murrow, Edward R.
profile of, 160–161
as radio reporter, 127–128
as television reporter, 111
*Muscle & Fitness*, 81
Music, radio, 125
Music videos, 249
Mutual Radio, 145
Muybridge, Eadweard, 197, 198

Nader, Ralph, 285, 288
Narrowcasting, 145
Nast, Thomas, 87
*Nation, The*, 88, 89
National Advertising Review Board (NARB),
321
National Association for the Advancement of
Colored People (NAACP), 88–89
National Association of Broadcasters, 487
National Broadcasting Company (NBC)
background of, 9, 157
establishment of, 129–130
libel suit brought against, 419, 423
loss of audience by, 172
news broadcasting by, 158
privacy issues and, 173
National Educational Television (NET), 174
National Electric Signaling Company, 115
*National Enquirer*, 58, 419
National Football League (NFL) games, 186
National media
magazines as, 83–84
newspapers as, 69, 72
radio as, 111–113
National News Council, 461
National Public Radio (NPR), 9
*National Review*, 88, 89
Native American newspapers, 46
Neal, Richard I., 411
Near, J. M., 405
*Near* v. *Minnesota*, 405
Networks
explanation of, 9
radio, 129–131, 145
television, 172, 180, 182–183
New American Library (NAL), 272, 273, 280
New Deal, 328–329
*New Era*, 47
*New Republic, The*, 88, 89
*New Woman*, 107
New World Information and Communications
Order (NWICO), 482–484
New York Associated Press, 50

*New York Daily News*, 57–58
*New York Gazette*, 39
New York *Journal*, 53, 56
*New York Ledger*, 302
*New York Sun*, 49, 297
*New York Times, The*, 49
background of, 53
as chain newspaper, 359
news service of, 73
publication of Pentagon Papers by,
405–406
*New York Times Co.* v. *United States*,
405–406
*New York Times* v. *Sullivan*, 399–400,
420–421, 424, 426, 435
*New York Tribune*, 49
*New-York Weekly Journal, The*, 39
New York *World*, 53
*New Yorker, The*
background of, 93–95
libel suit brought against, 422
misrepresentation of facts in, 443–444
press restrictions commentary in, 409
purchase of, 107
*New Yorker Staats-Zeitung*, 45
Newhouse, 107
News
blackout of, 408–412
and global information flow, 482–484
ideas conveyed by American, 368–369
presentation of, 365–369
radio broadcasts of, 127–129
television broadcasts of, 158–162, 175–179
News Corporation, 10, 14, 231, 233
News radio format, 144
News reporters, radio, 128, 159
News services, 50, 72
Newspaper advertising
audience and, 77
in daily papers, 18
overview of, 297–299
Newspaper Guild, 59, 74
Newspaper industry
future outlook for, 73–74
labor unions and, 58–59, 74
operations of, 65, 68
overview of, 17–18
ownership trends in, 75–77, 354, 356,
357, 359
present state of, 68–69
women in, 39–41
Newspapers
afternoon, 64
Civil War, 50–53
Colonial, 37–43
early 19th century, 44–50
early 20th century, 53–58
readership trends, 77
role of reporters in, 58–61
in television era, 62–67
Newton, Wayne, 419, 423
Nickelodeons, 199
Nicolay, Harry, 337
Nielsen ratings, 152, 167, 168, 188–189, 315
9XM, 118
Nipkow, Paul, 154
*Nipkow disk*, 154

Nixon, Richard, 175, 177, 179
Nixon-Kennedy debates, 385, 386
Noelle-Neumann, Elisabeth, 390
Nordgren, Sarah, 416–417
Noreen, Gary, 487
Normand, Mabel, 209
North African media systems, 473, 475–476
*North Star*, 47
*Northwood: A New England Tale* (Hale), 84
Norwood, Jennifer, 255
Novels
early publication of, 267–269
electronic, 290–291

O & O (owned-and-operated) stations, 180
Obscenity, 412, 414–415. *See also* Censorship;
Pornography
Ochs, Adolph S., 53
O'Farrill, Romulo, Jr., 481
Office of War Information (OWI), 59
Olszewski, Ray, 356
Ombudsman, 464
Onassis, Jacqueline Kennedy, 427
*Oregon Spectator*, 44
Oswald, Lee Harvey, 176
Otis, Harrison Gray, 35, 53
Overholser, Geneva, 451–452
Ownership. *See* Media ownership

Paine, Thomas, 267
Paley, William S.
role in recordings, 242, 243
role in television, 130, 156–158
*Pamela* (Richardson), 267–268, 392
Panavision, 220
Pantheon Books, 280
Paperback books
impact on publishing industry, 273–275
mass-market, 278–279
Papyrus, 23
Paramount Communications, Inc., 11, 205,
212
holdings of, 233
theater ownership by, 219
Parchment, 23
Parents Music Resource Center (PMRC), 253,
255
Parker, Dorothy, 93
Parker, Edwin, 379
Parker, George F., 327
Parsons, Dan, 107
Pass-along readership, magazine, 106
Passive people meters, 188–189
Patent medicines, 86
Pay-per-view television, 187
Payne Fund studies, 378
Payola, 134–135, 251–253
*PC Magazine*, 80–81
Peck, Abe, 63–64
*Pennsylvania Evening Post*, 43
*Pennsylvania Gazette*, 39, 41, 83
*Pennsylvania Journal*, 42–43
Penny arcades, 199
Penny papers, 49
Pentagon Papers, 405–406

# Credits

Photo on p. 4, © 1990 Orion Pictures Corporation.

Photo on p. 6, © Deborah Copaken/Contact Press Images.

Quotation on pp. 10–11 is reprinted by permission of Jeff Greenfield.

Photos on pp. 13 (all), 22 (bottom left), 45, 48, 54 (both), 55 (both), 61, 82, 85, 88, 92 (both), 95, 116, 126, 127, 129, 156, 159, 166, 176, 198, 199, 208, 218, 221, 240, 245, 250, 269 (right), 274, 285, 305, 330, 337, 338, 386, 402, 406, 407, 409, 413, 420, 453, are reprinted by the permission of The Bettmann Archive.

Photo on p. 14, reprinted by permission of Joe McNally.

Photo on p. 17, reprinted courtesy of *Glamour*. © 1985 by The Condé Nast Publications, Inc.

Photo on p. 22 (top): Louis S. Glanzman, © National Geographic Society. Used by permission.

Photos on pp. 22 (bottom right), 97, 104 (left), 143, 158 (right), 178, 190, 226, 264, 282, 285, 342, are reprinted by permission of Cliff Polland.

Photos on pp. 36 (left), 41, 42, 52, 57 (both), 59, 158 (left), 269 (left), are reprinted by permission of The Smithsonian Institution.

Photo on p. 36 (right), courtesy Massachusetts Historical Society.

Photos on pp. 46, 51, 113, 135, 241, 243, 298, 299, 328, are reprinted by permission of The Library of Congress.

Quotation on pp. 60–61 reprinted by permission of Scripps Howard News Service.

Photos on pp. 62, 256, 479, are reprinted by permission of AP/Wide World Photos.

Quotation on p. 67 is reprinted by permission of Scott Aiges, Music Writer for the *New Orleans Times-Picayune*.

Photo on p. 67, courtesy *The Dallas Morning News*.

Photo on p. 69, *USA Today* © Gannett Co., Inc. Reprinted by permission. All rights reserved.

Cover art on p. 94 from *The New Yorker* by Rea Irvin. Copyright 1925, 1953 The New Yorker Magazine, Inc.

Photo on p. 96, © 1983 Roger White, reproduced by permission of the Estate of Margaret Bourke-White and Scott Meredith Literary Agency, Inc., 845 Third Avenue, New York, NY 10022.

Photos on p. 102 (top, second from top, bottom), reprinted courtesy of World Wood, Database Programming & Design, Pulp & Paper, © 1991 Miller Freedman Publications.

Photo on p. 303, courtesy Lufthansa Airlines.

Photo on p. 306, © 1987 Revlon, Inc. Reprinted by permission.

Quotation on p. 308 is reprinted by permission of *The Wall Street Journal*, © Dow Jones & Company, Inc., 1990. All rights reserved.

Photo on p. 309, reprinted by permission of the American Association of Advertising Agencies, Inc.

Photo on p. 311, courtesy CTA Lasers and American Airlines.

Photo on p. 315, reprinted by permission of Inside Print.

Photo on p. 318, reprinted by permission of Carden & Cherry Advertising Agency.

Photo on p. 323, courtesy of Danny Villanueva.

Photo on p. 333, reprinted by permission of Bigger Than Life, Inc.

Quotation on p. 334, reprinted by permission of *The Cincinnati Enquirer*.

Quotation on pp. 338–339 © 1989 Dow Jones & Company, Inc. Reprinted by permission of *The Wall Street Journal*. All rights reserved worldwide.

Photo on p. 342, reprinted by permission of GTE.

Quotation on pp. 346–347, reprinted by permission of Robert Buchanan.

Quotation on pp. 360–361, reprinted by permission of *The Wall Street Journal*, © Dow Jones & Company, Inc., 1986. All rights reserved.

Photo on p. 364, reprinted by permission of Rick Reinhard/Impact Visuals.

Quotation on pp. 366–367, reprinted by permission of *The Los Angeles Times*.

Quotation on pp. 370–371, reprinted by permission of the *Washington Journalism Review*.

Chart on p. 372 courtesy of the Times Mirror Center for the People & the Press.

Cartoon on p. 380 is reprinted by permission of Doug Marlette and Creators Syndicate.

Quotation on pp. 388–389, reprinted by permission of *The Washington Journalism Review*.

Cartoon on p. 391 reprinted with special permission of King Features Syndicate, Inc.

Cartoon on p. 393 *Calvin and Hobbes* © 1991 Universal Press Syndicate. Reprinted with permission. All rights reserved.

Quotation on p. 395, from *Amusing Ourselves to Death*, by Neil Postman. Copyright © 1985 by Neil Postman. Reprinted by permission of Viking Penguin, a division of Penguin Books USA, Inc.

Cartoon on p. 409 reprinted by permission of Mike Luckovich and Creators Syndicate.

Quotation on pp. 410–411, "TV and the Gulf War" is reprinted by permission of the *Los Angeles Times*.

Quotation on pp. 416–417, is reprinted by permission of Associated Press.

Cartoon on p. 418 is reprinted by permission of Don Wright, *The Palm Beach Post*.

Quotation on pp. 424–425 is reprinted by permission of *The Washington Journalism Review*.

Photo on p. 431, courtesy Federal Communications Commission.

Quotation on pp. 446–447, reprinted by permission of *The Wall Street Journal*, © Dow Jones & Company, Inc., 1989. All rights reserved.

Photo on p. 447, courtesy Collins Publishers, San Francisco.

Cartoon on p. 451, *Bizarro* is reprinted by permission of Chronicle Features.

Photo on p. 452, © 1991 Des Moines Register and Tribune Company. Reprinted with permission.

Quotation on p. 455, © 1986 by The New York Times Company. Reprinted by permission of *The New York Times*.

Cartoon on p. 458, drawing by Vietor © 1987 The New Yorker Magazine, Inc.